TESI GREGORIANA

Serie Teologia

—— 106 ——

CHO HYUN-CHUL, S.J.

AN ECOLOGICAL VISION
OF THE WORLD

Toward a Christian Ecological
Theology for Our Age

EDITRICE PONTIFICIA UNIVERSITÀ GREGORIANA
Roma 2004

Vidimus et approbamus ad normam Statutorum Universitatis

Romae, ex Pontificia Universitate Gregoriana
die 3 mensis aprilis anni 2004

R.P. Prof. JOHN O'DONNELL, S.J.
R.P. Prof. GERALD O'COLLINS, S.J.

ISBN 88-7652-990-X

GREGORIAN UNIVERSITY PRESS
Piazza della Pilotta, 35 - 00187 Rome, Italy

DEDICATION
헌정

To my father and mother, with love and respect
사랑과 존경을 담아 어머님과 아버님께 드립니다.

ACKNOWLEDGEMENTS

In the first place, I express my sincere and deep gratitude to Fr. John O'Donnell, S.J. As my rector at the Weston Jesuit Community and my professor at Weston Jesuit School of Theology in Cambridge, Mass., U.S.A. and as my thesis director at the Gregorian University in Rome, Italy, he, with his scholarly brilliance and accuracy, always encouraged and empowered me to move forward in my studies. Without his generous concern and availability, this work could not have been completed successfully and promptly.

I thank Fr. Gerald O'Collins, S.J. He has always been a constant help during my stay in Rome. At the end of my doctoral research, he generously accepted to be the second reader of my thesis and took pains to read it. My thanks are further extended to Fr. Philip Rosato, S.J. He gave practical advices at the initial stage of my research in Rome.

I also express my gratefulness to all the Jesuit colleagues at Collegio S. Roberto Bellarmino where I lived for three years. I deliver my special acknowledgement to Fr. Lourdusamy Ambrose Jeyaraj, S.J. We started our doctoral studies together at the Gregorian University and have since encouraged each other to hold fast to our goal throughout this – sometimes tedious – period.

I am sincerely thankful that my province allowed me to complete this work. I owe a debt of gratitude to Fr. Jung Il-Woo, S.J. He has been accompanying me from my philosophical studies in various levels: as a spiritual director, as a superior, and most memorably, as a comrade in the latter part of my regency in the countryside. I deeply thank the farmers with whom I lived and worked at that time. Their life awakened me to a profound meaning of nature.

Finally, I cannot help finding in all these encounters God, «who created the world out of love», «became a creature out of love», and «is present in creation out of love from beginning to end».

PROLOGUE

«We live in a broken world where men and women are in need of integral healing, the power for which comes ultimately from God»[1]. «A broken world» appears to be an apt phrase to depict the present status of the earth. On the one hand, human beings are torn by such an extremely unbalanced distribution of wealth that some people indulge in astounding extravagance, while a great many suffer from absolute destitution. The human world is troubled with exploitation, alienation, starving, enmity, and violence. On the other hand, we are seized with such a perverted, anthropocentric perspective on nature that we have come to regard it merely as a source for commodities, while nature groans beneath our heedless extraction and extravagant waste of natural resources. The natural world is distressed with plunder, depletion, extinction, pollution, and disintegration. A grim prospect presses on the earth.

We live in a broken world where the integrity and harmony with which we believe God created the cosmos are lost. We need a healing from the wounds that we have inflicted on each other and nature. The healing that we need is an «integral healing» that considers every dimension of the human being. This integral healing mandates a reconciliation with nature as well as with other humans, which must be accompanied by some efficacious measures. Many of us may be doubtful and skeptical about this integral healing and reconciliation, seeing how grave the hurts that we have inflicted on one another and nature are. Many may feel overwhelmed and disheartened, perceiving how prevalent the consequences of these wounds are in the world. I acknowledge that it is an immensely formidable task for us to overcome

---

[1] The Thirty-Fourth General Congregation of the Society of Jesus, d. 6, n. 14. See SOCIETY OF JESUS, *Documents*, 89.

on our own the current, deep-seated and widespread sinfulness in this broken world and to recover the integrity of the world. As Christians, however, we believe and confess that God will eventually achieve the integrity of all creation to the full. Finally, we must remember as well that it is through creatures, particularly human beings, who are made in *imago Dei*, that God accomplishes it. I begin, standing firm on this faith in God, to wend my way in this broken world in search of a path that leads us to a more socially just and ecologically sustainable world.

INTRODUCTION

1. The Theological Significance and Purpose of the Study

I deal in this study with a Christian perspective on the world in the context of the global ecological crisis, with a view to forming an ecological vision of the world and cultivating ecological consciousness, which I believe to be essential for the well-being of all creation. The overall ecological situation of the earth has been deteriorating, due in great part to humanity's extravagant exploitation of the planet, to such a degree that the whole ecosystem has been severely degraded. Some species are disappearing at an alarming rate, and some others, including the human race itself, are on the brink of extinction. The crisis of nature that we face in the present is inextricably connected with the survival of humankind in the future. No one and no scholarly discipline can avert its eyes from the environmental devastation that threatens the human race with total destruction. One of most urgent, crucial, and unavoidable tasks of Christian theology today is, I believe, to observe what takes place on the earth, which God has created with joy, to reflect theologically upon it, and to present to us an alternative, more proper way of seeing and relating to nature.

I endeavor on the basis of the Christian theological tradition to overcome the tendency of the human's arrogant domination and reckless exploitation of nature and the consequent ecological crisis. Concretely speaking, I seek to obtain an alternative vision of the world for our age through the critical explorations of pertinent theological thoughts on nature. The alternative perspective thus obtained, i.e., an ecological vision of the world, is expected to be able to inspire ecological consciousness at least among Christians, against the current, excessively dualistic and utilitarian perspective on nature which I believe is to blame in great measure for the global ecological disruption in this age.

2. The Method of the Study

The method that I employ in this study is a method of correlation whereby we correlate a specific issue such as our concern and experience with the Christian tradition.[1] It can be held that the method of correlation has two functions: dialogic and apologetic. First, the method of correlation has a dialogic function. A dialogic function means that the correlative method brings the Christian tradition into an explicit dialogue with our concern and experience. This dialogic function takes place in a bilateral direction between the Christian tradition and our issue, providing a new insight and understanding to each other. In the first place, the Christian tradition speaks to our issue. We see and understand our specific issue in the light of Christian faith. Put otherwise, Christian faith illuminates and interprets what our concern and experience indicate, whereby we read «the signs of the times». We also learn how we, as Christians, must respond to that specific issue. In the second place, our issue in turn speaks to the Christian tradition. Christian faith is viewed from the vantage point of our concern and experience. This process requires us to (re)interpret and reclaim the Christian tradition. Therefore, one can say that the dialogic function of the correlative method is a hermeneutics between a concrete issue and the Christian tradition. Besides a hermeneutic method, sometimes it may be necessary to employ a more creative construction to grapple with our issue when the Christian heritage cannot respond to it properly and effectively, but always within a wider Christian tradition. Second, the correlative method has an apologetic function, primarily as a result of its dialogic function. Through the dialogic function of interpretation and construction, the Christian tradition that we have inherited from the past will become intelligible and convincing to our contemporaries. Otherwise, Christian faith would become so obsolete that one could hardly understand what significance it may have today.

I take up as a concrete issue the global ecological crisis in our times and seek to correlate it with the Christian theological tradition. I illuminate and interpret the environmental issue with appropriate Christian theological thoughts so that we may read the signs of the times that the crisis of nature reveals and learn how we, as Christians, must properly and effectively respond to this grave and challenging issue. Christian theological thoughts as well are critically explored by means of

---

[1] For a method of correlation as a theological methodology, see R. HAIGHT, *Dynamics of Theology*, 191-195.

(re)interpretation and construction. A concrete method employed in this study may well be illustrated by the following procedures. First, I present the main proposition to achieve the purpose of the thesis. Second, I present three subsequent propositions to support the main proposition. Third, I theologically explicate, develop, and support each subsequent proposition through critical reflections upon proper theological resources using an interpretative or a constructive method. Last, the main proposition as a conclusion of this study emerges again, theologically reinforced by the preceding, theologizing processes and permeated with its theological significance and implications. Therefore, the thesis starts with the main proposition, is unfolded around the three subsequent propositions, and finally returns to the main proposition.

3. The Context of the Thesis

The context of the thesis in which I locate myself can be described with three observations and a consequent challenge, which are rendered in detail in chapter one and two. The first observation is concerning the ecological crisis of the earth that we ourselves now experience and our various responses to it up until now. The second one is about the story of the universe and the earth that science tells us today. This is also regarding the worldview that this scientific account of the cosmos brings up, i.e., a dynamic and relational perspective on the world. The third is about an attitude toward others, both human and nonhuman, which I consider prevalent among us, i.e., a sense of disconnectedness and an excessive utilitarian attitude. As a result, these three observations present to us a challenge that we need such a radical change in our perspective to see the world that we may form and foster in ourselves an ecological vision of the world and ecological consciousness, which I believe are indispensable to the assurance of the integrity of nature.

4. The Propositions of the Thesis

I present one main proposition and three subsequent propositions around which the thesis is unfolded. All propositions, both main and subsequent, are grounded in the three observations and a challenge mentioned above. The main and three subsequent propositions are as follows:

The Main Proposition: A Christian perspective on the world provides an ecological vision of the world that awakens and cultivates ecological consciousness in human beings in the age of the global ecological crisis.

Proposition I: A Christian perspective on the world shows that all the finite beings in the world are interrelated and interdependent.

Proposition II: A Christian perspective on the world shows that all the finite beings in the world have their own intrinsic, though not absolute, value.

Proposition III: A Christian perspective on the world shows that concern for nature is compatible with concern for the poor.

The main proposition is inspired by all these three observations and by the challenge that we must radically change our way of grasping the world. The main proposition holds that we need an alternative vision of the world for this drastic change, and that Christianity can contribute to the formation of this new vision, i.e., an ecological vision of the world, which will instill in us ecological consciousness.

Proposition I is about relationships among finite beings in the world, and it is spurred by the first and third observations and based on the second one. This proposition takes notice in us of a deep sense of disconnectedness, despite a dynamic and relational perspective on the world which science presents today, and of its devastating effects to the earth. It claims, therefore, that we need to reclaim a sense of interconnectedness that all the finite beings in the world are interrelated and interdependent and that Christianity can contribute to the formation of this sensibility of relationality.

Proposition II is concerning the intrinsic value of finite beings in the world, and it is incited also by the first and third observations and grounded in the second one. This proposition takes heed in us of an extreme utilitarian attitude toward others, despite a dynamic and relational perspective on the world which science presents today, and of its ravaging consequences for the planet. It thus holds that we need to acknowledge and respect the intrinsic value of others, particularly that of nature, and that Christianity can help its cultivation.

Proposition III is regarding a difficulty and conflict that we may encounter when we hold fast to what the first and second propositions indicate. In fact, we already hear two seemingly different voices: a crying that ecological concern weakens our concern for the poor, which is still of utmost urgency, on the one hand; and a demand that we intensify concern for nature, even for our sheer survival itself, on the other. However, on the basis of the first proposition that all beings are connected with each other and the second one that every being is precious in one's own degree, the third proposition suggests that concern for nature be compatible with concern for the poor. Both nature and the poor must properly be regarded and respected according to their intrinsic value; one cannot be ensured without the other because of their interconnectedness. This proposition is intended to encourage and empower us to commit ourselves to the promotion of both ecological justice and social justice, with a conviction that we can pursue both without neglecting either.

5. The Theological Resources and Limit of the Study

This study seeks to demonstrate that Christianity can contribute to the formation and cultivation of an ecological vision of the world, which is vital to our world in ecological disruption. To achieve this goal, three propositions have been presented, which will subsequently be explored and solidified by pertinent Christian theological thoughts on nature. I have chosen four theologians as resource persons, who will provide theological materials to build up a theological foundation for each proposition: Karl Rahner, Jürgen Moltmann, Leonardo Boff, and Sallie McFague. The intention with which I employed these resource theologians needs to be made clear from the outset. It must be noted, in the first place, that I do not intend in this critical dialogue that the entire materials of each person pertinent to the propositions be examined or that the selected theological thoughts be explored as such[2]. Instead I will, in this study, engage myself in a critical dialogue with each of these theologians by selecting their theological thoughts which are directly or indirectly related to nature and making them fit to support those propositions theologically. In principle, therefore, any theologians can be employed in this study insofar as they bolster the three propositions theologically, whether they have explicitly mentioned environmental issues or not.

Rahner can be thought of as a theologian who rarely if ever mentioned the environmental issue. I think, however, it is probably because that issue was not acute in his age. He showed a deep concern about problems in his time. In fact, his numerous works came from his pastoral concern to respond promptly to new, often perplexing and

---

[2] It can be said that the immediate objects which are to be explored in this study are the propositions of the thesis.

embarrassing, topics for his contemporaries[3]. It seems evident to me that he was sensitive to «the signs of the times». He would express a serious concern for the natural environment and address the ecological issue theologically if he lived in these days. Moreover, though it is not manifested in a direct connection with the ecological issue, his theological perspective on the world has a great deal of potential to affirm an ecological vision of the world, which will be shown later. Therefore, one may have an advantage, in this case, to claim that Christianity is fundamentally pro-nature and can help us form and foster an ecological vision of the world even if it does not advocate nature explicitly.

The rest of the resource persons can be regarded as those who have considered and dealt with the environmental issue as a theological subject. There are other well known figures in this respect. However, not all of them provide sufficient theological materials to solidify those three propositions. Some aim to address the ecological issue to the general public, furnishing little theological materials[4]. Some others tend to remain by and large at the level of their experience, supplying few theological resources, although experience is a critical element to theology[5].

I must say that I took the third proposition into account in the selection of the resource persons. In other words, I sought and chose intentionally those who have expressed concern for the poor as well as for nature and dealt with both from a theological point of view. For I believe that, without serious consideration for poverty, any ecological discourse cannot help but be empty, particularly to those who suffer from poverty and are the victims of the ecological deterioration. All of the three resource persons, Moltmann, Boff, and McFague, have seriously responded to the suffering of the poor and extended their concern to nonhuman creation.

Finally, another element that was considered in the selection is a diversity of theologians, within a certain limit of number and without any attempt to exhaust all the different theological voices concerning

---

[3] For example, Rahner seemed particularly concerned for new scientific theories and discoveries, such as the evolutionary view of the world, and dialogues between theology and science, given that the influence of science on Christians could not be denied. Cf. K. RAHNER, «Natural Science and Reasonable Faith».

[4] One may name Matthew Fox for this case. See, for example, M. FOX, *Original Blessing*; ID., *The Coming of the Cosmic Christ*.

[5] One may name Sean McDonagh for this case. See, for example, S. MCDONAGH, *The Greening of the Church*; ID., *Passion for the Earth*.

the complex problem of ecology[6]. The resource theologians thus selected comprise Catholics (Rahner and Boff) and Protestants
(Moltmann and McFague), male (Rahner, Moltmann, and Boff) and
female (McFague), and a major voice in theological discipline (Rahner
and Moltmann) and a relatively minor one (Boff and McFague), with a
risk of oversimplification in the last category.

6. The Contents of the Thesis

The thesis consists of three parts and seven chapters: the first part,
composed of two chapters, corresponds to the introductory part of the
thesis; the second part, made up of three chapters, constitutes the main
body; the last, comprised of two chapters, the concluding part. Chapter
one deals with the ecological crisis of the earth. I present a summarized
ecological report on the earth and introduce diverse responses to the
ecological crisis from various quarters of the human world. This corresponds to the first observation. Chapter two provides two contrasting
perspectives on the world. The first one is a dynamic and relational
worldview that a recent scientific cosmology presents; the second is an
excessive, dualistic and utilitarian worldview which I believe is prevalent among us. These correspond to the second and third observations
respectively. I bring up, based on these three observations, a challenge
with an utmost importance: we must radically change our fundamental
perspective to grasp the world. Chapters three, four, and five explore
the three propositions theologically. In each chapter, I seek to explicate,
develop, and support each proposition through a critical engagement
with the relevant thoughts of the four resource theologians. Therefore,
each of the three chapters has four subchapters (sections), each of
which is to a certain extent a self-contained unit. These chapters are the
most substantial and theologizing portion of the thesis, where each
proposition takes on theological explications and significance. Chapter
six speaks of an emerging, alternative vision of the world as an outcome of the theologizing efforts of the three propositions: an ecological
vision of the world. With a view to assimilating what I examined and
reflected upon in the preceding three chapters, I concentrate on how
these three propositions have been solidified theologically. I then
confirm that these theologically strengthened propositions in turn
reinforce the main proposition with their theological significance and

---

[6] For an introduction of diverse environmental voices in philosophy and theology,
see P. SMITH, *What Are They*.

implications. Chapter seven thrust further an ecological vision of the world into the realm of Christian spirituality and life in order to explore and show how an ecological vision of the world can support them. A spirituality of life and peace and a commitment to social justice and ecological justice are the consequence of this final reflection.

PART I

OBSERVATIONS AND A CHALLENGE

CHAPTER I

The Ecological Crisis of the Earth

1. Preliminary Remarks on Ecology and Nature[1]

The word «ecology», coined by the German biologist Ernst Haeckel, emerged as a branch of biology in the late nineteenth century[2]. Etymologically, ecology derives from two Greek words, *oikos* and *logos*. *Oikos* means «house», more specifically a house common to all. In this regard, it may be interpreted as the household of living creatures with its life-supporting systems. *Oikos* is related to a whole, to which interactions among its parts are a critical element. *Logos* means «study» or «discourse». Therefore, simply speaking, ecology refers to the study of relationships among living organisms and the environment which sustains them. «The science of ecology looks at nonhuman nature, studying the numerous, complex interactions among its abiotic components (air, water, soils, atoms and molecules) and its biotic components (plants, animals, bacteria, and fungi)»[3]. Since the introduction of ecology to biology, the notion of ecology has widened to encompass and consider various aspects of humanity, which also belongs to living organisms. «Human ecology adds the interactions between people and their environments». Social ecology «analyzes the various political and social institutions that people use in relationship to nature and its resources»[4]. It can be said that this progress in the scope of ecology is

---

[1] What is intended here is not to provide the accurate definitions of these two terms but to make as clear as possible their meanings in diverse contexts in which they may be used.
[2] Cf. R. NASH, *The Rights of Nature*, 55.
[3] C. MERCHANT, *Radical Ecology*, 8.
[4] C. MERCHANT, *Radical Ecology*, 7-8.

in accord with its original, profound concern, that is, the whole of reality.

One may understand, in relation to *oikos*, the word «environment» as external conditions or surroundings which influence living organisms such as plants, animals, and human beings. Therefore, the notion of the environment assumes implicitly a distinction between that which surrounds and that which is surrounded, typically the natural world (the environment) and human beings. On the contrary, «ecological system (ecosystem)» or simply «ecology» encompasses both of them, i.e., the whole, as *oikos* indicates. Meanwhile, I will use interchangeably the adjectives «ecological» and «environmental» so that terms such as ecological crisis and environmental crisis have the same implication.

The word «nature» is a comprehensive term which has diverse meanings according to different contexts in which it is employed. The theologian Rosemary R. Ruether remarks that the term «nature» has been used in four distinct senses in Western philosophy and theology[5]. First, nature is understood as that which is «essential» to a being. Nature in the first sense indicates the essence of a being without which it cannot be what it is. Second, nature may mean «the sum total of physical reality, including humans». Nature in the second sense corresponds to the whole universe or the world. Third, nature may be conceived as «the sum total of physical reality apart from humans». Nature in the third sense points to the natural world, excluding humankind. Last, nature can be grasped as «the "created" world apart from God and divine grace». Nature in the last sense contrasts with grace. I will simply use the word «nature» in all these four cases unless its specific meaning needs to be clarified. «Nature» will be used in this study to refer most frequently to the second and third senses. Terms such as the whole creation (universe or world) and all creation will be used together for the second case; terms such as nonhuman creation, the natural world, and the (natural) environment for the third case; terms such as the world, the earth, the cosmos, and the universe for the second or the third case.

2. An Ecological Report on the Earth

The environmental disturbance and degradation of an ecosystem, such as the deteriorating quality of air, water, and soil, impact on all life forms in that ecosystem in one form or another, for example, the extinc-

---

[5] R.R. RUETHER, *Gaia and God*, 5.

tion or deformation of living organisms. Simply speaking, the global ecological crisis refers to a crisis of the earth as a single ecological system: «From Chernobyl radiation to the Gulf War oil spill; from tropical rainforest destruction to polar ozone holes; from alar in apples to toxics in water, the earth and all its life are in trouble»[6]. The effects of the ecological disintegration and deterioration on the earth are so comprehensive that they seep into almost every inch of the earth. They influence air, water, and soil, that is, the entire ecological system of the earth in such a way that changes in air, water, and soil affect further all other beings in them. Unfortunately, the general trend of the global ecosystem seems, at least up until now, to form a vicious cycle in regard to its status.

We live in the age of the global ecological crisis. The ecological problem is complex in its cause and process, involving human factors as well as natural elements. «Industrial production accentuated by the global reproduction of population, has put stress on nature's capacity for the reproduction of life. Pollution and depletion are systematically interlinked on a scale not previously experienced on the planet»[7]. The rapid growth of production in industry since the Industrial Revolution in the West, accelerated by scientific and technological development and forced by the fast increase of human population, not only has contaminated the global natural environment but also has been depleting the natural resources of the earth at an alarming rate. Human elements such as economic structures and political motivations are deeply embedded in the natural world and have a great influence on it.

Our predominant economic model is basically a capitalist market economy, which is based on the competition of individuals propelled by an insatiable desire for wealth and on the continuous supply of material resources for economic growth. This capitalist market economy originated in Europe; it has been expanded by the colonization of the day in that colonies at that time provided natural resources and cheap labor indispensable to economic development[8]. Although we cannot deal with the historical details that the current capitalist economy underwent, we can at least point out that capitalistic market economy, now globalized, has brought forth negative consequences epitomized by massive poverty and the global ecological devastation. Aside from poverty, a

---

[6] C. MERCHANT, *Radical Ecology*, 17.
[7] C. MERCHANT, *Radical Ecology*, 17.
[8] Cf. C. MERCHANT, *Radical Ecology*, 23-29.

fatal problem of global market capitalism in relation to ecological disruption lies in its inherent necessity for endless economic growth. This economic arrangement assumes the indefinite development of economy. Otherwise, massive unemployment would occur and the system itself would collapse. However, unlimited economic development needs the unlimited supply of natural resources, which is in fact impossible. This plain fact, though often overlooked, reveals that our present economy is not sustainable. It cannot last indefinitely. Capitalist market economy cannot help putting stress on the earth to squeeze ever more materials from nature. Global market capitalism is not only inextricably connected with the global ecological crisis but also inevitably causes it. A remark of Mahatma Gandhi hits the mark in this respect: «There are enough world resources for everyone's needs, but not for everyone's greed».

The ecological crisis of the earth reveals and reflects a crisis in the way we humans perceive nature, of which we are part. If we had understood nature fundamentally as that of which we are part, as that without which we cannot live, and as that for which we must care, our reckless exploitation of nature and the consequent environmental deterioration would not have happened, at least to the extent that we now witness and experience them. This point is that with which this study is most concerned: our perspective from which to view nature. I believe that ultimately the ecological crisis in our planet has originated in our inner realm, i.e., our way of perceiving the world and living in it. I have no doubt that insofar as we maintain the way we used to relate to nature, we can never find a way out of the present ecological crisis. In this regard, the ecological issue is a philosophical and theological issue as well, while we cannot deny or neglect its other dimensions such as technological, economic, and political. For our perspective on the world is profoundly influenced and formed by our theological and philosophical standpoints on the world.

I will now illustrate the current state of the earth in a way that we can grasp the gravity of the degradation of the world as a whole rather than various specific figures of the ecological crisis which continue to change[9]. In a passage of her book *The Death of Nature*, Carolyn Merchant succinctly describes how our planet is deteriorating day by day.

---

[9] Specific, updated data can be obtained by access to websites such as those of the Worldwatch Institute and World Resources Institute.

Today, a global ecological crisis [...] threatens the health of the entire planet. Ozone depletion, carbon dioxide buildup, chlorofluorocarbon emissions, and acid rain upset the respiration and clog the pores and lungs of the ancient Earth Mother, rechristened «Gaia», [...] Toxic wastes, pesticides, and herbicides seep into ground water, marshes, bays, and oceans, polluting Gaia's circulatory system. Tropical rainforests and northern old-growth forests disappear at alarming rates as lumberers shear Gaia of her tresses. Entire species of plants and animals become extinct each day[10].

The increase of the amount of carbon dioxide emission into the air, primarily owing to burning fossil fuels, causes the so-called greenhouse effect. The greenhouse effect is literally global: the temperature of the earth rises; the global weather pattern changes so that winter may become stormier and summer hotter and drier; sea level rises and many regions are flooded. Ozone depletion, mainly due to the emission of chlorofluorocarbons, which are used as refrigerator and air conditioner coolants, threatens living organisms in the planet with excessive ultraviolet rays from the sun. Acid rain is also generated by the industrial emission of sulfur dioxide, which in turn impacts on water, soil, and living organisms. «Toxic wastes, pesticides, and herbicides», which we produce for our convenience and discharge into the environment, contaminate the hydrosphere of the earth, which is indispensable to the survival of all life forms. Deforestation at an alarming rate allows the massive emission of carbon dioxide into the air, which in turn accentuates the greenhouse effect and accelerates the increase in the temperature of the earth. For one of the crucial functions of forest is to filter carbon dioxide by the process of photosynthesis. We now experience the impacts of the ecological disturbance and disintegration on living organisms: species of plants, animals, microbes, and fungi are reported to become extinct rapidly. Destructive changes in ecosystems lead to the extinction and deformation of diverse species; the loss of biodiversity breaks further the overall subtle equilibrium of the earth and worsens its ecological status.

One of the most serious dangers of the ecological disruption must be found in the fact that these unprecedented, dreadful phenomena in nature result from our ordinary way of living: «whenever our automobile air conditioner leaks, or we turn in an old refrigerator for a new one, we are inadvertently contributing to upper atmosphere ozone

---

[10] C. MERCHANT, *The Death of Nature*, xv. See also ID., *Radical Ecology*, 17-22.

depletion»[11]. The process of the ecological catastrophe is so unobtrusive and unnoticed that few if any perceive it at its early stage, but its effect is so extensive and fatal that few if any may escape from it. In this regard, the impact of war on ecological systems may awaken us to the seriousness of environmental disruption. Modern war instantly breaks and disrupts the ecosystem of a region with its annihilating power of weapons. While we must not forget this tremendous ravaging effect of war on ecosystems, it must be remembered as well that the consequences that our ordinary way of living brings about to the environment are no less dreadful, though more gradual, than those of war.

3. Responses from Humanity to the Ecological Crisis of the Earth

It is not long ago that ecological concern for nature was awakened. Until recently the pollution of air, water, and soil was regarded as a necessary evil for economic growth, which many believed would eventually bring them a better life. The American forester Aldo Leopold, who wrote *A Sand County Almanac* in 1949, a seminal book on the beauty of nature, and who is regarded as the pioneer of the so-called «land ethic» or «naturalist» environmental school, may be the first one in the modern era who evoked concern for nature. The American biologist and naturalist Rachel Carson raised a voice in 1962 with her book *Silent Spring*, a study of the effects of pesticides, to protest against the reckless exploitation of the environment for industrial development. It is said that she launched the environmental movement in the West. By the 1980s the ecological movement was well underway; ecological concern began to seep into the awareness of the public. For example, the Worldwatch Institute, which aims at an environmentally sustainable and socially just society, was founded by Lester Brown in 1974. It has since warned people of the gravity of ecological deterioration and issued the annual State of the World since 1984[12].

With the elevated awareness of the degradation of nature and its gravity increased the demands and efforts to deal with this difficult and perplexing problem. Considering that ecological issues are inevitably global, we will look at the efforts of international society to grapple with the deterioration of the global environment. From 1972 to 2002 were held three UN conferences on the environmental issue. The first

---

[11] C. MERCHANT, *Radical Ecology*, 19.
[12] Cf. B.R. HILL, *Christian Faith and the Environment*, 1-2.

one is the UN Conference on Human Environment in Stockholm in 1972. The Stockholm Conference stated that the natural resources of the earth must be preserved for the present and future generations; the capacity of the earth to produce renewable resources must be maintained, restored or improved; environmental concern must be considered in planning for economic development. In the years following the Stockholm Conference, two renowned reports regarding economic development and environment were issued, whose titles themselves are indicative of their contents: *The Limits to Growth* in 1972 by an international meeting known as the Club of Rome, composed of specialists in various fields; *Our Common Future* in 1987 by the WCED, also called the Brundtland Commission. The second one is the UN Conference on the Environment and Development in Rio de Janeiro in 1992. The Rio Conference, also called the Earth Summit, recognized a perpetuation of disparities between and within nations, a worsening of poverty, hunger, ill health, and illiteracy, and the continuing deterioration of the ecosystems. In the face of these human and natural calamities, it stressed the integration of the environment and development and that this cannot be achieved without a global cooperation for sustainable development. The third one is the UN World Summit on the Sustainable Development in Johannesburg in 2002. The Johannesburg Conference, addressing some of the most pressing concerns of poverty and the environment, contained in its outcome document targets and timetables to spur action on a wide range of issues: clean water, proper sanitation, the restoration of depleted fisheries, the reduction of biodiversity loss, the production and use of nontoxic chemicals, and increase in the use of renewable energy[13].

We need to listen to voices from religions as regards ecological issues. For religions are deeply involved in forming one's fundamental perspective on the world. While it is the case that religions inform a basic human attitude toward nature, it must be noted that throughout history, the relations of religions to nature have been ambivalent. It is true that religions have a potential power to contribute to building up a harmonious relationship of humanity with nature. However, some religions, Christianity in particular, have been criticized by some environmentalists as harmful rather than helpful to the well-being of nature.

---

[13] More specific details of the UN Conferences can be obtained by access to websites such as those of the UN Conference on Environment and Development and UN Division for Sustainable Development.

While it is controversial whether this criticism is true or not, religions have a great influence on human perspective on nature, either positively or negatively, at least at a theoretical level.

Religions may have a positive influence on human attitudes toward nature. First, most religions speak of a fundamental ground of all beings, explicitly or implicitly. Religions remind humans that all beings are interrelated and interdependent through this fundamental common ground, existing in all beings. In this regard, religions certainly help human beings cultivate an awareness of their interconnectedness with nature. For instance, Buddha-nature in Buddhism, *ch'i* in Confucianism, and the Holy Spirit in Christianity can be regarded as the respective fundamental ground of all beings in the universe.

Despite diverse Buddhist perspectives in various traditions, Buddhism in general teaches that there exists a Buddha-nature in all things that exist, even in nonsentient objects. For this reason, killing any life, however least it may be, is prohibited in principle. It emphasizes care and respect for the natural world for the same reason[14]. Furthermore, Buddhism sees that every being is connected with others in some way. Ultimately, there is no distinction between self and others: «life perdures only as a complex aggregation of multiple conditions»[15]. It holds that many people live in suffering because they do not realize this truth. According to Buddhism, salvation comes from the embodied realization of this truth: the oneness of all that exists in the universe. This can be a great source of ecological awareness.

Confucianism understands that the universe is a self-generating and organic process. It teaches that every life is sustained by *ch'i*, the unifying and generative material force in the universe. *Ch'i* is the fundamental source of all life forms and of transformation in the universe. Although Confucianism is criticized for being too patriarchal, its organic and unified cosmology holds potential to contribute to the formation of ecological consciousness[16].

Christianity, together with the other monotheistic religions of Judaism and Islam, believes that God created the universe and everything in it. Only God has the ultimate sovereignty and claim on the entire creation. Humanity may be God's steward or a ruler delegated by God. Human beings have no right to do any harm to nature, which belongs

---

14 Cf. L. LANCASTER, «Buddhism and Ecology», 13.

15 B. BROWN, «Toward a Buddhist Ecological Cosmology», 126.

16 Cf. M.E. TUCKER – J. BERTHRONG, ed., *Confucianism and Ecology*, xxxvi-xxxvii.

not to them but to God. While using with prudence the natural resources provided for their livelihood, humans have the responsibility to
take care of nature on behalf of God[17]. The doctrine of creation can
function as a constraint against the reckless human abuse of nature.
Moreover, the Judaeo-Christian tradition says that God not only created
the world but also sustains and renews it. Accordingly, God is at once
transcendent and immanent in relation to creation, which is bolstered
by the trinitarian doctrine of Christianity. God the Holy Spirit can be
perceived as the fundamental source and energizer for all beings in
creation. Understood this way, God is present in all beings without
exception because all creatures exist in virtue of the Spirit. The divine
immanence in all creation can play an affirmative role in reorienting
humanity's relationship to nature.

Second, many religions explicitly, or at least implicitly, teach mercy
to nonhuman beings and the love of them, which can make a positive
contribution to the well-being of nature. Buddhism, in particular,
teaches and stresses the importance of mercy which extends beyond
humanity. Respect for nonhuman beings comes out of its belief in the
existence of Buddha-nature in all things and leads to special respect for
life. Confucianism teaches *in* (meaning charity), which is one of the
most important virtues in Confucianism. *In* has potential to broaden its
scope beyond humanity to the natural world and to cultivate ecological
awareness.

The regulations of the sabbath day, sabbatical year, and jubilee in the
Judaeo-Christian heritage dictate the practice of concern not only for
human beings but also for other living beings and the land (cf. Lev. 25).
These insights and beliefs are critical for the cultivation of ecological
consciousness. In a similar vein, one of the most crucial teachings of
Christianity is love. The love which Jesus preached has been
understood to be a love only among human beings. No matter how we
may experience the love of Jesus, we must remember that it is
nonetheless the love of God of all creation that was manifested in the
person of Jesus. Therefore, ultimately, the love of God must be viewed
to reach the whole creation. In the Christian tradition, as in other
religious traditions, there are those who continue to be remembered for
being sensitive to nature, loving nature, and tasting a sense of God
through it: for instance, Hildegard of Bingen, Francis of Assisi, and
Meister Eckhart. Francis of Assisi, in particular, is well known for his

---

[17] Cf. E. KATZ, «Judaism and the Ecological Crisis»; R.E. TIMM, «The Ecological Fallout».

intimate relationship with other creatures such as the sun, the moon, birds, and even wolves, all of whom he referred to as his brothers and sisters. His love reached the whole creation beyond humanity. These pro-nature characters of religions, though sometimes neglected in the past, must be reclaimed today.

Admittedly, religions may also have a negative influence on human attitudes toward nature. First, an otherworldly tendency to emphasize the need of detachment from worldly things and to escape from the present material world to a spiritual world is found in most religions, except perhaps in Confucianism. Buddhism, for instance, teaches that one can arrive at the state of salvation, *nirvana*, only by removing all kinds of anxieties and evil passions in the present world. Notwithstanding its strong ecological motif of the oneness of all beings, it may then encourage people to depreciate the material world as a source of anxiety, passion, and suffering. Buddhists may easily become indifferent to the exploitation of nature by other human beings.

Christianity as well has shown a tendency of escapism in its history. Although acknowledging the goodness of creation by God, the ultimate Good, it has often depreciated or ignored nature. This tendency has probably originated in an ancient Greek worldview called hierarchical dualism, according to which, for instance, spirit (mind) and matter (body) are opposed: the former is good to pursue, the latter is evil and needs to be avoided[18]. During much of its history, one may say, Christianity's affirmation of the goodness of the natural world has actually remained in the shadow.

Second, some religions are predominantly human-centered in the sense that they consider their final goal to be the salvation of human beings (or human souls) alone. This anthropocentric idea of salvation in turn contributes to humanity's disregard to nature. Christianity in particular has severely been criticized by environmentalists for its strong anthropocentric tendency. Despite its affirmative attitudes toward the biophysical world, Christianity has shown, at the same time, the position that what is of ultimate importance is spiritual, and everything else will return to nothing. From this perspective, the rest of creation exists chiefly for humans, the only spiritual beings in the world. Nature has value solely in terms of usefulness for humankind. It is regarded as a backdrop in which human history unfolds and which will disappear in the end.

---

[18] Cf. E.A. JOHNSON, *Women, Earth, and Creator Spirit*, 10-12; R.R. RUETHER, *Gaia and God*, 22-26.

Confucianism has been anthropocentric in a different way from Christianity. In spite of its ecologically sound cosmology, Confucianism has been concerned primarily for the human world. It has made a great effort to explore how to live with harmony in society. Most of the classical literature in Confucianism is devoted to this theme such as ideal relationships between a monarch and a subject, among parents and children, and so forth. It is not clear, unlike anthropocentrism in Christian history, whether this human-centered propensity of Confucianism has substantially contributed to the human exploitation of nature.

Environmental awakening within Christianity was stirred in 1967, ironically, by a charge of the American historian Lynn White against Christianity for its responsibility for the ecological crisis[19]. White claimed that «the Judaeo-Christian tradition, with its emphasis on God's transcendence, the other-worldly destiny of the human, its orientation toward "progress," and its biblical notion of human "dominion" over the Earth, bore much of the blame for environmental devastation and degradation»[20]. His criticism provoked enormous controversies inside and outside Christianity, both pros and cons[21]. At the same time, it was an occasion to awaken the Christian churches to reflect upon themselves in relation to a pressing issue of the environment throughout the world[22]. Theologians began to review and reclaim their Christian traditions and to reframe their viewpoints on nature in an acute awareness of the impact and influence of religions and theologies on humanity's attitudes toward nature[23].

---

[19] Cf. L. WHITE, JR., «The Historical Roots».

[20] P. SMITH, *What Are They*, 72.

[21] Cf. P. SMITH, *What Are They*, 72-77.

[22] For a critical reflection on the Christian thoughts about nature, see P. SANTMIRE, *The Travail of Nature*. With two theological motifs, spiritual and ecological, Santmire examines prominent Christian thinkers in relation to nature. He finds in the history of Christian thought three dominant metaphors in this regard: a metaphor of ascent, fecundity, and migration to a good land. The first metaphor contributes to the spiritual motif; the third to the ecological motif; the second to both. He classifies those Christian thinkers into either of the two motifs, sometimes with their own ambiguities: Origen, Thomas Aquinas, Bonaventure, Dante, Luther, Calvin, Karl Barth, and Pierre Teilhard de Chardin to the spiritual motif; Irenaeus, Augustine in his later period, and Francis of Assisi to the ecological one.

[23] As some representative figures may be named Ian G. Barbour, Thomas Berry, Lenardo Boff, John Cobb, Jr., Matthew Fox, Elizabeth A. Johnson, Jay B. McDaniel, Sean McDonagh, Sallie McFague, Jürgen Moltmann, and Rosemary R. Ruether.

Aside from the theological circle, the Christian churches began to give their voices with regard to ecological issues. The WCC issued a document on «Just, Participatory and Sustainable Society» in the 1970s. Afterwards in the 1980s and 1990s, the WCC have worked on the theme «Justice, Peace and Integrity of Creation». The 1991 General Assembly of the WCC in Canberra took as its theme «Come Holy Spirit, Renew the Whole Creation». It maintained that the whole creation including the natural world as well as humanity must be renewed by the Holy Spirit in order to be liberated from all kinds of threats such as poverty, nuclear weapons, and the ecological collapse that threaten the life of all creation[24].

The Roman Catholic church as well started to address ecological issues. One could find the ecological concern of the Catholic church in various papal documents since Vatican Council II, but only in a scattered manner and in a context with a predominant concern for humanity[25]. The first substantial document must be attributed to Pope John Paul II's *Peace with God, Peace with All Creation*, the 1990 World Day of Peace Message, dedicated to peace and environmental issues[26]. This papal message describes the present ecological issue, complex as it is, basically as a moral issue that results from our lack of respect for life. It highlights the goodness and interdependence of all creation and an urgent need to preserve the integrity of creation, while it does not overlook the intimate relationship of poverty and ecological degradation. It emphasizes a concerted global solidarity and a common responsibility to solve this grave problem. Around this period Catholic Bishops' conferences in various countries, such as Dominican Republic (1987), Guatemala (1988), Northern Italy (1988), the Philippines (1988), Australia (1990), and the U.S.A. (1991), began to address environmental issues[27]. Ecological issues seem to have come into full blossom today.

---

[24] For the Protestan churches and ecological issues, see P. SMITH, *What Are They*, 72-77.

[25] For Catholic Magisterium and ecological issues, see P. SMITH, *What Are They*, 78-87.

[26] John Paul II already showed his ecological concern on other occasions. For example, see JOHN PAUL II, *Redemptor Hominis*, nn. 8.15.16; ID., *Centesimus Annus*, n. 37.

[27] Cf. The Appendices of D. CHRISTIANSEN – W. GRAZER, ed., *And God;* M. KEENAN, *From Stockholm to Johannesburg*.

CHAPTER II

Two Contrasting Perspectives on the World

1. A Scientific Perspective on the World

1.1 *The Significance of Cosmology*

In the twentieth century, we came to see from afar the earth as a whole, at least in its photographs taken by spaceships. The earth, thus taken, is often described as «a blue and white gem» spinning in the immense vastness of space. The earth, thus seen, looks beautiful, but fragile as well. We are now often told that this beautiful and tiny planet is undergoing severe ecological deterioration due to a species called humankind. With the ecological degradation of the earth, the role and significance that cosmology used to assume in the past come into the picture again. Before the modern period, «the story of the universe has given meaning to life and to existence itself. [...] It has been our fundamental referent as regards modes of personal and community conduct. It has established the basis of social authority»[1]. Regardless of their differences in specific contents, diverse cosmologies in various regions informed a perspective from which to see oneself, others, and the world and to find the ultimate meaning of life. In a word, cosmology used to provide a foundation of one's worldview.

Science such as astronomy, physics, biology, geology, and paleontology has revealed astoundingly new and significant facts about the universe and the earth, presenting a surprisingly different kind of cosmology. However, this new scientific account of the cosmos has been considered predominantly in relation to nature, apart from

---

[1] B. SWIMME – T. BERRY, *The Universe Story*, 1.

humankind. The story of humanity, i.e., history, has been regarded as strictly separated from the story of the universe. This is due in great measure to a dualistic worldview which divides the world into humanity and nature so thoroughly that these two are regarded as disparate realities. According to this dualistic perspective, humankind as the only subject is sharply contrasted with nature as an object. Because of a dichotomization of humanity from nature, a new scientific cosmology has had little influence on our perspective on the world. We have been left out of the contemporary universe story by stressing too much that we had another story proper to us, i.e., history.

We must seriously consider what the world is to us and how we are related to it in the face of the ecological disruption of the earth. For this, we need first to listen carefully to what science tells us today about the universe and the earth, which will provide a relatively objective foundation upon which we can form a proper attitude toward the world. This is true of a theological reflection on environmental issues, and theologians too must pay heed to the scientific account of the universe. As regards the relationship of theology and scientific cosmology, one can say, «Theology always presupposes some cosmology or another, and cosmology does make a difference to our theology's conceptualization of any God who possibly transcends and grounds the universe»[2]. Whether it is primitive or scientific, cosmology always bears theological implications; theologians speak within the context based on their cosmological assumptions. When one's cosmological presumption is out of date and no longer convincing to contemporaries, one's theological discourse and reflection would become sentimentally as well as intellectually irrelevant to them. For example, if a theologian today holds fast to the cosmology that the creation accounts of Genesis assumes, the theologian cannot talk in an intelligible and persuasive manner with his/her contemporaries, whose cosmological views are shaped by a substantially different version of cosmology such as an expanding universe and an evolving earth. With regard to the ecological issue as well, theologians must speak and talk in the terms and context which are generally accepted by their contemporaries in order that this issue may effectively be addressed.

This does not mean, however, that theology and religion must be examined and proved by science. This would mean an uncritical confla-

---

2 J.F. HAUGHT, *Science and Religion*, 41.

tion of theology and science, which can be called «concordism»[3]. For theology to appeal to science and to rely on it for a theological claim would be a risky and futile venture because scientific discoveries and conclusions always presume the possibility of revision in the future. Nevertheless, it is still true that although theology and science deal with different realms of reality, they can influence each other in a positive way that one deepens the other without intruding into one's proper area: «scientific knowledge can broaden the horizon of religious faith» and «the perspective of religious faith can deepen our understanding of the universe»[4]. Even from a historical point of view, Christianity has helped to shape the history of science in the West, and scientific cosmology has in turn influenced theology[5]. It is simply impossible to separate them completely. Nor is it desirable to do so.

As we begin the universe story, it needs to be remarked that I restrict myself to introducing and presenting an overview of the universe and the earth that is generally accepted in our times. Put otherwise, I will not deal with any advanced, but controversial, theory or discovery, which is definitely beyond my competency and the scope of this study. My intention consists in rendering a generally accepted scientific account of the universe and the earth and considering its significance and implications for our perspective on the world. What I expect here is that a perspective based on a scientific cosmology will provide a convincing, overall context within which one can theologically reflect on the world and a proper way of grasping the world in the age of the global ecological crisis.

1.2   The Story of the Universe[6]

What does science such as astronomy and physics tell us today about the universe? Let us start with our galaxy, the Milky Way, to which the

---

[3] For various perspectives on the relationship of theology (religion) and science, see I.G. BARBOUR, *Religion and Science*, 77-105; J.F. HAUGHT, *Science and Religion*, 9-26. According to Barbour (Haught), these diverse perspectives can be grouped into conflict, independence (contrast), dialogue (contact), and integration (confirmation).

[4] J.F. HAUGHT, *Science and Religion*, 18.

[5] Cf. J.F. HAUGHT, *Science and Religion*, 17-18.

[6] For a scientific account of the universe and the earth, I am indebted to I.G. BARBOUR, *Religion and Science*, 195-199.221-223; J.F. HAUGHT, *Science and Religion*, 100-105; D. EDWARDS, *Jesus and the Cosmos*, 11-19; ID., *Jesus the Wisdom of God*, 10-13; and B. SWIMME – T. BERRY, *Universe Story*, 7-15.

solar system belongs and whose size is such that it takes a hundred thousand years for light to cross it. The sun is just one of more than two billion stars in the Milky Way. The sun is an average-sized star with a diameter of 863,000 miles, located about 27,000 light years from the center of the galaxy; it travels in a circular orbit around the galaxy at a speed of 210 kilometers per second; it rotates around the galaxy once for about 250 million years. The American astronomer Edwin Hubble demonstrated in 1924 that the Milky Way is not the only galaxy in the universe. Astronomy says today that at least a hundred billion galaxies are observed in the universe.

How did this vast universe come into being at all? It is now generally accepted that the universe is not static but dynamic. The Dutch physicist Willem de Sitter found in 1917 a solution that predicted an expanding universe, while working on Einstein's general relativity equations. In 1929, the American astronomer Edwin Hubble discovered that the spectral lines of the light from distant nebulae are shifted to the red. This «red shift» of light could be explained only by the fact that these stars are moving away from us. For light from stars moving toward us is blue-shifted, while light from those moving away is red-shifted, due to the Doppler Effect. He showed that most galaxies move away from us, and he formulated Hubble's law that the velocity of the recession of a nebula is proportional to its distance from us. The distance between galaxies has always been increasing. We must not imagine, however, a universe which expands *in* space. Rather, these scientific facts affirm that the universe itself is stretching and inflating. Moreover, it is not only space that is expanding. Einstein's general theory of relativity holds that gravity is a distortion of space and time, indicating that time is inextricably linked to space. The universe is not static but dynamic in both space and time.

An ever expanding universe implies that the cosmic expansion might have begun from an extremely condensed state. The most commonly accepted scientific theory concerning the origin of the universe is the so-called «big-bang theory». According to the big bang theory, around fifteen billion years ago an «incredibly compressed pinhead of matter began to "explode," creating space and time in the process»[7]. With this primordial explosion, the universe came into being; it has since been expanding. Arno Penzias and Robert Wilson discovered in 1965 a low temperature cosmic background microwave radiation coming from all

---

7 J.F. HAUGHT, *Science and Religion*, 102.

directions in space, which might indicate the cosmic fireball's after-glow, cooled by its subsequent expansion. «This radiation was the clearest signal to date that a singular originating comic event had occurred some fifteen billion years ago»[8]. Tiny variations in back-ground microwave radiation, observed by the COBE satellite of NASA in 1992 and interpreted to account for the clumpiness of galaxies, further bolstered this theory[9]. Since the introduction of particle accel-erators to simulate the heat of the primordial explosion, high-energy physics too has provided, not only in theory but in experiment, indirect evidences in favor of the big-bang theory.

The story of the universe according to the discoveries and evidences from astronomy and high-energy physics may be reconstructed as follows. Around fifteen billion years ago, there occurred an explosion called «the big bang». A standard big bang theory does not give any explanation about the state of the universe at the moment of the explo-sion itself; that moment is regarded as a singularity to which the laws of physics cannot apply. It is surmised that at this phase the four basic forces of the universe (gravity, electromagnetic, and the strong and weak nuclear forces) constituted a single cosmic force. Theories are still more tentative regarding the first three minutes since the primor-dial explosion, because the state of the universe cannot be simulated in the laboratory. It is conjectured that within the first second the tempera-ture was so high that ordinary atomic nuclei did not exist. In this stage, individual subatomic particles, protons, neutrons, electrons, photons, and neutrinos came into being, as well as gravitational force, strong nuclear force, and weak nuclear and electromagnetic forces. It is said that the initial explosion took place with an incredible balance between expanding force and gravitational force: had one force been just slightly weaker than the other, the universe would have either fallen back upon itself or flown apart, without forming galaxies[10].

---

[8] J.F. HAUGHT, *Science and Religion*, 103.

[9] Cf. J.F. HAUGHT, *Science and Religion*, 104. The clumsiness or lumpiness of the universe refers to the fact that the universe is composed of «very unevenly distributed galaxies, clusters and super-clusters of galaxies, stars, planets, gases and other not yet fully understood kinds of matter».

[10] Cf. I.G. BARBOUR, *Religion and Science*, 204-205. The final fate of the universe may be predicted according to the balance of gravitational and expanding forces. The first possibility is the open universe that will expand forever; the second is the flat universe in which at some moment the two forces will come to a complete standoff; the last is the closed universe that will eventually collapse back upon itself (the big crunch).

It is estimated that within a few minutes from the explosion the nuclei of helium and hydrogen emerged out of the interactions of elementary particles such as protons and neutrons, as the universe continuously expanded and cooled down below a billion degrees. Eventually, the huge clouds of hydrogen gas began to coalesce due to the force of gravitation, forming first-generation gigantic stars. Inside these stars, nuclear reactions occurred owing to the rise of temperature caused by the pull of gravitation. They ultimately resulted in a huge explosion, which produced heavier atomic elements necessary for the present universe to be formed. These materials finally gave rise to second-generation stars, such as the sun. «Second-generation stars were richer in potentiality and more complex in internal structure because the primal stars had created the elemental beings of carbon, nitrogen, oxygen [...]»[11]. About five billion years ago, the solar system was brought into being. Its «parent nebular», as swirling particles of dust and gas, began to condense due to gravitational forces and caused density and temperature to be increased in its center. «Gravitational pressure eventually ignited the thermonuclear action of the Protosun. Rings of matter spun off from the nebula formed in individual units around the Sun, and their own forces of gravitation began to mold them into the spherical planets we know»[12].

In sum, the universe that science discloses to us is far beyond our imagination in its size, age, and process through which it has been formed as it is. The earth, seen from the vantage point of the whole universe, is really like a grain of sand in a vast sand field. Let us continue to listen to the story of the earth.

1.3 *The Story of the Earth*

What does science, such as geology, biology, and paleontology, tell us today about the earth? The earth, a satellite of the sun, is known to have come into being around 4.6 billion years ago. It is located at 93 million miles from the sun; its radius is 4,000 miles and its circumference 24,800 miles. Unlike other planets in the solar system such as Jupiter, Saturn, and Neptune, the earth is located at exactly the right distance from the sun which ensures an optimal temperature for the appearance of complex molecules and eventually life forms. The earth was formed through a process of accretion in which meteorites were

---

[11] B. SWIMME – T. BERRY, *Universe Story*, 8.
[12] D. EDWARDS, *Jesus and the Cosmos*, 14-15.

pulled together by gravitational forces. Gravitational pressure heated up the interior of the planet, and a molten core was formed. The core was surrounded by a mantle, which was in turn enclosed by a crust[13].

It was in the oceans that scientists believe that creative chemical interactions took place and eventually enabled the appearance of life forms. The fossil records inform us that the first life form emerged on earth in the form of blue-green bacteria 3.5 billion years ago in the early Precambrian period. They are believed to have been the main form of life for the next 2.5 billion years. During this period, oxygen is thought to have made its appearance, presumably because of these bacteria's consumption of hydrogen from water in the ocean. Oxygen in the atmosphere changed greatly the condition of the earth, in which these bacteria themselves could not endure. Out of this new condition emerged richer forms of life than before. We know by means of the fossil records that there appeared marine invertebrates as animal life between 600 and 700 million years ago around the end of the Precambrian period. We have plenty of fossils of various kinds of fish between 570 and 230 million years ago in the Paleozoic period. About four million years ago, simple vascular plants appeared; later in the same period, vertebrates in the form of marine amphibians began to live on land. By the end of this period, the first form of reptiles appeared. They dominated the earth during the next Mesozoic period between 230 and 65 million years ago. It was in this period as well that dinosaurs first appeared and proliferated. Toward the end of this period, birds and flowers came into being. Then, huge astronomical collisions with the earth took place and changed greatly the atmosphere and climate of the earth, which in turn forced the modification and extinction of nearly all life forms in that age. After this, many new forms of life began to thrive on earth. For instance, with the disappearance of dinosaurs, mammals took center-stage and multiplied. Mammals were able to regulate their body temperature so that they could inhabit other regions with different climates. In the Cenozoic period, which began about 65 million years ago, a wide variety of species appeared on earth. It is at the beginning of this period that the first primates appeared.

In Africa was found the fossil of human-like species called *Australopithecus*, which is believed to have existed from four to one million years ago. They stood erect, with a relatively small brain cavity. A next group is *Homo erectus*, which is thought to have lived from about two

---

13 Cf. D. EDWARDS, *Jesus and the Cosmos*, 15.

million years to 259 thousand years ago. They used fire and tools. Then, another group made its appearance, known as *Homo sapiens*, the Neanderthal subspecies, between 70,000 and 40,000 years ago. We have some evidences of modern humankind with a very large brain and small face and teeth between 30,000 and 40,000 years ago. It is estimated that somewhere in this course emerged human self-awareness.

Through new discoveries and theories in biology since the publication of *On the Origin of Species* by Charles Darwin in 1859, it is now generally allowed that all the appearances and transitions of diverse life forms on the earth have occurred out of evolutionary processes since the birth of the earth: from inanimate matter to primitive life forms to the human race with self-consciousness[14]. The appearance of humankind on earth was a genuinely and qualitatively new moment in the story of the earth in that although human beings have emerged out of the earth and are in this sense connected with it, they possess the unique qualities, such as mind and will, which drastically distinguish them from the rest of the earth. «Something radically different takes place when culture rather than the genes becomes the principal means by which the past is transmitted to the future and when conscious choice alters that future»[15].

Human beings began to form society in the form of tribe and to foster diverse cultures and civilizations, represented by Mesopotamia, Egypt, Greece, India, and China. Since the seventeenth century, European countries expanded their territories through colonization in other continents, supported by rapid developments of science and technologies, and the capitalist market economy came to thrive. In the twentieth century, we have seen further scientific developments at a dazzling speed; but, at the same time, we have also witnessed disastrous poverty imposed on a great number of people in the midst of splendid material affluence. The dropping of two atomic bombs in Japan by the U.S.A. around the end of World War II was the occasion that showed dramatically the astounding development which humanity has achieved in science and technologies, on the one hand, and the astonishing power and horrible consequence that the human race now possesses and can cause, on the other hand. In addition to the nuclear threat of destruction to humankind, we have now come to encounter another unprecedented

---

[14] For a historical and a theoretical expositions of evolution and its implications, see I.G. BARBOUR, *Religion and Science*, 49-74.

[15] I.G. BARBOUR, *Religion and Science*, 61.

threat of annihilation, not only to humanity but to almost all life forms on the planet: the ecological collapse of the earth.

1.4 An Emerging Perspective on the World: A Dynamic and Relational World

The scientific account today of the universe and the earth informs in a great measure our perspective on the world. The world seen from the vantage point of a new scientific cosmology is no longer static, nor is it a set of disparate individuals. The scientific cosmology reveals that the world is a dynamic reality. The universe is seen to expand and change continuously from the beginning. It also shows that the world is a relational reality. All things that exist in the universe are connected with each other due to the common origin and evolutionary process of the cosmos. All are interrelated not only spatially but temporally. The dynamic and relational aspects of the world come into the foreground by the scientific account of an expanding universe and an evolving earth. An expanding universe bluntly tells us that the universe is not a finished or fixed reality. The big bang theory holds that all things that exist in the universe came into being ultimately out of the primordial explosion. Hence, no matter how different things may appear from each other, their origins are one and the same. In this regard, all things are fundamentally linked with one another. Nature is now viewed basically as a reality in dynamism and relationality. An evolving earth solidifies this perspective on the world. The evolutionary theory casts light on nature as a state of flux rather than as a static structure of immutable forms.

A dynamic and relational perspective on the world implies a revolutionary turn from the classical, mechanistic viewpoint of the world. The mechanistic worldview, which was pioneered and developed by such figures as René Descartes and Isaac Newton, holds that nature, society, and the human body are composed of «interchangeable atomized parts that can be repaired or replaced from outside». According to this mechanistic viewpoint, nature is basically «a system of dead, inert particles moved by external rather than inherent forces»[16]. This mechanistic worldview has exerted, up until now, immense influence on our way of seeing and relating to nature. The mechanistic perspective, which perceives the world except the human being (or the human mind)

---

[16] C. MERCHANT, *Radical Ecology*, 48. For an exposition of the mechanistic worldview and its implications, see ID., *The Death of Nature*, 164-252.

as a machine made of separate material parts, inevitably bears a dualistic bias that breaks asunder humankind from nature. This mechanistic and dualistic worldview in turn gives us a sanction to manipulate and experiment on nature without constraints and to extract material resources out of it, because nature is grasped merely as a collective system of inanimate objects. This worldview cannot help but insinuate in us an anthropocentric posture toward nature. Nature turns into a warehouse for human beings.

On the contrary, recent scientific theories and discoveries show that all things are connected with each other due to the common origin of the universe. The evolutionary view of the earth confirms the interconnectedness of all things, especially that of humanity and nature. Interconnectedness implies that nature must no longer be viewed as a machine consisting of inert parts that can freely be extracted, replaced, and repaired. Instead, it brings to the fore nature as an organism in which all things are in organic interdependence. Interconnectedness indicates that one must not dichotomize matter from life and life from mind. In sum, a dynamic and relational perspective on the world, grounded in the recent scientific account of the world, raises a serious doubt on the validity of the mechanistic, dualistic, and anthropocentric worldview, which is to blame in great part for the ecological deterioration of the earth today.

A dynamic and relational perspective on the world also brings to the center the temporality of nature, which used to be grasped as a timeless reality. New scientific discoveries and theories make plain that nature has a continuously unfolding story, whose end we do not know yet. Each event is unique and irreversible in the evolutionary process of the cosmos. This means that the story of the universe has a historical character, like human history. The story of the cosmos emerges as cosmic history, i.e., the history of nature, an infinitesimal part of which is human history. Science reclaims historicity for nature. The story of nature is now generally accepted as an inconceivably long history which encompasses humanity as well as the earth.

An observation in the process of evolution bolsters this viewpoint. The importance of the role that «chance» plays in the evolutionary process leads us to view nature basically as an indeterminate reality incorporating spontaneity, novelty, and creativity rather than as a determinate reality ruled by rigid natural laws. «The past is built into the present, and it shapes the future, providing the starting point for further evolutionary change but not determining it»[17]. However, this does not mean a chaotic randomness of nature. It is now known that evolution as a whole has occurred, up until now, in a direction that it tends to increase the diversity, interiority, and complexity of beings, for example, from matter to life to mind. In this regard, nature seems to possess a self-organizing tendency. A bent toward the increase of diversity, interiority, and complexity in nature affirms further that the human race has appeared out of nature. Therefore, humankind is part of the earth, no matter how different it may seem from nature[18]. A bias toward the intensification of self-organization in nature confirms that natural history encompasses human history.

2. A Predominant Perspective on the World Today and a Challenge

We have been told in the second observation that all things in the universe are related to one another, without exception, owing to their common origin that the big bang theory conceives and to their gradual unfolding that the expanding universe and the evolving earth indicate. We generally accept that we humans have emerged from the earth through the process of evolution. We also admit that we are in this sense part of it. One may then expect that our realization of interconnectedness among all things instill in us a stronger motive than ever to care for the earth. For we may be inclined to appreciate the earth as that from which we have come into being. Contrary to this expectation, however, what we now witness and experience is the deterioration of nature throughout the world, as the first observation vividly shows. One must then ask why the ecological crisis happened to the earth and why it seems to be deepening. As already mentioned briefly, the ecological issue is, to be sure, a complex problem in which not a few factors are involved and considered. One may name a number of plausible causes such as selfishness, scientific and technological development, and economic and political systems. I believe, however, that all these are grounded in and influenced by our fundamental perspective to grasp ourselves, the entire humanity, the natural world, and finally the world as a whole.

I take heed of a sense of disconnectedness and an excessively utilitarian tendency as two prominent features in our attitude toward other

---

[17] I.G. BARBOUR, *Religion and Science*, 277.
[18] Cf. I.G. BARBOUR, *Religion and Science*, 55-56.

human beings and nature[19]. This observation is far from what one may expect as our attitude toward others, given that the scientific account of the world is taken for granted. Logically speaking, if we accept a new scientific cosmology, we must accordingly have a sensibility that we are connected with others and that these others in the world do not exist primarily for our sake. The story of the universe conveyed by science is not so much anthropocentric as cosmocentric. What we really experience and witness is, however, a strong sense that we are the center of the world. One cannot help admitting, in the face of this unexpected realization, that many accept what the scientific cosmology suggests, but only formally and theoretically and deny it, implicitly and practically. It seems to me that there exists a sense of deep division in us. Many rarely feel that they are somehow deeply related to others and dependent on them. Instead, a rigidly mechanistic, dualistic, and anthropocentric perspective which is inimical to the sensibility of interconnectedness prevails in us. We can hardly sense in this dualistic and anthropocentric viewpoint any inherent connection with others. It may then be natural that an attitude which would acknowledge primarily the instrumental (utilitarian) value of others becomes prevalent among us[20]. Others may have meaning, not as they are, but as a means to our benefit. An excessive utilitarianism makes it extremely formidable for one to recognize the intrinsic value of others. It tends to drive one to seek in the first place instrumental value in others, rather than to appreciate them as they are. A lack of the sensibility of interconnectedness and an immoderate, utilitarian attitude toward others make us blind to what our

---

[19] Some would not agree with what I recognize as predominant tendencies among us. For this understanding of our world depends on not so much some objective facts that can be proved as one's experience of the world and stance on it. I would say that my viewpoint is in accord with what the Thirty-Fourth General Congregation of the Society of Jesus in 1995 mentioned regarding our world in Decree 9: «Unbridled captialism produces disproportionate growth for some economic sectors, exclusion and marginalization for many others. Contemporary society is infected by consumerism, hedonism, and lack of responsibility. The values considered important today are personal fulfillment, competition, efficiency, and success at any cost» (n. 5); «in an egoistic world lacking a sense of responsibility for others [...]» (n. 18). See SOCIETY OF JESUS, *Documents*, 132-133.139.

[20] In this study, «utilitarian (value)» means «instrumental (value)», and these two terms will be used interchangeably. «Utilitarianism (instrumentalism)» in this thesis indicates an attitude in general that acknowledges predominantly utilitarian (instrumental) value in others, rather than precisely the ethical term «utilitarianism» such as the one with the slogan of «the greatest good for the greatest number of people».

scientific cosmology reveals today. They are likely to lead us to a reckless exploitation of other human beings and nature.

Given this, in order to grapple properly with the global ecological crisis in our times, we need drastically new minds, eyes, and behaviors whereby we may conceive, see, and act with others in a radically new way. We must differently think, see, and act. We need a conversion of heart, mind, and act. We must change in order that we may stop further ecological collapse. We are challenged to make a constant effort to change the way we used to relate to others in order to cultivate or regain a sensibility for the interconnectedness of all, which can be called ecological consciousness, and an integrated perspective on the world, which can be called an ecological vision of the world. This study is a response to this challenge we face. This thesis is an attempt, based on Christian faith, to overcome a tragic loss or lack of our sensibility for interconnectedness and an extremely utilitarian attitude toward others and to seek an ecological vision of the world that will instill in us ecological consciousness.

PART II

IN SEARCH OF
AN ALTERNATIVE VISION OF THE WORLD

CHAPTER III

The Interconnectedness of All Creatures

Proposition I: A Christian perspective on the world shows that all the finite beings in the world are interrelated and interdependent.

It is not self-evident that all the finite beings in the world are interrelated and interdependent. The first proposition depends in great measure on a perspective from which to see the world. We, as Christians, believe and confess that the world is the creation of God, who is «the maker of heaven and earth». However, this does not seem to be sufficient yet to affirm this proposition. For there can be different ways of grasping the world, granted that it is God's creation. After all, our way of seeing the world is closely connected with and deeply influenced by how we conceive God relates to creation.

As regards the relationship of God to the world, we Christians need first to look into what the Bible says about creation. It must be noted first of all that the theme of creation is not confined to the creation accounts of Genesis. Instead, this theme is found throughout the Scriptures, in diverse forms according to different purposes and contexts: for instance, Genesis, Deutero-Isaiah, Psalms, and wisdom literature in the Old Testament; gospels (especially, the gospel of John) and Pauline epistles in the New Testament[1]. Although a comprehensive review of creation texts in the Bible cannot be done here, two biblical perspectives on creation need to be noted here in relation to the first proposition. First, creation is not confined to those particular divine acts in the creation accounts of Genesis. Rather, the Scriptures view creation in the light of the continuous relationship of God with the world, ever

---

[1] Cf. A.M. CLIFFORD, «Creation».

since the beginning of creation. In this regard, the act of creation is closely linked to the way God relates to the order of creation. This creation theme is often expressed in the Old Testament through diverse historical experiences of Israel, a people which was deeply aware of God's presence in its history. Second, in connection with the first, the Scriptures declare that God is the unique origin, ground, and goal of creation. In other words, God is the creator, sustainer, and redeemer of the world. It means that creation, sustenance, and redemption are not three discrete events, but they constitute one single salvation history. We must understand these three aspects of the world in one continuous and dynamic horizon.

I will in this chapter deal with relationships among all the finite beings in the world, i.e., the interconnectedness of all creatures. I am particularly concerned for the relationship of humanity with nature. I intend to show, drawing on the four resource theologians, that the first proposition, which I think indispensable to an ecological vision of the world, is based on the sound Christian theological tradition and convincing to our contemporaries who are accustomed to a scientific worldview such as an evolutionary perspective. Especially since the Enlightenment in the West have we lost the sensibility of «being related to others», both human and nonhuman. One of its tragic consequences today is, I believe, the environmental disruption of the earth in the midst of unprecedented material affluence. Unless we recover this lost sense of interconnectedness, any suggestion to settle the present environmental deterioration of nature would be impractical or provisional, at best. It is naïve and unrealistic to expect people to relinquish their current, comfortable way of living to which they have long been accustomed, simply because they acknowledge the gravity of the ecological degradation of the earth. If one does not feel somehow fundamentally connected with nature, who bothers at all to make a drastic change for the sake of nature? A fundamental change in one's way of living is by no means facile. That change, if it is to occur and last, must originate from and be stimulated by a radical change in one's perspective on nature. We need a real change of heart, i.e., conversion. I believe that the first step toward this conversion would be to regain our sensibility of interconnected-ness with others. This is what the first proposition pursues.

1. The Interconnectedness of All Creatures from the Perspective of Karl Rahner

1.1 *Introduction*

Karl Rahner[2] was keenly aware of the scientific and intellectual milieu in his age and considered seriously some critical issues that it brought up. For instance, he was concerned about various challenges which science raised in his time and tried to grapple with them as a theologian[3]. He sought to provide theological responses for contemporary Christians perplexed or even discouraged by them. One may say that the evolutionary view of the world has been one of the most challenging and embarrassing issues to Christians. The evolution of the world means a revolutionary turn from the traditional, static viewpoint of the world from which nature was seen as a changeless and timeless reality. On the contrary, the world seen from the evolutionary viewpoint is basically a dynamic reality in a process of continuous change. The world is perceived as not so much fixed matter as fluctuating stream. Relationality and instability appear no less significant than individuality and stability. Such a drastic change that the evolutionary worldview effects would come into conflict with the traditional way of grasping the world. This was the case with Christianity.

At the heart of the controversy between Christianity and the evolutionary worldview was the issue of hominization, i.e., the evolution of humanity from nature[4]. To settle this controversial issue, the Catholic church held that a study of humankind's origin from the evolutionary perspective must be allowed only for the human body. The church claimed that the human soul cannot be an object of science because every human soul is directly created by God. The church recognized

---

[2] Karl Rahner, a German Jesuit priest, studied philosophy in Freiburg and completed doctoral and postdoctoral studies in theology in Innsbruck. He taught in Pullach, Innsbruck, Munich, and Münster. He was a peritus at Vatican Council II and a member of the editorial board of *Concilium*. In addition to his first two books, *Spirit in the World* and *Hearers of the Word*, most of his works, which are more than 3,500 items, are included in *Theological Investigations* (23 volumes).

[3] A glance at some of his works would show how sensitive and responsive Rahner was to the mindset and issues in his time: *Hominization: The Evolutionary Origin of Man as a Theological Problem*, «Natural Science and Reasonable Faith», «Christology within an Evolutionary View of the World», and «Christology in the Setting of Modern Man's Understanding of Himself and of His World».

[4] Cf. K. RAHNER, *Hominization*.

only the so-called «moderate evolutionary theory» that restricted the scope of evolution to the human body.

Rahner thought, however, that the way the Church sought to resolve this issue was problematic. He first pointed out that this issue could not be solved simply by declaring that God's immediate creation of the soul is a Catholic dogma and that therefore the Christian must allow and hold solely the moderate evolutionary view of the world[5]. For the acknowledgement of a moderate version of the evolutionary theory contradicted another teaching of the church. What the church demanded from the evolutionary theory presupposed that the human being is composed of soul and body and that they are separable from each other. What the church actually did is that it divided the human being into soul and body, surrendered the body to the evolutionary sphere and sought to maintain the soul intact. However, according to the Christian tradition, the human body and soul are inseparable, though distinct from each other. There is in the human person the substantial unity of body and soul. Therefore, once an argument is put forward about the human body, it is already meant for the human being as a whole. It follows from this that if the church acknowledges the evolution of the human body out of the natural world, it already comes to suggest in some way the evolution of the entire human being, i.e., body and soul. The soul cannot evade evolution once the body is involved in it. The problem thus remains unsolved because the church does not allow a dichotomization between soul and body, which it seems now to mandate: «It follows at once from the substantial unity of man that all problems are far from being solved when evolution of man's "body" is admitted, and excluded for his "soul"»[6].

Rahner worried that the contention that God immediately creates every human soul would appear, in the world where the idea of evolution was taken for granted, to be the «predicamental» intervention of God[7]. For him, it would be «a lazy compromise between a theological and a scientific statement» to leave this problem alone[8]. Given the substantial unity of body and soul, how can we coherently render God's immediate creation of the soul and hominization? This is what Rahner sought to answer.

---

[5] Cf. K. RAHNER, *Hominization*, 62.
[6] K. RAHNER, *Hominization*, 18.
[7] K. RAHNER, *Hominization*, 66.
[8] K. RAHNER, *Hominization*, 63.

Christology was another issue about which Rahner was greatly concerned, particularly in relation to the evolutionary viewpoint. He was not interested in the validity of the evolutionary view itself, nor was he competent in this scientific discipline. He was afraid, however, that the traditional christological formula of «the union of divine nature and human nature in the one divine person of Jesus Christ» might appear such an ancient myth to his contemporaries clothed with the evolutionary worldview that they would no longer consider it seriously. In order to cope with this problem, he focused on «whether Christology is compatible or can be compatible with it»[9] and whether there exists «the inner affinity of these two doctrines»[10], given the evolutionary worldview. He sought thereby to render the traditional christological assertion more intelligible.

In his effort to grapple with these issues, Rahner conceived an integrated perspective on creation from which he interpreted these traditional Christian assertions and rendered them compatible with what the evolutionary view of the world implies. Since the issue of the ecological crisis was not as vital in his time as it is now, it is understandable that he rarely if ever remarked on this topic. Nonetheless, his unified perspective on the world can bring to light the relationships of all finite beings in the world. With this in mind, I will in this section reflect on the relationship of humanity with nature from the standpoint of the unity of spirit and matter. I will then examine how evolution can be understood in connection with creation. It will be held that evolution in the world can be regarded as a process of active self-transcendence in creation and that nature and humanity can be viewed as the cosmic self-consciousness and cosmic bodily presence respectively.

Given the intrinsic connection of humankind with nature based on the unity of spirit and matter, one may be intrigued to ask what happens to one's relationship with nature after death. We know that the human being disappears in death from this world, at least physically. However, what happens to our relationship with the world? Is it still meaningful in some way, even after our death? I think that this question is not

---

[9] K. RAHNER, Foundations of Christian Faith, 178.

[10] K. RAHNER, «Christology», 158. Rahner is different in this respect from Teilhard de Chardin. Teilhard, as a paleontologist, made a contribution to the evolutionary research and was sure, to that extent, of the evolution of the world. It can be said that he tried to situate and understand Christian faith in the context of the evolutionary world, of which he was convinced. On the contrary, one may say that Rahner approached this issue purely as a theologian.

merely a matter of curiosity. Rather, it influences the way we view and relate to nature here and now. If our link to nature disappears in death, it may be formidable to find an enduring motive of ecological concern. One may wonder why we must bother to take care of nature if we have eventually no connection with it. In this context, at the end of this section, I will seek to reflect on the relationship of humanity to nature after death, based on Rahner's reflection on death. Death will be presented as a moment in which we become open to the entire cosmos and thereby widen and deepen our relationship with nature rather than lose it. Any reflection in relation to death cannot help being speculative in great measure. Despite this limitation, it may suggest how fundamentally and intrinsically interwoven humanity and nature are and what kind of relationship may continue to exist after death. This suggestion will throw, I hope, a new light on how we must relate to nature, here and now.

1.2 The Relationship of Humanity with Nature

1.2.1 Nature and the Human Being as the Unity of Spirit and Matter

A ground for the unity of creation can be found in the fundamental Christian faith that the only God created all things that exist. This belief means not only that

> everything in its variety stems from one cause [...] It means also that this variety shows an inner similarity and community: that the contents of this variety must not be simply regarded as essentially different or even contradictory but rather that this variety and difference be seen to form a unity in origin, self-realization and determination, in short: one world[11].

What we actually experience in the world is a myriad variety of things. Nonetheless, this diversity does not deny the unity which undergirds immensely diverse kinds of things and thereby maintains a certain integrity and harmony in the world, despite often chaotic appearances. For Christians, this unity originates in God the only creator of the cosmos, which is composed of innumerable creatures. It is the case that there exist in creation essential differences among diverse creatures, for example, among plants and animals. Nevertheless, it is not the case that they are so different that they are absolutely disparate realities and thus in no sense related to each other[12]. Insofar as God created all that exists,

---

11 K. RAHNER, «Christology», 161.
12 K. RAHNER, *Foundations of Christian Faith*, 184.

one must say, what is more profound than diversity and dissimilarity in creation is unity and harmony. Given that a community is grounded in both unity and diversity, which ensure coherence in a community (otherwise, it would be chaos) and the individuality of each member (otherwise, it would be a monad) respectively, creation can be regarded as a community whose unity and diversity stem from God. It is in virtue of unity and diversity that creation is called the cosmos[13].

Given the relationship of unity and diversity in the world, we need to heed the relationship between spirit and matter, two primary elements in creation, in order to delve more concretely into relationships among all creatures. One may first ask what is spirit and matter and how they can be experienced. It is in fact only in the human being that matter and spirit are manifested and experienced together. Since spirit and matter are indivisible in the human being, we cannot properly understand one without the other. One must be considered always in connection with the other. Hence, we must start from the human being as a whole. For Rahner, the human being is in the first place a spirit. Spirit is «the one man in so far as he becomes conscious of himself in an absolute consciousness of being-given-to himself»[14]. Spirit refers in this sense to self-presence and self-possession. In other words, when we are aware of ourselves, we already transcend, confront, and experience ourselves as something inevitably given to us. We, as spirit, transcend and possess ourselves, but not absolutely. Put otherwise, the human being is a finite spirit[15]. Conversely, matter can be regarded as what we, as spirit, experience as that which is unavoidably given to us. «A person experiences both himself and the world which directly encounters him as matter [...] insofar as every person includes what is foreign to himself and is not at his own disposal»[16].

---

[13] It may be worth mentioning the difference between unity and uniformity, particularly with regard to diversity. Every created being needs other beings in the sense that no creature is totally self-sufficient. One can then hold that creatures must be diverse in order that they may complement each other. In this regard, diversity is indispensable to a community in which no one is self-sufficient. Uniformity, however, does not allow the individuality of each member and forces all into the sameness. Uniformity is incompatible with and excludes diversity. On the contrary, unity does not reject but presupposes diversity. Diversity is in turn grounded in unity. See K. RAHNER, «The Unity», 161-162.

[14] K. RAHNER, «Christology», 162-163.

[15] K. RAHNER, Foundations of Christian Faith, 29-32.

[16] K. RAHNER, Foundations of Christian Faith, 183.

In this regard, we experience ourselves as spirit and matter, but always in unity. One may say that although they are essentially different from one another and irreducible to each other, spirit and matter are so profoundly and intrinsically interconnected that they form a profound unity: «a human person is not a contradictory or merely provisional composite of spirit and matter, but is a unity which is both logically and really antecedent to the differentiation and distinction of its elements»[17].

On the basis of this anthropological understanding, one may say, insofar as we are aware of the world as something inescapably given to us, we experience it as matter and thereby we, as spirit, are inseparably united with the world. We are «spirits in the world». We can never absolutely escape from the world, insofar as we are spirits in the world. We, as spirit, are connected with the world in the same way we are united with our body, in the sense that both of them are experienced as matter. One may now hold that the relationship of humanity with nature is tantamount to and rooted in the unity of spirit and matter. Put otherwise, human beings are connected with nature not extrinsically and incidentally but intrinsically and inevitably. This intrinsic link of spirit and matter implies that matter exists as far as spirit lasts, even at the moment of salvation: «the consummation of the finite spirit which is man must be thought of only in terms of the one (however 'unimaginable') consummation of his whole reality and that of the cosmos; yet the materiality of man and of the cosmos must not be simply eliminated from this consummation as if it were a merely temporary element»[18]. The unity of spirit and matter precludes the separation of one from the other. Nor does it permit the division of humanity from the natural world, even at the moment of consummation. Once the fulfillment of spirit is affirmed, matter is also involved in the fulfillment and assured of it owing to their intrinsic unity. Therefore, the consummation of spirit must always be construed as the fulfillment of the whole human being, not as that of the human soul alone. Moreover, it implies not the abandonment but the completion of the whole world, to which we belong and from which we are inseparable. The unity of spirit and matter in creation awakens us to the significance of nature. It brings to awareness the intrinsic relationship of humanity with nature that will last even to the moment of the future fulfillment of creation.

---

[17] K. RAHNER, *Foundations of Christian Faith*, 182.
[18] K. RAHNER, «Christology», 162.

1.2.2 The Dynamic Unity of Spirit and Matter:
Evolution in the World and Self- Transcendence in Creation

Assuming that evolution is basically about «change» in the world, one may expect that creation has a certain affinity with the idea of evolution. For all created beings are finite and the finite beings are supposed to change. Given evolution, Rahner reflects on how evolution as a scientific term can be related to creation as a theological term. The evolutionary worldview perceives the world in terms of a continuous and dynamic process of change, with the possibility of the emergence of radical novelties. Particularly, it brings to light the directionality of evolution toward the increase of complexity in species. A great merit of the evolutionary view is that it provides a comprehensive perspective on both nature and humanity whereby one can grasp in a single continuum matter, life, consciousness, and self-consciousness. It is also precisely here, however, that a conflict could occur between the Christian belief in creation and the evolutionary view of the world. Insofar as one holds fast to a static perception of creation that the universe was created in the beginning as it is now, evolution can hardly be incorporated in creation. This difficulty may be relieved if the idea of evolution discloses the often-forgotten, dynamic aspect of creation, that is, creation in a movement to its final goal. However, an evolutionary stance on the emergence of humanity from nature and the Christian doctrine of God's immediate creation of every human soul still hinder the incorporation of evolution in creation. Rahner delves into this dilemma in order to provide a theologically and metaphysically coherent response. It is worth noting for our purpose that this problem is not merely regarding how to understand the nature of the human being or the soul. Rather, it is deeply related to how we comprehend the place of humankind in the entire creation. For the human race, as the most evolved species, is the one in which the entire evolutionary process of the world is recapitulated, at least according to the evolutionary perspective.

Rahner holds that God, who is the transcendent ground of all creatures, must not be regarded simply as the first member of its causal nexus in creation. The activity of God itself is not «an item in our experience, but is present as the ground, implicitly and simultaneously affirmed, of every reality met with and affirmed, and as being, which is the ground of what is, but always present as mediated by finite things»[19]. God's presence in creation mediated by finite beings

---

[19] K. RAHNER, *Hominization*, 65.

demands that God be conceived to act in the world through secondary causes, although exceptional, divine interventions such as miracles may be allowed. This way of conceiving how God relates to creation throws doubt on the claim that God directly creates every human soul. For this claim as such seems to affirm God's immediate intervention at a certain moment in *every* natural, procreative process of the human being. It can be regarded as the «predicamental» intervention of God because it postulates «an event in which secondary causes within the closed causal series are suddenly replaced by God himself»[20]. Hence, God's immediate creation of the human soul seems to lose ground even in the light of the traditional Christian perspective on how God acts in creation, without mentioning the evolutionary viewpoint.

Rahner introduces the notion of active self-transcendence to explain the phenomenon of «change (becoming)» in the world and thereby eventually to overcome the apparent incompatibility between hominization and God's immediate creation of the soul[21]. He holds that becoming in a true sense, in which a being changes into a new being, is «not just the merely spatially, temporally and quantitatively transformed combination of basic elements which remain statically the same»[22]. Instead, becoming is «always and of its very nature a self-transcendence of the cause, effected by the lower itself; it is an active surpassing of self»[23]. However, if the self-transcendence of the lower must bring forth any intrinsic increase in its own being, this process cannot take place by the lower alone, according to the metaphysical principle of causality. For the cause is, in this case, lesser than the effect. *Self-transcendence* needs a greater being than what is surpassed. However, if this greater being worked from without, it would not be an *active self*-transcendence but merely «being surpassed» by another being. Active self-transcendence is possible when the greater causes the transcendence of the lesser, only in such a way that the greater works within the innermost part of the lesser so that transcendence can actively be achieved by the lesser and at the same time the greater does not become the constitutive element of the lesser in order to assure the lesser of its independence[24].

---

[20] K. RAHNER, *Hominization*, 66. See also ID., «The Unity», 173-174.

[21] For active self-transcendence, see K. RAHNER, *Foundations of Christian Faith*, 183-187; ID., «Christology», 164-168.

[22] K. RAHNER, «The Unity», 174.

[23] K. RAHNER, «The Unity», 174.

[24] Cf. K. RAHNER, «The Unity», 175. See also ID., «Christology», 165.

There is nothing, except God, that can act in such a manner within the inmost part of other beings. God alone is eligible for «the absolute act which without thereby becoming a constitutive element of the finite being itself, is interior to the finite being in its becoming and activity»[25]. Only the immanence and transcendence of God in relation to creation enable one to perceive that God acts in creatures in a way that God ensures them both self-surpassing power and their proper nature. In fact, God's immanence always presupposes God's transcendence, though they appear contradictory to each other. However, this apparent contradiction could be true only if one confused the divine transcendence with the categorical differences of finite created beings. God's transcendence is at once the absolute difference surpassing all creatures and, precisely as such, the absolute ground of them. The divine transcendence is «the difference which establishes the ultimate unity between God and the world, and the difference becomes intelligible only in this unity»[26]. God is absolutely immanent in creation precisely because God is absolutely transcendent. One can now say, without contradiction, that a being really transcends itself with its own power, on the one hand, and with the divine power, on the other hand. God works from within a being (due to the divine immanence), but God does not take over its constitutive element (due to the divine transcendence). Otherwise, God would impair either its active self-surpassing or its nature and independence.

One can assert that the notion of active self-transcendence encompasses even «transcendence into what is substantially new, i.e. the leap to a higher *nature*»[27]. In fact, active self-surpassing already implies *essential* self-transcendence that brings forth a change in one's nature, insofar as it occurs in virtue of God's immanent impulse. Since all beings were not created in the beginning as they are now, one can hold, based on the dynamic unity of spirit and matter, that matter has transcended itself into life and spirit through the process of essential self-transcendence. It is the case that matter, life, and spirit are essentially different realities. It is also the case, however, that this essential difference does not preclude the development of matter to life to consciousness to self-consciousness, insofar as essential self-development in virtue of the divine immanence is affirmed[28]. Essential self-surpassing

[25] K. RAHNER, «The Unity», 175.
[26] K. RAHNER, *Foundations of Christian Faith*, 63.
[27] K. RAHNER, «Christology», 165.
[28] K. RAHNER, «Christology», 166.

affirms that indeed matter develops into spirit. Spirit and matter are not only statically united in the human being. To the extent that matter develops into spirit, the unity of spirit and matter is dynamically maintained over time.

On the basis of essential self-transcendence are we entitled to assert that the human being of soul and body has appeared from the material world through the process of evolution (essential *active self-transcendence*), while we still maintain God's immediate creation of the soul (essential self-*transcendence* in virtue of the divine immanence). From the perspective of essential self-surpassing, the two assertions no longer contradict each other. Rahner presents «parents in procreation» as an example. The parents are «the cause of the one entire human being and so also of its soul», while God's creation of the soul is guaranteed. For they are «the cause of the human being in virtue of the power of God which renders possible their self-transcendence, and which is immanent in their causality without belonging to the constitutive factors of their essence»[29]. God does create every human soul, but only through its parents, that is, in such a way that God's power within the parents enables essential self-transcendence and at the same time retains itself distinct from the nature of the parents, whereby preserving their independent procreative activity and preventing predicamental intervention from without.

The notion of essential active self-transcendence shows that the whole human being, not the human body alone, has evolved from nature. To that extent and in that way, human beings, both individually and collectively, are connected with nature. Therefore, the idea of self-transcendence renders the idea of evolution, even that of hominization, to be compatible with and thereby incorporated in creation. Creation can now be regarded as the world in evolution; evolution can be understood as the process in creation of essential active self-transcendence in virtue of God's immanence.

1.2.3 Cosmic Self-Consciousness and Cosmic Bodily Presence

The notion of active self-transcendence provides a single framework of perspective from which to grasp in a coherent manner a myriad of things in the world, which appear essentially different and continuously change. One can grasp all these diverse things in this active self-surpassing process whereby matter develops into spirit. The dynamic

---

[29] K. RAHNER, *Hominization*, 99.

unity of spirit and matter helps us understand that all things in the world are related to and dependent on each other. The idea of essential active self-transcendence shows that the unity of spirit and matter found in the human being is not only static but also dynamic and that it is grounded in God's immanence in creation. The entire creation, seen from the dynamic unity of spirit and matter, demonstrates that all creatures and their relationships among themselves are grounded in God and formed through self-transcendence empowered by the divine immanence. Unity and diversity among all creatures come into view more plainly and specifically. One can say that not only all creatures but also their relationships among themselves originate in God. Moreover, these relationships are not externally granted to creatures by God. They must be seen to emerge from within creatures and are embedded in their innermost part, because they are caused and formed by true *active self*-transcendence. Therefore, all creatures are dynamically and intrinsically related to each other, in virtue of God's immanent power in each of them. The idea of essential self-transcendence also shows that no matter how advanced they are, the more evolved come into existence through the less evolved. This highlights the way creatures depend on one another, that is, creatures at higher level depend on those at lower level. Accordingly, humankind is always dependent upon nature in regard to existence, but not *vice versa*.

A coherent and dynamic perspective on nature and humankind presented by the idea of evolution and self-transcendence brings to awareness the historicity of nature, which in turn confirms the intimate association of humanity with nature. The world no longer appears in this standpoint as a static or cyclical reality. Instead, it reveals a temporal character that everything in the world is in the process of change through self-transcendence. Nature regains its own historicity, which has long been denied by human beings and regarded merely as a backdrop where human history unfolds. «The history of nature and the history of the spirit can be seen as *one* history without having thereby to deny the essential gradation of the world and of its development, and without having to embed the development of nature and the free personal history in dire opposition on one another»[30]. The perception of the world as a temporal reality in the process of self-surpassing integrates cosmic history and human history into a single history, while preserving their essential difference and more fundamental unity.

---

[30] K. RAHNER, «The Unity», 177.

The history of nature encompasses human history and *vice versa*. On the one hand, natural history involves human history in the sense that humanity has appeared from nature. On the other hand, one can understand that the entire history of nature is accumulated and recapitulated in humanity, in the sense that the history of nature is that of the self-surpassing process of matter into spirit. Therefore, it can be said that cosmic history is comprised in human history. This reciprocal association of natural history and human history leads us to appreciate properly the place of humanity in the world and *vice versa*. It is evident in the first place that humans as part of nature always need nature. Humanity is totally dependent on the material world for its basic needs. Nature exists without humanity, but not the other way around. On the other hand, humanity can be regarded as that in which the cosmos has achieved self-consciousness[31]. Put otherwise, humankind is the universe come to self-consciousness. In this regard, human self-consciousness can be understood as cosmic self-consciousness as well. Humanity is, in this sense, the representative of the cosmos. This reciprocal relationship between humanity and the world seems to be consistent with what Genesis tells us about creation. The two creation accounts tell us that human beings are created as part of the cosmos, while acknowledging a unique place of humankind as the image of God and a tiller of the garden that God planted. The awareness of being part of the cosmos will persuade us to have an attitude of due regard for nature. The consciousness of being representative of the cosmos will motivate us to have an attitude of responsibility for nature.

Cosmic self-consciousness, grounded in the dynamic unity of spirit and matter, casts light on the significance of the corporeality of the human being and the whole creation. Humans, as the recapitulation of the self-transcendental process of matter into spirit, are seen to assume cosmic presence in the world through their body, to the extent that the cosmos has self-consciousness in them. Every human being participates in the cosmos through one's cosmic bodily presence. Humanity and the material world are now seen to have such an internal and intrinsic link with each other that one can even speak of cosmic bodily presence and cosmic self-consciousness for humanity and nature respectively. This is possible only through corporeality common to humankind and nature.

For in his corporeality, every man is an element of the cosmos which cannot really be delimited and cut off from it, and in this corporeality he com-

---

[31] K. RAHNER, *Foundations of Christian Faith*, 188

municates with the whole cosmos in such a way that through this corporeality of man taken as the other element of belonging to the spirit, the cosmos
really presses forward to this self-presence in the spirit[32].

Human corporeality is an essential link that binds humankind with the
cosmos, without which no connection could be possible at all. The
human body is a bilateral medium whereby humans express themselves
in the world and the cosmos reaches the state of self-consciousness in
them. One may thrust to the end of time the materiality of the cosmos
and humankind, which has existed from the beginning and developed
into spirit over time. Since matter is intrinsically and dynamically
related to spirit by means of the process of self-transcendence in virtue
of the divine immanence, one can hardly imagine that matter will be
excluded from the final fulfillment of creation which will be achieved
ultimately by God. This eschatological perspective, based on the dynamic unity of spirit and matter, brings to a new light what the immortality of the soul implies in relation to matter. If the immortality of the
soul is properly understood, it is precisely «a finality and consummation of this very process by which the cosmos finds itself, and hence
must not be confused with the escape of a spiritual soul – an alien in
this cosmos – from the totality of that world which is always also
material and has always had and still has also a material history»[33]. The
inextricable link that self-transcendence brings forth in matter and spirit
precludes in salvation any idea that tends to separate soul from matter
such as «the escape of a spiritual soul». What will be consummated and
fulfilled is «this very process by which the cosmos finds itself» and in
which matter and spirit exist in inherent unity. As the world is at once
material and spiritual, so is its final fulfillment.

1.3 *The Relationship of Humanity with Nature after Death*

Traditionally, death is described in Christianity as the separation of
soul and body. The term «separation» in this description implies that
the human being no longer maintains after death the present relationship of soul and body. We know that the body perishes after death. We
believe, on the other hand, that the soul somehow endures after death.
Despite a grain of truth in it, Rahner regards this traditional rendering
of death as inadequate in some respects. Death is «an event which

---

[32] K. RAHNER, «Christology», 170.
[33] K. RAHNER, «Christology», 171.

strikes man in his totality»[34]. However, the traditional depiction of death as the separation of soul and body does not do justice to death as an event embracing the whole human being. For example, this depiction does not consider «an absolute determination» that one's «free, personal self-affirmation and self-realization achieves in death»[35]. In other words, the personal and spiritual aspects of death are not properly considered in that description. Moreover, it leaves ambiguous what separation means and gives no specific account of what happens to the relationship of the soul with the body and, through it, with the world[36].

The human being is grasped as the inseparable unity of soul and body, which are the organizing principle of the body and the material ground of the soul respectively. As already mentioned, it is through the corporeality of the human body that we, as at once spirit and «an element of the cosmos», form some connection with the world and experience it: «the soul, as united to the body, must also have some relationship to that "whole" of which the body is a part, that is, to that wholeness which constitutes the unity of the material universe»[37]. The soul no longer retains in death its current relationship with the body. For the body is bound to pass away in death. As regards the relationship of humanity with nature, we may ask whether our connection with the world perishes too with the dissolution of the body. If so, the soul will become «a-cosmic» and lose the relationship it has with the world through the body. Or one may suppose that the soul enters into «deeper, all-embracing openness» in which the association of the soul to the universe is more fully realized. Rahner argues that although the soul is separated in death from bodily structure, it does not imply that the soul becomes absolutely a-cosmic, without any connection with the world. Rather, he holds that the soul establishes a wider, deeper, and more intimate link with the entire universe than the present connection that is inevitably restricted by the spatial and temporal limit of the body. In death, the human soul becomes «all-cosmic», that is, pan-cosmic[38].

Rahner draws, for his claim for pan-cosmic soul, on the argument that the soul has «a transcendental relationship», i.e., «a relationship which endures even after death»[39]. He holds, based on the substantial

---

34 K. RAHNER, *On the Theology of Death*, 21.
35 K. RAHNER, *On the Theology of Death*, 26.
36 Cf. K. RAHNER, *On the Theology of Death*, 25-26.
37 K. RAHNER, *On the Theology of Death*, 26.
38 K. RAHNER, *On the Theology of Death*, 27.
39 K. RAHNER, *On the Theology of Death*, 28.

unity of soul and body, that the act of the soul to form relationship with the body is an act not by accident but by nature: «the soul's own substantial existence is, so to speak, grafted upon the material reality, so that the act of informing matter is not really distinct from the existence of the soul»[40]. It is not merely «an activity of the soul, but is her substantial act»[41]. The soul is then expected to maintain in some way a connection with matter as long as the soul exists. For an essential character of the soul consists in forming some relationship with matter. Therefore, what occurs in death must not be the disappearance of the relationship that the soul maintains with matter. Instead, it must be a radical change in the range and manner of the relationship of the soul to matter. One can conceive in this change a pan-cosmic relationship that the soul extends, in death, its relationship into the whole world[42].

Rahner presents three grounds that could support his argument for pan-cosmic soul. First, the doctrine of angels affirms that a spiritual being without materiality in itself can still have a certain relationship with the world[43]. Second, the doctrine of purgatory suggests some involvement of the soul in matter. According to this doctrine, only material beings can commit venial sins, which are to be purified in purgatory. Therefore, the endurance of the consequences of those venial sins implies some bodily involvement of the soul after death[44]. Finally, the resurrection of the body firmly holds that death does not indicate a complete release from the body and a departure from this material world. The spiritual body that is formed in the resurrection will not abandon the pan-cosmic association of the soul (cf. 1 Cor. 15): «such a new bodily form in the resurrection is, of course, not to be conceived as a surrender of that openness of the spirit to the world as a whole which is attained in death»[45]. The idea of pan-cosmic soul in turn fleshes out the spiritual body in terms of relationship: «The glorified body seems to become the perfect expression of the enduring relation of the glorified person to the world as a whole»[46]. Although the spiritual body possesses a bodily character, it would not be identical with the body at present, which is restricted in time and space. It would be open to the

---

[40] K. RAHNER, *On the Theology of Death*, 28.
[41] K. RAHNER, *On the Theology of Death*, 28.
[42] Cf. K. RAHNER, *On the Theology of Death*, 30.
[43] Cf. K. RAHNER, *On the Theology of Death*, 31-32.
[44] Cf. K. RAHNER, *On the Theology of Death*, 32-33.
[45] K. RAHNER, *On the Theology of Death*, 34.
[46] K. RAHNER, *On the Theology of Death*, 34.

entire world, as is implied in the idea of pan-cosmic soul. The spiritual body seems to enjoy, beyond any physical restrictions, the cosmic relationship with the whole universe.

One may point out some limitations of this reflection upon death. Any thought on death cannot help being speculative in great measure, because we cannot experience death as long as we are alive. The argument is developed, moreover, based on a dualistic framework that separates soul and body, although this would be inevitable, given the character of the issue. I think, however, that despite these drawbacks, this reflection on death can illuminate and deepen the relationship of humanity with nature. It shows that humans and nature are so fundamentally and intrinsically interwoven that their relationship continues to exist even after death. It in turn urges us to ponder on how we must relate to nature, here and now.

First, a claim for pan-cosmic soul confirms again that all creatures are not extrinsically but intrinsically related to each other through the process of active self-transcendence in virtue of the divine immanence. All the relationships that we form and maintain with nature are so intrinsically embedded in us and nature that they will become deeper and wider, rather than vanish away to nothing, after death. Moreover, this enduring connection of the soul with the material world adds credibility to the eschatological perspective that the final fulfillment of creation includes not only the human soul but also entire material world, which the dynamic unity of spirit and matter strongly supports.

Second, the notion of pan-cosmic relationship broadens and matures our perspective on nature. If we acknowledge that we become open to the entire cosmos through pan-cosmic association, it will help us turn our excessive, anthropocentric perspective on the world into a more nature-centered one. It can invite us to cultivate a more responsible and mature attitude toward nature. We will become in death «a co-determining factor of the universe» in which other creatures, without mentioning other humans, continue to live[47]. We can be motivated and encouraged to retain an enduring concern for nature by anticipating the deeper and wider relationship that we will form with the cosmos after death. If we accept that, even after death, we will not be completely separated from the world, we have a good morale to develop a continuing concern for nature.

---

[47] K. RAHNER, On the Theology of Death, 31.

One may ask how the disintegration of the body to nothingness after death can be grasped, in relation to the soul in the light of all-encompassing cosmic relationship. One can consider the dissolution of the body in line with the soul which attains a broader connection with the world. It is evident that the material elements of the body disperse after death into the earth, out of which they come. In accordance with the way the soul gets into contact with the whole universe, this can be interpreted as a process that the body enters into a wider and deeper association with the cosmos. It can then be held that the soul will still maintain a connection with the body, even after death, but now always by the medium of the cosmos. It follows from this that after death, the human being as a whole, not only the human soul, comes to establish a wider and deeper relationship with all creation. In sum, the viewpoint of pan-cosmic relationship in death provides us a perspective from which to confirm and strengthen the intimate relationship of humanity with nature[48].

2. The Interconnectedness of All Creatures from the Perspective of Jürgen Moltmann

2.1 Introduction

The theological work of Jürgen Moltmann[49] began with and was influenced by his own experience of suffering during World War II. He has since been sensitive and responsive to the suffering of people in the world[50]. The theme of suffering has been at once a catalyst for and a leitmotif in his theology. This is also true of his theology of creation in

---

[48] This pan-cosmic perspective on death has another merit that it helps us envision death more serenely. Provided that death is regarded as a process through which we widen and deepen our relationship with the entire universe, we can accept our spontaneous, negative feelings about death, such as fear and anxiety, as the typical, psychological movements which occur when we enter into a new relationship. They may reach their maximums when we are confronted with death. For, from this perspective, we establish after death a pan-cosmic relationship, which means a radical change in the way we relate to the world. Cf. J.F. HAUGHT, «Ecology and Eschatology», 60-63.

[49] Jürgen Moltmann, a German Protestant theologian, studied and gained his doctorate in Göttingen. He taught theology in Tübingen more than twenty years until his retirement. He was a member of the board of directors of *Concilium*. He is best known for his trilogy, *Theology of Hope*, *The Crucified God*, and *The Church in the Power of the Spirit*. His other works include *The Trinity and the Kingdom of God*, *The Spirit of Life*, *God in Creation*, *The Way of Jesus Christ*, *God for a Secular Society*, *The Coming of God*, and *Experiences in Theology*.

[50] Cf. G. MÜLLER-FAHRENHOLZ, *The Kingdom and the Power*, 15-25.

the sense that he approaches it with a keen awareness of the ecological disruption of the earth. He confronts the pressing issue of the ecological crisis with the Christian belief in creation: «Faced as we are with the progressive industrial exploitation of nature and its irreparable destruction, what does it mean to say that we believe in God the Creator, and in this world as his creation?»[51] It is difficult to pin down what is to blame for the deterioration of nature throughout the world today. We may consider diverse plausible factors, such as socio-economic, psychological, and religious ones. They could range from the development of science and technology to capitalist market economy to our inner attitude toward nature. Each of these in turn includes many subordinate elements. The ecological issue is a complex problem. From a theological viewpoint, Moltmann finds problematic our predominant way of conceiving how God relates to creation. He holds that we have viewed God principally as the absolute and transcendent subject in relation to creation. Eventually, this has driven God completely out of the world.

> Through the monotheism of the absolute subject, God was increasingly stripped of his connection with the world, and the world was increasingly secularized. As a result, the human being – since he was God's image on earth – had to see himself as the subject of cognition and will, and was bound to confront his world as its ruler[52].

It is difficult to find in this absolutely transcendent, monotheistic notion any intimate connection between God and the world, once creation is completed. God is virtually alienated from God's own creation. Creation, stripped of the divine vestige, is likely to be secularized and turned into a passive and inert, material world that humans can waste without constraint. Humankind, now as the only subject in the world, replaces God, the absolute subject who is conceived to exist solely in heaven.

Moltmann seeks an alternative way of conceiving how God relates to the world in response to the ecological crisis of the earth. Drawing on the trinitarian conception of God, he takes heed of the way God the Spirit acts in creation. Focusing on the immanence of the Spirit, he tries to develop an ecological doctrine of creation. He hopes that the «discernment of the God who is present in creation through his Holy Spirit

---

[51] J. MOLTMANN, *God in Creation*, xiii.
[52] J. MOLTMANN, *God in Creation*, 1. Cf. R.R. RUETHER, *Gaia and God*, 237-238.

can bring men and women to reconciliation and peace with nature»[53]. He holds that the pneumatological vision of creation can bridge a huge gap between God and humanity, on the one hand, and the rest of creation, on the other hand. Only then can the whole creation recover a harmonious and symbiotic fellowship. Only then will peace prevail in creation.

I will in this section deal with the pneumatological vision of creation. I will reflect, for this, on the relationship of God the Spirit with creation and evolution. I will first concentrate on the Spirit in creation and creation in the Spirit, presenting God and creation as the cosmic Spirit and a web of relationships respectively. The interconnectedness of all creatures will be highlighted in this reflection. I will then consider the Spirit in evolution and evolution in the Spirit, suggesting evolution as the self-movement of the Spirit and as the self-transcendence of creation. The interconnectedness of all creatures will be spotlighted again, reclaiming the historicity of nature. Finally, I will remark on how evolution influences the relationships embedded in creation and how the human race, the most evolved species at present, must live and act in the world.

2.2 Creation and the Spirit: The Pneumatological Vision of Creation

2.2.1 The Spirit in Creation: The Cosmic Spirit

Moltmann makes a criticism, in relation to the traditional pneumatological conception, that «there is a tendency to view the Holy Spirit solely as *the Spirit of redemption*»[54]. What he means by this remark is that the traditional Christian theology has a bias to dissociate the Spirit from nature and the human body. This tendency in turn restricts and relegates the role of the Spirit only to a spiritual realm, that is, the redemption of the soul[55]. It is likely to weaken one's concern for the present world, because this world is viewed to be discarded in the final analysis. It can hardly provide any rationale or motive of concern for the world, and consequently, it tends to make blunt our ecological awareness. From the biblical perspective, however, this viewpoint on the Spirit is distorted, though prevalent at present. For the Bible speaks

---

[53] J. MOLTMANN, *God in Creation*, xiv.

[54] J. MOLTMANN, *The Spirit of Life*, 8.

[55] A tendency of spiritualization has been notable in the history of Christian theology, particularly since theology came into conflict with science around the Enlightenment. Cf. A.M. CLIFFORD, «Foundations», 21-22.

of the cosmic Spirit, i.e., the Spirit in all creation. According to the biblical standpoint, the cosmic dimension of the Spirit that has been in the background must be rediscovered, recovered, and brought into the foreground.

Moltmann notes that all the divine activities in the biblical tradition are pneumatic in their efficacy: «It is always the Spirit who first brings the activity of the Father and the Son to its goal»[56]. The Spirit in the Scriptures is intrinsically connected with the creative activities of God. It is through the Spirit that creatures actually come into being and continue to exist. The Nicene-Constantinopolitan Creed enunciates this respect by naming the Holy Spirit «the giver of life». The Old Testament gives no emphatic reference to God as the Spirit. There are, however, not a few occasions in the Old Testament where the Spirit is implicitly referred to. In these instances, diverse images are employed from nature, such as breath, wind, water, fire, and dove in order to portray the activities of the Spirit[57]. The first creation account of Genesis says that at the moment of creation God's *ruah*, i.e., God's spirit as wind, was hovering over the waters (cf. Gen. 1:2)[58]. According to the second creation story, when God breathed the breath of life into man's nostrils, the man became a living being (cf. Gen. 2:7). When God takes away creatures' breath, they die; when God sends forth God's *ruah*, things are created and God renews the earth (cf. Ps. 104:29-30; Job 34:14-15). God is the fountain of living water (cf. Jer. 2:13; 17:13) and makes the thirsty land spring up like a green tamarisk (cf. Isa. 44:3). This image of water is adopted again in the New Testament when Jesus is depicted as «a spring of water gushing up to eternal life» (John 4:14). It also refers to the Spirit as the water and wind that cleanse people to be reborn and renewed (cf. John 3:5-7). The Spirit is also likened to the fire and wind which bring forth mutual understanding beyond the language barrier among different peoples (cf. Acts 2:4-6). The Spirit is pictured as a dove purifying the world; Jesus, who will take away the sin of the world, will baptize people with this Spirit (cf. John 1:29-33). In sum, the biblical imagery of the Spirit is filled with dynamic power and vitality. The world is not only created in the power of the Spirit.

---

[56] J. MOLTMANN, *God in Creation*, 9.

[57] Cf. M.I. WALLACE, «The Wounded Spirit», 58-59.

[58] Cf. R.J. CLIFFORD – R.E. MURPHY, «Genesis», 10. Hebrew word *ruah* literally means «air in motion»; hence, it is used to indicate «wind», «breath», and «spirit».

The Spirit also dwells in creation, empowering and vivifying it, purifying and renewing it, and sustaining it.

Moltmann seeks to construe the Spirit as the metaphor of energy and power: «The experience of the divine Spirit as an *energy* and *vital power* goes back to the Hebrew *ruah* concept»[59]. Simply speaking, energy refers to a source of power whereby one lives and acts. Energy keeps life forms alive and active. If energy is exhausted and no longer supplied, they cannot exist; they die. Energy is invisible, but it does exist. It must be understood not as visible, discrete, and static matter but as invisible, continuous, and dynamic flow. In this regard, energy may be conceived to penetrate and permeate the world. «Everything that is, exists and lives in the unceasing inflow of the energies and potentialities of the cosmic Spirit. Through the energies and potentialities of the Spirit, the Creator is himself present in his creation. He does not merely confront it in his transcendence; entering into it, he is also immanent in it»[60]. The Spirit is the source and ground of «everything that is» at every moment of its existence as well as at the moment of creation. The Spirit is the fountain of energy without which nothing can exist. It is «in the unceasing inflow of the energies» that the Spirit becomes the source and ground of every being. To understand the activities of the Spirit as the divine energy flow is to perceive «the Spirit in creation» and «creation in the Spirit».

The Spirit as the one who sustains and vitalizes creation through the divine energy suggests the way God relates to the world. Anyone can assert that if God the creator exists, God is transcendent over creation in the sense that the creator and creation are absolutely different. However, this statement alone regarding God's relationship with creation is not sufficient for the Judaeo-Christian faith in God. It lacks what is no less important than God's transcendence, i.e., God's immanence. God the creator is immanent in creation by virtue of the Spirit. It is no longer possible, in the light of the cosmic Spirit, to conceive God simply as the absolute and transcendent being completely disconnected from creation. God is at once transcendent and immanent in relation to creation. God's transcendence and immanence, which seem mutually exclusive, are in fact compatible with each other in virtue of the Spirit.

---

[59] J. MOLTMANN, *The Spirit of Life*, 274. Moltmann suggests four kinds of metaphor for the Spirit, each of which comprises three related images: personal metaphor (lord, mother, and judge); formative metaphor (energy, space, and *Gestalt*); movement metaphor (tempest, fire, and love).

[60] J. MOLTMANN, *God in Creation*, 9.

A dichotomy between God and creation is shattered. Insofar as God is seen to pervade the whole creation, we may freely say that God is in creation and creation in God.

2.2.2 Creation in the Spirit: A Web of Relationships

The view of creation in the light of the Spirit, i.e., the pneumatological vision of creation, challenges our dominant, dualistic way of perceiving God and creation. The pneumatological perspective on creation holds that God does not merely confront creation from above nor is God indifferent to it. Instead, this pneumatological vision holds that God cares for creation in the power of the Spirit. This becomes more evident when one considers why God created the cosmos at all. Since God is perfect and self-sufficient, God is never obliged or compelled to create something. Therefore, one must say that God created the cosmos with perfect freedom. This implies that creation itself does not necessarily have to exist. The world as creation is a contingent reality. As Moltmann points out, however, «God's freedom is not the almighty power for which everything is possible. It is love, which means the self-communication of the good»[61]. Seen from the horizon of creation, the divine freedom is absolute without limit and obligation. At the same time, when it is viewed from the vantage point of God, the divine freedom cannot mean arbitrariness. God is not free to act against God's nature because God is always faithful to the divine nature. God is perfectly free in the sense that the will of God always corresponds with the nature of God[62]. We are told that God is love (cf. 1 John 4:16). Therefore, to create with the divine freedom is identical with to create with the divine love. God creates the world with the divine freedom and love. And God has pleasure in it (cf. Gen. 1:1-2:4a).

Love has a propensity to unite rather than disunite. A lover is inclined to be with a beloved. The lover cares ceaselessly for the beloved that it may live well. The divine love, a consequence of which was manifested as creation, never leaves it alone. God is with and in creation in virtue of the Spirit. God as the cosmic Spirit takes care of creation. God gives life to the world abundantly; the world receives it gratefully. Creation praises God; God rejoices over creation (cf. Ps. 104). Moreover, love runs the risk of vulnerability for the beloved. God

---

[61] J. MOLTMANN, *God in Creation*, 75.

[62] Cf. J. MOLTMANN, *The Trinity*, 55-56 and 105-106. See also ID., *God in Creation*, 82-83.

became, in the loving power of the Spirit, a human being with all human weakness (cf. John 3:16). God's love encompasses even God's suffering with and for God's beloved creation. Jesus, in whom God's love was supremely manifested, surrendered himself on the cross out of his love through the eternal Spirit (cf. Heb. 9:14). God continues, by virtue of the Spirit, to be with all creatures in suffering, both human and nonhuman.

The pneumatological vision of creation does not separate God from the world. Rather, this perspective leads us to perceive creation in the Spirit, who is love, and the Spirit in creation, which is God's beloved. It is underscored that God the creator and creation are intimately related to each other in the power of the Spirit. «If the Creator is himself present in his creation by virtue of the Spirit, then his relationship to creation must rather be viewed as an intricate web of [...] relationships»[63]. Relationships originate in the Spirit in creation. The Spirit unites the Father and the Son that they may interpenetrate each other (cf. John 17:21). Likewise, the Spirit brings forth relationships in the world where the Spirit resides. All creation is imbued with relationships or their potentialities in virtue of the omnipresence of the Spirit. The Spirit creates the indissoluble connection of God with creation. The Spirit also links internally all creatures together through the relationships which come into being by the divine presence in them. This is conceivable since the Spirit is seen as energy or power which interpenetrates and permeates every creature. Creation turns into a web of relationships in virtue of the Spirit in creation.

The Spirit as the one who brings forth relationships in creation sheds light on an ecological vision of the world and ecological consciousness. A web of relationships formed by the cosmic Spirit, in which all creatures exist, awakens us to a vision that human and nonhuman creatures are interrelated and interdependent, i.e., an ecological vision of the world. It is definitely false, according to the pneumatological and thus ecological vision of the world, to assume that humankind and nature are disparate realities. Such a division is not possible in the pneumatological vision of creation nor is it conceivable in an ecological vision of the world. It is one and the same power of the Spirit that interpenetrates both humans and nature. It is that same Spirit who interconnects them together in a single community called creation. Every creature exists, without exception, in diverse relationships with others, in virtue

---

[63] J. MOLTMANN, *God in Creation*, 14.

of the Spirit. Humankind too exists and lives together with nonhuman creatures in the same community of creation. The uniqueness of humanity is never meant to negate the essential character of relationality to all creatures. An ecological vision of the world, grounded in the presence of the Spirit in creation, throws light on the affinity of all beings. The interconnectedness of all creatures is vague and hidden in the shadow, essential as it is. In order to sense and appreciate it, one needs an ecological consciousness stimulated and fostered by an ecological vision of the world. Only then will the relationality of the world come into view. «Being created» always means «being created in relationships» and «existing in relationships».

One may even say that what God first and foremost creates is a community in the sense that, since the very beginning of creation, all created beings are interrelated in the ever-permeating power of the Spirit. «If the Holy Spirit is 'poured out' on the whole creation, then he creates the community of all created things with God and with each other, making it that fellowship of creation in which all created things communicate with one another and with God, each in its own way»[64]. Everything is created not as a monad but in relationships with others. The significance of relationships in creation comes to the surface when one considers how a living creature exists. One must say that every life form receives life-sustaining power from the Spirit. One can also say, however, that every creature always gets this life-giving energy from and within the community of creation, upon which the Spirit pours out the divine energy without cease. It must be noted that the energy of the Spirit is poured out «on the whole creation», not on each individual creature in isolation. The Spirit sustains every individual creature, but only as a member of the community formed by the divine power. No one, except God, is self-sufficient for one's existence; everyone depends on others to exist. This calls to mind that God, as the primary cause, works in creation always through secondary causes. The Spirit sustains and empowers every single creature, but always through others. It can be said that there exists a chain of relationship in the order of creation. This chain of relationship is not that which may or may not exist but that without which any single life form cannot live. It is a life-sustaining link, the source of which is God the Spirit. Again, «being created» always means «being created in relationships» and «existing in relationships».

---

64 J. MOLTMANN, *God in Creation*, 11.

The pneumatological vision of the world gives us a new light on relationship. Viewed in terms of the Spirit, relationships are not merely a secondary phenomenon which comes into view only after individual beings come together in multitude. Rather, we must hold that individual beings are steeped so deeply in relationships and relationships penetrate individual beings so thoroughly that both of them are equally primal. «'Thing' and 'relation' are complementary modes of appearance, in the same way as particle and wave in the nuclear sector. For nothing in the world exists, lives and moves of itself. Everything exists, lives and moves in others, in one another, with one another, for one another, in the cosmic interrelations of the divine Spirit»[65]. Some observations in physics may clearly illustrate what being and relationship are like[66]. The classical Newtonian physics of matter employed a particle model to explain certain physical phenomena with mechanical laws. In the nineteenth century, physicists introduced another type of model called wave in order to account for a different group of phenomena such as light and electromagnetic field. In the twentieth century, however, it was discovered that electrons, always viewed as individual particles, possess the character of wave and that light, always conceived as continuous wave, moves like a stream of discrete particles. Particle and wave are completely distinct in their basic characteristics: «Waves are continuous and extended, and they interact in terms of phase; particles are discontinuous, localized, and they interact in terms of momentum»[67]. Nonetheless, light and electron are discovered to show in themselves these two distinct, apparently contradictory, features. Light

---

[65] J. MOLTMANN, *God in Creation*, 11.

[66] Cf. J.F. HAUGHT, *Science and Religion*, 9-26. As already mentioned, we must be aware of the risk of «concordism» that theology uncritically appeals to science to prove its validity. This would be an uncritical and futile conflation of theology and science, no matter how well scientific theories or discoveries seem to fit in with what theological assertions claim. For science always assumes the possibility of revision in the future; otherwise, science would become an ideology or a belief system called scientism. However, there is another way in which theology and science may benefit from each other. On the one hand, for instance, a new scientific discovery about the universe challenges and stimulates theologians to reflect upon their previous conception of God, creation, and their relationship from a new angle, because theology always presumes one cosmology or another. In this sense, a new scientific cosmology can widen the horizon of theology. On the other hand, the theological claim that «the universe is a finite, coherent, rational, ordered totality, grounded in an ultimate love and promise, provides a general vision of things that consistently nurtures scientific quests» in the midst of apparently perplexing realities (at 22).

[67] I.G. BARBOUR, *Religion and Science*, 166.

and electron exhibit both particle-like and wave-like characters, but we are still speaking of one and the same entity of light or electron[68]. Hence, we must view them from both perspectives to understand them properly. In our case, a discrete particle and continuous wave may be seen to correspond to an individual being and its relationship respectively. Being and relationship interpenetrate each other, and in that measure, they are equally primal, though they are different in kind and irreducible to one another. They must be understood as two different modes of one and the same reality. This holds again that to exist means to exist in relationships[69]. This example elucidates the pneumatological vision of the world that relationship is inherently embedded in the nature of every individual creature due to the Spirit, who permeates all creatures and connects them together. All created beings are, in virtue of the Spirit, interrelated and interdependent.

It can even be said that «everything real and everything living is simply a concentration and manifestation of its relationships, interconnections and surroundings»[70]. This means that an individual being is eventually the totality of the relationships in which this being is born and which it builds up. It is true that individual beings form relationships among themselves. It is also the case, on the contrary, that these relationships in turn influence and shape individuals. For example, we are influenced and shaped by diverse kinds of relationships that we maintain with others in the world. Our future as well as our present depends on our relationships and is determined by them. This does not mean, however, that we lose our own individual identity and disintegrate and disappear into a web of relationships. What is meant is that our unique identity is influenced and formed by them. The pneumatological perspective on creation holds that the Spirit permeates creation and is present in creation. However, this does not mean, either, that the Spirit is dissolved into the world and thereby becomes undistinguishable from it. What is meant is that the Spirit and the world are not separated from each other, although they are absolutely distinct from each other and irreducible to one another. We must say exactly the same as regards one's individuality and relationships with others. The

---

[68] I.G. BARBOUR, *Religion and Science*, 17-19.165-170.

[69] In the atomic world, particles called quarks exhibit a literal example for this. See I.G. BARBOUR, *Religion and Science*, 174: «free quarks have never been observed, and it appears that a quark cannot exist alone [...] Quarks are parts that apparently cannot exist except in a larger whole».

[70] J. MOLTMANN, *God in Creation*, 3.

Spirit at once steeps all creation in relationships in virtue of the divine immanence and guarantees the uniqueness of every creature.

It is worth noting that God does not bring about relationships in an extrinsic way. Rather, they are intrinsically formed and embedded in all creatures through the power of the Spirit. «It is the powers and energies of the Holy Spirit that bridge the difference between Creator and creature [...] This certainly does not make creation divine, but it is nevertheless brought into the sphere of the Spirit's power, and acquires a share in the inner life of the Trinity itself»[71]. If one considers relationships in creation in the light of the Spirit, who bridges «the difference between Creator and creature», they will be grasped in a radically new way. If the Spirit founds relationships among all creatures by connecting them in virtue of the divine immanence, they are brought into «the sphere of the Spirit's power» and acquire «a share in the inner life of the Trinity itself». These relationships thus formed are not divine. Nonetheless, they originate in the inner life of the triune God. To the measure that they have a share in the divine life, they resemble the divine relationship of the triune God.

Moltmann describes this trinitarian relationship in terms of *perichoresis*, the principle of mutual interpenetration or indwelling (cf. John 10:30; 14:11): «The Father exists in the Son, the Son in the Father, and both of them in the Spirit, just as the Spirit exists in both the Father and the Son»[72]. The idea of *perichoresis* keeps both the identity and unity of each divine person, thereby without making them totally distinct or the same. Likewise, relationships in all creation, stemming from God's *perichoresis*, place all creatures both in unity and diversity. The entire creation maintains unity as one community while preserving immensely diverse creatures. Anyone, particularly humankind, cannot claim these relationships as one's own. Nor can anyone arbitrarily change or demolish them for one's own sake. God alone can lay claim to them.

The fact that humanity is part of nature and dependent on it has in great measure been denied or forgotten since the Enlightenment in the West. The pneumatological vision of creation that all creatures exist in the intricate web of relationships in the power of the Spirit awakens us to this obvious but forgotten fact. In fact, one may hold, at the heart of the ecological degradation of nature today is the loss of sensibility for

---

[71] J. MOLTMANN, *Trinity*, 113.
[72] J. MOLTMANN, *Trinity*, 174-176. See also ID., *God in Creation*, 16-17.

«being interconnected». Moltmann notices that the present massive environmental destruction began only with modern scientific and technological development for the last four hundred years[73]. This development depends in great part on basic human convictions about the meaning and purpose of life. According to him, it was generally accepted that the meaning and purpose of life consisted in the acquisition of power. Power meant power *over* others, both human and non-human; it implied the conquest and domination of others. Science and technologies were, in this regard, the most effective means of the pursuit of power[74].

The motive of domination is reflected in the type of knowledge that science employed. The type of knowledge that science employed is objectifying, analytical, and reductionistic. This type of knowledge is characterized by «separation and division». In the first place, it separates «I» as a subject from an entity as an object. It divides the object into smaller parts and analyzes them, until the subject has a full knowledge and control of it[75]. One can hardly find in this epistemological process any concern for intimate relationship. Rather, it must be dispelled because it is not «clear and distinct». Humankind has no longer remained as one member of nature. It has become the conqueror and ruler of nature. Humans, as the lord and master of nature, have come to think themselves entitled to plunder and lavish it. Nature has become their property. What will happen in the end, however, is the destruction of all as well as humanity. For what they are now demolishing is the life-giving relationship itself.

In the face of this imminent catastrophe, we need a profound change in our way of seeing, knowing, and relating to the world. If we are to view nature primarily not as resources for commodities but as creation,

---

[73] Cf. J. MOLTMANN, *God in Creation*, 26. Moltmann does not agree with the criticism that the biblical view of the world or Jewish-Christian tradition as a whole is responsible for the present destructive exploitation of nature: «Yet this allegedly 'anthropocentric' view of the world found in the Bible is more than three thousand years old, whereas modern scientific and technological civilization only began to develop in Europe four hundred years ago at the earliest». Instead, he presents as a major factor to blame «the new picture of God offered by the Renaissance and by nominalism».

[74] Cf. J. MOLTMANN, *God in Creation*, 20-27.

[75] Scholars in science and philosophy hold today that this subject-object, analytic, and reductionistic kind of knowledge does not always do justice to realities and phenomena in the world. See, for instance, D. BOHM, *Wholeness and the Implicate Order*, 1-26.48-64.

we are asked to perceive nature as a community where all its members are imbued with the divine breath and thereby interrelated and interdependent. We must recognize the primary importance of relationships in nature. Only then will we want to know nature not to conquer and dominate it but primarily to live in harmony with it.

2.3 *Evolution and the Spirit:*
The Pneumatological Vision of Evolution

2.3.1 The Spirit in Evolution: The Self-Movement of the Spirit

The pneumatological vision of creation brings to light the aspect of creation as a web of relationships. Creation is viewed as a community in which all creatures, imbued with the power of the Spirit, are inherently interrelated and interdependent. This conception of the world leads us to an ecological vision of the world and ecological awareness that all beings are virtually interconnected. It can be said that up until now, all beings in the world and their relationships have been considered predominantly from a spatial perspective. However, the Spirit, who has been forming, fostering, and embedding relationships in creation since the beginning, leads us to see them also from a temporal perspective. When we grasp the world temporally, what we first encounter in the world may be «change». We experience in the first place ordinary changes in our daily life. We are told, however, about another type of change called evolution. Simply speaking, evolution refers to the fact that a species in the midst of gradual changes undergoes the so-called «qualitative leap» when certain conditions are fulfilled, whereby a drastic change occurs in the nature of the species. It is now generally accepted that the evolution of inert matter to life forms to humankind with self-consciousness through great spans of time has occurred on the earth. Moreover, astrophysics today informs us of the expansion and dynamic change of the universe since the beginning.

The scientific accounts of the earth and the universe present us a dynamic and relational picture of the world. Nature seen as a relational reality (i.e., a web of relationships) is now seen as a dynamic reality as well. The world is conceived as ceaselessly fluctuating flow with continuity/discontinuity, stability/instability and order/disorder. The interconnectedness of all creatures is not static but dynamic. What significance does this dynamic characteristic bring up to the picture of the world toned with interconnectedness? How does this dynamism of the world influence the interconnectedness of all beings? Will this dynamic feature widen and intensify relationships in the world? Or will it dwindle and disturb them? May the astounding uniqueness of humanity, achieved through the process of evolution, deny any connection with nonhuman nature? We need to reflect upon how the Spirit is related to the evolution of the world in order to answer these questions. For the Spirit is the ground of all relationships in creation.

One must first ask whether the notion of evolution is compatible with the doctrine of creation and thus theologically acceptable. Moltmann himself takes it for granted that evolution occurs in creation. He points out that the notion of evolution does not contradict the Christian belief in creation because «evolution has nothing to do with 'creation' itself»[76]. He holds that the biblical understanding of «creating» is different from that of «making» and that evolution belongs to the latter. Furthermore, creation depicted in the Scriptures is not a static reality, completed once and for all at the very moment of «creating» the cosmos. Rather, creation is a dynamic reality longing in travail for its renewal and perfection in the future, which we believe was already anticipated and ensured in the resurrection of Jesus (cf. Isa. 43:16-21; Rom. 8:19; Col. 1:18): «the creation of the world has been so designed that it points in the direction of the kingdom of glory [...]»[77].

How can the evolution of the world be theologically interpreted, given this dynamic perception of creation? One may ask, in the first place, what enables evolution to occur at all. Assuming that the Spirit empowers, vivifies, and renews all creation, one may have a good reason to construe the changes that evolution effects in the world as the consequence of the activities or movements of the Spirit in creation. This pneumatological vision of evolution enables one to comprehend the Spirit as the fundamental ground and source of a radical change or newness that evolution brings about. Moltmann notes that evolution is composed of multilateral, complex processes and occurrences: «The process of evolution of systems of matter and life is not a unilinear chain of causality. It more nearly resembles a growing and spreading web of elementary particles and structures»[78]. As regards this aspect of evolution, one may recall that the power of the Spirit is poured out on the whole creation and pervades it. This implies that the Spirit works in an individual creature, but always through other creatures to which it is

---

[76] J. MOLTMANN, *God in Creation*, 196.
[77] J. MOLTMANN, *God in Creation*, 19.
[78] J. MOLTMANN, *God in Creation*, 202.

related, forming not so much one-to-one as one-to-many connections. One may now regard «the concept of evolution as a basic concept of the self-movement of the divine Spirit of creation»[79]. The power of the Spirit, which is the ground of the communal relationships of all creatures, is at the same time the source which brings forth essentially new, but still connected, creatures out of existing ones.

It is worth noting that the pneumatological vision of evolution allows one to acknowledge both a radical discontinuity leading to the diversity of creation and a profound continuity retaining the unity of creation. For the Spirit is seen to create, sustain, and renew all creation (cf. Ps. 104:29-30). All creation is simultaneously in the process of self-preservation due to God's sustaining power and self-transcendence owing to God's renewing power. These two aspects of creation are what we observe in the world: «Self-assertion and integration, self-preservation and self-transcendence are the two sides of the process in which life evolves»[80]. We experience both continuity and discontinuity in the evolving world. It must be remembered that evolution accompanied by radical changes or discontinuities does not negate the continuous stability of individual beings and relationships among them. The relationships of an individual with others are reliably maintained in the evolutionary world over a substantial span of time so that one's identity and individuality may be ensured. Otherwise, they would be disintegrated into the fluctuating flux of change. Evolution does not deny one's individuality or relationship with others. On the other hand, it is also the case that profound changes do occur so that radically new species may emerge out of existing ones. Otherwise, we could never see all the diverse species in world today.

2.3.2 Evolution in the Spirit: The Self-Transcendence of Creation

A new species with a new nature evolves out of an existing species in due time and condition. This drastic change of «quality leap» can be referred to as *self*-transcendence in that a species surpasses itself in its nature and turns into another. As the term self-*transcendence* implies, it has been observed that evolution, though influenced by chance and natural selection, tends to happen in a direction that the interiority and complexity of species increase. A new species possesses a more developed, i.e., a more interiorized and complex, inner structure and

---

[79] J. MOLTMANN, *God in Creation*, 19.
[80] J. MOLTMANN, *God in Creation*, 100.

organizational principle than the previous one[81]. In a word, «a greater» comes out of «a lesser» in the process of evolution. It must be noted, however, that evolution does not take place in such a way that a gap between the greater and the lesser is filled up from without. It is not known yet, scientifically, exactly how this radical change happens: for example, how life and mind has come out of matter and life respectively. However, one may say, metaphysically, that a gap is replenished from within the lesser (otherwise, it could not be called *self*-transcendence) and at the same time by that which is still distinct from the lesser (otherwise, it would not be possible for the lesser to transcend itself into the greater). What can then be said, theologically, concerning self-transcendence? One may immediately take notice of a resemblance between the way the Spirit acts in a creature and the way a species achieves self-transcendence. It is the power of the Spirit that sustains, vivifies, and renews all creatures. Every creature needs the life-giving breath of the Spirit. However, this divine breath must not be conceived as an object which is externally given to a creature. Rather, one must say that the Spirit steeps the creature in the divine breath. It is in virtue of the divine power that the creature (the lesser) is seen to transcend itself and turn into a new one (the greater). The pneumato-logical vision of creation that the Spirit is at once immanent (within the creature) and transcendent (distinct from it) renders intelligible the process of self-transcendence.

One can understand in the light of self-transcendence the appearance of life and mind out of matter and life respectively, which seem at the first glance to be disparate realities. The pneumatological perspective on self-transcendence enables one to accept their radical and essential difference without losing one's sense of their interconnectedness. Both immense diversity and profound unity in the world originate from the Spirit. It is the power of the Spirit in the form of self-surpassing process for ages that made possible the appearance of human beings out of nature and keeps them in intrinsic connection with it. This pneuma-tological vision of evolution elucidates the relationship of humanity with nature. A species called the human race appeared in the power of the Spirit to such a degree that it has come to possess mind. This unpar-alleled phenomenon allows a unique place in the world for humanity. Nonetheless, the pneumatological viewpoint of evolution discloses plainly that there exists profound unity between humanity and nature,

---

[81] Cf. J. MOLTMANN, *God in Creation*, 200-204.

and that these two are inherently connected with each other. Characteristics proper to humanity, such as self-consciousness and free will, do not nullify its intrinsic association with the material and biological world, which has been formed in the power of the Spirit and out of which it has come. Nor do they permit humankind to take a superior and arrogant attitude toward nature. If we are to hold fast to the pneumatological vision of creation and evolution, we must say that humanity is the recapitulation of the whole evolutionary process of the world. Again, the recapitulation of the world must not lead us to assume a domineering posture to nature. Instead, according to the pneumatological perspective, it is a powerful symbol that humanity has appeared out of nature. It must evoke warm affection and deep concern for nature, if it is properly understood.

From the perspective of history, one can arrive at the same conclusion about the relationship of humankind with nature. Nature used to be conceived as passive and timeless matter in a cyclic process. But science today, especially evolutionary theories and discoveries, denies this static and cyclic conception of nature. Instead, it holds that nature is characterized by dynamic and irreversible flux. It is not only humanity that experiences a chain of temporally unique events. Nature as well undergoes moments that are not repeated temporally. If history is made of «unique happenings and series of events which are characterized by an irreversible direction in time», nature as a whole, not only humankind, exists in a historical process[82]. This evolutionary perspective on nature challenges the human-centered conception of history. This anthropocentric perception of history allows neither the historicity of nature nor its proper significance, but only its instrumental usefulness as resources for human beings. However, the evolutionary view of the world reclaims historicity to nature. The evolutionary standpoint says plainly that the human race appeared through a long, gradual, and complex evolutionary process of inorganic sphere to biosphere and finally to noosphere[83]. Insofar as it has emerged from nature, humankind is obviously part of nature. As long as nature has its history, we cannot find, except in nature, any time and space for human history. This cosmic perspective on history is needed for a comprehensive understanding of humanity: «we must start with the complexes and

---

[82] J. MOLTMANN, *God in Creation*, 199.
[83] For theological issues in evolution in general, see I.G. BARBOUR, *Religion and Science*, 57-63.

milieus in which human beings appear and from which they live; and that means beginning with the genesis of the cosmos, the evolution of life, and the history of consciousness, not with the special position of human beings in that cosmos»[84]. Human history began at certain moments in certain places on the earth, but still within a single movement of irreversible and unrepeatable events in nature. Humanity emerges from nature; to that extent, human history belongs to the history of nature. In this regard, there is only one unified history of the world, in which human beings undergo diverse events in their own way and thus make human history, but always within the history of nature.

One may think of salvation history from the pneumatological perspective on creation. This pneumatological and thus ecological vision of the world sees clearly that there is no salvation history of humanity alone, apart from nature. If one recognizes in nature as well as in humans those unique and irreversible events and movements caused by the power of the Spirit, one must say that salvation history began with creation. The vision of the world in the light of the Spirit does not allow any bifurcation of humankind from the rest of creation. There is only one salvation history, in which each one is guided in one's own way by the Spirit, but always within the whole creation upon which the divine power is poured out. This standpoint is consistent with the biblical perspective and reinforced by it: the prophet Isaiah proclaims the salvation of nature as well as humanity (cf. Isa. 35:1, 5-7); St. Paul says that the natural world, together with humans, has been waiting for its salvation (cf. Rom. 8:19-23).

The radical changes that self-transcendence effects in evolution do not diminish or destroy the relationships of all things in the world. On the contrary, a new species brings forth new connections with others, as seen in the emergence of humanity. One must say that evolutionary processes increase and enrich interconnectedness in the world. Evolution has been observed to take place in a direction to augment interiority and complexity. The more complex a species becomes, the more diverse and complex its relationships with others become due to the growing capacity of communication: «with the complexity of the structure, the capacity for communication grows»[85]. This will in turn

---

[84] J. MOLTMANN, *God in Creation*, 186.

[85] J. MOLTMANN, *God in Creation*, 204. See also I.G. BARBOUR, *Religion and Science*, 174: «As more complex systems are built up, *new properties* appear that were not foreshadowed in the parts alone. New wholes have distinctive principles of

intensify and deepen interactions among them, stimulating additional new appearances and relationships in the world. For example, the world is entering into a more complex and intimate web of relationships by means of sophisticated, computer-aided communications. As a result, every part of the world relies on each other more and more; and accordingly, the significance of relationship increases. According to the pneumatological vision of evolution, the Spirit brings into being a new kind of creature out of those which already exist and thereby creates, sustains, and vivifies new relationships in creation. The interconnectedness of all creatures is advanced and becomes abundant even in an unexpected and surprising way in virtue of the Spirit. In sum, as evolution proceeds, the interrelatedness and interdependence of all creatures are enlarged and intensified. Therefore, it can be said that the pneumatological vision of evolution reinforces an ecological vision of the world and ecological consciousness which the pneumatological vision of creation presents.

It must be remarked, finally, that the tendency of evolution to increase interiority and complexity brings forth a negative effect as well. In other words, the more sophisticated a system becomes, the more vulnerable and fragile it becomes: «if with growing complexity the range of possibility grows, the degree of vulnerability and destructibility of course increases at the same time»[86]. As a system develops into a more sophisticated one with more complex and delicate subsystems, the degree of the interactions and interdependence of subsystems grows. The possibility of new forms and relationships in the future increases as well. At the same time, however, it becomes more unstable and vulnerable to external and internal disturbances. It may easily come to breakdown or collapse. On the contrary, a simple system is in general unlikely to change and is more stable to that measure. This fact brings a significant implication to us in the face of the global ecological deterioration. The present earth as an ecosystem is much more complex than the earth when humankind, such a sophisticated species, did not appeared yet. It means that the earth as a whole has become more complex, delicate, and vulnerable. The earth and its subparts need more care than before. In the pneumatological vision of creation and evolution, one may say that the Spirit will care for them all. We must recall,

---

organization as systems and therefore exhibit properties and activities not found in their components».

[86] J. MOLTMANN, *God in Creation*, 203.

however, that the Spirit reaches and sustains each creature through the divine power permeated in creation. The Spirit relates to each one through other creatures, i.e., through one's relationships with others. It may be said, in this sense, that human beings influence the movements of the Spirit in creation. For human beings alone with self-consciousness and freedom, unlike all the other creatures, are able to act either for or against the movement of the Spirit. We have a choice of either abundant life in ever-richer fellowship or impending death (cf. Deut. 30:15-20). It is all the more so today when humanity has come to possess the annihilating power of nuclear holocaust and to pursuit a lifestyle that depletes natural resources and degrades the environment of the earth at an alarming rate.

3. The Interconnectedness of All Creatures from the Perspective of Leonardo Boff

3.1 *Introduction*

Leonardo Boff[87] has in recent years shown concern for the environmental deterioration of the earth. He has widened, one may say, the scope of his concern as a liberation theologian from the poor to nature[88]. He is particularly concerned for one's way of envisioning the world. In relation to the issue of ecology, one may conceive the world either from a dualistic perspective to bifurcate it into humanity and nature or from an integrated perspective to regard both of them basically as a single continuum. Boff claims that the latter, which will be tantamount to an ecological vision of the world, must be our perspective on the world in this age. He advocates adamantly this unified perspective not as an

---

[87] Leonardo Boff, a liberation theologian and a former Franciscan priest from Brazil, received his doctorate in Munich, Germany. He taught at the Petropolis Institute for Philosophy and Theology and was a member of the editorial board of *Concilium* (1970-1995). He is the author of many books, which include *Jesus Christ Liberator, Liberating Grace, Ecclesiogenesis, Church, Power and Charism, Trinity and Society, Ecology and Liberation,* and *Cry of the Earth, Cry of the Poor.*

[88] Boff has published two books devoted to ecological issues: *Ecology and Liberation* and *Cry of the Earth, Cry of the Poor.* He addresses in these volumes the issue of the ecological crisis basically as a liberation theologian. Put otherwise, he views nature, like the poor, as that which is exploited, and he thus maintains an intrinsic connection between poverty and the exploited environment. This aspect will be brought to light in detail in chapter five.

option but as a mandate without which the human race may perish in the near future[89].

I will in this section reflect on the trinitarian perspective on creation. This reflection will disclose and highlight the aspect of interrelatedness and interdependence of all creatures inherent in the world. I will first review ecology, an ecological perspective on the world, and the prime cause of the present ecological crisis, as Boff understands it. This will reveal the way he basically grasps the world. I will then examine a scientific basis in which he grounds this ecological perspective on the world: the universe story that science today conveys to us. I will then explore the doctrine of the Trinity with an emphasis on the relationship of the triune God. I will consider what significance and implications this trinitarian relationship may bring to our understanding of creation. It will be held that an ecological perspective on the world based on the scientific account of the universe is theologically supported and solidified by the doctrine of the Trinity.

3.2 *Ecology and an Ecological Perspective on the World*

Ecology as a scholarly discipline seeks to understand reality primarily in terms of relationship, as already mentioned at the outset of this study. Hence, ecology is «the study of the interrelationship of all living and nonliving systems among themselves and with their environment»[90]. The prime significance of ecology consists in relationships:

> Ecology stands for the relations, interaction, and dialogue of all existing creatures (whether alive or not) among themselves and with all that exists. Nature (all living things as a whole), from elementary particles and primordial energy all the way to more complex forms of life, is dynamic; it comprises an intricate network of connections on all sides[91].

Ecology sheds light first and foremost on the relational character of all things that exist. It is interested primarily in how individual beings influence one another in a particular region. Ecology regards all things as fundamentally interconnected and interdependent. It stresses that there is no exception in this aspect of relationality «from elementary particles [...] to more complex forms of life». The remark that nature is «dynamic» and consists of «an intricate network on all sides» indicates

---

[89] In fact, throughout the two books mentioned above, Boff emphasizes the importance of the integrated perspective on the world and an urgent need to adopt it.

[90] L. BOFF, *Cry*, 3.

[91] L. BOFF, *Ecology and Liberation*, 9.

that all things are interlaced temporally as well as spatially. It is not only at the present moment that ecology brings to the center the interconnectedness of all. It also throws into relief the evolutionary character of the world «from elementary particles [...] to more complex forms of life». An evolutionary worldview is taken for granted in ecology. All things that exist at present are connected with those in the past; the future appears out of the present. It must also be noted that due to its concern for the interconnectedness of all, ecology is inclusive of humanity, too. Therefore, it pertains to both an individual human person (human ecology) and humankind (social ecology) as well as to the natural world (natural ecology)[92]. In short, ecology views all realities from a relational and inclusive perspective.

An ecological perspective on the world is characterized by the relationality and inclusiveness that ecology brings to the center. This ecological standpoint refers, owing to the relational and inclusive character of ecology, to a perspective from which we grasp in a single web of relationships ourselves, all others in nature, and nature as a whole. «Consequently, the basic concept of nature seen from an ecological standpoint is that everything is related to everything else [...]»[93]. This ecological viewpoint bears a holistic character as well. «Ecology, as paradigm, entails taking a basic stance, always thinking holistically; that is, continually seeing the whole, which does not derive from the sum of the parts but from the organic interdependence of all the elements»[94]. Therefore, ecology and an ecological perspective on the world anticipate a radical change in our conventional epistemology whereby we observe the world. The ecological standpoint pays attention in the first place to a reality as a whole rather than to its individual

---

[92] L. BOFF, *Ecology and Liberation*, 9. What Boff basically means by human ecology and social ecology is that humanity and society are part of nature and inevitably related to the natural world: «Human beings and society always establish a relationship with the environment». Human ecology refers, simply speaking, to a viewpoint that human beings are «the result of a long biological process» (ID., *Cry*, 6). «Social ecology is primarily concerned about social relations as belonging to ecological relations; that is, because human beings [...] are part of the natural world their relationship with nature passes through the social relationship of exploitation, collaboration, or respect and reverence» (ID., *Cry*, 105). The task of social ecology would then be «to study social systems in interaction with ecosystems» (ID., *Ecology and Liberation*, 26). For a detailed account of social ecology, see ID., «Social Ecology: Poverty and Misery».

[93] L. BOFF, *Ecology and Liberation*, 10.

[94] L. BOFF, *Cry*, 41.

parts. In this regard, it is synthetic rather than analytic. The ecological viewpoint holds that the whole is not merely the total sum of all parts, but more than that, due to the «organic interdependence of all the elements». Relationships among beings are, in this standpoint, as real as beings themselves. They make a real difference between the whole and the total sum of its parts. This holistic perspective on reality calls into question a deterministic and reductionistic epistemology, which has up until now prevailed in the West since the Enlightenment, that a reality is entirely determined by all of its parts and completely known in a process in which the reality is dissected into already known parts[95]. An ecological perspective holds, on the contrary, that one cannot arrive at the proper comprehension of a reality with the knowledge alone of all the individual parts which constitute the reality. It claims that it is only when both the whole reality and relationships among its parts, as well as the parts themselves, are taken into due consideration that it is rightly known[96].

According to this relational and holistic perspective, we cannot properly understand who we are, as long as we consider ourselves in separation from nature. The ecological standpoint supports an anthropological understanding of humankind «in and with», rather than «apart from», nature. It will be shown that this viewpoint, which considers seriously interrelatedness and consequent interdependence, has a sound scientific and theological ground.

Our current, predominant perspective to grasp the world contrasts well with this ecological perspective on the world. The ecological viewpoint stimulates us to see, with ecologically awakened eyes, our prevalent way of perceiving the world and of living and acting in it. Our present worldview today is so dualistic that it is taken for granted that humanity stands apart from nature. We may have access to it whenever material needs arise. We have come to recognize nature mainly as material resources for commodities, not as that from which we have appeared and in which we live. One of the root causes of the ecological crisis today can be found in the loss of an ecological sensibility with which we feel and view ourselves as part of nature. Many have been accustomed, due to a deep-seated dualistic worldview, to precisely the opposite perception that we are separate from nature. We

---

[95] Cf. J. MOLTMANN, *God in Creation*, 2-3. See also I.G. BARBOUR, *Religion and Science*, 35.

[96] Cf. D. BOHM, *Wholeness and the Implicate Order*, 1-26.

must learn how to appreciate a sense that we belong to nature and thereby how to maintain harmonious relationship with it. We need, for this, an integrated perspective on the world.

3.3 A Root of the Ecological Crisis

In the face of the ecological degradation of the earth today, we must reach the root cause of this problem if we are to deal with it properly and effectively. Otherwise, any approach would be but provisional and superficial. What is at the root of this ecological deterioration of the earth? Diverse diagnostics may be possible. The claim that science and technologies are responsible in great measure for the present ecological crisis has a grain of truth. It would be naïve, however, to insist that the so-called eco-technologies, which may be developed and replace the current, ecologically harmful or insensitive ones, can prevent further deterioration of nature. Technologies are not neutral and value-free. What kinds of technologies are to be developed and adopted are influenced and determined by a model of development which we choose and pursue. What kind of developmental model is to be employed in turn depends on what sort of society we want to build. The character of society is greatly informed by our basic convictions and values about our life and the world[97]. For instance, we may choose, according to our basic conviction about life, either economic development and competition or distribution and cooperation as a primary goal to be pursued in our society. This basic perspective fundamentally orients our attitude toward others, both human and nonhuman. It is at this inner dimension that we must confront the issue of the ecological crisis.

Boff regards anthropocentrism and androcentrism as our present, distinctive attitudes to nature[98]. The consequence has turned out to be disastrous. It is destructive not only because these attitudes have brought about the ecological degradation of the earth today. It is devastating also because human beings are «impoverished, drained of life, enclosed in their own limits, which today threaten their very life and

---

[97] Cf. L. BOFF, *Cry*, 64-81.

[98] Cf. L. BOFF, *Cry*, 71. Boff does not intend to distinguish strictly anthropocentrism from androcentrism as deep ecologists and ecofeminists do. He simply mentions that anthropocentrism «when considered historically is exposed as androcentrism». Rather, his primary concern consists in the tragic consequences that the isolation of human beings (or human males) from the rest of the world has brought about. Anthropocentrism and androcentrism will be examined in detail in the fourth section of chapter five.

future. Finally, they display a boundless aggressivity, for they are threatened on all sides»[99]. We have long since lost a sensibility for connectedness, which used to link us with nature, of which we are part. We have lost our root. Anxiety, which has become a typical mental symptom of modern humanity, may be a sign of the loss of our root, which used to give us belongingness and stability. Anxiety is likely to turn into aggressiveness. «The violence and aggression in the environment grow from roots deep down in the mental structures that have their genealogy and ancestry within us»[100]. Boff comes to a conclusion that we are sick in our relationship to the natural world as well as with other humans.

Boff believes that the present ecological crisis depends in great part on our perspective on the world; he holds that we must regain a sensibility for the interconnectedness of beings in the world to cope with this crisis. He is especially concerned for the role that religions can play in recovering this sensibility of interconnectedness. «The mission of a religion [...] is to reinforce the perception that [...] everything is interconnected [...]; and finally, it is to give a name to the Fount of being and meaning, origin of all [...]»[101]. As far as the relationship of humanity with other beings in the world is concerned, it can be said that religion has a great potential of supporting and fostering an ecological perspective on the world. For most religions provide a profound ground of a sensibility for the interconnected-ness of all beings by emphasizing «the Fount of being», which somehow undergirds all things that exist. It is particularly true of the Jewish-Christian tradition, since it explicitly believes that God created and sustains all creatures and will lead them to their final destination. God is the only origin and end of all creatures and creation as a whole. It is plain in this conception of God that all things are, somehow in a fundamental way, connected with one another. All creatures are seen to form and express unity in the midst of diversity, in virtue of this conception of God and the world.

3.4 *An Ecological Perspective on the World and the Universe Story*

Boff unfolds his perspective on the world, based on the universe story that science conveys to us today. I will not deal in detail with his account of the universe, because a common version of the universe story has already been presented in chapter two, which he himself

---

[99] L. BOFF, *Cry*, 71.
[100] L. BOFF, *Ecology and Liberation*, 32.
[101] L. BOFF, *The Prayer of Saint Francis*, 24.

adopts as his own. Rather, I will mention only what is significant to our concern from his exposition of the cosmos. Today, astrophysics generally asserts that since its beginning, «the universe has been dynamic; its natural state is evolution rather than stability, change rather than immutability. [...] The universe displays a self-organizing capability»[102]. Likewise, geology and biology now hold that since its birth, the earth has been in the process of evolution, which can be distinguished into the lithosphere (rock), the hydrosphere (water), the atmosphere (air), the biosphere (life), and the noosphere (spirit)[103].

From a perspective informed by this scientific account of the universe, the universe can be seen as a dynamic organic whole in which all things that exist are interconnected and interdependent due to the common origin out of which they have come into being and the evolutionary process which they have undergone. It is in the common origin and evolution of the universe that a ground for the interconnectedness of all creatures can be found. In this regard, we can hold in accord with Boff that «the snail by the roadside» is connected to «the farthest galaxy»[104]. The common origin of all things in the universe does not mean, however, that «we are all alike. As the expansionary process moves forward, the matter and energy in the universe tend to become ever more complex»[105]. Therefore, one must say that the common origin of the cosmos is the ground of unity out of which immense diversity has appeared in the universe, particularly on the earth due to the process of evolution. At present, human beings have reached a level of such complexity and interiority that one can hardly notice any inherent connection with other beings. Nonetheless, no matter how complex and developed they are, it is still the case that every being in the world is related to others in a profound sense.

From the perspective of the common origin and evolution of the universe, inanimate matter and animate life forms are distinguished, but they are not completely disparate realities. Rather, one must say that they exist in a single, though complex, continuum of evolution. On the one hand, life forms have appeared out of matter, and on the other hand, their qualities are really distinct from each other[106]. The evolutionary process includes both continuity and discontinuity. «Life thus repre-

---

[102] L. BOFF, *Cry*, 44.
[103] Cf. L. BOFF, *Cry*, 48-49.
[104] L. BOFF, *Cry*, 42.
[105] L. BOFF, *Cry*, 50.
[106] Cf. L. BOFF, *Cry*, 51.

sents the realization of a possibility present in the original matter and energy»[107]. It can be held from this standpoint that «matter is seen to be no longer inert». It can also be said that «matter possesses interiority and life», at least in the form of possibility[108]. Life forms become complex as evolution continues: «The more it progresses the more complex it becomes; the more complex it becomes the more it is unified, the more it is unified the more it becomes conscious of itself»[109]. At last, some life forms have evolved into a species which possesses self-consciousness: the appearance of humanity. This account of the universe grounded in the common origin and evolution helps us integrate and grasp all beings in the cosmos in one comprehensive perspective.

At the center of the controversy about human identity in the universe is the self-consciousness of the human being. «Man and woman are the most recent shoot on the tree of life, the most complex expression of [...] the history of Earth and the history of the universe»[110]. This understanding of humanity results from the coherent and comprehensive perspective on the universe. Humanity is seen, in this standpoint, as a recapitulation of the entire evolutionary history of the universe. It bears in itself the whole evolving process from inert matter to the most current stage of the universe, which is characterized by self-consciousness. Self-awareness is such an unparalleled quality that it confers on the human race a unique place, at least on this planet. However, this uniqueness does not eradicate, although it frequently obscures, the common ground which humankind shares with other species. In a sense, humankind is the universe come to the stage of self-awareness, and the universe has reached in humanity the phase of self-consciousness. This is not an arrogant anthropocentric stance on the universe. This conception of humanity and the world stems from the integrated perspective on the world that humankind has emerged out of the natural world in virtue of evolution, which tends to increase complexity and interiority. Human distinctiveness originates in the continuity of humanity with nature. Cosmic unity precedes and undergirds human uniqueness.

Human beings possess various kinds of knowledge based on experiences, observations, reflections, and so forth. In addition, owing to self-awareness whereby we confront ourselves, we know that we know

---

[107] L. BOFF, *Cry*, 50.
[108] L. BOFF, *Cry*, 52.
[109] L. BOFF, *Jesus Christ Liberator*, 234.
[110] L. BOFF, *Cry*, 51-52.

something and what we do. We have free will to choose this or that. In short, we are an ethical being responsible for our deeds. Therefore, it is we ourselves that eventually decide our basic attitude toward nature, although we are influenced by other factors around us.

> Each can transform his or her entire experience and knowledge in his or her way in an act of love; in other words, in an act of acceptance and affirmation of the universe [...] Each person can also refuse all of this, make his or her life-project one of rebellion against the meaning of the universe, and assume exclusionary stances[111].

The universe story today stresses that we are part of nature and cannot be separated from it. Our stance on nature may be an affirmation of this account. We will then begin to see nature, from which we have originated and without which we cannot live, with respectful heart and loving eyes. Or our stance can be a denial of it. We will then hardly overcome the present anthropocentric perspective to see nature with greedy heart and arrogant eyes, and nature will remain primarily as a warehouse for commodities. The consequence of this choice will be our responsibility.

A perspective on the world, grounded in the universe story characterized by the common origin and evolution of the universe, brings to the center the interconnectedness of all things in the world in the midst of their diversity. The world is conceived to be permeated by interrelatedness and interdependence. Humanity is not an exception in this network of relationships. Rather, human beings illuminate in themselves the whole process of this relational and evolving universe from the initial stage to the most developed one. In sum, the contemporary scientific account of the universe brings forth and supports an ecological perspective on the world.

3.5 *An Ecological Perspective on the World and the Doctrine of the Trinity*

An ecological perspective on the world that the contemporary universe story presents can further be bolstered and deepened by the doctrine of the Trinity. One may ask, first of all, what an ecological perspective on the world has to do with Christian theology in general and a theological rendering of the Trinity in particular. In fact, one may find a reciprocal relationship between theology and ecology: theology is ecological and ecology is theological. We must first recall that ecol-

---

[111] L. BOFF, *Cry*, 60.

ogy is relational and inclusive. Theology is then held to be ecological in two senses[112]. First, theology is ecological in the sense that it speaks of the God who is triune, i.e., the three divine persons in one and the same Godhead, which reveals supreme relationality. Theology is ecological due to its relationality. Second, theology is ecological in the sense that it deals primarily with the God who creates and sustains all creatures, and consequently, it includes all of them in its scope. Theology is ecological due to its inclusiveness. On the other hand, «ecology is eminently theological by nature»[113]. For ecology is first and foremost regarding relationship, the perfection of which is disclosed to us through Jesus Christ in the Holy Spirit, i.e., the Trinity. In other words, the triune God is the absolute exemplar of relationship, which is the core of ecology and an ecological perspective on the world. The trinitarian doctrine of God «affirms the one nature of the Godhead, but at the same time maintains the diversity of the divine Persons without in any way «multiplying» God as a number of gods»[114]. The trinitarian relationship is «the eternal relationship of the three divine Persons, the infinite communion of Father, Son and Holy Spirit [...]»[115].

Boff holds that the Greek term *perichoresis* expresses most fittingly the incomprehensible relationship of the triune God.

> the Greek word *perichoresis* [...] mean cohabitation, co-existence, inter-penetration of the divine Persons by one another. There is a complete circulation of life and a perfect coequality between the Persons, without any anteriority or superiority of one over another. Everything in them is common and communicated one to another, except what cannot be communicated: what distinguishes one from the others[116].

All the features of *perichoresis* such as cohabitation, co-existence, interpenetration, circulation, and coequality are emblematic of relationship. They denote the perfect unity of the three divine persons without losing each one's distinctive identity, i.e., «what distinguishes one from the others». Envisaged from an ecological perspective, *perichoresis* can be compared to relationships in creation, which form and maintain unity in the midst of diversity, although their respective degrees of unity are different. *Perichoresis* is the mutual indwelling in its fullness of the triune God of the Father, the Son, and the Holy Spirit, as «co-

---

[112] Cf. D. EDWARDS, *Jesus the Wisdom of God*, 2.
[113] L. BOFF, *Ecology and Liberation*, 11.
[114] L. BOFF, *Ecology and Liberation*, 48.
[115] L. BOFF, *Ecology and Liberation*, 11.
[116] L. BOFF, *Trinity and Society*, 93.

habitation, co-existence and interpenetration» indicate. A case can be made that the divine mutual indwelling presumes and is based on perfect openness among the three divine persons. Without one's openness to others, one can never establish relationship with others. Hence, I assert here that perfect openness exists among the three divine persons so that each divine person fully dwells in one another.

Perichoresis with an emphasis on openness brings up a few implications. First, I hold that *perichoresis* with perfect openness is the principle of life. Life can be viewed as a continuous emergence of newness. Life appears and endures, in this sense, only in circulation with others, i.e., in one's openness with others. Life disappears when one separates and closes oneself from others. In this regard, openness, whereby one comes into contact with others and thereby lets newness spring up, is an indispensable condition of life. *Perichoresis* is the way the triune God is life and the source of life (cf. Ps. 36:9; John 14:6).

Second, I hold that *perichoresis* with perfect openness is the principle of love. Each divine person completely gives oneself to the others in virtue of perfect openness, and thereby they dwell fully in one another and enjoy perfect communion with each other. The trinitarian relationship is, in this sense, an expression of perfect self-offering, which is the divine love. *Perichoresis* is the way the triune God is love and loves one another (cf. 1 John 4:8). Life and love are in fact inseparable: love always tends toward life; life is the supreme actualization of love.

Third, I hold that *perichoresis*, as the principle of life and love, is also the principle of inclusiveness. Life and love, by the nature of circulation into others and the nature of self-offering to others respectively, are not exclusive but inclusive of others, rendering all in communion. The meaning of «three» in the Trinity must be understood as «an affirmation that the name of God means differences that include, not exclude, each other; that are not opposed to each other, since they are set in communion; a distinction that makes for union»[117]. Inclusiveness is an essential condition for communion, which means «union with (com-union)». *Perichoresis* is «the principle of inclusiveness of differences and individual identities» and thus the principle of communion as well[118]. *Perichoresis* is the way the triune God embraces all that exists.

Fourth, I hold that *perichoresis* is the principle of equality. The divine persons are in perfect equality in virtue of perfect openness among them. This is already suggested by *perichoresis* as the principle

---

[117] L. BOFF, *Trinity and Society*, 3.
[118] L. BOFF, *Trinity and Society*, 5.

of life, love, and inclusiveness. Perfect equality among the divine persons points to a community where one lives *with*, not *over*, others. *Perichoresis* is the way the triune God forms a perfect egalitarian community on the basis of life, love, and inclusiveness.

Last, I hold that *perichoresis* is the principle of creation. The communion of the triune God the creator is an open communion in virtue of the divine openness. Therefore, the divine communion includes creation; creation participates in the divine communion. «Through being an open reality, this triune God also includes other differences; so the created universe enters into communion with the divine»[119]. Furthermore, creation can be regarded as an outcome of the trinitarian creative process: «In the act of creation the three Persons act together, but each one does so personally with the properties of its own Hypostasis. The Father creates *through* the Son *in* the Holy Spirit»[120]. In this trinitarian formula of creation, we can understand «*through* the Son» as the principle of individuation and diversity in creation and «*in* the Holy Spirit» as the principle of communion and unity[121]. Creation comprises a myriad of diverse creatures, which are profoundly related to one another in the Spirit and thereby form unity. However, creation as a trinitarian process does not only suggest diversity in unity as its fundamental character. Creation as a trinitarian event also implies that the whole creation bears within itself a vestige of the triune God. «The entire universe emanates from this divine relational interplay and is made in the image and the likeness of the Trinity»[122]. This means that life, love, inclusiveness, and equality, which I will call the trinitarian values, are reflected in the whole creation, though to a deficient degree.

For instance, the perfect equality among the divine persons is seen to be reflected and actualized in creation as due regard to every creature. One may also say that inclusiveness is manifested in the world as

---

[119] L. BOFF, *Trinity and Society*, 3. Cf. *Ibid.*, 149.

[120] L. BOFF, *Cry*, 166.

[121] One can imagine the influence of St. Bonaventure, a Franciscan theologian, on Boff's conception of creation, given that Boff himself used to be a Franciscan priest. Bonaventure understood creation as a trinitarian event. He asserted that the Father generates the Son (the Word) coeternal with Himself and expresses the likeness of the Father in the Son and that in this process the Father expresses all the things that he could create. The world may then be viewed as an actualization of possibilities given in the Son from eternity. The world is in this sense a «mirror reflecting God». See H.P. SANTMIRE, *The Travail of Nature*, 99.

[122] L. BOFF, *Ecology and Liberation*, 11.

«generosity in the space»[123]. Generosity urges and encourages us to share with others, both human and nonhuman, space for living and thereby let them live with us. In this regard, generosity originates in love. By virtue of generosity, we let others enter into our space and live with us. This act of sharing space for living is equivalent of sharing life. Hence, this act is a supreme expression of love. The trinitarian value of inclusiveness is reflected in creation as generosity, which lets others flourish with us.

Although the whole creation is a reflection of the triune God, it is true that the human being assumes a unique place in it. «God especially sacramentalizes the life of every human individual, because there we find intelligence, will, and sensibility [...]»[124]. One can say, moreover, that the trinitarian structure in creation reaches its apex and bears maximum visibility in Jesus Christ. For he, as the incarnate Son of God, lived in perfect union with and under the guidance of the Holy Spirit[125]. Jesus made divine communion palpable in his relationship with God. However, this prominent status of the human being, especially that of Jesus Christ, in the reflection of the Trinity must not eliminate or obscure the relationship of other creatures with humankind and God their creator. For the trinitarian relationship is the principle of inclusiveness and communion based on life and love. Jesus Christ, who entered into creation and became part of it through the incarnation, elucidates the unity of the whole creation, not only of humanity, with God.

Insofar as creation is a trinitarian event and reflection, the community of the triune God «becomes the prototype of the human community dreamed of by those who wish to improve society and build in such a way as to make it into the image and likeness of the Trinity»[126]. However, the trinitarian community is not confined only to the model of the human world. It is the exemplar of community for all creation. The trinitarian relationship of *perichoresis* must be regarded as the ideal form of all kinds of relationships in the entire creation. *Perichoresis*, in virtue of perfect openness to each other, brings to light trinitarian values such as life, love, inclusiveness, and equality. A community grounded in these values can be imagined as a perfect egalitarian and just community where one lives *with* others, not *over* others. In this regard, one may find in the trinitarian relationship a strong theological

---

[123] L. BOFF, *Trinity and Society*, 151.
[124] L. BOFF, *Ecology and Liberation*, 48-49.
[125] Cf. L. BOFF, *Jesus Christ Liberator*, 254.
[126] L. BOFF, *Trinity and Society*, 7.

motif of liberation from all kinds of hatred, oppression, and exploitation in the world[127]. All social structures which tend to facilitate and
promote the alienation and abuse of others are directly against what the
trinitarian relationship suggests and will be condemned as sin. The
trinitarian community criticizes «all closed systems in all fields because
everything must be image and likeness of God – communion, an absolutely open and processive reality»[128]. *Perichoresis* is «the source of the
utopia of equality – with due respect for differences – full communion
and just relationships in society and in history»[129]. As a reflection of the
Trinity, creation aspires to liberation.

It can now be held that an ecological perspective on the world based
on the universe story has a sound theological ground. The ecological
standpoint on the world is not only a scientifically reasonable but also a
theologically sound way of viewing the world. It can further be held
that the trinitarian doctrine provides additional pivotal elements for the
building of a peaceful and just world in our age. The ecological view of
the world illuminated by the trinitarian relationship of *perichoresis*
highlights the hidden values in the world of life, love, inclusiveness,
and equality, which the scientific account of the universe alone does not
reveal to us. We may dream, on the basis of these trinitarian values, of a
socially and ecologically just world. We can hope that this dream will
come true, insofar as we live according to an ecological perspective on
the world imbued with the spirit of *perichoresis*.

4. The Interconnectedness of All Creatures
from the Perspective of Sallie McFague

4.1 *Introduction*

4.1.1 Metaphor and Metaphorical Theology

Sallie McFague[130] has consistently been concerned about the use of
metaphor in theology. She holds that a metaphor is an indispensable

---

[127] This aspect will be dealt with in detail in the third section of chapter five.

[128] L. BOFF, *Cry*, 156.

[129] L. BOFF, *Trinity and Society*, 93.

[130] Sallie McFague received her doctorate from Yale University. She is the former
Carpenter Professor of Theology at Vanderbilt Divinity School, Nashville, Tennessee,
where she taught for thirty years. Her research interests include ecological theology,
feminist hermeneutics, and Christian doctrine. She is the author of *Speaking in
Parables, Metaphorical Theology, Models of God, the Body of God, Super, Natural
Christians*, and *Life Abundant*.

element to theology due to the nature of metaphor. Assuming that Christian theology is a discourse on God, who was supremely revealed in the person of Jesus of Nazareth, we see that the gospels are prime materials for access to this God. For the gospels are witnesses to and reflections on Jesus in the light of the Easter event. The focal point of the gospels, at least in the synoptic gospels, is the kingdom of God, which Jesus taught mainly by means of the so-called parables. As a form of language, these parables belong to the category of metaphor. Therefore, insofar as theology deals with the God of Jesus, no one can evade encountering a metaphor. It can be held, in this sense, that metaphorical theology is not only permitted but called for in theological discourses[131]. Since our main concern here is not metaphor itself, I will not consider the details of metaphor in language theories. Instead, I will review what McFague means and intends by metaphor and metaphorical theology only to the extent that we can understand the process of metaphorical theology. For we will employ and follow this process with a view to theologizing the three proposition of this study.

Simply speaking, a metaphor is «seeing one thing *as* something else, pretending "this" is "that" because we do not know how to think or to talk about "this," so we use "that" as a way of saying something about it»[132]. When we think of an unfamiliar object in terms of a familiar one, we think *metaphorically*. «Thinking metaphorically means spotting a thread of similarity between two dissimilar objects», one of which is better known and the other lesser known[133]. Hence, religious language, which deals with the transcendent and divine, cannot help being inherently metaphorical. For God is beyond the scope of human understanding and language. In this regard, the parables of Jesus concerning the kingdom of God are typically metaphorical. God's kingdom is a divine reality and as such unknown immediately to people, but he sought to convey its meaning to his contemporaries through familiar stories.

In a strict sense, most ordinary language as well is metaphorical. The only difference is that we no longer perceive ordinary language as a metaphor because we are already accustomed to its metaphorical character. In other words, a metaphor in ordinary language is a dead metaphor[134]. It can be claimed, based on the metaphorical character of ordinary language, that «metaphor is indigenous to all human learning

---

[131] Cf. S. MCFAGUE, *Metaphorical Theology*, 14-15.
[132] S. MCFAGUE, *Metaphorical Theology*, 15.
[133] S. MCFAGUE, *Metaphorical Theology*, 15.
[134] Cf. S. MCFAGUE, *Metaphorical Theology*, 15-16.

from the simplest to the most complex», for example, children's acquisition of a meaning of a new reality as well as philosophy and science[135]. The way we think and learn is essentially metaphorical.

A metaphor and a reality to which a metaphor refers are similar but
not identical. They have both similarity and dissimilarity in tension. A
metaphor has the aspect of «it is» with regard to a reality which it
indicates, but it has at the same time the aspect of «it is not»[136]. In
addition, «a metaphor not only lives in the region of dissimilarity, but
also in the region of the unconventional and surprising»[137]. Put otherwise, a dissimilarity between a metaphor and a reality evokes unex-
pectedness in a metaphorical statement. For example, a metaphor or a
metaphorical assertion may surprise hearers by means of unexpected
extraordinariness, which is drawn from ordinariness. In this regard, too,
the parables of God's kingdom are typically metaphorical[138]. The
parables employ an ordinary object or event to deliver the meaning of
God's kingdom. At the end, the parables shock, disturb, and destabilize
hearers; the parables upset their conventional thoughts and expectations
with an extraordinary conclusion or consequence. The parables stimulate the imagination of hearers and challenge them to make a certain
decision in their own context or to accord their way of being and living
in the world with what God's kingdom demands.

A model is basically a metaphor. Specifically, a model is regarded as
«a dominant metaphor, a metaphor with staying power»[139]. If a metaphor is frequently used and gains ground, that metaphor is employed as
a model. A model tends to move beyond a metaphor toward the conceptualization of an entity with more abstract and precise terms. Therefore,
a model is situated between metaphor and concept in referring to an
entity. Once a new model is formed in regard to a reality, one seeks to

---

[135] S. MCFAGUE, *Metaphorical Theology*, 32.

[136] S. MCFAGUE, *Models of God*, 33.

[137] S. MCFAGUE, *Metaphorical Theology*, 17.

[138] Cf. C.H. DODD, *The Parables of the Kingdom*, 5: «At its simplest the parable
is a metaphor or simile drawn from nature or common life, arresting the hearer by its
vividness or strangeness, and leaving the mind in sufficient doubt about its precise
application to tease it into active thought».

[139] S. MCFAGUE, *Metaphorical Theology*, 23. Cf. I.G. BARBOUR, *Religion and
Science*, 358. Barbour describes a model as follows: «An imaginative representation
of characteristics of an entity that is not directly observable and that is postulated by
analogy with entities in a more familiar domain». Therefore, a model belongs to the
category of metaphor in that a model uses a familiar entity to point to an unfamiliar
one.

see and comprehend the reality through this model. A theological model can be regarded as a «combination of metaphorical and conceptual language that provides grids or screens for interpreting the relationship between the divine and the human»[140].

The notion of paradigm is known to have developed in the realm of science, and it is deeply related to model[141]. It may be enough, for our purpose, to say that a paradigm is what «constitutes the most basic set of assumptions within which a tradition, in this instance, a religious tradition, functions. It is the unquestioned framework or context for its normal operations; [...]»[142]. For example, we Christians live within the Christian paradigm established and characterized by Jesus Christ. As members of the Christian community, our way of being in the world, i.e., the way we think, live, and act, is expected to be consistent with this paradigm, despite individual differences. In relation to a model, a paradigm is a tradition that «sets the limits on the range of acceptable models»[143]. If a newly proposed model is to be Christian, it must remain within the scope of the Christian paradigm. In other words, the model must be compatible, in critical points, with the Christian paradigm. If an existing paradigm is changed, the models which presuppose that paradigm must be changed as well. Hence, the change of a paradigm also means a radical change of our way of seeing and comprehending reality.

It can be held, grounded in these features of metaphor, that «metaphorical theology is appropriate and necessary for two reasons: metaphor is the way we think, and it is the way the parables – a central form of expression in the New Testament – work»[144]. It is critical to metaphorical theology that a metaphor has both similarity and dissimilarity in relation to a reality to which a metaphor refers. A metaphor is not an exact correspondence to a reality. Nor is it a literal description. A metaphor is imperfect, relative, and pluralistic in referring to a reality.

---

[140] S. MCFAGUE, *Metaphorical Theology*, 129.

[141] Cf. T. KUHN, *The Structure of Scientific Revolutions*, 175.182.187. According to Kuhn, a paradigm refers in a broad sense to «the entire constellation of beliefs, values, techniques, and so on shared by the members of a given community», and in a strict sense, it refers to «one sort of element in that constellation, the concrete puzzle-solutions which, employed as models or examples, can replace explicit rules as a basis for the solution of the remaining puzzles of normal science».

[142] S. MCFAGUE, *Metaphorical Theology*, 108.

[143] I.G. BARBOUR, *Myths, Models and Paradigms*, 124, as quoted in S. MCFAGUE, *Metaphorical Theology*, 109.

[144] S. MCFAGUE, *Metaphorical Theology*, 31.

Therefore, an old metaphor is supposed to be replaced with a new metaphor, when the old one can no longer express a reality properly. It is generally the case, however, that a religious metaphor makes resistance to a new metaphor. Once a metaphor settles in a religious community, it tends to become an idol, losing its tension between similarity and dissimilarity and pretending to be a literal reference to divine reality or its description.

A good example is the metaphor of «father» for God, which is often understood literally as if God were male. One of the negative consequences of this personal metaphor is, as feminist theologians criticize, that God is thought of exclusively as masculine. Besides, they argue that the metaphor of father is now irrelevant, because it is no longer proper and convincing to the mindset of many today. Regardless of a plausible controversy around this claim, it must be stressed that there is a perennial need for a new metaphor by the very nature of metaphor itself[145]. The nature of metaphor which is imperfect, relative, and pluralistic indicates strongly an enduring necessity of constructing or adopting a new metaphor. Therefore, the construction of a new metaphor and experiment with it in a new context are essential in metaphorical theology.

The characteristics of metaphorical theology can be drawn from the nature of metaphor. First, metaphorical theology does not «demythologize» but «remythologizes» the Christian tradition. It does not seek to replace the Christian tradition delivered to us in the «language of its concrete, poetic, imagistic, and hence inevitably anthropomorphic, character» by more abstract terminology. Rather, metaphorical theology attempts to remythologize Christian faith with a new metaphor, which can express it more properly and effectively in our age[146]. Second, metaphorical theology is a heuristic theology in that it «experiments and tests» with a new metaphor for the relationship of God to the world in a new context. «It will not accept on the basis of authority but will acknowledge only what it finds convincing and persuasive [...]»[147]. Third, metaphorical theology is hermeneutical in that it is bound to show that a proposed metaphor is «an appropriate, persuasive expression of Christian faith for our time»[148]. It must be engaged in the process of interpretation to demonstrate that a new metaphor is compatible

---

[145] Cf. S. MCFAGUE, *Metaphorical Theology*, 1-10.
[146] S. MCFAGUE, *Models of God*, 32.
[147] S. MCFAGUE, *Models of God*, 36.
[148] S. MCFAGUE, *Models of God*, 36.

with the Christian tradition (if they are to remain as Christian theology) and is more appropriate than an old metaphor for our age. Fourth, metaphorical theology is constructive in that «it claims that a valid understanding of God and the world for a particular time is an imaginative construal built up from a variety of sources»[149]. It insists that theology must not be satisfied simply with hermeneutics, i.e., an interpretation of the tradition, if it is to be effective in a new context. Metaphorical theology deconstructs an existing, not-working-well metaphor, constructs a new one, and experiments with it in a new context. Finally, metaphorical theology is experimental, imagistic, and pluralistic precisely due to the nature of a metaphor[150].

4.1.2 The Construction of a New Metaphor: Doing a Metaphorical Theology[151]

I will divide, for convenience, the whole process of metaphorical theology into three stages. The first is a stage of analyzing a reality and estimating an existing metaphor for that reality. A reality to be analyzed may be a particular issue in our age, and we review and analyze it in this phase. We then examine and estimate whether an existing metaphor is still proper and effective for our issue. The second is a stage of constructing a new metaphor. Once we conclude that an existing metaphor does not work properly for our issue, we must find and propose a new metaphor which is competent to deal with the issue. The third is a stage of validating, shaping, and experimenting with a new metaphor. We validate a proposed metaphor by showing that it is compatible and consistent with the Christian tradition. We also shape a new metaphor by the Christian tradition. A new metaphor may in turn bring the Christian tradition to a new light or awareness which is needed for a new situation. Hence, the third stage is a phase in which a new metaphor and the Christian tradition enrich each other. Finally, we experiment on a new metaphor to see if it works properly for our issue or in a new context. A new metaphor which undergoes this process is expected to express Christian faith more properly with regard to a specific pressing

---

[149] S. MCFAGUE, *Models of God*, 37.

[150] Cf. S. MCFAGUE, *Models of God*, 37-40.

[151] For a general introduction of metaphorical theology, see S. MCFAGUE, *Models of God*, chapters one and two.

issue in our times[152]. As McFague writes, «metaphorical theology is a kind of heuristic construction that in focusing on the imaginative construal of the God-world relationship, attempts to remythologize Christian faith through metaphors and models» appropriate for our age[153].

It will be held that our two predominant metaphors for the relationship between God and the world are no longer proper in our age, which is characterized by the ecological degradation of the earth. These two metaphors must be discarded. A new metaphor, which can work better in the age of the global ecological crisis, must be sought and constructed. A new metaphor thus proposed is validated in terms of the Christian tradition. A proposed metaphor is shaped as well by the Christian tradition; conversely, the former also make a contribution to the latter. A new metaphor thus acquired is expected to express Christian faith more properly and effectively in our age. The Christian tradition is remythologized.

I will, from now on, seek to follow the process of metaphorical theology to find a new metaphor for the relationship between God and the world, which is more suitable for our times. I will in this section deal with the first and second stages of metaphorical theology: the analysis of a reality, the estimation of an existing metaphor, and the construction of a new metaphor. The final stage of the validation, shaping, and experiment of a new metaphor will be mentioned in chapters four and five. I will first raise the necessity of a new metaphor for the relationship among God, the world, and humanity because the existing, monarchical and mechanistic metaphors are no longer proper in our age. A new metaphor will then be proposed, grounded in what is called the common creation story. I will in this process reflect on what a new metaphor may imply with regard to the interconnectedness of all creatures. This section will be a place where Christianity learns, rather than teaches, from a proposed metaphor. It is expected to awaken the Christian tradition to some vital aspects in order to grapple with the ecological crisis of the earth.

---

[152] Cf. S. MCFAGUE, *Models of God*, 49; ID., *The Body of God*, 83; ID., *Life Abundant*, 146; ID., *Super, Natural Christians*, 164-169.

[153] S. MCFAGUE, *Models of God*, 40. Remythologization can be understood as reconceiving of the relationship of God to the world through a new metaphor which is more suitable for our issue and more intelligible and convincing to our contemporaries. Cf. ID., *The Body of God*, 81.

4.2 *A Search for a New Metaphor in a New Context*

4.2.1 Monarch and Machine:
Two Predominant Metaphors for God and the World

Given that one of the most urgent issues in our age is the deterioration of the environment by human beings, it is critical to examine how we conceive God relates to the world. For this exerts a great influence upon our own way of seeing and relating to the world[154]. It is primarily through a metaphor (model) that we conceive how God acts in the world. We must then ask what has been the most influential metaphor for the relationship of God to the world and how it now works. We must review whether that metaphor is still compatible with the dominant worldview of our contemporaries, including non-Christians, and thus convincing to them. We must examine whether it functions in a positive way as regards the present ecological crisis. That metaphor must also help to cultivate in us ecological consciousness and responsibility for nature. Otherwise, we must discard it and seek a new metaphor, which is more proper for our times. In fact, McFague estimates that the present, predominant metaphors, which influence the formation of our worldview, are dualistic and hierarchical and contribute in great measure to the current environmental destruction. Therefore, we must discard them and search for a more proper metaphor, which can bring forth an integrated worldview. A comprehensive perspective thus attained will lead us to a more elevated ecological concern and responsibility.

One of the most traditional and influential metaphors for the relationship of God and the world in the Jewish-Christian tradition is the monarchical metaphor, in which God is conceived as king and human beings as subjects[155]. The monarchical model dates back to the ancient Jewish tradition. The idea of God as the king of the universe was developed in Jewish thought. God's omnipotence was stressed in medieval Christian thought; and God's sovereignty was emphasized in the Reformation, especially by Calvin[156]. This metaphor depicts God as an all-powerful king who dominates and controls his subjects with domination and benevolence.

---

[154] McFague presents five models as major models in the Christian tradition for the relationship of God to the world: the deistic, dialogic, monarchical, agential, and organic models. See S. MCFAGUE, *The Body of God*, 136-141.

[155] Cf. S. MCFAGUE, *Models of God*, 63-69.

[156] Cf. I.G. BARBOUR, *Myths, Models and Paradigms*, 156.

It can be held that this king-subject metaphor does not work effectively to alleviate the present ecological crisis. First, God as an almighty king is not seen to live closely with human beings in the world. God is the supreme being who is remote from the world. God relates to the world only from without and is not involved in the world. As a result, God becomes worldless and the world Godless. The desacralization of the world may in turn give a sanction to humanity's plunder of the world, which is regarded as Godless. The natural world and our effort to protect it from the environmental deterioration will not be considered important because God is absent from the world. The so-called otherworldly tendency is likely to be promoted in us, and we are inclined to depreciate the corporeality of the world. Second, according to the monarchical metaphor, God relates only to humanity and shows no concern for nonhuman creation. In this regard, this metaphor is excessively anthropocentric and can hardly contribute to instilling in us ecological concern. Third, the monarchical metaphor, in which a superior king rules and inferior subjects obey, corresponds to a typical hierarchical dualism. This hierarchical dualism «has fueled many kinds of oppression, including (in addition to that of the nonhuman by the human) those arising from the cleavages of male/female, white/colored, rich/poor, Christian/non-Christian, and mind/body»[157]. Fourth, the image of the absolute king who rules by means of domination and benevolence evokes in us militarism or passivity. It does not help us foster a sense of responsible care for others, especially for nonhuman creatures.

In sum, concerning God, the monarchical metaphor does not express any salvific will or power of God for creation; regarding the world, this metaphor does not express any concern for the entire creation, but at best, only for humanity; as regards humanity, it does not help to form and foster a caring and responsible attitude toward nature. Above all, it is critical to note that the relationship of God to the world that the monarchical metaphor indicates is external and temporal, rather than intrinsic and permanent, that it can be removed whenever God (and thus humans as well) wants to do so. We can hardly perceive in this metaphor any intimate relationship of God to the world. Nor will any sense of the intimate relationship of humanity with nature germinate out of this metaphor. Hence, a case is now made that the monarchical

---

[157] S. MCFAGUE, *Models of God*, 67.

metaphor must be discarded and we must find or construct a new metaphor, which can serve more properly in our age.

Another traditional and powerful metaphor for the relationship of God to the world is the mechanistic metaphor (model), which came into being around the Scientific Revolution in the West[158]. The world and God in the mechanistic metaphor are seen as a machine and its designer respectively (for instance, a clock and a clockmaker). Isaac Newton made a great contribution to this mechanistic way of seeing the world and God. Basically, he understood the world as a law-abiding machine which God created. The appearance of the mechanistic metaphor and its gaining ground signify the retreat from the perspective of seeing the world as a living organism, which was influential in the Middle Ages.

The mechanistic viewpoint grasps the world as a machine, which is composed of inert objects and governed by external forces and laws. Nature is seen to be controlled, dominated, and managed freely only if we know those laws abiding in it. Hence, Francis Bacon insisted that nature must be interrogated through scientific methods such as dissection so that order may be extracted from disorder[159]. René Descartes, in pursuit of the certainty of knowledge, sharply separated the human mind from both the human body and nature. The material world was viewed as a system composed of passive, dead, and inert parts moved by external forces[160]. At first, when this mechanistic perception of the world emerged, God's intervention in the world was acknowledged for special occasions and God's providence was attempted to be secured. In the final analysis, however, it came to hold that once God starts the world as a machine, then God leaves it to run by itself[161]. As in the monarchical metaphor, the world has become *de facto* Godless, though God is admitted as the creator of all that exists.

The mechanistic metaphor too discloses some problems with regard to our concern. First, it must be noted that the mechanistic metaphor was influenced by a dualistic worldview and grounded in it. The first division takes place between God and the world; the world has eventually become the world without God. The desacralization of the world provides a fertile soil for the subsequent domination, control, and exploitation of nature by human beings. God's continuous care for the

---

[158] Cf. S. MCFAGUE, *Models of God*, 137-138. See also I.G. BARBOUR, *Religion and Science*, 18-19. 21-23.

[159] Cf. C. MERCHANT, *The Death of Nature*, 164-165.

[160] Cf. C. MERCHANT, *The Death of Nature*, 203-205.

[161] I.G. BARBOUR, *Religion and Science*, 36-38.

world cannot be imagined, except sporadic interventions at best. The second separation occurs between the human being (or the human mind) and nature (or both the human body and nature); the former is regarded as the only subject in the world and the latter as an object that the former conquers and controls. This anthropocentric attitude opens the door wide to the devastation of nature by humanity. We begin to regard nature simply as resources for commodities and to plunder it. The mechanistic metaphor does not help us form and cultivate a caring and responsible attitude toward nature.

Second, as nature is conceived as a machine composed of inanimate and externally connected objects rather than as a living organism, it is virtually impossible to see that all things in the world are intrinsically interrelated and interdependent as perceived in a living organism. Rather, all things are viewed as separate and replaceable parts moved by external forces. The mechanistic metaphor functions as a sanction to the reckless exploitation and extravagant waste of nature by humans. Historically, this metaphor supported social, economic, and political activities such as commercialism, colonialism, and capitalism at that time, which still remain today in different guises[162]. The mechanistic metaphor of the world has helped humans exploit nature and still influence our way of viewing and dealing with nature.

In short, the mechanistic metaphor discloses similar problems with regard to nature, as the monarchical metaphor does. We must discard it and seek a new metaphor for the world and God, which can work positively for the world suffering from the ecological disruption.

4.2.2 The Body of Christ: A Traditional Christian Organic Metaphor

When we think of an alternative metaphor to the monarchical and mechanistic metaphors, we must pay attention to whether a new metaphor can bring forth the intimate relationship of God and the world and evoke in us deep concern and mature responsibility for others, both human and nonhuman. These requirements may immediately recall us to the organic worldview which was prevalent in the Middle Ages[163]. This organic perspective on the world conceived nature principally as a living organism. Nature was perceived as a nurturing, benevolent

---

[162] Cf. C. MERCHANT, *Earthcare*, 76-80.

[163] Cf. C. MERCHANT, *The Death of Nature*, 1: «for sixteenth-century Europeans the root metaphor binding together the self, society, and the cosmos was that of an organism».

mother feeding all creatures. However, another opposing image of nature as «wild and uncontrollable disorder», which causes natural disasters and therefore needs to be tamed, existed together[164]. Also in the Christian tradition, a strong organic metaphor has existed: the church as the body of Christ and Christ as the head of the body (cf. 1 Cor. 12:12-31; Col. 1:18). With the emergence and domination of the mechanistic metaphor and the disappearance of the organic metaphor since the Enlightenment, we have lost «the sense of belonging in our world and to the God who creates, nurtures, and redeems this world and all its creatures, and we have lost the sense that we are part of a living, changing, dynamic cosmos that has its being in and through God»[165].

Given the requirements for a new metaphor, the church as the body of Christ, a traditional Christian organic metaphor, discloses some problems despite its relational viewpoint of reality. It is worth reviewing them before we seek a new organic metaphor[166]. First, the church as the body of Christ is modeled on the human body and therefore principally concerned with human (especially male) forms of community and organization. This body metaphor does not show concern for nature and women; both of them are excluded in this metaphor. In this sense, this metaphor is anthropocentric and androcentric, organic as it is. Second, this metaphor does not encompass all human beings, but only Christians. Non-Christians, the majority of the population of the earth, are excluded. Third, this metaphor does not include the whole human being, either. Only the rational and spiritual part of the human being is recognized and appreciated, while its material part tends to disregarded and depreciated, as Christ as the *head* of the body implies. In short, this body metaphor discloses «a dualistic, hierarchical notion of exclusion», although it is ostensively organic. This metaphor can hardly be expected to foster a perspective which regards all creatures as interconnected and interdependent. Nor will it help us appreciate the importance of the corporeality of the world. Instead, it may promote a tendency to divide the world into two unequal parts and to view one part as superior and the other inferior: for example, mind/body, Christians/non-Christians, male/female, and humanity/nature. Moreover, this

---

[164] C. MERCHANT, *The Death of Nature*, 2-3. The metaphor of a nurturing mother gave way to the image of disorder as the Reformation and the Scientific Revolution proceeded. The disorder of nature must be conquered and curbed by new sciences and technologies, and the order of nature must be regained (See *Ibid.*, 127.164).

[165] S. MCFAGUE, *The Body of God*, 34.

[166] Cf. S. MCFAGUE, *The Body of God*, 36-37.

traditional organic metaphor, rooted in one ideal human body, would have difficulty in considering seriously the freedom and diversity of individual members in the body. For it tends to subordinate the members of the body as parts to the whole; the members must conform themselves to the one head. This is likely to force them into a uniform way of thinking and thereby to weaken a sense of responsibility in their deeds.

When we seek a new metaphor, we must consider all the drawbacks of the traditional, predominant metaphors so that they can guide us and provide some hints in a negative way. Against the traditional Christian organic metaphor, for example, a new metaphor must be inclusive of nature, female, non-Christians, and corporeality. It must be a comprehensive metaphor. It must preserve and respect the diversity of individuals, and thereby it must foster their freedom and responsibility. We may imagine a metaphor which derives not from one ideal human (male) body but from a cosmic body comprising many bodies in itself. Diverse individual bodies in one cosmic body may be seen to form unity in virtue of their organic interconnectedness. All these must be critical aspects that we must consider with regard to a new metaphor for the world and God. The contemporary scientific account of the universe and the earth is now presented as a source for a new metaphor.

4.2.3 The Common Creation Story:
The Universe Story of Contemporary Science

The origin and history of the universe and the earth based on science today, which McFague calls «the common creation story», need not be repeated in detail, because a common version of the universe story has already been mentioned in chapter two, which she herself adopts as her own. I will mention only some critical points of the story pertinent to our concern. Theories and discoveries in astrophysics today say that the universe came into being from «one infinitely hot, infinitely condensed bit of matter» about fifteen billion years ago and has since been expanding. The universe is estimated to comprise «one hundred billion galaxies, each with its billions of stars and planets». Modern geology and biology disclose that the earth was brought into being around four billion years ago and underwent since then evolution whereby myriad kinds and levels of life forms including humankind have appeared[167].

---

[167] Cf. S. MCFAGUE, *The Body of God*, 38-47. Today most people, though not all, seem to agree with this general scheme of the universe story. Therefore, McFague

What may this universe story imply in regard to a new metaphor for the world? First of all, to acknowledge this scientific account would alleviate our excessive, anthropocentric worldview and foster a more balanced and humble attitude toward nature with a heightened cosmo-centric awareness. For example, according to the universe story, the history of the universe and human story are not disparate or separable from each other. Rather, human history assumes an infinitesimal part of the history of the earth, without mentioning cosmic history. At the same time, the story continues, at least on this planet, the human race is the only species which possesses self-awareness and freedom. The universe story makes clear that we are not the center of the cosmos. It is the case, nevertheless, that we are the most evolved species so far in the world. As such, we are conscious of our unique and special place and role in the world. This must be all the more so today when we possess enor-mous power to dominate, control, and even eradicate most of creatures including ourselves.

Second, we may analogously say that the universe as a whole is a living reality in that it is not static and inert but still growing and thus dynamic. Moreover, all things that exist in this living universe can be viewed as organically related to and dependent on one another. Their interrelatedness and interdependence in diversity are possible due to their common origin. The pattern of dependence among species at different evolutionary levels shows that species at higher levels gener-ally depend on those at lower levels. Therefore, humankind, the most evolved species on the earth, depends for its survival on other species, but not *vice versa*. This pattern of dependence helps us reflect soberly on our place in the planet[168]. Humanity is the most developed, but at the same time, the most dependent, member of the earth. In short, the entire universe can be envisioned as one cosmic organism in which all indi-vidual beings are organically interconnected.

The most critical point of the common creation story in regard to our new metaphor lies in its emphasis on the intimate and internal links of all beings due to their common origin and evolution. «All things living and all things not living are the products of the same primal explosion and evolutionary history and hence interrelated in an internal way right from the beginning. We are distant cousins to the stars and near rela-

---

claims that Christian theology must conceive and formulate Christian faith in a renewed fashion in the light of this viewpoint of the universe, thereby rendering it more convincing to people today (cf. *Ibid.*, 107).

168 Cf. S. MCFAGUE, *The Body of God*, 106.

tions to the oceans, plants, and all other living creatures on our planet»[169]. All things that exist in the universe are, without exception, characterized by radical unity and diversity. Their radical unity originates from «the same primal explosion» in the beginning of the universe. Their radical diversity originates in the «evolutionary history» of the universe, i.e., the subsequent expansion of the universe and the evolution of the earth. The common origin of all beings and the evolutionary history of the universe inseparably link unity and diversity. Ultimately, all things come into being out of the ashes of the same stars at the primordial explosion. Diverse species with different levels of complexity and interiority have emerged on the earth through evolution: from matter to life forms, to consciousness, to self-consciousness. All are interrelated and interdependent «in an internal way right from the beginning».

It is critically important to note that the relationships of all beings in the universe are not accidental or external but inevitable and internal owing to their same origin and the continuity of evolution. Their relationships are not something that may exist or not. Nor can they be arbitrarily revoked. Being and relationship are at once distinct and inseparable from each other. A being cannot exist without its relationship with other beings. The astounding diversity of the universe in radical unity is a critical aspect, which the traditional Christian organic metaphor lacks[170]. This suggests that we may find on the basis of the common creation story a new organic metaphor which can overcome the drawbacks of the old organic metaphor. A resultant metaphor will be the one that acknowledges and manifests unity through intimate relationships among individuals, without thereby sacrificing their diversity in the name of the organic oneness.

The view based on the common creation story that human beings are connected to the rest of the universe, without mentioning the earth, is not romantic or naïve. Rather, it is realistic in that it is grounded in the observations that contemporary science provides. Moreover, this account of the universe is not only scientific: «it is, implicitly, deeply moral, for it raises the question of the place of human beings in nature, and calls for a kind of praxis in which we see ourselves in proportion, in harmony, and in a fitting manner relating to all others that live and

---

[169] S. MCFAGUE, *The Body of God*, 104.
[170] Cf. S. MCFAGUE, *The Body of God*, 55.

all the systems that support life»[171]. The consequence that this universe story brings regarding the place of the human race may be described as «a decentering and a recentering of human beings»[172]. The common creation story disturbs and decenters the position of humanity in the world which we have traditionally assumed. It then adjusts and re-centers our place in the world. It implies a drastic change in the way we perceive ourselves in the world. To acknowledge and accept this story would mean that we, who used to regard ourselves as the center of the world and its master, are willing to express a humble gratitude to the world and a responsible concern for it. It is a sober realization that we are not the center of the universe nor does the universe exist principally for our sake. It means the renunciation of our anthropocentric view of the world. At the same time, it also indicates that as the only species, at least on this planet, which is aware of this marvelous story of the universe and which is inextricably related to and dependent upon all the other beings, we humans are responsible for the future of nature.

4.3 *The Body of God: A New Metaphor in a New Context*

4.3.1 The World as the Body of God
       and God as the Spirit of the Body

McFague proposes the body of God as a new metaphor for the world and its relationship with God. This new metaphor is organic, and it seeks to overcome the drawbacks of the traditional organic metaphor. It has been remarked that the traditional Christian organic metaphor is anthropocentric, androcentric, excessively spiritual, and confined only to Christians. It does not allow or encourage freedom, spontaneity, and responsibility. To handle these problems, a new metaphor is conceived as a cosmic body that involves «bodies, all the diverse, strange, multi-tude of bodies [...] that make up the universe»[173]. One can imagine, based on the common creation story, a cosmic whole which comprises an immense number of individual cosmic bodies, i.e., all things that exist in the universe – a myriad of stars and planets and innumerable things in them, animate and inanimate. This cosmic whole is seen as one organic body in which all its members are organically interrelated and interdependent. All individual bodies in this one cosmic and or-ganic body maintain a profound unity and a myriad diversity due to

---

[171] S. MCFAGUE, *The Body of God*, 111.
[172] S. MCFAGUE, *The Body of God*, 108.
[173] S. MCFAGUE, *The Body of God*, 37.

their common origin and the evolving process from which they have appeared. We humans are no exception to this cosmic interrelatedness and interdependence. We are related to other beings in our origin and dependent upon them in our existence at every moment. The organic body metaphor conceived in this way is radically inclusive. What was excluded from the concern of the previous organic metaphor, that is, nature, women, and non-Christians, is included in this metaphor. It considers seriously the corporeality of the world because the body metaphor itself is material.

If the universe is regarded as the body *of God*, how must we conceive God relates to the world? This influence directly and profoundly the way we see and relate to the world. The monarchical and mechanistic metaphors perceive that God is remote or absent from the world. God is not involved in the world, nor is God interested in it. At most, God is envisaged as intervening in the world from without and sporadically. The world is related to God, only externally and occasionally. This connection can arbitrarily be revoked. On the contrary, the world seen as the body of God offers an astoundingly different account of the relationship of God to the world.

One's relationship to one's body is a good analogy to God's relationship to the world as God's body. First of all, «I» am not entirely identical with my body in the sense that I am conscious of my body. I am more than my body to the extent that I transcend my body. It is still the case, however, that my body is not completely different from myself. I and my body are distinct but also inseparable. I am intrinsically related to my body: my body is not what is imposed upon me from without; I cannot refuse or revoke my body. I do not deal with my body as an outer object nor am I indifferent to it. My body is precious to me, and I appreciate its presence. I am concerned and care for my body, indeed, its every part. This understanding of my relationship with my body can analogically be applied to God's relationship with the world. If the world is God's body, one must not conceive that God relates externally to the world and is indifferent to it. Rather, God must be seen to relate to the world internally and intimately. Since it is God's body, the world is precious to God, and God appreciates its presence. God is concerned and cares for God's body, indeed, every part of the world. It must be noted that this perception of the relationship between God and the world has a strong affinity with the biblical perspective of the world as God's precious creation and God's intimate concern for it, as seen in the creation stories of Genesis.

The metaphor of God's body brings about a fundamental change in our way of conceiving how God relates to the world. The monarchical or mechanistic metaphor, i.e., the metaphor of king or clockmaker for God, is no longer appropriate for the God who relates to the world intimately and intrinsically. We need also to find a new metaphor for God, which is in accord with a new organic metaphor. One may spontaneously recall spirit as a competent candidate for the metaphor of God's body. For we regard ourselves as unity of spirit and body[174]. McFague remarks that the word «spirit» connotes vigor, courage or strength in its ordinary use, for instance, a person's spirit. They express diversely the power of life immanent in a living creature. In this regard, spirit can be understood primarily as what gives life, i.e., the life-giving breath. Moreover, spirit as the life-giving breath has solid biblical grounds. However, the metaphor of spirit will not immediately be related to the Holy Spirit because the term «Holy Spirit» has been used predominantly in relation to human beings, especially Christians. If we confine the scope of the spirit metaphor to humankind or Christians, it will not befit the body of God, which is meant to embrace the entire cosmos.

Nonetheless, we can still draws on another biblical tradition of spirit: «the spirit of God, the divine wind that "swept over the face of the waters" prior to creation, life-giving breath given to all creatures, and the dynamic movement that creates, recreates, and transcreates throughout the universe»[175]. This cosmic spirit must be understood not only as the spirit of living creatures but as the spirit of all that exists, including inanimate creatures, although it is in living creatures that the power of spirit is most noticeable. The divine, creative, and cosmic spirit in the whole creation creates, sustains, and renews all creatures through its life-giving breath (cf. Gen. 2:7; Ps. 104:29-30). A living creature cannot exist without breath. All living creatures owe their existence to the spirit who gives breath[176]. The metaphor of spirit stresses that the relationship between God and creation is formed at the most profound level, i.e., existence and life. Spirit is seen to permeate all creatures in the form of breath, to sustain them, and to enliven them.

It is important to note how spirit acts in creation. Spirit is envisioned to penetrate all creatures and thereby knitting them together. Although

---

174 Cf. S. MCFAGUE, *The Body of God*, 143-145.
175 S. MCFAGUE, *The Body of God*, 143.
176 Cf. S. MCFAGUE, *The Body of God*, 143-144.

it is distinct from creation, spirit relates to creatures neither externally nor occasionally. Rather, one must say that spirit is always present and work internally in all creatures. For spirit does not occasionally approach them from without. Instead, it penetrates them. The spirit that is grasped in this way does not only render God's relationship with the world intimate and intrinsic. It also provides a solid ground for relationships among creatures. All of them are regarded as interrelated and interdependent in virtue of this immanent spirit. This all-penetrating and all-encompassing spirit is the ultimate ground for the interconnectedness of all creatures. Therefore, in common with the metaphor of God's body, the metaphor of spirit indicates that God acts intimately and internally in regard to the world and that all creatures in the world are interconnected.

It needs to be mentioned that the metaphor of spirit for God is not only a spontaneous choice. It is also an intentional and considerate selection, because there are other candidates befitting the metaphor of body, such as self, mind, heart, will, and soul[177]. A critical reason for selecting spirit as a new metaphor for God is that the metaphor of spirit «undercuts anthropocentrism and promotes cosmocentricism»[178]. We can notice that that all the other candidates are used only for human beings, whereas spirit is relatively an amorphous term which can be used for the entire world as well as for humankind. Spirit bears a cosmic significance and its meaning is much broader than what those anthropological terms signify. It can be held, for our concern, that «mind» must especially be avoided, because it has often been understood and used with a view of dichotomizing the world into mind (subject) and matter (object) and of controlling matter (body), as is typical in the Cartesian tradition. If a new metaphor for God were decided as mind, God would be viewed as the dominator and controller of the world. On the contrary, the metaphor of spirit perceives and expresses God as the source of life and the empowerment of creation. A different metaphor does make a difference with regard to our way of conceiving how God relates to the world.

> The connection is one of *relationship* at the deepest possible level, the level of life, rather than *control* at the level of ordering and directing nature. And since, as we recall, our tendency is not only to model God in our image but to model ourselves on the models with which we imagine God, the

---

[177] Cf. S. MCFAGUE, *The Body of God*, 144-145.
[178] S. MCFAGUE, *The Body of God*, 144.

metaphor of breath rather than mind might help us to support, rather than control, life in all its forms[179].

The spirit metaphor for God allows us to see the relationship of God to the world at the level of life, and thereby we come to perceive this relationship as internal and profound. The significance of this spirit metaphor comes to the fore if it is considered that we tend to adopt, in forming our relationship to the world, our way of conceiving how God acts in the world. If God is perceived to dominate and control the world, we humans, as the only species in this planet which has self-consciousness, are likely to act in a similar way. On the contrary, if God is conceived to sustain and enliven all creation from within, we too are more inclined to act in this way. Hence, the metaphor of spirit helps us recognize the intrinsic and intimate link of human beings and nature. This recognition will in turn contribute to forming and fostering in us ecological awareness.

4.3.2 The Metaphor of God's Body: Pantheism or Panentheism

When the body of God is presented as a metaphor for the world and its relationship with God, this metaphor may immediately evoke a pantheistic impression in Christians. It is the case that this body metaphor seems to be closer to pantheism than the monarchical and mechanistic metaphors. But it must be noted that the metaphor of God's body does not identify God with the world, as we are not completely identified with our body. We are not simply our body, although body is an essential part of us. The fact that we are aware of our body confirms that we are not entirely identical with our body nor are we completely absorbed into our body. The metaphor of spirit for God, in which spirit is seen at once to permeate the world and to be distinct from it, also precludes a pantheistic understanding of this body metaphor. Without rendering God and the world the same, it can be held, in virtue of the spirit metaphor, that God is present in the world as God's body. Hence, it can also be claimed that all creatures exist in God in the sense that they have their origin, sustenance, and liveliness from God, while retaining their distinction from God.

This understanding of God and the world corresponds to neither pantheism nor absolute monotheism. Rather, it pertains to the notion of panentheism: «Everything that is is *in* God and God is *in* all things and

---

[179] S. MCFAGUE, *The Body of God*, 145.

yet God is not identical with the universe, for the universe is dependent on God in a way that God is not dependent on the universe»[180]. All things exist in God; God exists in all things. Panentheism holds that all creatures and God are mutually present in one another and internally related to each other. However, they are not identical with each other. All creatures are dependent on God, but not *vice versa*. They are internally but *asymmetrically* related to each other. It can be said that the proposed spirit/body metaphor is consistent with the configuration of God and the world which panentheism suggests. The fact that the metaphor of God's body is not pantheistic but panentheistic provides a ground for its compatibility with Christianity. One may say that the trinitarian doctrine of Christianity maintains both God's transcendence and immanence in regard to creation. The body/spirit metaphor can also be seen to maintain the divine transcendence and immanence in the relationship between God and the world. In this regard, the metaphor of God's body fits in with the trinitarian conception of God, which is properly Christian[181].

4.4 *Ecological Unity: A Basic Perspective of God's Body*

Ecological unity, which an immense number of individual bodies form in virtue of their interrelatedness and interdependence, is the most important and basic perspective of the metaphor of God's body grounded in the common creation story. This body metaphor conceives the world as one organic body in which a myriad of individual things exist in a web of interconnectedness. The metaphor of God's body brings to light the intrinsic and internal relationship of all things in the world. The body metaphor stimulates us to realize that we are related to nature and dependent on it. We do belong to the cosmos and are part of it. It will be explored here what ecological unity grounded in the common creation story may imply further in the light of the metaphor of God's body.

4.4.1 Bodies in Relationships: An Ecological View of Space

It has been mentioned that the corporeality of the world is seriously considered in the metaphor of God's body. The material aspect of the world calls to mind that a body needs space. For a material body must

---

[180] S. MCFAGUE, *The Body of God*, 149.
[181] The compatibility of the metaphor of God's body with the Christian tradition will be discussed in detail in the fourth section of chapter four.

occupy space to exist. The issue of space comes to the fore in this body metaphor. First, everybody needs space to exist, because it is an embodied, physical being, not a purely spiritual one. Second, life forms need space in another sense that they must obtain from space their basics for living. They must be nourished. This conception of space contrasts well with a disengaged notion of space in mathematics. «Space is not an empty notion from an ecological perspective ("empty space"), but a central one, for it means the basic world that each and every creature inhabits»[182]. In this regard, space is a habitat. Space is the most basic foundation for the existence of all life forms. Therefore, the world as God's body must be in good shape to provide healthy habitats to all individual bodies in it.

Since the world is viewed as the body of God, it can be held that God provides sufficient space for all individual bodies. It is true from the biblical perspective that God makes every provision for all creation. The first creation account of Genesis shows the God who prepares a proper habitat for various kinds of creatures including humanity. God creates various life forms, but always with an appropriate environment for them: plants and trees on the earth; fishes and birds in the water and sky; all kinds of animals on the earth; and finally human beings, who are dependent upon all these. God's provision is hinted at also when God blesses living creatures for multiplication. God is praised for God's benevolent providence for creatures, especially for human beings (cf. Isa. 55; Ps. 8; 104; Job 38-39). Jesus is also reported to have expressed deep trust in God that God prepares whatever is needed for all creatures, even for the lilies in the field and the birds in the sky (cf. Matt. 6:26-29).

We must not forget, however, that the world as the body of God is not infinite in its space and that all cannot maintain whatever space they want. «The category of space reminds us not only that each and every life-form needs space for its own physical needs, but also that we all exist together in one space, our finite planet [...]»[183]. The earth, one tiny body among an immense number of stars and planets in the universe, is definitely a limited space. It is limited in its size and resources. Therefore, all must share the given space and resources of the earth. It

---

[182] S. MCFAGUE, *The Body of God*, 99. See also J. MOLTMANN, *God in Creation*, 148: «space is primarily a living space. That is to say, it is the environment to which a particular life is related, because it accords that life the conditions in which it can live».

[183] S. MCFAGUE, *The Body of God*, 100.

is essential for all to recognize their own space and stay in it in order that everybody may have space to exist. The metaphor of God's body makes clear, by its interrelatedness and interdependence, that if one seeks to attain excessive space for one's sake, it encroaches directly on others. The relationships among all creatures which God the spirit forms and fosters must be regarded as part of God's provision for the whole creation. For the ecological unity of the world comes into being due to the way God the spirit resides and acts in creation. God wants all creatures to prosper in a web of interconnectedness.

Understanding space in the context of the environment for one's living and co-living invites us to reflect upon the way we view the world and act with others, both human and nonhuman. Do we acknowledge that the earth must remain in good shape for all, and do we behave accordingly? Do we stay in our proper space so that other species and the whole earth may stay in good condition? In confrontation with what happens to the ecology of the earth today, we cannot help admitting that we have made intrusion into the space of others. We are also ruining the earth itself by polluting the soil, air, and water. Interrelatedness and interdependence warn us that we too will become the victims of the ecological disruption that we ourselves bring about.

4.4.2 Bodies in Relationships: An Ecological View of Well-Being

Another issue which the metaphor of God's body may raise is the well-being of the body. Every creature is supposed to be concerned and care for one's own body, which is indispensable to one's well-being. Ecological unity, which is a basic perspective of the body metaphor on the world, immediately reminds us that we cannot maintain our body in good shape and thereby our well-being without the well-being of other bodies, with which we are intimately connected. The ecological viewpoint of space highlights this aspect once again. An ecological perspective on space warns us that if we pursue excessively our well-being by infringing on the space of others and thereby their well-being is threatened, our well-being cannot be guaranteed, either, in the long run. To stay in one's place is a key factor for the well-being of all. We must recall that ecological unity is not imposed on us from without so that we may remove or refuse it. According to the proposed body/spirit metaphor, ecological unity is embedded in all creatures by the spirit which interpenetrates and connects them intrinsically. Therefore, our well-being is inextricably linked with that of other creatures.

Again, this conception of well-being calls upon us to reflect on the way we view others, both human and nonhuman. The metaphor of God's body challenges us to change the way we act in regard to others. It warns us that we must have concern for our body, but always with a concern for other creatures. Do we acknowledge that the well-being of the earth must be respected, and do we behave accordingly? Do we admit that we must share the limited space and resources of the earth with all the others that they may retain their well-being, and do we act accordingly? In the face of the ecological degradation of the earth today, we cannot help accepting that we have not been concerned for the well-being of others on the earth and of the earth as a whole. We must confess that we have satisfied our indulgence at the cost of others and its consequence is the environmental deterioration throughout the world. However, insofar as all are connected with one another in one organic body and we are part of this body, we too cannot evade the calamity that this ecological devastation will bring about.

4.4.3 Bodies in Relationships: An Ecological View of Sin

From the biblical perspective, sin is understood basically as a violation of one's relationship with God established by God's covenantal love. In other words, sin is a refusal to live out the gift of the divine love[184]. Our refusal of God's love tarnishes our relationship with God. This may be referred to as the transcendent dimension of sin in the sense that sin is understood in relation to God. On the other hand, we can rarely experience our relationship with God except through our involvement in the world, particularly in other human beings. Our relationship with God is always mediated through and manifested in our experience in the world, primarily with other human beings. We violate our relationship with God or refuse God's love generally in our relationship with other human beings. This may be called the immanent dimension of sin in the sense that sin is understood with regard to the world[185]. This link between the transcendent and immanent aspects of sin is more clearly disclosed in the conception of the world as God's body. «Sin in the Christian tradition has usually been, first of all, against God; it is in our reflections also, for in the model of the universe (world) as God's body, sin against any part of the body *is* against

---

[184] Cf. R.M. GULA, *Reason Informed by Faith*, 90-92.
[185] Cf. R.M. GULA, *Reason Informed by Faith*, 101.

God»[186]. The way we act in regard to others is immediately related, in an analogical sense, to God and *vice versa*, since the world is seen as the body of God.

The conception of sin from the standpoint of God's body has an advantage over the traditional understanding of sin. Traditionally, sin is understood to be committed only among human beings and thereby to God. Only the anthropological dimension of sin has been brought to awareness. However, in this age when almost all life forms are threatened to death by the deterioration of the environment, this traditional comprehension of sin is too narrow, inappropriate, and ineffective. The present situation of the earth demands that a cosmic dimension of sin be taken into a serious account. In accord with this requirement, the metaphor of God's body widens the scope of sin to the entire creation and thereby brings to the fore the cosmic dimension of sin.

As the continuation of the preceding reflections on space and well-being in the light of ecological unity, one may speak of an ecological view of sin. If our sinful act is thought of as that which puts the well-being of other species and the earth as a whole into danger, sin means primarily «our unwillingness to stay in our place, to accept our proper limits so that other individuals of our species as well as other species can also have needed space»[187]. In this regard, sin is a denial of ecological unity, which is the most fundamental relationship among all creatures in the world by virtue of the spirit of God in creation. Sin is to disregard the most vital fact, vague as it is, for the living and well-being of all: all things are interrelated and interdependent in the one and the same space called the earth; all must stay in their own proper space so that all may prosper. This ecological aspect of sin may be expressed in a single word: selfishness.

---

[186] S. MCFAGUE, *The Body of God*, 114.
[187] S. MCFAGUE, *The Body of God*, 113.

CHAPTER IV

The Intrinsic Value of All Creatures

Proposition II: A Christian perspective on the world shows that all the finite beings in the world have their own intrinsic, although not absolute, value.

It is not self-evident, like the first proposition, that all the finite beings in the world have their own intrinsic value. The second proposition too depends on a perspective from which to see the world. For instance, if we view the world primarily as a source of materials for the sake of humanity, we will hardly acknowledge that «all the finite beings in the world» have any value for their sake. They will be regarded to exist principally for us; what is likely to be recognized is their value for our sake, i.e., instrumental value. On the other hand, if we view the world as God's creation, which is permeated by the power of the Spirit, we will be inclined to admit that «all the finite beings», i.e., all creatures, have value for their sake in virtue of God's presence in creation.

In accord with latter viewpoint, the biblical perspective on creation endorses emphatically the goodness of the world. The first creation account of Genesis ends every creative act of God with the affirmation of the goodness of what was created. God blessed all living creatures for their fruitfulness and multiplication. What God created is the cosmos, a harmonious system, which God saw was good (cf. Gen. 1:1-2:4). After the flood, God established a cosmic covenant with both humans and animals in which God promised that the earth would never be destroyed (cf. Gen. 9:9-11). It is God's promise that God will sustain all creation to the end. Prophets such as Isaiah proclaimed the transformation of the world defiled and disfigured by human sins, implying that creation is essentially good and would be renewed (cf. Isa. 40-66). Jesus announced that the kingdom of God began in this world through him, suggesting that it would be brought to completion through the transformation of the world, which is fundamentally good (cf. Mark 1:14-15; Matt. 11:5-6; Luke 4:16-21). He also affirmed that God is concerned even for least creatures in nature like the birds of the air and the lilies of the field, hinting that the entire creation is entrusted to God's love and care (cf. Matt. 6:26-28)[1].

Before we further explore the second proposition, the term «intrinsic (inherent) value» needs to be clarified at the outset. Many assume, even though implicitly, that only human beings have value in themselves, i.e., intrinsic value. It is often presumed that all nonhuman beings have simply utilitarian (instrumental) value because they exist for the sake of humanity, not for their sake. This argument implies that human beings can judge and decide the value of nonhuman beings. This presumption discloses a strong bias toward anthropocentrism. Most environmental philosophers are opposed to this anthropocentric assumption about value. Instead, they uphold the intrinsic value of nonhuman beings, although they maintain differing opinions in details[2]. Given that one's value originates in one's goodness, utilitarian and intrinsic values depend on «goodness for whom». It may be held that one's utilitarian value is one's goodness «for others», whereas one's intrinsic value is one's goodness «for oneself»[3]. Intrinsic value indicates the value which one has in and for oneself, regardless of the perception, valuation, and need of human beings[4].

What I mean by the phrase in the second proposition, «intrinsic, though not absolute value», is that though all the finite beings in the world have their own intrinsic value, they are not absolute (divine) or equal with each other in the degree of value. In the Christian context, God can be regarded as the fundamental ground for the intrinsic value of all creatures. For God created all creatures out of love, sustains them,

---

[1] Cf. R.J. CLIFFORD, «The Bible and the Environment».

[2] Deep ecologists insist, for instance, that every being in the world, without exception, has the same intrinsic value and thereby equal right. All must be equally considered and treated. On the other hand, ecocentric environmental philosophers are inclined to attach more weight to ecosystem as a whole rather than each individual. See P. SMITH, *What Are They*, 5-18.47-56; M.S. NORTHCOTT, *The Environment and Christian Ethics*, 86-163; I.G. BARBOUR, *Ethics in an Age of Technology*, 57-82.

[3] Cf. J. M. GUSTAFSON, *A Sense of the Divine*, 55-57.

[4] Cf. L. GRUEN, «Revaluing Nature».

and will lead them to the future fulfillment. However, the second proposition with this phrase rejects the argument that all beings possess precisely the same degree of intrinsic value and must be treated, accordingly, exactly the same way. Rather, what this proposition means is in accord with the remark that «all things have value in themselves because of their relationship with God»[5]. This assertion affirms that the dignity of all created beings originates from God, while it maintains that each one has a different inherent value depending on one's own relationship with God. This standpoint of intrinsic value holds that we must envision all beings primarily as God's precious creatures, but at the same time, we need to relate to them with due concern properly informed by their difference.

It is the case that the interconnectedness of all creatures implies that each one has a dimension of instrumental value for the sake of others. No creature in the world is totally self-sufficient. Every creature needs others. Conversely, each one contributes to the existence and living of others in virtue of the interconnectedness of all. In this regard, it is legitimate that we humans use nonhuman nature for our living. But we must remember, at the same time, that there is a limit within which we must remain. Beyond this limit, «use» would degenerate into «abuse». The second proposition concerning intrinsic value warns us that utilitarian value must be considered always in the light of intrinsic value. Instrumental value must be allowed only insofar as both one's right based on one's intrinsic value and the harmony of all are preserved.

I will in this chapter deal with the intrinsic value of all the finite beings in the world, i.e., the value which is inherent in all creatures. I intend to show, drawing on the resource persons, that the second proposition, which I think is indispensable to build an alternative vision of the world together with the first proposition, is grounded in the sound Christian theological tradition. I perceive that an excessively utilitarian standpoint that originates from self-interest, both individual and collective, now prevails in this world. I believe that this immoderate, instrumental tendency is deeply engaged in pathological phenomena in our age, such as the lack of respect for life and the reckless exploitation of nature. An extreme, utilitarian view of the world overshadows the dignity and intrinsic value of all creatures. In this regard, I hold that the second proposition is a requirement for the sake of the whole creation. This proposition suggests that a fundamental attitude which we must

---

[5] D. EDWARDS, *Jesus the Wisdom of God*, 154.

cultivate in this age is mutual respect based on the acknowledgement of the intrinsic value of others, the origin of which is God. Mutual respect does not deny one's utilitarian aspect for others. It does allow for instrumental value, but always with due consideration of intrinsic value. What it rejects is a thoughtless and excessive use of others, because it infringes on their right based on their inherent value and destroys the overall harmony of the world. If we are to acknowledge that we are interrelated and interdependent, our basic attitude toward others must be gratitude and respect for them.

1. The Intrinsic Value of All Creatures from the Perspective of Karl Rahner

1.1 Introduction

Given that the intrinsic value of all creatures originates in God the creator and depends on one's own relationship with God, the most supreme relationship of creation with God that Christians can conceive is the hypostatic union of the incarnation, in which divine nature and human nature are united in the one divine person of Jesus Christ. One may say, in this sense, that the doctrine of the incarnation (or christology) can provide a profound ground for affirming the intrinsic value of all creatures. Rahner holds that since it is christology that makes Christian theology properly Christian, creation too must be viewed in the light of christology in order that the meaning of creation may rightly be revealed in the Christian context[6]. In other words, the doctrine of creation alone cannot do justice to what creation means in a specifically Christian sense.

The incarnation, if considered seriously, has a great potential of affirming profoundly the goodness and intrinsic value of all creation, particularly in relation to its materiality. One of the contributions that Rahner made in christology is that he provided a perspective from which to view the incarnation coherently within an evolutionary view of the world. In regard to christology, he was particularly concerned about the tendency of his contemporaries to conceive the human nature of Jesus as not genuine but merely a way of manifesting God in the world. He denounced for two reasons any thoughts that would give this impression[7]. First, these ideas would tarnish the validity of salvation

---

[6] Cf. K. RAHNER, «Incarnation», 110.

[7] Some examples in the early church may be Docetism, Apollinarianism, and Monophysitism. Rahner argues that these mythological understandings of christology

that the incarnation has established, because we are saved precisely by God's assuming «somber facts of historical existence with its limits, dependency and baseness, without which there can be no true and full humanity»[8]. It can be said, with a more cosmic nuance, that the whole creation is redeemed by God's assuming precisely as God's own reality what creation is. Second, these thoughts would make the story of Jesus appear as a myth with an abrupt intervention of God from without, and thus his contemporaries would not have considered it seriously[9]. In the face of this problem, Rahner attempted a transcendental christology, which explores «the transcendental possibility for man to take the question of a God-Man seriously»[10]. What I heed in this transcendental christology is that it can also bring to light the significance of creation. A serious regard for the incarnation would greatly influence our way of conceiving creation. It would lead us to consider soberly that God assumed as God's own a portion of creation, which is absolutely distinct from God. We would then deeply accept that all creation was fundamentally transformed through the effect of the incarnation.

In his transcendental reflection on christology, Rahner sought to demonstrate that the idea of the incarnation is conceivable in the evolutionary view of the world and compatible with it. The incarnation thus conceived is revealed to be inextricably connected with creation. The incarnation is viewed as the goal and consummation of creation in the process of self-transcendence. He stresses, at the same time, that the transcendental idea of Christ is possible precisely because we have already experienced the incarnation in a historical figure called Jesus of Nazareth. It must be remembered that salvation comes from the concrete event of Jesus Christ, not from an abstract idea of the incarnation. Nonetheless, this does not invalidate the role and significance that transcendental christology assumes: «Transcendental Christology allows one to search for, and in his search to understand, what he has already found in Jesus of Nazareth»[11].

---

may still be implicit in the minds of many Christians. See K. RAHNER, «On the theology of the Incarnation», 118.

[8] K. RAHNER, «Christology Today?», 29. Cf. ID., «On the theology of the Incarnation», 116: «the fact that he pronounces as his reality precisely that which we are, also constitutes and redeems our very being and history».

[9] Cf. K. RAHNER, «Current Problems in Christology», 155-158; ID., «On the theology of the Incarnation», 116-118.

[10] K. RAHNER, Foundations of Christian Faith, 178.

[11] K. RAHNER, Foundations of Christian Faith, 212.

I will in this section reflect on the significance of the incarnation for creation by means of the idea of the absolute savior. Creation will be viewed in the light of the history of God's self-communication to creation. This perspective on creation will demonstrate that the incarnation is intrinsically related to creation and transforms it from its innermost part. I will then consider the historical event of the incarnation, with the same concern in mind. The incarnation will be seen from the perspective of God's self-emptying, that is, God's love. This will show that creation and the incarnation are two different phases of one and the same process of God's outward self-communication and that creation is directed toward the incarnation. This will disclose the goodness and worth of creation grounded in the incarnation.

At the end, I will ponder the consequence of the death of Jesus for creation, drawing on Rahner's reflection on death. If we understand death, as in chapter three, as a moment in which we become open to the entire cosmos and thereby widen and deepen our relationship with nature, then the death of Jesus, in whom the divine nature and the human nature are united, must have a special significance to creation. If it is in the life of Jesus that we experience concretely what the incarnation means to creation and how it transforms the world, his death must have an immense influence on creation. For his life, like others', is finalized in his death. I expect that this reflection on the relationship of Jesus' death to creation will flesh out the significance and effect of the incarnation on creation which transcendental christology has disclosed.

1.2 God's Self-Communication to Creation: Creation's Self-Transcendence to God

It has been shown in chapter three that creation can be viewed in the light of the dynamic unity of spirit and matter. This dynamic unity is achieved in the process of self-transcendence in which matter develops into spirit in virtue of God's immanence. Creation is grasped as moving toward ever-increasing complexity and interiority. From this perspective of dynamic unity, humankind is seen to appear out of nature. Creation comes thereby to form one coherent history of self-development from matter to life, to self-consciousness. The final goal of this movement in the Christian tradition is the consummation of the whole creation encompassing both humanity and nature, which is strongly suggested by the dynamic unity of spirit and matter: «the Christian knows that this history of the cosmos as a whole will find its real consummation [...] and that its finality as a whole will also be its consummation»[12]. Christianity speaks plainly of the eschatological hope for the fulfillment of the whole creation.

However, this dynamic conception of creation from beginning to end does not yet reveal its Christian significance properly. In order to comprehend profoundly what creation means in the Christian context, one must view creation from the perspective of God's salvation history, the supreme moment of which is the incarnation. The Christian understanding of the world grounded in the history of salvation says that creation is an outcome of God's outward self-communication out of love in freedom: «God creates the *ad extra* in order to communicate the *ad intra* of his love»[13]. God created the world in order that God may offer the divine self outwardly. God's self-bestowal begins, from this standpoint, from the outset of creation. Salvation and creation are then seen to be reciprocally related. God's self-communication is the ground of creation, because the former is the motive and purpose of the latter. It is also the case, however, that salvation history, i.e., the process of the divine self-communication, unfolds in the world[14]. The world is the physical ground of God's salvation history. Seeing creation in regard to salvation history, one may conceive why the eschatological promise and hope for the final fulfillment are already inherent in creation. «God does not merely create something other than himself – he also gives himself to this other. The world receives God, the Infinite and the ineffable mystery, to such an extent that he himself becomes its innermost life»[15]. God the infinite offers the divine self to the world; creation the finite receives God. The world is granted the dignity that is rooted in the self-offer of God. One can adds that creation is continuously elevated toward its final goal. For God does not leave it alone insofar as God created the world out of the divine love. The love, in case of genuine love, does not abandon the beloved. Rather, the lover seeks to lead the beloved to perfection.

Since self-transcendence is a dynamic process which occurs in the innermost part of a creature by virtue of God's immanence[16], the whole dynamism of creation in self-transcendence can be regarded as the other aspect of God's self-communication to creation: «the whole

---

[12] K. RAHNER, «Christology», 168.

[13] K. RAHNER, «Incarnation», 111.

[14] Cf. K. RAHNER, «Incarnation», 111.

[15] K. RAHNER, «Christology», 171-172.

[16] Cf. K. RAHNER, «The Unity», 175-176.

dynamism which God has instituted in the very heart of the world's becoming by self-transcendence [...] is really always meant already as the beginning and first step towards this [God's] self-communication and its acceptance by the world»[17]. God's self-bestowal must have begun from the outset of creation since it is the motive and ground of creation. However, given that communication presupposes a response (acceptance or rejection), God's self-communication is completed only by the appearance of spiritual creatures with self-consciousness and free will. In other words, God's self-communication is brought to completion only when humankind appears in the world. It is still valid, nonetheless, to speak of God's self-communication to the *whole* creation from the standpoint of the dynamic unity of spirit and matter. For nonhuman creation is seen to develop into humankind (cosmic self-consciousness), and humanity is viewed as appearing out of creation (cosmic bodily presence).

Given that the divine self-communication to creation supposes a free response from humankind, which has emerged out of the self-surpassing process of creation (the evolutionary process of the world), Rahner postulates the appearance of the so-called absolute savior in the history of God's self-communication (creation's self-transcendence):

> in so far as this self-communication must be conceived as free on the part of God and of the history of the human race which must accept it, it is quite legitimate to conceive of an event by which this self-communication and acceptance attains an irrevocable and irreversible character in history – an event in which the history of this self-communication realizes its proper nature and in which it breaks through[18].

What is meant by «the absolute savior» is that we can legitimately conceive in history of a human being in whom God's self-communication and its acceptance (the self-transcendence of creation to God) occur absolutely, i.e., «irrevocably and irreversibly» and that the idea of what Christianity calls the incarnation is conceivable. In the light of the absolute savior in the history of the divine self-communication and the self-transcendence of creation, the incarnation is construed as the ultimate goal of the self-transcendence of creation to God. Therefore, the historical event of the incarnation can be understood as the realization in history of the idea of the absolute savior.

---

[17] K. RAHNER, «Christology», 173.
[18] K. RAHNER, «Christology», 175.

The idea of the absolute savior leads us to recognize the incarnation as the definitive and supreme moment in the history of God's self-communication and of creation's self-transcendence. The incarnation from the standpoint of the absolute savior recapitulates how salvation history in the world has proceeded toward the final goal from the outset, in the process of the divine self-communication to creation and the self-surpassing of creation to God. The incarnation also shows how salvation history reached its culmination. In short, the conception of creation from the viewpoint of salvation history provides a coherent perspective from which one can clearly perceive the intrinsic connection between creation and the incarnation. As a consequence, the goodness and value of creation is profoundly affirmed.

1.3   Creation and the Absolute Savior

In order to understand the relationship of creation and the incarnation and thereby to appreciate rightly the goodness and value of creation, it is critical to keep in mind that the absolute savior is a figure in history. Insofar as the savior is viewed to appear at a certain moment of salvation history in the world, the savior appears out of the world and belongs to it. The savior is part of creation. «He is a moment of the history of God's communication of himself to the world – in the sense that he is a part of this history of the cosmos itself. He must not be merely God acting on the world but must be a part of the cosmos itself in its very climax»[19]. This historical aspect of the savior becomes obvious if we recall that God's self-communication to creation is the other side of creation's self-transcendence to God. Then the absolute savior is clearly seen to emerge out of the self-surpassing process of creation and is as such part of creation. Hence, the conception of the absolute savior in the light of God's self-offer and creation's self-surpassing precludes the possibility of regarding Jesus as merely dressed up in the livery of human nature[20]. Moreover, what the absolute savior indicates in this regard corresponds exactly to what Christianity states about the incarnation: «Jesus is true man; he is truly a part of the earth, truly a moment in the biological evolution of this world, a moment of human natural history [...]»[21]. Therefore, the idea of the absolute savior helps us

---

[19] K. RAHNER, «Christology», 176.
[20] K. RAHNER, «Christology», 176.
[21] K. RAHNER, «Christology», 176.

accept soberly that the incarnation did occur in and out of the world, God truly took on a segment of creation, and Jesus is truly like us.

One may now understand how creation and the incarnation are related to each other. The idea of the absolute savior asserts plainly that the savior is part of the world and thus dependent on it. In fact, insofar as the incarnation took place in and out of the world, the incarnation needs creation as its physical ground. Creation is the material ground of the incarnation, and in that measure, the incarnation is dependent on creation. At the same time, given the supreme, i.e., irrevocable and irreversible, realization of God's self-communication and its acceptance in the absolute savior, one may hold that the savior is the final goal of God's salvation history, although it does not mean the temporal end of the world.

> Insofar as a historical movement already lives in virtue of its end even in its beginnings – since the dynamism of its own being desires its end, carries its goal in itself [...] – it is absolutely legitimate [...] to think of the whole movement of God's communication of himself to the human race [...] as something based on this event [...][22].

We must recall that the conception of creation from the standpoint of salvation history indicates that creation comes into being with God's self-communication and that creation's self-transcendence to God is possible by virtue of God's self-offer. Creation is aligned toward God from the outset, and this dynamism of creation occurs in virtue of God's immanence. Therefore, «the whole movement of God's communication of himself to the human race», and thereby to the whole creation due to the dynamic unity of spirit and matter, is grounded in the event of the absolute savior. It can be held, accordingly, that the incarnation is the ground and goal of the entire dynamism of creation to God.

The consideration of the incarnation in the light of the absolute savior sheds light on the significance of creation. The idea of the savior tells us straight that creation is good and precious. The emergence of the savior out of creation affirms profoundly that the world is good to such a measure that it can become a corporeal ground of the incarnation, which is God's self-expression in creation. The self-transcendence of creation reaching its goal in the savior implies that creation is good to such an extent that a fragment of creation is assumed by and united with the divine in the incarnation. If one recalls that all creatures are interconnected through the dynamic unity of matter and spirit, one must

---

[22] K. RAHNER, «Christology», 175.

say that the effect of the incarnation that assumes a segment of creation spreads to every single part of creation. The whole creation is virtually united to God due to the dynamic unity of spirit and matter, and thereby it is divinized and sanctified in virtue of the incarnation. What happens in the incarnation is for the sake of all creation. Given the inherent continuity of the absolute savior and the divine self-communication, the incarnation is «precisely the way in which the divinization of the spiritual creatures is and must be carried out if it is to happen»[23]. The incarnation is the exemplar of how the divinization and sanctification of creation take place. Moreover, as God's self-offer is poured out on all creation, so is the gift of the incarnation, insofar as the incarnation is the supreme moment of God' self-bestowal. «In Christ, God's self-communication takes place basically for all men»[24]. The incarnation is the most unique and highest conceivable event in the history of God's self-offer to creation. As such, the incarnation is the absolute expression of God's will of salvation for all creation.

One must be aware that although the absolute savior is the unambiguous, supreme moment of salvation history in the world, in which creation as a whole undergoes a profound change due to its intrinsic connection to the savior, this does not necessarily mean the temporal end of the world. Rather, one may say that what the savior brings to the world is not the end of the world but «the end of the previous history of salvation and revelation» and «the fullness of time» (cf. Mark 1:15)[25]. This means that the world after the appearance of the savior is temporally continuous with but qualitatively different from the world before this moment. It is in this transfigured world in virtue of the incarnation that we now live.

---

[23] K. RAHNER, «Christology», 179.

[24] K. RAHNER, «Christology», 182. One may still ask why the incarnation is necessary at all. Why does not God come directly into each one of us? Why cannot the human being as a spirit transcend directly into God and arrive at its goal? According to Rahner, except for the case of the beatific vision, «every self-manifestation of God takes place through some finite reality [...] which belongs to the finite realm of creatures» (*Ibid.*, 182). In this sense, the incarnation is the achievement of creation's final goal in the concrete history of the world. See also J. O'DONNELL, «The Mystery», 312-313: «Man as transcendence or spirit never exists apart from the world and history. Therefore there can be no fulfillment of man's transcendence which by-passes history. The marvel of the Incarnation is that by God's taking on our human history, human transcendence finds its fulfillment in a way which is faithful to itself as being-in-the-world».

[25] K. RAHNER, *Foundations of Christian Faith*, 194.

1.4 *Creation and the Incarnation*

We have sought, up until now, to understand the incarnation and its implications for creation in the light of the absolute savior, who appears out of the history of God's self-communication to creation. However, insofar as we Christians believe and confess that the incarnation did occur in world history, i.e., in a concrete place and moment, we need to face directly what the statement of the incarnation literally means. In confrontation with the statement that God became a human being, one cannot evade the question of how God in immutability can *become* what is other than God. Rahner points out here that if we started with God's assuming something as God's own, we could not succeed in resolving the dilemma of immutability and becoming. For these two terms obviously contradict and thereby reject each other. Rahner goes on to say that the only way of resolving this contradiction is to begin with God's self-emptying, which is grounded in our faith that God is love[26].

The conception of the world from the standpoint of salvation history tells us that creation is an outcome of the divine will for outward self-communication[27]. On the one hand, one may then construe creation as God's bringing into existence what is other than God. On the other hand, one may conceive the incarnation as an event in which God brings into existence what is other than God and accepts it as God's own reality in such a way that the assumed corporeal part of creation truly expresses God and thereby lets God be present historically in the world[28]. This perception of creation and the incarnation shows clearly their intimate connection. Viewing creation and the incarnation in one single trajectory of salvation history, we can regard creation as «a part-moment in that process of God's coming-into-the-world», i.e., the incarnation.[29] The whole process of creation is disclosed to be directed to the incarnation. Creation and the incarnation can now be regarded

> not as two disparate, adjacent acts of God 'ad extram' [sic] which in the actual world are due to two quite separate original acts of God, but as two moments and phases in the real world of the unique, even though internally

---

[26] Cf. K. RAHNER, «On the Theology of the Incarnation», 112-117.

[27] Cf. K. RAHNER, «Incarnation», 110.

[28] Cf. K. RAHNER, «On the Theology of the Incarnation», 115; ID., «Christology», 177.

[29] K. RAHNER, «Christology», 177.

differentiated, process of God's self-renunciation and self-expression into what is other than himself[30].

Creation and the incarnation are equal in their origin and motive: both originated in and stimulated by the outward self-expression of God out of love. However, they are different in their degree of union with God: creation is an incomplete phase of the process of God's outward self-communication, whereas the incarnation is the perfect moment of this process. But we must not simply conclude from this that creation is inferior to the incarnation and the incarnation superior to creation. Rather, we must pay attention to the fact that creation, as an uncompleted reality, is still in a process toward its completion by virtue of the incarnation. In other words, the incarnation reveals that God intends to bring creation to perfection. The incarnation is a divine pledge for this intention.

This understanding of creation and the incarnation discloses again that creation is a corporeal ground of the incarnation, without which the incarnation itself cannot occur: «the creature is endowed, by virtue of its inmost essence and constitution, with the possibility of being assumed, of becoming the material of a possible history of God»[31]. Creation as the material foundation and condition of the incarnation confirms in «its inmost essence and constitution» the goodness and value that the incarnation pledges to creation. Creation is meant to be a means and condition, not an obstacle, to the perfect expression of God. This perception of creation powerfully awakens us to the goodness of creation.

The incarnation further confirms the goodness and worth of creation, because it announces that the possibility of God's assuming creation is actualized in the world. The incarnation is the perfect union of the infinite and the finite: «the finite itself has been given an infinite depth and is no longer a contrast to the infinite, but that which the infinite himself has become, to open a passage into the infinite for all the finite [...]»[32]. The whole creation is, in virtue of the dynamic unity of spirit and matter, transformed by the incarnation. The corporeality assumed by God, i.e., the human nature of Jesus, has become a passage into God. Insofar as we are beings in the world, there are no other ways to reach God except this passage. In addition, the passage is for all creatures.

---

[30] K. RAHNER, «Christology», 177-178.

[31] K. RAHNER, «On the Theology of the Incarnation», 115.

[32] K. RAHNER, «On the Theology of the Incarnation», 117.

The gift of the incarnation is meant to be for the whole creation. What took place in such a small segment of creation affects the whole creation. If we recall the dynamic unity of spirit and matter in the world, we can conceive «why the total reality of the world is *ipso facto* touched to its very roots by the Incarnation [...]»[33]. If we understand what the incarnation really means, we can perceive both God's salvific will for creation and the intrinsic goodness and value of creation. If we comprehend what creation truly means, we can also appreciate its intrinsic goodness and value. Ultimately, the incarnation and creation tell us one and the same truth: God is love.

1.5 *Creation and the Death of Jesus*

An anthropological reflection on death shows that death has both an active dimension and a passive one[34]. Death is active in the sense that one can take a stance on one's death. As Rahner says, «death – and only death – is the event by which freedom's choice becomes definitive»[35]. In other words, death is a final manifestation and act of one's freedom. On the other hand, death is passive as well, in the sense that one cannot help but confront and undergo it. Death is an unavoidable destiny of all. The active and passive aspects of death have in common that one's life is definitively and permanently decided in one's death. Once we die, we no longer have any chances to make choice and thereby to change our life. One's life is completely determined in death.

This is true of Jesus of Nazareth, insofar as he is a real human being. If he is conceived as the ultimate manifestation of God's will for the salvation of creation, his death too must have a definitive significance for the redemption of creation: «Jesus' death is of fundamental importance to salvation history because it makes final the acceptance of God's offer of himself to Jesus (and in him to humankind)»[36]. Given that Jesus is the incarnated Logos in the world, what is meant by the incarnation was revealed and actualized in his life and completed in his death. Put otherwise, his death makes definitive the meaning and consequence of the incarnation in regard to creation. It can also be held that the goodness of creation, launched by the incarnation, was solidified in a more radical way, when he completely surrendered himself to

---

[33] K. RAHNER, «Christology in the Setting», 219.

[34] Cf. J. O'DONNELL, *The Mystery of the Triune God*, 66-67.

[35] K. RAHNER, «Christology Today», 226.

[36] K. RAHNER, «Christology Today», 226. See also ID., «Christology Today?», 33.

God on the cross and accorded his will perfectly with the will of God. The resurrection of Jesus, which can be understood as a consequence of his death in total surrender and commitment to God, powerfully manifests and confirms the transfiguration of creation in virtue of the incarnation. Here is found a single coherent movement that starts with creation and leads to the incarnation, to Jesus' life, to his death, and finally to his resurrection, i.e., the beginning of the new creation. All these events were motivated, effected, and are threaded together by God's love, which is manifested in the world as God's self-communication, the culmination of which is the incarnation. It can be held that creation is located at the center of these events in the sense that all the other events can be seen to occur for the sake of creation. God does love creation.

The idea of pan-cosmic soul and relationship that Rahner introduces in his reflection on death can help to conceive more concretely the significance and effect of Jesus' death to creation. As mentioned in chapter three, it is in death that a human being, whose connection with the universe is restricted in bodily structure, enters into «an open, unrestricted relationship to the world as a whole». It is in this cosmic relationship in death that one «in some way introduces as his contribution the result of his life» into the world[37]. In other words, one spreads over the whole world what one has achieved in one's life, in virtue of a pan-cosmic relationship. This speculation may be applied to Jesus and his death: «through Christ's death, his spiritual reality, which he possessed from the beginning, enacted in his life, and brought to consummation in his death, becomes open to the whole world and is inserted into this world as a permanent destiny of real-ontological kind»[38]. The spiritual reality which Jesus had from the outset, practiced throughout his life, and fulfilled in his death, but which was still constrained in his bodily arrangement, is poured out over the entire creation after his death. Jesus is inserted, in death, together with this pan-cosmic contribution of his spiritual reality, into the cosmos to such an extent that he becomes the permanent destiny of the world.

In regard to the incarnation as an event in which God assumed a fragment of creation (the human nature of Jesus) and united it to the divine nature, it can be held that Jesus' death infused the effect of the incarnation into every single part of creation, but at this time, directly through his pan-cosmic relationship, not indirectly through the inter-

---

[37] K. RAHNER, *On the Theology of Death*, 71

[38] K. RAHNER, *On the Theology of Death*, 71.

connectedness of all creatures. It can be said, in this sense, that Jesus' death deepens what the incarnation brings about to creation. Although what is meant by Jesus' spiritual reality is not obvious, a critical element of his spiritual reality that he possessed from the beginning, enacted in his life, and fulfilled in his death, can be conceived as his relationship with God, i.e., the sonship that he supremely demonstrated on the cross by accepting God's will even to his death. The perfect union of Jesus with God, which was dispersed in his death to the entire creation, led the world to a deeper union with God. Jesus became the permanent destiny of the world.

It must be noted that it is by being «inserted into this world», not by departing from it, that Jesus led the world more deeply toward God. What the Creed says about Jesus' deeds after his death can help to grasp what his insertion to the world indicates. Creed mentions Jesus' descent into the realm of the dead, his resurrection, and ascension to heaven[39]. Jesus descended after death into the place of the dead, «establishing contact with the most intrinsic, unified, ultimate and deepest level of the reality of the world»[40]. This implies that the transformation of creation launched by his death begins from the remotest part of the world which Jesus reached in his death. It is significant that the transformation begins from the remotest and most forgotten part of the world, given that Jesus stood in with the marginalized in his life. Jesus is always, during his lifetime and after death, with the least ones (cf. Matt. 25:31-46).

His resurrection and ascension too can be viewed as different expressions of God's supreme salvific act that his death definitively initiated. Resurrection does not indicate in this standpoint that Jesus left and abandoned the world. For it is precisely in body that he rose and appeared. No matter how transfigured he was in resurrection, his body still belongs to the cosmos. As the body of the risen Jesus shows, the transformation taken place in creation is the transfiguration and liberation of creation from all the bondages that have disfigured it. Jesus' ascension to heaven does not mean, either, that he left the world alone. Rather, it must be understood as a further confirmation of the transformed state of creation that there is no longer a wide gap between God and creation. Creation becomes a transfigured world in virtue of Jesus' death, which is in turn confirmed by his resurrection and ascension. It can be held, in this sense, that Jesus became more faithful to the world

---

[39] K. RAHNER, «A Faith That Loves the Earth», 78-83.
[40] K. RAHNER, *On the Theology of Death*, 72.

after death. Jesus, who had walked on the earth during his lifetime, descended into the depths of creation after death. It implies that creation is touched and transformed every inch by this movement of Jesus.

Jesus became after death a permanent «destiny» and «intrinsic principle» of the world by grafting his whole reality into it[41]. He entirely penetrated the world in his death. «When the vessel of his body was shattered in death, Christ was poured out over all the world; he became actually, in his humanity, what he had always been according to his dignity, the heart of the world, the innermost center of creation»[42]. Besides the destiny and intrinsic principle of the world, Jesus is now perceived as «the heart of the world, the innermost center of creation». What these four titles mean could be suggested by the phrase «what he had always been according to his dignity». The significance and dignity of Jesus with regard to creation is revealed to us in his resurrection, which could not have occurred without his death. We are told that all things have been created *in, through,* and *for* Christ (cf. Col. 1:16). Jesus is the heart and center *in* which all things were created. He is the principle *through* which all things were created. He is the destiny *for* which all things were created. As the center of creation, he holds together all creatures in himself (cf. Col. 1: 17). As the heart of the world, he gives life to all creatures, which are held together in him. As the destiny and intrinsic principle of creation, he leads the world to himself. We must not forget, however, that Jesus became the heart and center of creation through his descent into the realm of the dead. It is precisely by his reaching the most forsaken and forgotten part of creation that he became its heart and center. There is no part of creation that is not touched or cared for by him. The entire creation shines forth with its ineffable dignity, which originates in Jesus Christ, who is the destiny, intrinsic principle, heart, and center of creation.

2. The Intrinsic Value of All Creatures from the Perspective of Jürgen Moltmann

2.1 *Introduction*

Moltmann confesses that he personally experienced Jesus Christ while he was imprisoned after World War II[43]. He grasped that Jesus is the divine brother who is with those in forsakenness and brings hope to

---

[41] K. RAHNER, *On the Theology of Death*, 73.
[42] K. RAHNER, *On the Theology of Death*, 74.
[43] Cf. J. MOLTMANN, *Jesus Christ for Today's World*, 1-3.

those in despair. For Jesus himself underwent forsakenness and despair in the extreme on the cross. The Christ for Moltmann is, in the first place, the crucified Jesus. The experience of the risen Jesus is possible for him only in the struggle out of love against forces of darkness, that is, through the crucified one. It in turn inspires unyielding hope in him. The more deeply we experience the Christ of liberation, the more acutely we become aware of disastrous realities in the world such as destitution, enmity, oppression, and war. However, the experience of the risen Jesus, who proclaims victory over death, infuses us with hope. It encourages us to stand firmly on the side of the victims in the world and to struggle against the power of evil to the end. In this regard, christology is not so much a speculative theological discipline as a process in which one seeks and follows the way of Jesus. A genuine encounter with Christ would invite us to a serious reflection on his way of living. This will in turn lead us to Christ-centered life with renewed and strengthened faith. Christology and christopraxis stimulate and solidify one another[44].

With this relationship of christology and praxis in mind, how can we expand the scope of christology from humanity to the whole creation in the face of the ecological crisis of the earth? In relation to this question, one may first ask why Jesus stood on the side of the poor, the sick, and the outcast. Jesus was sent by God, who is love, to proclaim to the good news of the kingdom of God. Jesus firmly believed that all human beings are God's beloved creatures with ineffaceable and undeniable dignity. He witnessed, however, that many were disregarded, abused, and trampled by the powerful. He believed that these people needed more urgently than others the love, protection, and consolation of God. It can be said that the universal love of God was actualized and manifested in the world as the preferential option of Jesus for the marginalized.

Today nature, which is also God's creation, is plundered and crushed by those who regard it merely as unclaimed property. They must be accused of an act of usurpation. For nature as God's creation belongs to

---

[44] It is liberation theology that holds typically this viewpoint. However, this is also true of Christian theology in general. As far as Christian theology is a critical reflection on Christian life in the light of Christian faith, it can be held that experience always comes first and theology follows. Theology reveals the significance of one's experience in the light of faith and leads one to Christian life with renewed vigor. Theology as reflection and Christian life as praxis are reciprocally related to each other. See G. GUTIÉRREZ, *A Theology of Liberation*, 5-12.

God, not to them. «If God is the creator of heaven and earth, then heaven and earth are his property and must as such be considered holy, and respected»[45]. All creatures, not only human beings, have their own value granted by God. But we have since long regarded nature simply as a warehouse for commodities and acknowledged only the instrumental value of nature. Nature is deprived of its dignity and value, as are the poor; it is abused and abandoned, as are the marginalized. A case can now be made that both of them are victims today without voices. The Christ who is sent by the God of all creation would stand in with nature as well as with the poor. This demands that christology today manifest a deep concern for nature groaning beneath the violent exploitation of human beings. We need a cosmic christology, which can instill in us concern, care, and responsibility for nature. At the same time, christology itself needs this cosmic consideration. Since Christ is the Christ of God, the creator of the entire cosmos, christology could not be complete without its being engaged in nature. It is all the more so in the age of the global ecological crisis.

I will in this section deal with the christological vision of creation. I will first examine the significance of Jesus Christ to creation. It will be mentioned that we need a dynamic perspective to understand creation properly. In this regard, three aspects of creation will be presented: the original (initial) creation, continuous creation, and the new creation. I will envision each aspect of creation from the vantage point of Christ, focusing on the unity and diversity of creation, the renewal of creation, and the redemption of creation respectively. Finally, I will remark on the two significances that the christological vision of creation brings up: a dynamic and inclusive perspective on creation and the cosmic discipleship of Christ.

2.2 Creation and Christ: The Christological Vision of Creation

Moltmann explores cosmic christology with a deep consciousness of nature in deterioration[46]. He demands that cosmic christology be retrieved, renewed, and revitalized in the age of the global ecological crisis. He criticizes christology in the past for its excessive, anthropological bias. For this tendency caused christology to be indifferent to the environmental degradation of the earth by humans. Anthropological christology needs, even for its own sake, a cosmic dimension in its

---

[45] J. MOLTMANN, *The Way of Jesus Christ*, 311.
[46] Cf. J. MOLTMANN, *The Way of Jesus Christ*, 274-280.

scope. For we humans are always a being in nature and, as such, we are part of nature. If we are to be healed, nature, which was plundered and ruined by us, must be healed; if our integrity is to be recovered, that of nature must be recovered, too. Hence, an important responsibility of cosmic christology today is «to confront Christ the redeemer with a nature which human beings have plunged into chaos, infected with poisonous waste and condemned to universal death»[47]. Such cosmic christology would perceive Christ to be on the side of nature under the violence of humans, not on the side of those who ravage nature. If it is to be of significance, cosmic christology today must challenge people to face the ever-worsening reality of the earth, to rethink their way of conceiving God and creation, and to practice what is needed to rid nature of destructive power. In this regard, cosmic christology, like any other christology, must demand from us a profound conversion in order to follow the way of Christ.

2.2.1 The Cosmic Christ and the Three Aspects of Creation

What significance may Christ have in regard to creation? How does christology influence our fundamental perspective from which to grasp the world and to act in it? The christological vision of creation refers, literally, to view it in the light of Christ. It is in the experience of the risen Jesus and faith in him that the relevance and significance of Christ to creation have been found. The experience of the risen Jesus as the redeemer of creation led his followers to recognize him as the foundation of creation as well. The risen Jesus was understood as Christ for all creation, not only for humanity. The risen Jesus was regarded as the cosmic Christ. Therefore, it can be held that the epistemological foundation for the cosmic Christ is the resurrection of Jesus. It has since quite early been considered that resurrection is closely linked with creation. The God of creation is the same God of resurrection (cf. Rom. 4:17). Only the experience of «the firstborn from the dead» (Col. 1:18) leads to the confession of «the firstborn of creation» (Col. 1:15). Christological hymns and passages scattered in the New Testaments show how the cosmic Christ was understood at that time (cf. John 1:1-18; Col. 1:15-20; 1 Cor. 8:6; Heb. 1:2) We must remember, at the same time, that the ontological foundation for the cosmic Christ is the death of Jesus. Put otherwise, it is by his death on the cross that Jesus became the cosmic Christ in the sense that his death bears universal

---

[47] J. MOLTMANN, *The Way of Jesus Christ*, 275.

significance. His death brought about the reconciliation of all creatures to God (cf. Col. 1:20)[48]. This cosmic christology of the New Testament can be regarded as wisdom christology. Wisdom in the tradition of the Old Testament is intimately connected with the creative work of God[49]. In short, the christological vision of creation is meant to view creation in the light of the cosmic Christ who was effected by Jesus' death, recognized in the event of his resurrection, and envisioned as Wisdom.

Moltmann remarks that cosmic christology in the past was concerned mainly for the original creation (*creatio originalis*) and ignored other aspects of creation, i.e., the historicity of creation (*creatio continua*) and the eschatology of creation (*creatio nuova*). This bias toward the original creation tended to separate the theme of creation from that of salvation. This division had a propensity to downplay the status of creation merely as a preliminary stage of the salvation of the human being (or the human soul). Creation used to be viewed as that which would be discarded in the final stage of redemption. This conception of creation contributed to our ecological insensitivity and responsibility and even justified them[50]. Redemption was regarded at best as the restoration of the initial creation. Neither fits in well with the biblical perspective on salvation, which articulates an eschatological hope for the new creation, which was anticipated, inaugurated, and manifested in the bodily resurrection of Jesus (cf. Isa. 65:17).

From the static viewpoint that considers only the initial (original) aspect of creation, we cannot comprehend creation appropriately. To understand it properly, we must perceive creation as a dynamic process «extended over time and open to future»[51]. Creation is not that which is

---

[48] Cf. J. MOLTMANN, *The Way of Jesus Christ*, 281-282.

[49] For a detailed account of wisdom in the Old Testament, see R.E. MURPHY, *The Tree of Life*; D. EDWARDS, *Jesus the Wisdom of God*, especially chapter one. See also J. MOLTMANN, *The Trinity*, 102-103; ID., *The Way of Jesus Christ*, 280.

[50] Cf. J. MOLTMANN, *The Way of Jesus Christ*, 286. In addition, there are other important theological and historical factors for the separation of creation from redemption. Historically, the challenge of modern science to the Christian teaching on creation forced Christianity to surrender the realm of nature to scientists and to turn its attention only to the salvation of the human being (or the human soul). Theologically, the argument of some biblical scholars, such as Gerhard von Rad, that creation theme in the Old Testament was employed, only after the salvation theme of Israel and as an aid to widen its salvific horizon to the cosmos, led to the neglect of creation. See A.M. CLIFFORD, «Foundations», 21-22; R.J. CLIFFORD, *Creation*, 153.164.168-169.

[51] J. MOLTMANN, *The Way of Jesus Christ*, 301.

finished at a certain moment once and for all. It contains in itself immense possibilities in the future. Creation must be viewed as a promise-laden process that evokes hope for its fulfillment in the future. This process can be divided into three phases: the beginning, the interim, and the end. Moltmann presents three differentiated notion of Christ according to these three aspects of creation: «the ground of the creation of all things», «the moving power in the evolution of creation», and «the redeemer of the whole creation process»[52].

> If Christ is described only as the ground of creation, this world, which is often so chaotic, is enhanced in an illusory way, and transfigured into a harmony and a home. If Christ is described solely as the "evoluter," the evolutionary process itself takes on redemptive meaning for the initial creation; but the myriads of faulty developments and the victims of this process fall hopelessly by the wayside. If, finally, we look simply at the coming Christ who is to redeem the world, we see only this world in its need of redemption, and nothing of the goodness of the Creator and the traces of his beauty in all things[53].

We need all these three aspects of Christ, if we are to maintain in balance the intrinsic goodness of God's creation as we believe, the negativities of the world as we see, and the future fulfillment of creation as we hope for. The lack of any one aspect would not do justice to the multifold significance of creation. We need realistic eyes to see the world as it is, a warm heart sympathetic to its victims and an eschatological vision to embrace them, and a firm belief to perceive the goodness of creation.

2.2.2 The Initial Creation and Christ: The Unity and Diversity of Creation

One may first draw on the first creation account of Genesis to understand the initial creation. This creation story tells us that God created a myriad of diverse creatures. At the same time, given that all of them were created by one and the same God, one must see in creation an overall unity underlying an immense diversity. From the trinitarian (which is properly Christian) perspective on creation, Moltmann seeks to find unity and diversity in the original creation, which are definitely distinct but inherently interwoven features.

---

[52] J. MOLTMANN, *The Way of Jesus Christ*, 286.
[53] J. MOLTMANN, *The Way of Jesus Christ*, 287.

If all things are created by the one God through his Wisdom/Logos and are held together in that, then underlying their diversity in space and time is an immanent unity in which they all exist together. [...] All things have their genesis in a fundamental underlying unity, which is called God's Wisdom, Spirit or Word. The fellowship of all created beings goes ahead of their differentiations and the specific forms given to them, and is therefore the foundation underlying their diversity[54].

The perception of unity and diversity in the initial creation is based on the trinitarian understanding of creation. Unity precedes and undergirds the diversity of all creatures because their origin is one and the same God. Both unity and diversity are essential factors to form creation. A world, which has diversity without unity, would be a chaos; a world, which has unity without diversity, would be a monad. Neither is what God created, according to the first creation story. What God created is a system in which diverse creatures exist and live in overall harmony: the cosmos. The diversity and unity of creation may well be described by the trinitarian formula that God creates through the Word in the Spirit[55]. «The Word specifies and differentiates through its efficacy; the Spirit binds and creates symmetries, harmonies and concord through its presence»[56]. As unity and diversity are inseparable in creation, so the Word and the Spirit are indivisible in divine creative activities[57]. Christ, the mediator of creation, through whom all things have been created, is the ground of the initial creation with diversity in unity (cf. Col. 1:16).

The perception of unity and diversity, grounded in the trinitarian perspective on creation, is an effective, interpretive tool to grasp the initial creation theologically. However, the picture of the original creation alone cannot do justice to the world that we actually experience at present. Nature does not always appear good or benevolent to us. Rather, it often emerges as a life-threatening reality to us as we experience it in natural catastrophes. The world, as it is now, seems ambiguous to us. At the same time, we ourselves do not relate to nature in a way that we may ensure its integrity. We must admit that the natural world has suffered from the disturbance and degradation that

---

[54] Cf. J. MOLTMANN, *The Way of Jesus Christ*, 288.

[55] J. MOLTMANN, *God in Creation*, 9.

[56] J. MOLTMANN, *The Way of Jesus Christ*, 289.

[57] Moltmann uses Wisdom, Spirit, and Word interchangeably. Wisdom in the Old Testament is construed as both the Word and the Spirit, as in the Wisdom of Solomon: «wisdom, the fashioner of all things» and «she is a breath of the power of God» (7:22. 25).

our improper attitude and activities brought about. We too, as we are now, appear ambivalent to nonhuman creation. We need another picture of creation whereby we may better understand all these ambiguities.

2.2.3 Continuous Creation and Christ: The Renewal of Creation

It is now generally taken for granted that the world has evolved in a direction that complexity and interiority are increased. The evolutionary view of the world shows us a picture drastically different from that which the initial creation depicts. The original creation presents basically a static world with unity and diversity. On the contrary, the evolutionary picture of the world unfolds a dynamic world in continuous change. The world in this new picture is much more complex than the previous, static one. The idea of continuous creation can be employed to understand theologically this dynamic, spontaneous, and multidirectional process of the world, provided that the ultimate power of evolution originates from God. «Continuous creation is creation's ongoing history. In this historical creation God 'renews the face of the earth' (Ps. 104:30), looking towards the final new creation of all things»[58]. Christ is «the moving power in the evolution of creation of all things». Continuous creation does not only indicate that what was created in the beginning is sustained. Then, there would be no change at all. Insofar as it is continuous *creation*, newness must continue to appear. All creation is renewed through God's life-giving breath while looking forward with hope to the final fulfillment. Continuous creation means both the sustenance and the renewal of the original creation. Christ, the upholder of creation, in whom all things hold together, is the source of continuous creation (cf. Col. 1:17).

If one thinks of justice in society as part of the cosmic harmony that God implanted in the initial creation, an important renewal in the human world will be the promotion of justice by those who commit themselves to the cause of justice and peace, empowered by the Spirit. Justice has been distorted and many have been denied justice in history. God «creates justice for those who have never known justice. He raises up the humble and obscure. He fulfils his promises in historical experiences»[59]. It can be held that every moment when justice is promoted, the human world comes closer to its fulfillment.

---

[58] J. MOLTMANN, *The Way of Jesus Christ*, 291.
[59] J. MOLTMANN, *The Way of Jesus Christ*, 291.

Evolution can be understood, in a similar context, as a renewal in the natural world. Evolution is then viewed as a process in which nature moves toward its goal in virtue of the divine power in the world. The evolving world is a symbol and promise of the consummation of creation in the future. The dynamic picture of the world in continuous creation complements in this way the static picture that the original creation presents. It facilitates us to perceive the inherent goodness of creation and to retain hope despite the often malevolent face of nature. However, there still remains a problem that many fail to survive and disappear in the history of evolution including human history. Then, competitive survival rather than symbiotic coexistence will characterize creation, overshadowing its goodness. We still need another picture of creation to grapple with this formidable issue epitomized by the survival of the fittest in evolution.

2.2.4 The New Creation and Christ: The Redemption of Creation

We will here seek to settle the issue of survival and failure in continuous creation with the last aspect of the cosmic Christ, «the redeemer of the whole creation process». Regarding as victims all those which fail to survive in evolution, Moltmann argues that all the victims will be redeemed in the final analysis by Christ, the redeemer of creation[60]. However, if they are regarded as victims, we will encounter a

---

[60] Moltmann criticizes Rahner, together with Teilhard de Chardin, on the account that Rahner did not consider seriously the death of Jesus in his cosmic christology (J. MOLTMANN, *The Way of Jesus Christ*, 292-301). Moltmann writes: «the passion and Christ's death by violence on the cross play hardly any part. [...] Christ stands on the summit of successful self-transcendencies in the history of nature and human beings [...] He does not stand beside the self-transcendencies which have miscarried and been thwarted» (J. MOLTMANN, *The Way of Jesus Christ*, 300). He appears to claim that Rahner was not aware of negative aspects in the process of self-transcendence (evolution).

While agreeing with Moltmann that cosmic christology must be concerned about those negative aspects, one may still say that the primary motive of Rahner in his cosmic christology must be found in «the transcendental possibility for man to take the question of a God-Man seriously» (K. RAHNER, *Foundations of Christian Faith*, 178). Rahner was «not concerned in the first instance with a presentation of Catholic Christology, nor with [...] an "evolutionary view of the world"» (K. RAHNER, *Foundations of Christian Faith*, 178). He reflects in his cosmic christology on «a question of the possibility of correlating» christology and the evolutionary view of the world (K. RAHNER, «Christology», 157). Moltmann's requirement seems to deviate from what Rahner intended in his cosmic christology.

dilemma that Christ is somehow involved in producing these victims. For Christ is «the moving power of evolution». This does not fit well with the aspect of Christ, either, who is the ground of all creatures and, as such, sustains and empowers all of them. We need to distinguish real victims from those which fail to survive in evolution, while agreeing with Moltmann that all creatures that have once existed will be redeemed at the consummation. Without mentioning human victims, nonhuman victims too exist in the world. We know, for example, that countless nonhuman creatures are sacrificed due to their mistreatment by humans such as in factory farming of animals or immoderate animal experiments. They are real victims. In this regard, it may be helpful to recall that the second proposition suggests that we must relate to and deal with nonhuman creatures with due concern properly informed by their difference in intrinsic value. A creature will be named a victim, according to this viewpoint, when its proper inherent value is disregarded and violated, as we see in the human abuse of animals.

As St. Paul points out, the whole creation is in travail. At the same time, it is also in the hope that it will be «set free from its bondage to decay and will obtain the freedom of the glory of the children of God» (Rom. 8:21-23). It is still the case, however, that evolution in the world appears a continuous process without end. On what ground, then, can we hold that this apparently endless process will be brought to completion? The assurance of the fulfillment of creation must be found in the cosmic Christ, too. Christ, the lord of creation, for whom all things have been created, is the assurance of the new creation (cf. Col. 1:16). It can be held that the cosmic Christ is particularly concerned for the redemption of those who failed to survive in the entire history of the world, not merely for the salvation of some competent, victorious survivors. This is in accord with the fact that the earthly Jesus stood on the side of the vulnerable in society. However, the process of evolution cannot be envisioned to redeem them, because «a perfect being at the

---

Moreover, one may even hold that Rahner was aware of the negative dimension of creation when he said, «In so far as this history of the cosmos is the history of the free spirit, this history – like that of man – is posed in freedom as guilt and trial» (K. RAHNER, «Christology», 168). There are other occasions as well in which he manifested explicitly his concern for «the passion and Christ's death». In fact, he shed light on the significance of Jesus' life and death in christology, which he believed was not properly dealt with in classical christology. After all, it is the actual and specific reality of Jesus' life and death that «we experience first of all, and it is this that we grasp in faith and hope as what is saving and liberating for ourselves» (K. RAHNER, «Christology Today?», 29-30; cf. ID., «The Two Basic Types»).

end of evolution is certainly conceivable, but not the perfection of all created beings»[61]. All those failed would be forgotten and abandoned forever. From the vantage point of those failed, this would not be the perfection of all creation. All those who disappeared in the midst of the evolutionary history, including countless, nameless and voiceless victims, are not the concern of our present world where only winners in vehement competition are praised and remembered. Those who failed will simply be forgotten and disappear.

However, we must remember again that the ultimate significance and value of all creatures depend not on their competence but on their relationship with God. All creatures are precious to God the creator and have inherent value regardless of their fitness in competition: «every single person, and indeed every single living thing in nature, has a meaning, whether they are of utility for evolution or not»[62]. How will all these creatures be redeemed and their own significance and value be reclaimed? History, which always proceeds forward and leaves the past behind, cannot save the loser in the past. For the unilateral flow of history cannot be reversed. It is here that one must conceive an eschatological event which can achieve what no historical event can bring about.

> What is eschatological is the new creation of all things which were and are and will be. What is eschatological is the bringing back of all things out of their past, and the gathering of them into the kingdom of glory. [...] God forgets nothing that he has created. Nothing is lost to him. He will restore it all[63].

Moltmann envisions the eschatological, redeeming movement that is counter to the direction of evolution from the past to the future. Put otherwise, the eschatological power will burst into creation from the future to the past. Christ will save all creatures, sweeping the entire time span of creation in the reverse direction. «It is the divine tempest of the new creation, which sweeps out of God's future over history's fields of the dead, waking and gathering every last created being»[64]. It

---

[61] J. MOLTMANN, *The Way of Jesus Christ*, 303.

[62] J. MOLTMANN, *God in Creation*, 197.

[63] J. MOLTMANN, *The Way of Jesus Christ*, 303.

[64] J. MOLTMANN, *The Way of Jesus Christ*, 303. A similar vision may be found in Matt. 27:52-52: «The tombs also were opened, and many bodies of the saints who had fallen asleep were raised. After his resurrection they came out of the tombs and entered the holy city and appeared to many». See also Ez. 37:1-14; 1 Cor. 15:20-23.

is the coming of God to creation[65]. This divine gust will save in God's eternity all those abandoned in the past. The world will completely be transfigured into the new creation. It is at this moment that the authentic significance and value of all creatures are revealed and realized. Only then can we have the complete picture of creation.

2.3 *The Significance of the Christological Vision of Creation*

2.3.1 A Dynamic and Inclusive Perspective on Creation

If the christological vision of creation is to view creation in the light of Christ, through, in, and for whom all things have been created, it can be held that this vision is at once dynamic and inclusive[66]. It is dynamic in the sense that the christological vision of creation conceives that the initial creation is in a dynamic movement (continuous creation) toward the new creation. This dynamic perspective on creation implies that creation is on the way to the final fulfillment. Creation is, in this sense, a promise for the future completion confirmed by Christ. The world as a promise is the anticipation in the present of the new creation; the new creation is the realization in the future of the promise. Creation as a promise and anticipation for the future fulfillment helps us appreciate and accept the value and significance of nature despite its ambivalence

---

[65] For a detailed account of his cosmic eschatology, see J. MOLTMANN, *The Coming of God*, 259-319. He emphasizes in cosmic eschatology that the new creation will be achieved through the transformation of the world. This transformation must be understood to include the redemption of all those failed to survive in evolution.

[66] The relationship of the christological vision of creation to the pneumatological vision is disclosed by the relationship of Jesus and the Holy Spirit. According to the gospel of Luke, the Spirit is inseparable from Jesus: from his conception to baptism to ministry and finally to his death and resurrection. Jesus was born into the world through the Holy Spirit (cf. 1:35) and was guided by the Spirit (cf. 4:1). The mission of Jesus to proclaim good news and liberation originated in the Spirit (cf. 4:18-19). His ministry such as healing, exorcism, and fellowship with the outcast led people in affliction to new life. In this regard, Jesus can be compared to the Spirit, who sustains and renews creation. Jesus offered, through the Sprit, his life on the cross. The Spirit raised him from the dead (cf. Rom. 8:11). The risen Jesus has become a life-giving spirit (cf. 1 Cor. 15:45). In short, Jesus was entirely taken by the Spirit. Christ and the Spirit are inextricably interwoven. Hence, the christological vision of creation is intrinsically united with the pneumatological vision. Each vision provides a dynamic and inclusive perspective on creation. One can even find in the life of the earthly Jesus an integrated way of viewing the world in virtue of his unity with the Spirit and his life encompassing all, especially the marginalized. For the relationship of Jesus and the Spirit, see J. MOLTMANN, *The Way of Jesus Christ*, 73-94; J. O'DONNELL, *The Mystery of the Triune God*, 48-53.

at present. Promise refers basically to what is not yet realized and accordingly, not perfect. The world is not created once and for all. It is deficient in many respects as long as it is in the process toward completion. If we conceive creation as a not-yet-fulfilled-promise, we can accept the current realities of creation with tranquility and without despair. Besides, the world as a promise justifies and confirms its own value, imperfect as it is now. Insofar as the world as a promise is the potentiality of the future fulfillment, it already contains in itself the ultimate goal and value in the future, unrealized as it is now[67]. We must then deal with creation with every concern and care. Otherwise, the very ground of the future fulfillment would be lost.

The christological vision of creation is inclusive as well in the sense that throughout the dynamic process of creation, all creatures without exception are seen to be under the concern and care of Christ, who is the firstborn of creation, the reconciler of creation, and the firstborn from the dead (cf. Col. 1:15-20). The inclusive perspective on creation tells us that Christ cherishes all creatures, reconciles one another, and will save all of them. As the firstborn of creation, Christ can be considered as the eldest brother of all creatures. As such, he regards all of them, especially those vulnerable, with affectionate concern and care. All are his beloved brothers and sisters. The all-encompassing concern of Christ is in accord with the love of Jesus, in whom the universal love of God was actualized as his preferential option for the poor. The cosmic love that Christ manifests to all creatures, particularly to exploited and abused ones, is the same love that Jesus expressed to all human beings, especially to the marginalized. As the reconciler of creation, Christ can be viewed as the advocate of all creatures. As such, he offered his life and achieved the reconciliation of them with God. Christ's self-sacrifice for the sake of creation powerfully testifies that he himself acknowledged and appreciated deeply, despite all its negativities, the inherent goodness and value embedded in creation by God. It must be remembered that whenever we mistreat and impoverish creation, we tarnish the reconciliation that Christ has achieved with his blood and that we stand opposed to him in that measure. As the firstborn from the dead, Christ can be regarded as the pioneer and assurance of the new creation. As such, he made the eschatological promise of the new creation present and palpable in this world through his resurrection. The resurrection of Jesus is the beginning of the new creation in this

---

[67] Cf. J.F. HAUGHT, «Ecology and Eschatology», 56-60.

world. Hence, Christ is the pledge for the future fulfillment of all creatures. As such, he is also the savior of all the dead, particularly all the abandoned in the history of creation. Indeed, Christ was, is, and will be with all creatures from beginning to end.

2.3.2 The Reconciliation of Humanity with Nature: The Cosmic Discipleship of Christ

A promise inspires a hope. As promise for the future fulfillment of creation is grounded in Christ, hope for that promise originates in him. This hope consists in our unyielding faith in Christ that he will finally bring all creation to redemption and completion. In this regard, our hope is an eschatological hope. This cosmic and eschatological hope encourages us to change our world today. «Christianity is eschatology, is hope, forward looking and forward moving, and therefore also revolutionizing and transforming the present»[68]. A change initiated by the eschatological hope cannot be mediocre. It must be radical and even revolutionary. The promise and hope that the christological vision of the world evokes lead us to such a profound conversion that we can participate in the cosmic endeavor of Christ for all creatures. The love to which the christological vision of the world awakens us calls for our participation in the cosmic concern of Christ. In short, the christological vision of creation adds a cosmic significance to the discipleship of Jesus, i.e., the cosmic discipleship of Christ.

The comic discipleship of Christ today includes as an essential element one's commitment to the practice of ecological concern and care. This can be regarded as a continuation of the cosmic reconciliation which Christ has achieved. This cosmic reconciliation is a consequence of his death: «through himself God was pleased to reconcile to himself all things [...] by making peace through the blood of his cross» (Col. 1:20; cf. Rom. 5:6-12; 2 Cor. 5:19). It is this reconciliation to which God invites all creatures, particularly human beings. It is an invitation of all creatures into the peace that Christ has achieved through his death. It must be noted, however, that reconciliation among creatures is indispensable and prerequisite for the reconciliation of all with God (cf. Matt. 5:22-25). In fact, one may say, Jesus aspired to and struggled for reconciliation among human beings by obliterating all that entraps them into the darkness of sin and enslaves them. We confess, therefore, that Christ died for us sinners (cf. Rom. 5:8).

---

[68] J. MOLTMANN, *Theology of Hope*, 16.

It has been held, at the same time, that Christ is the lord of all creatures, for whom all things have been created. However, the lordship of Christ, who offered his life for all, must not be understood as the exercise of the mighty power of a king (cf. Mark 10:42-45). Rather, his lordship that has been achieved by his death on the cross consists in «his conquest of enmity and violence and in the spread of reconciliation and harmonious, happily lived life»[69]. The lordship of Christ is found in making peace and imbuing the entire creation with the peace of Christ in order that all may be reconciled to one another. We are invited to participate in this lordship and to continue it. This lordship can be actualized today in our effort to reconcile ourselves to nature and to admit and appreciate the beauty, goodness, and value of nature.

However, we cannot face away from the evil power which seems to dominate our world, no matter how adamantly we advocate the goodness of creation. Nature as well as the human world shows such a grim prospect that many of us may lose the courage to continue that for which Jesus strove. Nevertheless, we must not lose sight of the goodness of creation nor must we abandon hope for the world, insofar as we have faith in Christ. The Christ in whom we believe is at once the lord of peace and the reconciler of creation. As Jesus stood on the side of the poor, the sick, and the outcast, Christ is now «present not only in the human victims of world history but in victimized nature too»[70]. Christ will never give way to the violence that is infringed on nature. As the lord of peace, he embraces and consoles wounded nature in his peace. He infuses the entire creation with the spirit of peace. It is in this peace that the reconciliation of all creatures, particularly between humanity and nature, is finally achieved by Christ the reconciler of creation. With this peace and reconciliation of Christ, all creatures will recover their goodness and value, which have been defiled and disregarded.

The cosmic reconciliation with God which Christ achieved through his death is an indispensable element in the new creation. The world in a movement toward the new creation suggests that the reconciliation of the world is not achieved once and for all as far as history continues. Rather, it is an enduring mission that must be carried out until the consummation of the world. The ministry of cosmic reconciliation demands from us a profound change of heart, i.e., conversion, since this

---

[69] J. MOLTMANN, *The Way of Jesus Christ*, 279.
[70] J. MOLTMANN, *The Way of Jesus Christ*, 279.

task is dependent in great measure on the way we relate to and act in nature. Given that it is deeply connected with the restoration of damaged relationships, reconciliation is possible only when we renounce our current way of seeing and dealing with nature, which has brought about violent and immoderate exploitation. Reconciliation is possible only when we seek and adopt a more harmonious and symbiotic way of seeing and relating to nature. This is in turn possible only when we acknowledge nature primarily as it is and admit that we are dependent on it. This acknowledgement will lead us to gratitude and humility in our relation to nature. Only then can we admit from the depth of our heart that nature is God' creation with its own goodness and value, not simply raw materials for our commodities. Only then can the true reconciliation of humanity and nature begin.

3. The Intrinsic Value of All Creatures from the Perspective of Leonardo Boff

3.1 *Introduction*

At the root of the present ecological crisis of the earth, I believe, is the loss of our sensibility for the connectedness of all beings in the world[71]. With the loss of this sensibility, we began to conceive that humankind and nature are disparate realities. Nature has turned into a collection of inert objects, which may freely be used as natural resources for our sake. This has contributed in great measure to the disruption of the environment. Moreover, the loss of sensibility has effected «a kind of blindness, a real lobotomy of the human spirit, which has become insensitive to the message of the beauty and grandeur of the universe»[72].

In the face of deteriorating nature and the loss of our capability to appreciate nature as such, Boff presents an integrated perspective on the world in order to deal with this problem at its root. An integrated worldview leads us to change radically the way we envision the world. We must replace our dualistic way of seeing the world, which splits the world into humanity and nature, by an ecological way of viewing the world, which grasps a reality primarily in the light of relationship. An ecological perspective perceives the world as one organic whole in which all things are in constant interactions in virtue of their intercon-

---

[71] Cf. L. BOFF, *Cry*, 63-85.
[72] L. BOFF, *The Prayer of Saint Francis*, 89.

nectedness. The world appears as a dynamic and organic, rather than static and inert, reality due to internal interactions. This ecological perception of the world will positively acknowledge the intrinsic value of nature while it does not deny completely its utilitarian aspect. The interrelatedness and interdependence that the ecological standpoint perceives in the world indicate that no one is self-sufficient. Every being needs other beings. If we really admit that we are dependent on others for our existence, our attitude to others must be, in the first place, respect and gratitude. Therefore, this organic and integrated perspective on the world denounces an excessively utilitarian attitude toward nature and calls for our proper regard for nature as it is. «We are refusing to reduce Earth to an assortment of natural resources or to a physical and chemical reservoir of raw materials. It has its own identity and autonomy as an extremely dynamic and complex organism»[73]. With an ecological perspective on the world, nature with its own significance and intrinsic value comes into view.

In our capitalist and market-oriented society, it is formidable for us to hold fast to a perspective that acknowledges the intrinsic value of nature and discovers and appreciates its aesthetic dimension. It means that we stand against the current, consumeristic society strongly supported by global market capitalism. We must not expect that we can accept an alternative viewpoint on the world and embody it in ourselves without difficulty. For many of us are the very ones who profit from the current, predominant socio-economic structure. Therefore, we must seek an efficacious means that can actualize an alternative perspective.

Boff presents as an effective means a sense of the sacred in nature, without which he believes our new perspective on the world would remain as a mere dream: «Without the sacred, affirming the dignity of Earth and the need to set limits on our desire to exploit its potentialities remains empty rhetoric»[74]. What is meant by «the sacred» is «that quality of things and in things that in a comprehensive way completely takes hold of us, fascinates us, speaks to us of the depths of our being and gives us the immediate experience of respect, fear, and reverence»[75]. With a sense of the sacred in nature, we will come to acknowledge that all things in nature and nature as a whole are penetrated and permeated with that which originates in God. This helps us perceive

---

[73] L. BOFF, Cry, 12.
[74] L. BOFF, Cry, 115.
[75] L. BOFF, Cry, 116

that nature is charged with such wonder that we cannot help perceiving the source of the wonder, i.e., the divine presence in nature. The sacred of nature can be referred to as the sacramentality of nature in the sense that nature is understood as that through which the divine (God) is perceived and disclosed to us[76]. Nature as a sacrament of God awakens us to recognize that nature has its own reason to exist in association with God and apart from human needs. It will bring to light the intrinsic value of nature grounded in its relationship with God.

St. Francis of Assisi (1182-1226) is a renowned figure in Christian history for his love of nature[77]. It is well known that he loved all creatures to such an extent that he called them even as his brothers and sisters. He did not love them for any other purposes or reasons. He simply loved them as themselves. He recognized and cherished their beauty and preciousness; he acknowledged to the full their intrinsic value. Where did such loving care for nature come from? It may be held that his universal brotherhood and sisterhood are based on his perception in nature of God the creator, one and the same origin of all creatures. His outstanding sensitivity to the presence of God in nature is the basis of his cosmic kinship.

I will in this section regard and employ St. Francis as a stepping stone to explore how Boff thinks of the intrinsic value of nature, assuming that as a former Franciscan priest, he himself was influenced by St. Francis or interested in him in this respect[78]. It means that I will approach him in this regard through the lens of St. Francis. I will first examine how he understands St. Francis in relation to nature. The sensibility of St. Francis to the presence of God in nature and his cosmic kinship with all creatures will be emphasized. I expect in this discourse that a ground for the intrinsic value of all creatures can be affirmed on the basis of their own relationship with God. I will hold that Boff's understanding of St. Francis in regard to nature is consistent with the perspective on the world that he has presented in chapter three. I will then consider his exposition of panentheism as a theological articulation and reinforcement of the sacramentality of nature. It will be

---

[76] Cf. R.P. MCBRIEN, *Catholicism*, 787-790.

[77] St. Francis of Assisi was proclaimed in 1979 as the saint of those who promote ecology. Cf. JOHN PAUL II, *Peace with God the Creator*, no. 16.

[78] This assumption is supported by the fact that Boff has published some books about St. Francis of Assisi, such as *The Prayer of Saint Francis* and *Saint Francis: A Model for Human Liberation*. Besides, Boff frequently mentions St. Francis on other occasions.

held that panentheism can be a theological ground and source for the dignity and intrinsic value of nature. In the end, I will ponder on further implications that the intrinsic value of nature may bring up: first, a balance between intrinsic value and utilitarian value from the panentheistic perspective; second, the significance of voluntary poverty as a way of actualizing cosmic kinship.

3.2 Nature as a Sacrament of God: A Ground for the Intrinsic Value of Nature

3.2.1 St. Francis of Assisi: A Champion of Cosmic Kinship

The human perceptivity of the divine presence in nature has been eclipsed to a great measure, though not totally, as we lost a sense of our connectedness with nature and began to conceive it primarily as natural resources. This subsequently brought about our aggressive and violent exploitation of nature: «This [divine] transparency is tarnished and obscured by the aggression that one creature, the human being, practices on other creatures, and, tragically indeed, on his or her own kind»[79]. This in turn accelerated our instrumental perspective on nature. Nature has lost its sacredness and degenerated into an inert object at our disposal. We may find in St. Francis a clue whereby we can reclaim our sensibility for both the divine presence in nature and the interconnectedness of all things, particularly humanity's link with nature. «He created a synthesis that Christianity had lost: the encounter with God, with Christ and with the Spirit in nature, and accordingly the discovery of the vast cosmic kinship [...]»[80]. It is important to note that it is by his deeds rather than his words that St. Francis has become an exemplary figure to appreciate the divine presence in nature and an intimate association of human beings with nature. His great significance lies in that he showed us in his life that it is possible to live in communion with God and nature. St. Francis is the one in whom our dream for «a simple love for all things, experienced as brothers and sisters [...]» has been achieved[81]. «He lived a new relationship with nature in a way that was so moving that he became an archetype of ecological concern for the collective unconscious of humankind»[82]. It may be said that the ecological standpoint of the world was so fully actualized in him that St.

---

[79] L. BOFF, *Ecology and Liberation*, 77.
[80] L. BOFF, *Cry*, 208.
[81] L. BOFF, *The Prayer of Saint Francis*, 1.
[82] L. BOFF, *Cry*, 204.

Francis felt all beings in the world as his brothers and sisters. In this sense, he is an embodiment or personification of an ecological perspective on the world.

Due to his sensitivity to cosmic kinship, St. Francis loved all creatures in an extraordinary manner and to an astounding measure. Where did this cosmic kinship come from? Two movements, vertical and horizontal, can be found in him with regard to his attitude to nature. As to vertical movement, we are told: «He admired in every thing its Author and in all events he recognized the Creator [...]»[83]. It is witnessed in other occasions as well that he had a striking capability to perceive the presence of God in nature. It is reported, for instance, that St. Francis let a portion of land free and uncultivated so that all the herbs could grow there «so that [...] they might announce the beauty of the Father of all things» and «so that they would bring those who look upon them to the memory of the Eternal Sweetness»[84]. «Everything makes up a grand symphony – and God is the conductor»[85]. For St. Francis, all creatures were connected with one another and harmonized in the presence of God the creator of the universe. This illuminates his extraordinary sensitivity to nature as a sacrament of God. He invited us to «contemplate God and the splendor of God's grace and glory in the extensive wealth of creation, which is the great sacrament of God and Christ»[86].

It is also observed in his relation to nature that St. Francis moved in not only a vertical but also a horizontal direction. We are told again: «Finally, he called all creatures brother, and in a most extraordinary manner, a manner never experienced by others [...]»[87]; «He was filled with a greater gentleness when he thought of the first and common origin of all beings, and he called all creatures, no matter how small they were, by the name of brother or sister, because he knew that they all had in common with him the same beginning»[88]. It is in this cosmic kinship that the uniqueness of St. Francis must be found.

---

[83] L. BOFF, *Saint Francis*, 37.

[84] L. BOFF, *Cry*, 211.

[85] L. BOFF, *Cry*, 211.

[86] L. BOFF, *Cry*, 205.

[87] L. BOFF, *Cry*, 210.

[88] L. BOFF, *Saint Francis*, 37. See also H.P. SANTMIRE, *The Travail of Nature*, 108-109: «there was much more in Francis's relationship to the creatures of nature than an aesthetic delight and a theocentric devotion, although those elements were certainly there. Francis loved those lowly creatures as brothers and sisters». Santmire emphasizes not so much St. Francis's appreciation of the divine presence in nature as

It can be said that what occurred first in St. Francis was a perception of the divine presence in nature (sacramentality). Only then, owing to his sacramental perception of nature, cosmic kinship appeared in him. For his cosmic kinship with all creatures resulted from his own experience of the common origin of all beings. It can be held that the universal parenthood of God undergirded his cosmic relationship with other creatures. It is the case that the sacramentality of nature grants a solid ground for the intrinsic value of nature. However, it is important to note that sacramentality does not necessarily ensure in practice intrinsic value to nature. Even if we arrive at the presence of God thanks to the sacramentality of nature, it is still possible that we disregard nature, assuming that the (instrumental) purpose of nature is achieved. In this regard, nature has importance and meaning only for our ascent to God, not for its own sake[89]. This means that nature is regarded predominantly as a means despite our acknowledgement of the sacramentality of nature. We can conceive nature to be excluded from the ultimate stage of salvation in the future and deal accordingly with it at present. Humankind alone, for which salvation is meant, would have importance for its own sake. On the contrary, St. Francis proceeded further, based on his perception of the divine in creatures, to such a measure that he acknowledged and cherished their preciousness before God the creator, independently of his needs to ascend to God.

We have briefly seen that the cosmic kinship of St. Francis was grounded in God's presence in nature and stemmed from it. His cosmic brotherhood and sisterhood were based on the sacramentality of nature. It needs first to be mentioned, however, that the sacramentality of nature is not self-evident. The perception of God's presence in nature is

---

his universal brotherhood and sisterhood. For him, all creatures are not merely «an instrument for his own and his fellow's ascent to God». «He rested his affection in them. They were for him, in a certain sense, centers of value in their own right».

[89] Cf. H.P. SANTMIRE, *The Travail of Nature*, 97-104. Santmire holds that a representative figure for this case is, albeit ironically, St. Bonaventure, who is himself a Franciscan as well as an eminent theologian and wrote a biography of St. Francis: «the whole world is charged with the glory of God. [...] Bonaventure consistently emphasizes the divine immanence in the created order» (at 98); «They [creatures] are, in fact, left behind at lower rungs of the ladder of being, as humans ascend to perfect spiritual communion with God above» (at 102). This standpoint on Bonaventure's thoughts on nature is disputable. However, my emphasis is placed on his remark that our perception of the sacramentality of nature does not always lead to and guarantee our acknowledgement of nature's own integrity, purpose, and value, apart from its utility for us.

possible only through one's faith in God the creator. It is faith in God the creator that «creates in human beings the viewpoint that enables them to see the presence of God in things and history. [...] Then the world, with its things and events, undergoes transfiguration. It is more than just world; it is now a sacrament of God»[90]. Strictly speaking, it is our perspective to see the world, rather than the world itself, that undergoes a radical change in virtue of our faith in God. Only in this drastic change in our perspective on the world, we can perceive what we did not perceive before and what was hidden in the world from our sight: the presence of God in nature.

It was mentioned that although the sacramentality of nature is acknowledged, it does not necessarily guarantee the intrinsic value of nature. Then, how can we still hold the sacramentality of nature as a ground of intrinsic value? We need first to recall that it has been presupposed that one's intrinsic value is based on and dependent on one's own relationship with God. A case can then be made that the sacramentality of nature is a ground for its intrinsic value. For all things in nature reflect God, but always according to one's own sacramentality, which depends on one's relationship with God. Put otherwise, sacramentality becomes a ground for intrinsic value because it is understood to indicate one's own relationship with God.

A sacrament signifies and mediates the divine to us. For this, a sacrament must be related, somehow intrinsically, to the divine[91]. It must be recalled that the whole creation is a reflection of the Trinity from the trinitarian perspective on creation. It must also be remembered that the divine persons of the Father, the Son, and the Holy Spirit reflect perfectly each other in the trinitarian relationship of *perichoresis*. This trinitarian relationship is embedded and embodied, though deficiently,

---

[90] L. BOFF, *Sacraments*, 89-90.

[91] We can suppose two different cases in which one signifies another. The first case is that in which there is no intrinsic relationship between a signifier and a signified. In this case, one signifies the other, but simply through an arbitrary designation. An example may be the colors of traffic signals and their corresponding meanings. There exists no compelling reason why red color necessarily means «stop». The second case is that in which there is an intrinsic connection between these two. One signifies the other, in this case, not arbitrarily but by its nature. A dream that reveals what is beneath one's consciousness or one's body that expresses oneself may be an example. A sacrament belongs to the second case. Cf. K. RAHNER, «The Theology of Symbol», 222-234; R. HAIGHT, *Dynamics of Theology*, 130-135. Rahner distinguishes between these two cases, calling the first signifier a (mere) sign and the second a (real) symbol.

in the entire creation as a trinitarian reflection. This embedment and embodiment of the trinitarian relationship in creation can be interpreted as the relationship of creation with God. To this measure, creation as a whole reflects the triune God. It can be held that every creature reflects God according to one's own relationship with God. For instance, the human being forms a unique and special relationship with God, as the image and likeness of God (cf. Gen. 1:26-27). God breathed the divine breath of life into the nostrils of the human being (cf. Gen. 2:7). We reflect God according to our own relationship with God characterized by divine image, likeness, and breath. To that extent, we are a sacrament of God. One can further claim that Jesus Christ, the incarnate Son, reflects God perfectly by virtue of his supreme identity (his own relationship) with God (cf. John 10:30; 14:9). In this regard, Jesus Christ is *the* sacrament of God.

In short, one's sacramentality, which is the measure of one's reflection of God, depends on one's relationship with God. Everyone reflects God and is a sacrament of God, but only according to one's own relationship with God. Therefore, the sacramentality of creation becomes a crucial ground for intrinsic value insofar as intrinsic value is rooted in one's relationship with God. Again, it is still the case that sacramentality may be used only as a ladder to God and then be left behind in the final analysis.

Cosmic kinship is in accordance in critical respects with an ecological perspective on the world. We have seen that the ecological standpoint on the world is grounded scientifically in the contemporary universe story and reinforced theologically by the doctrine of the Trinity. The ecological perspective that «the universe is made up of a vast network of relationships in such a way that each one lives through the other, for the other, and with the other [...] that the Divinity itself is revealed to be an all-relational Reality» calls to mind nature as a divine sacrament and the cosmic kinship of all creatures in St. Francis[92]. From an ecological perspective, the world comprises a myriad of things, but always in an intricate network of relationships. The world is not a collection of disparate, individual things, but one organic whole in virtue of those intrinsic relationships, the source of which is the triune God who is perfectly relational. An obvious influence of St. Francis on Boff is found when he renders the ecological viewpoint as follows:

---

[92] L. BOFF, *Cry*, 20.

we all proceed from the Creator's one and the same act of love. That means that there is a universal brotherhood and sisterhood among all beings. All creatures bear within themselves traces of the divine hand that shaped them [...] This means that creatures are sacramental. They are symbols of a Presence that inhabits the universe[93].

Relationships in the universe, i.e., the interconnectedness of all things, can be understood as the cosmic kinship of all creatures, which are reflections of God according to their own manners and in varying degrees. The ecological view of the world, grounded in the universe story and strengthened by the trinitarian doctrine, reinforces this understanding. The universe story affirms that all things in the universe, from «the snail by the roadside» to «the farthest galaxy», are connected with one another due to their common origin and evolutionary process[94]. The trinitarian relationship of *perichoresis* presents all creatures as reflections of the triune God, confirming the interconnectedness of all things in the universe story and highlighting the cosmos as a sacrament of God.

Cosmic kinship brings to light the intrinsic value of nature. Cosmic kinship can be viewed as a concrete manifestation of one's keen perception of the intrinsic value of all. If we regard all creatures our brothers and sisters, like St. Francis, we will take it for granted that they have their own value for themselves. Our brothers and sisters do not exist primarily for our sake. They are precious to us simply because they are our brothers and sisters. An ecological perspective on the world can be considered, too, in relation to intrinsic value. Then, the ecological worldview also brings into relief the intrinsic value of nature, as cosmic kinship does. An ecological perspective conceives that all things in the world support each other in their own way due to their interconnectedness. At first glance, a utilitarian standpoint seems to appear. However, what eventually comes into view is the intrinsic value of all things. If we really realize and admit that we are related to and dependent on others for our existence, we must profoundly appreciate the existence of others and humbly express our respect and gratitude for them, albeit in various degrees and ways. An ecological perspective on the world highlights the intrinsic value of nature, as the universal kinship of St. Francis did. Boff finds in the life of St. Francis, characterized by his cosmic kinship and solidarity with all creatures, «a distinct

---

[93] L. BOFF, *Ecology and Liberation*, 77.
[94] L. BOFF, *Cry*, 42.

way of being-in-the-world, not over things, but together with them, like brothers and sisters of the same family»[95]. This way of being and living in the world means that we see others not with greedy eyes that seek in others only our own interest but with a loving heart which appreciates their presence in the world as they are. The same conclusion is drawn from an ecological perspective on the world. A difference may be that his perception of cosmic kinship presents much more vivid and warm-hearted expressions and that he lived that perception and embodied it in his life.

3.2.2 Panentheism:
A Theological Ground for Sacramentality and Cosmic Kinship

We have seen that Boff affirms the intrinsic value of nature on the basis of St. Francis's sensibility for the divine presence in nature and his cosmic kinship. I hold that his affirmation of intrinsic value is compatible with and theologically bolstered by his exposition of panentheism, as his ecological way of viewing the world is consistent with and theologically reinforced by the trinitarian doctrine. The panentheistic perception of God and the world can be seen as an alternative to both the pantheistic and the excessive, transcendent conceptions of God.

Boff's turn to the ecological conception of the world away from a dualistic worldview already suggested a radical change in his way of conceiving how God relates to creation. The ecological view of the world brings to the foreground the relationality of creation, which used to be eclipsed in the background. An emphasis on the interconnectedness of all beings stimulates us to review how we conceive God relates to the world. A classical, monotheistic conception of God «tended to show God as a Being so absolute, self-sufficient, perfect, and transcendent that it was unaffected by the world. A worldless God easily paves the way for a Godless world»[96]. As God receded from creation, we as the image of God also separated ourselves from nature. A vertical dichotomization of God from the world brought about a horizontal separation of humanity from nature. In conjunction with other socio-economic circumstances particularly since the era of the Scientific Revolution in the West, the traditional features of God such as absoluteness, self-sufficiency, perfection, and transcendence, which were emphasized in the Judaeo-Christian tradition to distinguish God from

---

[95] L. BOFF, *Saint Francis*, 35.
[96] L. BOFF, *Cry*, 141.

finite creatures, caused a bifurcation of God from the world and subsequently the degradation of nature[97].

In confrontation with the recession of God from the world, the consequent loss of the divine presence in the world, and their devastating effects to the natural world, we must seek another way of conceiving God which can overcome the alienation of creation from God. An ecological perspective on the world has already shown a possibility of abolishing a fatal division between humanity and nature. In this regard, apart from an absolute monotheistic perception of God, we must recall that Christianity has another conception of God, which is properly Christian, i.e., the triune God. The trinitarian perspective on God and creation holds that the three divine persons dwell in each other in perfect communion and brought the cosmos into being through the trinitarian process: «The Father creates through the Son in the Holy Spirit. This means that creation is introduced into trinitarian communion by the Holy Spirit, which is always active in creation»[98]. If it is recalled that the trinitarian relationship of *perichoresis* is the principle of inclusiveness in virtue of the divine openness to others, we must not simply say that the whole creation exists in separation from the triune God, who is absolutely open to all and thereby inclusive of all, although God is absolutely distinct from creation. Rather, one must say that God embraces creation and creation participates in the divine, trinitarian community in virtue of the divine openness and inclusiveness. «The world emerges not as a mere otherness from God, but as the receptacle for God's self-communication. The world begins to belong to the history of the triune God»[99]. The whole creation is conceived to be in God and God in creation. The panentheistic perception of God and the world emerges out of this trinitarian conception of God and the world. The panentheistic perspective holds that «God is in all and all is in God. [...] God and world are different. One is not the other. But they are not separated or closed. They are open to one another. They are always intertwined with one another»[100]. Panentheism describes appro-

---

[97] For a detailed account, from a historical standpoint, of the change in the perception of nature in the West, see, for instance, C. MERCHANT, *Earthcare*, 75-87.

[98] L. BOFF, *Trinity and Society*, 223.

[99] L. BOFF, *Trinity and Society*, 113.

[100] L. BOFF, *Cry*, 153. Boff distinguishes explicitly panentheism from pantheism: «Pantheism maintains that everything is God, and that primordial energy, atoms, stones, mountains, stars, and human beings form part of the deity»; «Panentheism, however, starts from the distinction between God and the creature, yet always main-

priately how God embraces the universe and the universe participates in God.

The panentheistic relationship can be understood as an outward manifestation of the trinitarian relationship to creation. One may say that when we extend to creation the relationship of *perichoresis* within the trinitarian community, we come to encounter the relationship of God to creation which is conceived by panentheism. It must be noted, however, that there is a difference between the trinitarian relationship of *perichoresis* and the panentheistic relationship. While there is a perfect mutual reciprocity in *perichoresis* within the divine community, there is no such one in the panentheistic relationship of God and creation. For God is infinite and creation is finite. This is not a symmetric but asymmetric relationship. *Perichoresis* is a perfect mode of the panentheistic relationship; the latter is a deficient mode of the former. A reflection of the trinitarian community, i.e., creation, is different from the trinitarian community itself. Nonetheless, in the panentheistic perspective, God is in all creatures and all creatures are in God in virtue of the divine openness to creation and the outpouring of the divine presence over creation.

The panentheistic perspective on creation brings to the fore nature as a sacrament of God: «God flows through all things; God is present in everything and makes of all reality a temple»[101]. It has been remarked, however, that the sacramentality of nature does not always assure nature of its own significance and intrinsic value. It is still possible that we regard nature as of no significance once we achieve a purpose of our ascent to God by means of nature. Sacramentality can be used only as an instrument. In this regard, the panentheistic vision of creation has the merit to hold back this excessive, instrumental approach to sacramentality and to reveal its further significance. The panentheistic perspective on creation makes obvious, first of all, that it is the triune God who penetrates the whole creation and turns it into a divine reflection and sacrament. The sacramentality of nature is not what we can create or imagine on our own. What the panentheistic perspective stresses is that the divine presence in nature is as real and enduring as nature itself, regardless of the way we perceive it. «The world is not only a bridge to God»[102]. The panentheistic viewpoint reminds us that

---

tains relation between them. The one is not the other. Each of them has his/her/its own relative autonomy yet is always related». See ID., *Ecology and Liberation*, 50-51.

[101] L. BOFF, *Ecology and Liberation*, 51.

[102] L. BOFF, *Ecology and Liberation*, 51.

the world is a place in which God *is* present. Only then can we say that we meet God in and through the world.

The pantheistic way of perceiving creation further informs us that the sacramentality of nature does not simply refer in a detached manner to the presence of God in nature. What the panentheistic perception of God and the world in the light of *perichoresis* brings forth is the affective and affectionate presence of God in nature. *Perichoresis* is a relationship biased toward life, love, inclusiveness, and equality. When the trinitarian relationship of *perichoresis* is expressed outwardly, these trinitarian values are seen to be poured upon the whole creation. Sacramentality asserts, from the panentheistic standpoint, that creation is suffused with life, love, inclusiveness, and equality. *Perichoresis* does not indicate a disengaged relationship of God with the world. These trinitarian values in creation urge us to acknowledge the intrinsic value of nature so that they may be preserved and promoted. Only with the acknowledgement of intrinsic value may we move in the direction that life is secured, everyone is loved as such, no one is marginalized, and all are justly dealt with.

One can simply say, by logic, that all creatures are brothers and sisters to one another because all of them originate from God and exist in God. However, this will not touch us by the heart to such an extent that we may feel, in a measure, cosmic kinship with nature. This logical ground for cosmic kinship will take on flesh with the panentheistic view that creation is steeped in the presence of the triune God with life, love, inclusiveness, and equality. All creatures can now be seen to live under the loving care of God. If one perceives nature as a community infused with these values, one may also experience in nature cosmic kinship in varying degrees. This is what happened in St. Francis to an astounding extent. The panentheistic perspective on creation vindicates theologically both his sensibility for the divine presence in nature that he demonstrated and the cosmic kinship that he himself lived.

3.3 *Further Reflections on the Intrinsic Value of Nature*

3.3.1 A Balance between the Intrinsic and Utilitarian Values of Nature

A ground for the intrinsic value of nature, from the panentheistic perspective, is theocentric in the sense that the mutual presence of God and creation originates not from nature but from God in virtue of the divine openness. The fact that the source of intrinsic value is God puts a curb on an excessive, anthropocentric attitude toward nature. It lays restraints also upon an extreme claim of biocentrism or ecocentrism that seeks to render nature as the absolute reality. This theocentric viewpoint of intrinsic value makes moderate these two extreme perspectives on creation. It enables us to have a balanced attitude toward the intrinsic value as well as the instrumental value of creatures. First, the pantheistic perspective makes plain that nature is not divine and cannot claim for itself intrinsic value in the absolute sense. It does allow and justify our instrumental conception of nature. Second, however, the panentheistic standpoint mandates a proper way of approaching and using nature. It maintains that nature exists in the presence of God, prior to our sake. It awakens us to an attitude of due regard and care for all creatures, in which God is present. It is eventually our share and task to recognize the sacramentality of nature, cosmic kinship with all creatures, and consequent intrinsic value, and to act accordingly. «It is up to human beings – it is part of their function in the cosmos – to know how to read the book of creation in order to be joyful and celebrate, to thank and praise the Creator»[103]. On the contrary, an unrestricted and extravagant way of living will obscure from our sight the sacramentality of nature, cosmic kinship, and intrinsic value, all of which originate in God.

3.3.2 Voluntary Poverty: A Way of Living Cosmic Kinship

We cannot become what we are meant to be, until we achieve «a friendly and fraternal relationship with our natural world»[104]. For the human being is a being in nature as well as a personal and social being. A prophetic vision in the Scriptures even envisions that all creatures, human and nonhuman, in the world live together in peace, although this points to an eschatological ideal (cf. Isa. 11:6-9). Boff understands in this sense «to-be-in-the-world-with-all-things» as the basic structure of humanity[105]. We have witnessed a figure in whom this eschatological ideal of human identity was realized: St. Francis. How did the eschatological dream of cosmic kinship come true in St. Francis? One may simply say that he was born with an exceptionally outstanding, aesthetic sensitivity for nature and all creatures in it. It is, however, in his life of poverty and renunciation that the fundamental source of his cosmic kinship must be found. His love for all creatures as his brothers

---

[103] L. BOFF, *Cry*, 151.

[104] L. BOFF, *Saint Francis*, 46.

[105] L. BOFF, *Saint Francis*, 46.

and sisters was «only possible by means of a profound asceticism and an interrupted [*sic*] effort at purification and denial of the desire for the possession and domination of things»[106]. He chose a radical, ascetic way of living because he sought ardently to follow Jesus Christ. His radical option for poverty stemmed from his passion to follow and imitate Christ, who had possessed nothing in order to love all (cf. Luke 9:58; Mark 10:17-22). In this sense, his love for nature was never naïve or romantic. Rather, one must say that his cosmic love for all was possible only as a consequence of his intense imitation of the Christ who lived a life of radical poverty. It can be held, therefore, that there was a strong christological aspect in his cosmic kinship[107].

Poverty, not forced but voluntary, now comes into view as a way of actualizing cosmic love. In our possession or desire to possess is found a deep-rooted orientation to dominate and control others at our disposal. Possession tends to divide human beings and put them into conflict with each other: «Possession is what engenders the obstacles to communication between human beings themselves and between persons and things». Poverty, freely chosen, can achieve the opposite. Poverty leads one to liberation from the possessive attitude whereby one seeks to dominate others: «Poverty is a way of being by which the individual lets things be what they are». Poverty is an outward expression of a way of being *with* others, instead of *over* others. Poverty will lead all to become what they are meant to be. «The more radical the poverty, [...] the easier it is to commune with all things, respecting and reverencing their differences and distinctions. Universal fraternity is the result of the way-of-being-poor of Saint Francis»[108]. Poverty, as a way of living and being with others in the world, will liberate us from an obsession to dominate, possess, and use others for our sake. It will in turn lead us to the appreciation of others primarily as they are, not as what they are for us. Only then can we have respect and reverence for otherness and difference in other beings. Only then can we acknowledge that they are precious as they are, not as what they are for us.

---

[106] L. BOFF, *Saint Francis*, 38.

[107] Cf. H.P. SANTMIRE, *The Travail of Nature*, 112-113. Santmire shares this understanding of St. Francis's cosmic love. «Francis was not romantic. He did not go directly to nature, at least at first. At first he went directly to Christ. This meant that the only way to see nature as it truly is, as universally blessed and cared for by the Creator, was the way of *humility* again, the way of Lady Poverty».

[108] L. BOFF, *Saint Francis*, 39.

4. The Intrinsic Value of All Creatures from the Perspective of Sallie McFague

4.1 *Introduction*

The body of God was proposed in chapter three as a new metaphor for the world and its relationship with God. This body metaphor conceives the world as a cosmic organism in which a myriad of diverse individual bodies are organically interconnected. The metaphor of God's body spontaneously evokes an impression that God loves the world. For the world is *God's* body. Corporeality matters to the God who is conceived to relate to the world as God's body. This body metaphor stands opposed to any tendency to depreciate body and matter, which has somehow existed in the Christian tradition, explicitly or implicitly, to various extents[109]. This metaphor implies that God created the material world and that God cherishes and nourishes it. God is concerned about the basic needs of all the individual bodies in God's body (i.e., all creatures in the world) for their existence. It suggests that God is somehow present in all creatures and creation as a whole, as one's relationship with one's body implies. The metaphor of spirit for God indicates that God is related to the world internally and intimately rather than externally and superficially. God is envisaged to be immanent in the world and to knit all creatures together from within. God is omnipresent in God's body. All creatures are intrinsically connected with each other and linked with God, in virtue of the spirit of God. This body/spirit metaphor can provide a solid ground for the intrinsic value of all creatures. For God's body alludes to the God who cherishes the world (God's body) and all creatures in it (individual bodies in God's body); God's spirit indicates God's omnipresence whereby all creatures without exception form their relationship with God, in varying ways and degrees.

This section corresponds to the final stage of metaphorical theology where a proposed metaphor is validated and shaped in regard to the Christian tradition. I will first examine in what sense the metaphor of God's body is compatible with the Christian tradition. If it is to be called Christian, this body metaphor must be grounded in and compatible with the Christian tradition. I will then reflect on the story of Jesus of Nazareth, from which the vision of Jesus (the Christic vision)

---

[109] For a review of the biblical and theological thoughts about nature in Christianity, see H.P. SANTMIRE, *The Travail of Nature*; C.E. GUNTON, *The Triune Creator*.

emerges. The Christic vision will be seen from the perspective of God's body, and *vice versa*. The metaphor of God's body will render the Christic vision more proper for the age of the ecological crisis; conversely, the body metaphor will take on a new, specifically Christian shape. The metaphor of God's body and the Christic vision affect and enrich each other in this phase of metaphorical theology. A ground for the intrinsic value of all creatures will be found in the renewed Christic vision and the metaphor of God's body.

4.2 The Body of God and Jesus' Death and Resurrection

Christianity claims that God is manifested in the person of Jesus of Nazareth in an unparalleled way and measure. For Christians, he is the supreme symbol of God. Jesus is *the* sacrament of God. In this regard, he is the paramount way God reveals and communicates the divine self to the world. However, the revelation of God in and through Jesus may be grasped in this age not as clearly as in that age. For, as a historical human being who lived at a particular time and place, Jesus too is deeply involved in his age and culture. In other words, a context matters to our encounter of God, insofar as it is historically mediated to us. We must ask how we may better comprehend in our own historical context the way God relates to the world, which was manifested through this historical figure called Jesus[110]. We need our own way of grasping and expressing God's relationship with the world which is effective and proper in our times and, at the same time, which is based on and consistent with what was revealed in Jesus[111]. We proposed the body of God as a new metaphor for the world and its relationship with God, and we examined it to see if a proposed metaphor works well in our concrete context called the ecological crisis. We must now ask if a

---

[110] S. MCFAGUE, *Models of God*, 56.

[111] Cf. S. MCFAGUE, *Models of God*, 40-41; D. TRACY, «Theological Method». There are always two constants to be interpreted or correlated: tradition and a concrete situation. This task can be fulfilled in two ways. First, a hermeneutical method interprets the Christian tradition in the light of a new situation so that contemporaries can understand it better. Second, a constructive method employs variety of resources including metaphors and models, and it attempts to render the Christian tradition more intelligible in a new context. This attempt is examined for its effectiveness and compatibility with the Christian tradition grounded in Jesus Christ in order to see if it can be accepted in Christian faith community. The method of construction too has a hermeneutical dimension in that it is examined, in the final analysis, by the Christian tradition. See also R. HAIGHT, *Dynamics of Theology*, 191-195.

proposed metaphor is consistent with the relationship of God with the world that was revealed in Jesus. The body of God is conceived as one cosmic organism composed of an immense number of individual creatures organically interwoven by the spirit of God. How can the metaphor of God's body be linked to the Christian tradition? Put otherwise, where can we find a significant affinity of a new organic metaphor to the Christian tradition, particularly to Jesus of Nazareth? I assert that a meaningful link between the metaphor of God's body and the Christian tradition is found in the death and resurrection of Jesus.

4.2.1 The Body of God and the Death of Jesus: An Expression of the Divine Compassion

The body of God as a metaphor for God's relationship with the world hints at the way God relates to creatures in suffering. This body metaphor indicates that God is concerned for the world, particularly for parts of the world in affliction. For the world is the body of God. It alludes further to the way God acts for the sake of the world. The body of God does not imply God's care for the world from without. Instead, it strongly suggests that God is together *with* all afflicted creatures. The suffering of creatures is somehow intrinsically connected with God precisely because the world is the body *of God*. The suffering of our body is intrinsically related to us, although we are not completely identical with our body. We are inseparable from our body, and to that extent we are linked to the suffering of our body. The suffering of our body is our suffering. We suffer when our body suffers. Analogically, we may conceive how God is related to the suffering of the world. It can be said, analogically, that the suffering of God's body is God's suffering and that God suffers when God's body suffers.

The intimate connection of God with God's body in suffering recalls us to what compassion means. Epistemologically, the word «compassion» means to share suffering. It does not refer simply to a sense of pity that one may have for someone in distress. Rather, what compassion implies is to share with (*com*) those who are in suffering (*passion*) by means of being together with them and standing on their side. In this regard, compassion is voluntary suffering out of love for and with others. Compassion is precisely what Jesus manifested and actualized throughout his life, especially on the cross. Compassion is the love of God, who is with all creation and willing to share with all those in suffering. God's love is compassionate love for all creatures. Jesus identified himself out of compassion with those in distress whom he met, such as the poor, the sick, the possessed, and the outcast. His death on the cross is a culminating and supreme moment of God's love, which embraces the suffering of all creatures, without exception.

A case can now be made that the metaphor of God's body has a significant affinity with Jesus' life, particularly his death on the cross. Both of them bring into relief the most radical type of love called compassion. The metaphor of God's body «emphasizes God's willingness to suffer for and with the world, even to the point of personal risk. The world as God's body, then, may be seen as a way to remythologize the inclusive, suffering love of the cross of Jesus of Nazareth»[112]. This body metaphor implies that God shares the suffering of the world. The way God loves all creatures by sharing their suffering was eminently expressed in the life of Jesus, especially in his death. It may seem powerless, but the power of God comes exactly from this powerlessness, i.e., being with the vulnerable and sharing their suffering, epitomized by the death of Jesus. This is the power of the cross. We must remember that it is not the divine omnipotence but the divine vulnerability that will transform the whole creation into the new creation, as was manifested in the resurrection of Jesus, the beginning of the new creation.

4.2.2 The Body of God and the Resurrection of Jesus:
An Expression of the Divine Omnipresence

In the resurrection of Jesus can be found another allusion to a significant connection of the metaphor of God's body with the Christian tradition. We need, for this, to pay heed to the relationship of Jesus with the Spirit. According to the gospel of Luke, Jesus was completely taken and led by the Spirit from the beginning (Mary's conception of Jesus) to the end (his death on the cross). He is the bearer of the Spirit. We are also told that Jesus promised to send the Spirit to his disciples after his death (cf. John 14:15-26; 16:5-15). The Spirit is the Spirit of the risen Jesus. The Spirit who took and led Jesus during his lifetime is the Spirit sent by Jesus after his death. It is in Jesus that his followers experienced the Spirit while he was living; it is in the Spirit that we now experience Jesus once he died and was raised. A difference between the earthly Jesus and the risen Jesus lies in the way he exists in the world. As the one like us, he used to exist as a historically conditioned human

---

[112] S. MCFAGUE, *Models of God*, 72.

being; as the risen one, he now exists in the whole world in virtue of the Spirit. The risen Jesus is present everywhere and in every moment. If we recall that the metaphor of God's body conceives the world as a cosmic organism permeated with the spirit of God, another significant affinity of this body metaphor with the Christian tradition is found in the omnipresence of the risen Jesus in the world. The body of God suffused with the spirit of God can be a vivid, palpable expression of the way the risen Jesus is present in the whole creation by virtue of the Spirit.

The resurrection of Jesus as the divine omnipresence in the world can be appreciated in another direction. McFague makes a criticism that the traditional interpretation of resurrection as a definitive eschatological event is confined to the past (the resurrection *of Jesus*) and the future (the resurrection of *elected individuals*), and the significance of resurrection to the present is absent[113]. Hence, one can hardly find in the traditional understanding of resurrection its significance with regard to this world. Our comprehension of resurrection tends to be nostalgic (toward the past) or otherworldly (toward the future). Moreover, the notion of resurrection in this view pertains only to human beings. Salvation in this respect is predominantly anthropocentric and exclusive of nonhuman creation. It can be held that the traditional perspective on resurrection and salvation is not effective and proper for our age. For it is critical today to emphasize the importance of *this* world and to cultivate our concern for nonhuman creation. It can be held further, for this reason, that we need to interpret the resurrection of Jesus in a new light. In this regard, Jesus' resurrection may be interpreted as God's palpable promise to be present in all places and moments in this world[114].

We must draw on the resurrection narratives of the gospels for a new interpretation of Jesus' resurrection. There are two kinds of resurrection narratives: the empty tomb and the appearances of Jesus. We are told by the appearance stories that the risen Jesus appeared to his disciples, but in a mysterious way: closed doors were no obstacles to his presence; he disappeared in front of the two disciples (cf. John 20:19-29; Luke 24:13-35). This mode of appearance implies a radical change in his way of being in the world. The way he appeared to his disciples indicates that the risen Jesus, unlike the earthly Jesus, is now present everywhere

---

[113] Cf. S. MCFAGUE, *Models of God*, 60.
[114] Cf. S. MCFAGUE, *Models of God*, 59-60.

in this world. Moreover, as McFague points out, St. Paul's testimony to the appearance of Jesus to him implies further that the risen Jesus is present especially to the least, given that he considered himself the least of the apostles (cf. 1 Cor. 15:8-9)[115]. This suggestion is reinforced by the fact that the risen Jesus appeared to those who were in disappointment, sorrow, fear, and without hope, such as Mary Magdalene and his disciples (cf. John 20:11-23).

McFague is skeptical, however, about the effectiveness of the empty tomb stories for a new interpretation of Jesus' resurrection. For they bring to light, according to her, the aspect of Jesus' absence in this world and transition into anther world. She holds that this would not encourage us to interpret Jesus' resurrection as his omnipresence in this world. Nonetheless, I think that the empty tomb accounts too can strengthen rather than weaken what the appearance stories indicate. It is the case, to be sure, that the empty tomb stories by themselves give only an ambiguous sign about the resurrection of Jesus: for example, seeing the empty tomb, Mary Magdalene thought that someone stole the body of Jesus (cf. John 20:2.13. 15). However, if they are considered in connection with the appearance stories, the empty tomb stories affirm explicitly the resurrection of the whole of Jesus, not merely the immortality of his soul. Therefore, it can be held that the empty tomb stories too reinforce the importance of the corporeal aspect of Jesus' resurrection in that the corpse of Jesus was not left behind and what was raised is not his soul alone but his totality. These stories then indicate that resurrection reached and transformed the whole Jesus and that corporeality is still important to the risen Jesus.

It follows that Jesus, who was raised from the dead, is still with us in this world, but in a mode radically different from the way the earthly Jesus used to be, as the appearance stories indicate. The risen Jesus is the same Jesus who used to live on the earth, but he now exists in the world in a totally different way. One can now make a case that the metaphor of God's body fits in well with this understanding of Jesus' resurrection. For this body metaphor also implies strongly the divine presence in the entire creation[116]. The relationship of God with the

[115] Cf. S. MCFAGUE, *Models of God*, 60.

[116] It must be recalled that we cannot expect a metaphor to fit reality in every respect (cf. S. MCFAGUE, *Metaphorical Theology*, 34; ID., *Models of God*, 33-34). That would not be a metaphor but a definition. What is important here is that a proposed metaphor is compatible and consistent with an important, the most important in a sense, aspect of the Christian tradition and functions well in our times. For

world indicated in the new interpretation of Jesus' resurrection is intimate and inclusive, as it is in the metaphor of God' body.

4.2.3 The Divine Omnipresence: Another Expression of the Divine Compassion for Creation

The metaphor of God' body sheds light from a new angle on the meaning of the divine omnipresence in the world. This body metaphor has been disclosed to have an affinity with the death and resurrection of Jesus. The body metaphor shares the character of compassion for the world with his death, and it shares the character of omnipresence in the world with his resurrection. This metaphor, as a common denominator, suggests that there is an intrinsic connection between the divine compassion and omnipresence, thereby confirming that Jesus' death and resurrection are inextricably linked to each other. The metaphor reveals that the divine omnipresence is another expression of the divine compassion for the entire creation. God is present in the whole creation because God loves all creatures, particularly the vulnerable. A case can now be made that the omnipresence of Jesus in virtue of his resurrection is a spatial and temporal extension of his compassion which was supremely revealed in his death, but which was restricted within his physicality during his lifetime. The divine omnipresence in creation is a palpable manifestation of the divine love for all creation. Therefore, the resurrection of Jesus is not only the glorification of Jesus as an individual. Rather, it must be viewed as a drastic change in his way of being in the world whereby he radically widened his compassionate love of human beings to the whole creation. The metaphor of God's body makes explicit what was implicit in the earthly Jesus. The resurrection of Jesus in the light of God's body discloses that the love of God revealed in him is the cosmic and inclusive love which is concerned for all creatures, especially for the least.

---

instance, the metaphor of God's body does not fit in well with Jesus as a divine person who has assumed the human condition, because this metaphor is not a personal metaphor. On the contrary, this metaphor fits well in the omnipresence of the risen Jesus in the world. If this cosmic metaphor loses its appropriateness or competency later, it will be replaced by another metaphor that is evaluated more suitable for a new situation. This is the way a metaphor works. A really serious problem takes place when a certain metaphor persists as the best for all ages and regardless of historical contexts. This is not a correct perspective on a metaphor; it is nothing but an idolatrous viewpoint.

It can now be asserted that the metaphor of God's body is in accord with the God who was revealed in the person of Jesus, in regard to God's relationship with the world. At the same time, we have found a solid ground for the intrinsic value of all creatures, which is dependent on one's relationship with God. From the perspective of God's body, the divine omnipresence in virtue of the spirit is eventually God's compassionate concern and care for every single creature and creation as a whole. All are God's beloved, and as such, they deserve God's compassion. For the world is the body of God. The body metaphor tells us that God's infinite love for the entire creation is the ground of the relationship between God and all creatures. All creatures are in such intimate and profound relationships with God that God embraces and shares the suffering of all creatures, as was shown in Jesus. All creatures, especially the least, are precious to God. The understanding of Jesus' resurrection in the light of God's body disturbs our conventional, anthropocentric perspective on the relationship with God, which excludes nonhuman creation. The metaphor of God's body indicates that all creatures have intimate relationship with God in their own way and degree and thereby have their own value in themselves.

4.3 *The Christic Vision:*
Destabilization, Inclusiveness, and Nonhierarchy

For Christians, the gospels bear a privileged witness to the love of God, which was revealed in Jesus of Nazareth in his life, death, and resurrection. This Jesus whom we confess as the Christ is what makes our faith specifically Christian and the most fundamental ground for Christianity. We Christians must understand the relationship of God to the world primarily through Jesus. In other words, Jesus is the Christian paradigm whereby we conceive how God reveals the divine self and loves all creatures. «To see the story of Jesus as paradigmatic means to see it as illuminative and illustrative of basic characteristics of the Christian understanding of the God-world relationship»[117]. It is the case that there may be diverse interpretations and understandings of Jesus' narrative according to different contexts. Otherwise, Christian faith could not render itself intelligible to those who live in different situations. Nonetheless, they must always maintain and manifest «demon-

---

[117] S. MCFAGUE, *Models of God*, 46.

strable continuities» with the Christian paradigm, if they are to be Christian[118].

From the standpoint of liberation, McFague holds, the gospels can be epitomized as «a destabilizing, inclusive, nonhierarchical vision of Christian faith»[119]. This Christic vision is *an* interpretation of the gospels from a specific perspective, and we must examine this interpretation to see whether it is in continuity with the paradigmatic Christian story of Jesus. To demonstrate that the paradigmatic story of Jesus bears a destabilizing, inclusive, and nonhierarchical vision, she suggests that the story of Jesus be characterized by his speaking in parables, his table fellowship with the outcast, and his death on the cross: «the parables illuminate the destabilizing aspect of the good news of Christianity; the table fellowship its inclusive character; and the death on the cross its nonhierarchical emphasis»[120]. Insofar as these three aspects feature the life of Jesus, the proposed Christic vision must be examined to see whether it is based on and consistent with these aspects.

Although, like other feminist theologians, McFague is keenly aware of oppression and exploitation as historical realities when she speaks of the destabilizing, inclusive, and nonhierarchical Christic vision, her wording of the Christic vision needs to be qualified more precisely. First, not all dualistic worldviews and structures but only exploitative ones must be destabilized so that exploitation can be eradicated. Second, likewise, not all hierarchies but only oppressive ones must be denounced so that oppression may be eliminated.

4.3.1 The Parables of Jesus:
The Destabilization of Exploitative Dualistic Worldviews

The parables that Jesus used to illustrate the kingdom of God may be regarded as extended metaphors in that they tell us in a narrative form «something about the unfamiliar, the "kingdom of God," in terms of the familiar». The way these parables influence hearers can be described as three phases of «orientation, disorientation, and reorientation». Parables begin with the ordinary world, standards, expectations, and language (orientation); in the course of narration, they surprise listeners with unexpected or radically different perspectives, «often by means of surrealistic extravagance» (disorientation); in the end, they lead hearers

---

[118] S. MCFAGUE, *Models of God*, 46.
[119] S. MCFAGUE, *Models of God*, 48.
[120] S. MCFAGUE, *Models of God*, 49.

to a radically new way of being and living in the world (reorientation). The parables of God's kingdom are meant to «invert and subvert» a conventional way of living in the world. They suggest that «the way of the kingdom is not the way of the world»[121].

The kingdom parables challenge hearers to opt for the way of the kingdom instead of the way of the world. For instance, the parable of the owner of a vineyard brings to light a sharp contrast between the way of God's kingdom and the way of the world (cf. Matt. 20:1-16). The way the owner calculates wages for workers is drastically different from the ordinary way in the world. The parable makes plain that the way of viewing reality in God's kingdom is radically different from the one in the world. This parable presents to us «a radically egalitarian, nondualistic way of being in the world»: all deserve to live. The kingdom parables intend to shatter all kinds of dehumanizing, dualistic perspectives, which divide human beings and put them in conflict. It is important here to note that «what is distinctive in the parables is not primarily a reversal that elevates the «unworthy» but a destabilization of *all* dualism»[122]. A mere reversal would create another division. It cannot end fatal separations prevalent in the world, always putting a part of the whole into oppression and exploitation by the other. What is first required is the destabilization of all dualistic structures, both mental and social, that bring about endless conflict and enmity. This goal can be achieved only by the destabilization, not the reversal, of exploitative dualistic structures. A case is now made that the destabilizing aspect of the proposed Christic vision is compatible and consistent with the Christian paradigm grounded in Jesus.

It must be recalled that we Christians must see the relationship of God with the world in the light of Jesus Christ, who is the fundamental ground of the Christian paradigm. We can then hold that, as revealed in the destabilizing goal and effect of Jesus' parables, God wants to destabilize and abolish all dehumanizing, dualistic structures in the world whereby one group dominates, oppresses, and exploits the other. The parables make obvious that God is against whatever dualistic perspectives or structures that dehumanize human beings. This demands that we change radically the way we view other human beings. It requires that we deal with other human beings in the same way we treat ourselves (cf. Matt. 7:12). We must acknowledge, for this, that they have

---

[121] S. MCFAGUE, *Models of God*, 50.
[122] S. MCFAGUE, *Models of God*, 51.

the same human dignity and value as ours, regardless of their race, gender, religion, and so forth. This destabilizing vision grounded in the kingdom parables needs to be widened to encompass nonhuman creatures, i.e., nature, in order that it may be effective in our age. This is what the metaphor of God's body will carry out. Only then can the destabilizing Christic vision become a vision for all creation, not only for human beings.

4.3.2 The Table Fellowship of Jesus: The Inclusiveness of All

Jesus not only taught destabilizing parables but also lived them out. He actually destabilized those dehumanizing, dualistic perspectives and structures in his age by his table fellowship with the outcast, which assumed the center of his ministry together with his healing activity. It can be said that «the destabilization of the parables becomes an "enacted parable" as Jesus invites the outcast of society to eat with him»[123]. To understand his table fellowship with the outcast as an enacted parable is bolstered, one can hold, by the fact that the table fellowship follows the same procedure of the parables: eating together with someone belongs to the ordinariness (orientation); then comes an unexpected event of eating with the outcast (disorientation); and finally it challenges the worthy to review their dualistic perspective and socioeconomic structure that trap many in the category of the unworthy (reorientation).

We need to heed another important significance of the table fellowship in addition to the actualization of destabilization. Jesus realized in anticipation, in the act of eating with the alienated, his parable of a wedding banquet in the kingdom of God in which all are invited and included (cf. Matt. 22:1-14; Luke 14:16-24). His table fellowship not only symbolizes but also actualizes the radical inclusiveness of God's kingdom. We are told that Jesus began his ministry with the passage of the prophet Isaiah that proclaims good news to the poor, release to the captives, healing to the sick, and finally, the year of the Lord's favor (cf. Luke 4:18-19). One can hold that these diverse tasks were dramatically expressed and achieved in his invitation of the outcast to a festive meal[124]. In fact, it can be held that all these ministries have and manifest the inclusive character of the table fellowship. The captives are released; the sick are healed; and the possessed are released from the

---

[123] S. MCFAGUE, *Models of God*, 51.
[124] Cf. S. MCFAGUE, *Models of God*, 52.

evil spirits. All can now go back to their community and join it again. This is what «the year of the Lord's favor» indicates. Jubilee aims at the restoration of the original good order and harmony in creation, both human and nonhuman (cf. Lev. 25). The table fellowship of Jesus with the outcast makes explicit the inclusive character of God's kingdom that is implicit in his other ministries. A case is now made again that the inclusive character of the proposed Christic vision is compatible and consistent with the Christian paradigm grounded in Jesus.

It must be recalled again that the relationship of God with the world must be viewed in the light of Jesus Christ. We can then claim that, as disclosed in the inclusive, as well as destabilizing, effect of Jesus' table fellowship, God wants to destabilize and abolish alienating, dualistic structures in society and thereby to invite and gather everyone to a festive meal in the kingdom of God. This inclusive vision can be realized in anticipation in this world to the measure that the privileged welcome the marginalized and provide them with an efficacious means to participate in society. But this is possible only when the powerful acknowledge the vulnerable as human persons like them, with the same human dignity and value. Again, this inclusive vision grounded in the table fellowship of Jesus needs to be broadened to embrace nature in order that it may become effective in our age. Only then can the inclusive Christic vision become a vision for all creation, not only for human beings.

4.3.3 The Cross of Jesus: A Radical Rejection of Oppressive Hierarchies

Jesus' death on the cross can be understood in accordance with his parables and table fellowship with the outcast. His parables, which were enacted in his table fellowship with the outcast, came to a culminating conclusion in his death on the cross. The cross shows his way of actualizing in this world a destabilizing and inclusive vision and the price to pay for it. «The destabilization of the parables that is fleshed out in the invitation to all, especially to the "unworthy" and the outcasts to share in the feast of life, is radicalized further in the cross. Here the way necessary to bring about this new mode of being is suggested. The way is radical identification with all others»[125]. The way Jesus implemented this vision is «radical identification with all others». It requires us to oppose firmly all hierarchical systems that oppress human beings.

---

[125] S. MCFAGUE, *Models of God*, 53.

Oftentimes, this requirement is accompanied by persecution. The denunciation of Jesus against oppressive hierarchical orders incurred violent reaction from the ruling class which definitely wanted intact the social structures established for their sake. His violent death was somehow anticipated in his attempt to destabilize the established hierarchical, dualistic social structures that dehumanize human beings and in his commitment to building a more inclusive, just society. The cross is a risk to run when we identify with the alienated in an oppressive society. «The cross epitomizes the retribution that comes to those who give up controlling and triumphalist postures in order to relate to others in mutual love»[126]. Again, a case is now made that the nonhierarchical aspect of the proposed Christic vision is compatible and consistent with the Christian paradigm grounded in Jesus.

It needs to be recalled again that the relationship of God with the world must be viewed in the light of Jesus Christ. We can then claim that, as demonstrated by the death of Jesus on the cross, God wants to obliterate all dehumanizing, hierarchical perspectives and structures. Jesus dedicated himself totally and unyieldingly to opposing and abolishing those structures. Such a life demands a radically new way of being in the world, and the cross is the price that we must pay for this new way of living. The cross suggests that a new way of being and living in the world requires two-fold praxes: solidarity and compassion. To bear the cross means to express solidarity with the oppressed and marginalized, identifying with them and enduring disadvantages that it demands, even suffering and death. This is an active aspect of the cross. Jesus chose to stand on the side of the unworthy because Jesus was convinced that God regards them as worthy and wants them to recover their dignity. Jesus challenged the privileged to acknowledge that the unprivileged also have the same human dignity and value. The powerful in the world reacted furiously to him to retain their interests. To the God who is love, there is no option in this occasion except bearing persecution. Here comes compassion, the love to share voluntarily the suffering of others. In fact, compassion is another expression and consequence of solidarity and identification with the marginalized to whom violence and persecution are an ordinary experience. This is a passive aspect of the cross. Jesus' death on the cross, as a result of his solidarity with the oppressed even to the threat of death, reveals supremely how deeply God loves and cherishes all human beings,

---

[126] S. MCFAGUE, *Models of God*, 53.

especially the vulnerable and marginalized, as already shown in Jesus' parables and table fellowship. Once again, this nonhierarchical vision based on the cross of Jesus needs to be extended to include nature in order that it may become effective in our age. Only then can the non-hierarchical Christic vision become a vision for all creation, not only for human beings.

4.4 *The Body of God and the Christic Vision: A Cosmic Concern for the Least*

The metaphor of God's body and the Christic vision will enrich each other, if one is viewed from the perspective of the other. What the body of God may suggest to the Christic vision will first be examined. I hold that this metaphor will help the Christic vision serve more properly in our times. The Christic vision, seen from the standpoint of God's body, will take on a cosmic significance whereby it can address more effectively the disruption of nature. The Christian tradition is enriched by the metaphor of God's body. Conversely, then, what the Christic vision may contribute to the metaphor of God's body will be considered. I hold that the Christic vision will help this metaphor work more in accord with the cause of Jesus in our age. The metaphor of God's body, grasped from the viewpoint of the Christic vision, will bear a specifically Christian significance. The body metaphor is shaped by the Christian tradition. At the same time, this reflection will reinforce the intrinsic value of all creatures, especially that of the vulnerable.

4.4.1 The Christic Vision from the Perspective of God's Body

The destabilizing, inclusive, and nonhierarchical Christic vision can effectively serve for the liberation of those who are oppressed and exploited. It must be noted, at the same time, that this Christic vision lacks a concern for nature and is predominantly focused on human beings. The Christic vision, as it is now, does not seem to work efficaciously in this age characterized by the ecological crisis. However, if the Christic vision is viewed from a new angle of God's body, its scope is widened to the entire world. The conception of the world as God's body composed of an immense number of creatures leads us to realize some vital facts in our age. Humanity is not the center of the entire cosmos; other nonhuman beings exist with us in one and the same space called the earth, primarily not for us but for themselves; and we are so deeply related to and definitely dependent upon other creatures that our life and well-being are not possible without theirs. The recognition of these facts motivated by the metaphor of God's body will infuse us with concern for nature. This metaphor illuminates the Christic vision by an all-embracing and relational character and thereby widens its scope to the entire world. The Christic vision now turns into a destabilizing, inclusive, and nonhierarchical vision, which denounces the hierarchies and dualistic structures that are exploitative and oppressive, for the *whole* creation, not only for humanity.

First, if the scope of the destabilization is extended to nature, the Christic vision will require the end of our aggressive, anthropocentric, and dualistic perspective and structure with regard to nature. The Christic vision with a cosmic destabilizing effect demands that we make a profound conversion toward nature. It requires that we shake off the presumptuous stance that we are the center of the world and nonhuman creation exists only for the sake of humanity. We must learn to perceive nature for its own sake; we must admit that nature has its own value as God's creation, independently of its utility for us. The Christic vision, enriched by the metaphor of God's body, tells us that God wants the recovery of the goodness and value of nature for its own sake.

Second, if the scope of inclusiveness is broadened to nature, the Christic vision will suggest that every creature must have its own place to exist in the world. That all are invited to the festive meal of Jesus indicates that all have the right to live. The Christic vision, illuminated by the metaphor of God's body, throws light on a simple, but frequently forgotten or ignored, fact that God loves all creatures, which constitute God's body. God's love is the fundamental basis of God's relationship with the world, seen in the light of God's body. God created the world out of love; God sustains and will fulfill it because God loves it. The universal love of God for creation, revealed in Jesus' invitation of the outcast to his meal, is directed primarily toward the vulnerable and alienated because of their urgent need. The inclusive Christic vision based on the universal love of God already includes in itself a preferential option for the poor. The marginalized in society are not acknowledged as the human being. They are denied human dignity and value. They cry for their own place in which to live. The Christic vision with cosmic inclusiveness urges us to acknowledge that nature is a new marginalized being which is denied its proper regard and value and plundered by humans. As Jesus' table fellowship is the enactment of his parables, the Christic vision with a cosmic inclusive effect demands that we put into practice our conversion of heart toward nature that the destabilizing Christic vision brought about.

One may make a criticism that the Christic vision which is inclusive of nature is but a naïve ideal in the present situation in which a great number of human beings are starving. As regards this criticism, we need simply to recall a fact that without the earth and its resources, the invitation of all human beings would be impossible. Instead, only the invitation of some chosen individuals would be possible[127]. It must be remembered that an ecological sensibility which promotes our concern for nature is deeply related to the well-being of all human beings. One may then make another criticism that an ecological concern comes out of a utilitarian motive. Regarding this, we can respond that a utilitarian motive must not be criticized indiscriminately nor is it excluded from ecological consciousness. An ecological sensibility needs as its critical element «an aesthetic appreciation for the intrinsic value of all forms of life»[128]. Nonetheless, it never denies the utilitarian value of nature. Rather, it is always taken for granted due to the ecological unity of all things, i.e., the interconnectedness of all creatures. Every creature exists and lives in interdependence with others. Meanwhile, an ecological sensibility calls upon us to revise fundamentally our way of viewing and using nature. It requires that we attain and use material resources from nature with an acknowledgement that we are part of nature and as such dependent on it. This appreciation will in turn instill in us a sense of gratitude and respect for nature. This ecological sensibility helps us appreciate the intrinsic value of nature, while allowing for its utilitarian aspect.

Third, if the nonhierarchical Christic vision is widened to nature, it will imply that the solidarity and compassion which Jesus had for the marginalized and were climatically expressed in his death on the cross must be understood to include all creatures in the world. At the same time, it warns us sternly that our solidarity with groaning nature may cause negative, often violent, reactions from those who have appropriated nature, as Jesus' solidarity and identification with the poor brought persecution to him.

---

[127] Cf. S. MCFAGUE, *The Body of God*, 52.
[128] S. MCFAGUE, *The Body of God*, 52.

4.4.2 The Body of God from the Perspective of the Christic Vision

The body of God has originally been proposed as a substitute metaphor for the monarchical and mechanistic metaphors for God's relationship with the world, because they are no longer proper in our age characterized by the ecological crisis. It has been demonstrated that the metaphor of God's body overcomes successfully a sense of God's remoteness or absence from the world in those two traditional metaphors. For God is conceived to be concerned for the world as God's body and to be present in the world in virtue of the spirit. The metaphor of God's body brings us a sense that God is present in the world and loves the world. We have also seen in the metaphor of God's body that ecological unity is formed in virtue of God's spirit which interpenetrates and interconnects all creatures. Hence, this metaphor reminds us that human beings are part of creation and dependent upon nonhuman creatures. Ecological unity is a basic perspective of the body metaphor from which to conceive the world. However, the metaphor of God's body does not deliver yet a specifically Christian meaning of ecological unity among all creatures in the world, particularly between humanity and nature. It is when the metaphor of God's body is viewed in the light of the Christic vision that the significance of ecological unity is revealed in the Christian context. Put otherwise, the metaphor of God's body is shaped by the Christic vision.

When it is viewed from the horizon of the Christic vision, ecological unity can be understood as a cosmic manifestation and actualization of the destabilizing, inclusive, and nonhierarchical Christic vision, rooted in the universal love of God. The Christic vision discloses that «the direction of creation is toward inclusive love for all, especially the oppressed, the outcast, the vulnerable»[129]. In this light, the spirit of God is seen to interconnect all creatures so that even a single creature is not marginalized in the world. The interconnectedness of all creatures originates from God's «love that overturns conventional dualistic hierarchies to reach out to the outcast and the victim»[130]. This is what the Christic vision indicates with regard to ecological unity. Ecological unity does not only show that all creatures are interconnected. It also reveals that they are interconnected in order that all of them, especially even the least creatures, may exist in virtue of ecological unity. In this regard, ecological unity is an expression of God's universal love

---

[129] S. MCFAGUE, *The Body of God*, 160.
[130] S. MCFAGUE, *The Body of God*, 165.

manifested in the destabilizing, inclusive, and nonhierarchical love of Jesus, which denounces the hierarchies and dualistic structures that are exploitative and oppressive. The vulnerable in the world too are precious to God in their own way and degree. Therefore, ecological unity illuminated by the Christic vision does not hold simply that we are part of nature. It requires us to admit also that every creature, no matter how trivial it may look, has the right to exist, which we cannot fully understand at present. In other words, ecological unity can be regarded as an invitation for us to give due regard to all creatures, especially the vulnerable: «even microorganisms have their place in creation, a place that is not merely their usefulness (or threat) to human beings»[131].

Ecological unity in the light of the Christic vision persuades us that we must seriously consider the intrinsic value of nonhuman creatures. However, this invitation or persuasion does not mean naïvely that all forms of being have the same rights so that one can insist on «such absurdities as speaking of "oppressed" mosquitoes or rocks»[132]. Rather, it holds soberly that all creatures have their own reason for their existence which does not depend on human beings. In practice, however, nature has been impoverished. For we have exploited nature violently and used it extravagantly only for our sake, strictly speaking, for the sake of a few. Ecological unity seen from the Christic vision urges us to acknowledge that even the least in the world must be given their due regard. Ecological unity is now seen as a relationship embedded in creation, which is meant to assure all creatures of their own intrinsic value. In sum, the metaphor of God's body shaped by the Christic vision conceives that all creatures are organically connected with one another in virtue of God's immanence motivated by God's compassionate love so that even the least creatures may not be alienated or lose ground for their existence.

---

131 S. MCFAGUE, *The Body of God*, 165.
132 S. MCFAGUE, *The Body of God*, 166.

CHAPTER V

The Compatibility of Ecological Concern and Social Concern

Proposition III: A Christian perspective on the world shows that concern for nature is compatible with concern for the poor.

The third proposition that concern for nature is compatible with concern for the poor is a critical and practical issue with which we must grapple, insofar as we envision the world from the perspective that the first and second propositions present and we seek to live accordingly. We hear today two seemingly different voices calling for our concern and commitment: one voice comes from the poor and the other from nature. Some argue that we need to make a choice between these two voices because it would exceed our ability and available resources to respond to both. But a case can be made, grounded in the two preceding propositions, that concern for nature is compatible with concern for the poor. Poverty and the deterioration of nature must be dealt with and settled together; otherwise, they cannot be resolved at all. In other words, they are not two different issues out of which we must select one or which we may separately handle. First, the second proposition of intrinsic value suggests that both the poor and nature deserve our concern because nonhuman creation as well as humanity has intrinsic value, though they are different from each other in value. Second, the first proposition of interconnectedness implies that we must be concerned for both nature and the poor because they are interrelated and interdependent. In this sense, the first and second propositions undergird the third. A closer look into the issue of poverty and ecology would disclose that they are so intimately interwoven that one cannot properly be solved without due consideration for the other.

The Bible presents an integrated perspective on humanity and non-human creation. The story of the Garden of Eden tells us that not only humankind but also nature was destined to suffer because human beings did not remain faithful to God and God's ordinances (cf. Gen. 3:17; 6:5-7). This biblical standpoint implies that the human world and the natural world are so closely connected with each other that they influence one another. It understands that if the divine order that God established in society breaks down, the divine order in nature collapses, too. The Scriptures warn us that if justice is not maintained in society, the integrity of nature is not retained, either. This perspective is developed and explicitly expressed in a variety of biblical texts (cf. Hos. 4:1-3; Jer. 9:1-10; Ps. 107:33-42). For instance, the prophet Hosea condemns Israel: «There is no faithfulness or loyalty, and no knowledge of God in the land. Swearing, lying, and murder, and stealing and adultery break out; bloodshed follows bloodshed. Therefore the land mourns, and all who live in it languish; together with the wild animals and the birds of the air, even the fish of the sea are perishing» (4:1-3). It is we humans who commit a sin against God and against each other, but the effect of a sin reaches the rest of creation: the land, the animals in it, the birds of the air, and the fish of the sea. This biblical passage reminds us that humanity and nonhuman creation, which are created by one and the same God and intimately intertwined, face the common destiny. This theme is further articulated in the ordinances of the sabbath and jubilee in the Mosaic covenant[1]. These ordinances dictate how to restore the original order implanted by God in society and nature. The Bible understands that the well-being of society and that of nature are so interdependent that one cannot be achieved and sustained without the other.

In reality, there exists a conflict between the issue of destitution and that of ecology. From the global perspective, this is often referred to as and reflected in the conflict of South and North[2]. The poor and those who work for them look with suspicion at increasing concern for ecology and ecological movements. What they denounce is that the rich have achieved and enjoyed material affluence at the cost of the poor and the natural environment and that they speak now of the need of ecological awareness, whereas an immense number of human beings

---

[1] The significance of the sabbath in this regard will be dealt with in detail in the second section of this chapter.

[2] Cf. D.G. HALLMAN, «Beyond "North/South Dialogue"».

are still starving. It is understandable that ecological concern is nothing
but a luxurious slogan for those who are on the brink of starvation. On
the other hand, those who work for ecology stress that we have an
urgent need to protect nature from further deterioration not only for the
rich but also for the poor. For the ecological destruction of the earth
means the end of all human beings. What they criticize is that those
who are on the side of development maintain an anthropocentric attitude toward nature, acknowledge in nature mainly instrumental value,
and are not sensitive to the environmental degradation throughout the
world.

Some now hold that social impoverishment and ecological devastation are so inextricably entangled with each other that we must grapple
with them together[3]. For example, one may trace the origin of mass
poverty and global ecological devastation back to the lack of respect for
life[4]. It can be held that a tendency prevalent in us to disregard life
enables the current, exploitative economic system. It in turn brings
about both economic injustice such as an extreme unbalance in the
distribution of wealth and ecological crisis such as the depletion of
natural resources and the pollution of the environment. As another
example, poverty in a rural area inevitably causes the exhaustive use of
the soil. Poverty compels farmers to clear new land at the cost of the
environment such as deforestation. It may also force them to move into
urban areas where they end up in the urban poor. Besides, the poor
almost always suffer from the degradation of the environment where
they live because they cannot afford to move to another area with a
better environmental quality[5]. Poverty and environmental devastation
are interrelated, structural problems.

Social destitution and ecological degradation are in the final analysis
issues of social justice and ecological justice. The term «social justice»
appears in diverse ways in Catholic social teaching. For example,
Quadragesimo Anno connects the proper distribution of wealth in
society with social justice: «By these principles of social justice one
class is forbidden to exclude the other from a share in the profit»; «the
distribution of created goods must be brought into conformity with the
demands of the common goods and social justice»[6]. *Justice in the*

---

[3] Cf. D.G. HALLMAN, «Beyond "North/South Dialogue"», 5.
[4] Cf. JOHN PAUL II, *Peace with God the Creator*, n. 7.
[5] Cf. USCC, *Renewing the Earth*, 225
[6] PIUS XI, *Quadragesimo Anno*, nn. 57.58. Cf. VATICAN COUNCIL II, *Gaudium et Spes*, n. 67-72.

World recognizes various types of structural injustice and stresses the necessity of structural change[7]. Social justice casts light on a structural change that can effect and ensure a just socio-economic order in society. The term «ecological justice» is relatively new and used as a term for the natural world corresponding to social justice for the human world[8]. Social justice and ecological justice connote and demand a change in the unjust socio-economic system which brings about mass poverty and ecological degeneration. They aim at the just distribution of wealth in society and the integrity of nature. With an escalated awareness of ecological disruption, the Catholic church began to give an emphatic voice to the ecological crisis. It is remarkable that while their immediate subject is the environmental issue, most ecclesial documents do not forget emphasizing that ecological concern by no means sets aside concern for human dignity[9]. They recognize clearly that these two issues are intimately connected with each other.

If the common good is understood as «the sum total of those conditions of social living» for integral human perfection and, as such, the good to be enjoyed by all human beings, the importance of ecological concern must be recognized in the idea of the common good[10]. In other words, ecology must be regarded as the planetary common good and dealt with as such in the sense that it must be shared by the whole humankind. Its planetary (global) character is further disclosed by the fact that grave ecological problems such as the depletion of ozone layer and the greenhouse effect influence the entire planet[11]. Nature, seen from the global perspective, warns us that the present capitalist economy on the assumption of endless economic growth and the limitless supply of natural resources cannot be sustained indefinitely. For the natural resources of the earth are limited. It is only an illusion that all human beings can enjoy in the future thanks to economic development the material standard of living that some enjoy in affluent countries in the present. In a word, the current, predominant economic system and prevalent way of living are not sustainable.

---

[7] Cf. SYNOD OF BISHOPS, *Justice in the World*, n. 20-26.

[8] Cf. R.R. RUETHER, *Gaia and God*, 2-3.

[9] Cf. The Appendices of D. CHRISTIANSEN – W. GRAZER, ed., *And God*.

[10] JOHN XXIII, *Pacem in Terris*, n. 58: «the common good of all embraces the sum total of those conditions of social living whereby men are enabled to achieve their own integral perfection more fully and more easily». Cf. VATICAN COUNCIL II, *Gaudium et spes*, n. 26.

[11] Cf. USCC, *Renewing the Earth*, 232-233.

Since the report of *Bruntland Commission* in 1987, the term «sustainable development» has gained ground[12]. We must not forget, however, that there always exists a tension and conflict between the two terms «sustainable» and «development», insofar as development means the traditional, linear economic growth without limit[13]. Insofar as we hold fast to this conception of development, we can hardly put into practice sustainable development. This suggests that we must seriously consider an alternative notion of development that ensures the integrity of nature as well. The notion of authentic development that Catholic social teaching presents may provide a hint in this regard[14]. Authentic development aims at the good of both an individual human being and humanity as a whole. It indicates the integral growth of the human being, not merely economic development. From the viewpoint of authentic development, the current model of economic development must be criticized in two respects. First, it failed in the just distribution of material affluence that it achieved, and it deepened the gap between the rich and the poor. Conflict among them has been worsened. Second, it failed to bring a sense of genuine happiness and satisfaction even to the rich and instead implanted an insatiable desire in them, making them ever greedier. On the contrary, authentic development considers seriously other elements, such as love, solidarity, freedom, balance and moderation in life, and the contemplation of nature, in addition to economic wealth. These elements have a substantial potential of contributing to the sustainability of nature as well. For the idea of authentic development contains, «unlike the reductionistic notion of economic development, built-in restraints and limits that help it readily cohere with an ecological reading of the common good»[15].

One thing that we must bear in mind is that the present economic system which has caused social impoverishment and ecological deterioration will not automatically be reformed even if we acknowledge its serious drawbacks. For many of us are deeply involved in the

---

[12] Cf. WCED, *Our Common Future*, 43: «sustainable development is development that meets the needs of the present without compromising the ability of future generations to meet their own needs». It can be held that the perspective of the commission is still anthropocentric in that only the need of future generations and that of the present generation are considered in the two terms «sustainable» and «development» respectively. It lacks any serious concern for the integrity of nature.

[13] This problem will be mentioned in detail in the third section of this chapter.

[14] For the key texts of authentic development, see PAUL VI, *Populorum Progressio*, nn. 12-21; JOHN PAUL II, *Sollicitudo Rei Socialis*, nn. 27-34

[15] C.F. HINZE, «Catholic Social Teaching», 185.

present system and benefit from it. We need, in this sense, a profound conversion to make a substantial change. Only a radical conversion from the depth of our heart could lead us to renounce our interests and to commit ourselves to a fundamental change of the present socio-economic system. I believe that the two preceding propositions can be a ground and motive of conversion. The first proposition regarding the interconnectedness of all creatures can contribute to the formation of solidarity in us with nonhuman creation as well as with other human beings. The second one concerning the intrinsic value of all creatures can help us replace a deep-rooted anthropocentric perspective on nature by a theocentric perspective with a deep acknowledgement and appreciation of the dignity and intrinsic value of nature. Only then can we proceed toward social justice and ecological justice for the sake of the poor and nature. I intend in this chapter to show that the third proposition, which I think is indispensable to build an alternative vision of the world together with the first and second propositions, is based on the sound Christian theological tradition. With this intention in mind, I will explore the resource persons to reinforce theologically the third proposition.

1. The Compatibility of Ecological Concern and Social Concern from the Perspective of Karl Rahner

1.1 *Introduction*

It has been remarked at the outset of this study that Rahner rarely if ever mentioned ecological concern and its relationship with social concern[16]. This is not surprising, given that the environmental issue was

---

[16] Even if some fragments of his writings regarding ecological concern are found, they will not be of much significance for our purpose. One may hold, for example, that he had an anthropocentric attitude toward nature, based on his saying that «the demythologization and secularization of the world [...] has turned the world into a material which man himself can manipulate technologically» (K. RAHNER, «Christology», 190). However, this utterance could be understood as an expression of the optimistic expectation that his contemporaries had in common about science and technology, rather than as his explicit stance on nature. He cannot be judged by this fragmentary writing alone with regard to this issue. In fact, he expresses, in this essay as a whole, an integrated view of the world that stresses an intrinsic connection between nature and humanity, despite the absence of an explicit ecological concern. Moreover, one can find in his writings counter-evidences to an anthropocentric tendency. For instance, he seemed to be aware that the natural environment is in trouble because of human greediness when he said that «the earth bears children

not as acute in his day as it is now. On the contrary, his concern for social issues, such as poverty, is observed in his essays[17]. I hold that despite the lack of his writings about the third proposition, his plausible stance on it can at least be inferred from other pertinent materials. I will draw, for this, on his view of social concern and his theological perspective on the world, which has been explored in chapter three. For instance, if he regards the world as the two disparate realities of society and nature, it will not be possible to draw his feasible stance on the third proposition from his view of social concern. On the other hand, if he conceives the world as a reality in which society and nature are intimately related to each other, one may conjecture without violence his plausible stance on the third proposition, grounded in his standpoint on social concern.

I will in this section seek to infer a viewpoint which Rahner might have had on the third proposition on the basis of his thought on freedom, his concern for the poor, and his perspective on the world. I will first consider freedom, which he regards ultimately as a fundamental option for God and the love of God. I will then focus on the unity of the love of God and of neighbor, in which the former is actualized in the latter. I will take heed of a social dimension of the love of neighbor, an example of which would be concern for the poor. Finally, I will conjecture his plausible stance on ecological concern and its relationship with social concern, grounded in his integrated perspective on the world.

1.2 *Freedom: A Transcendental Ground for Social Concern*

1.2.1 Freedom as a Fundamental Option for God

Rahner holds that freedom, together with knowledge, is a basic feature of the human being as a being in transcendence. Freedom is «a transcendental mark of human existence itself»[18]. It is not merely an act of choosing one thing or another. Rather, it refers in a profound sense to «the capacity of the one subject to decide about himself in his single

---

whose hearts know no limits [...] the earth becomes a fertile source of its children's guilt, for they try to tear more from the earth than it can rightly give» (ID., «A Faith That Loves the Earth», 78). In short, these fragments by themselves do not provide any reliable materials which may disclose his stance on the third proposition.

[17] For a collection of Rahner's writings in this aspect, see H. VORGRIMLER, ed., *Dimensioni Politiche del Cristianesimo.*

[18] K. RAHNER, «Theology of Freedom», 184. For Rahner's anthroplogy, see ID., *Foundations of Christian Faith*, 26-39;

totality»[19]. Freedom is an act of self-determination and self-actualization by making a choice among finite objects. As we select this or that in our daily life, we shape ourselves. We determine and form who we are in the exercise of our freedom.

This freedom, like knowledge, always presupposes the infinite horizon which makes us free with regard to any finite realities in the world. Without it, we could not help but be limited by finite realities and would not be free. This infinite horizon, which we call God, is the condition of possibility of freedom; it is within this horizon that we exercise our freedom. Given this, it can be held that in every act of freedom not only do we actualize and form ourselves but also make our stance on God, at least implicitly[20]. In other words, when we make a choice among finite things, we unthematically but ultimately say «yes» or «no» to God. For what we choose in our freedom can be understood as «the historical concreteness of the encounter and projection of this source and goal that support our transcendence»[21]. The concrete realities that we encounter and choose everyday, however trivial they seem, mediate us to God explicitly or implicitly. Our fundamental attitude toward God is gradually determined as we make our decision and choice with respect to concrete objects in our life. Hence, our freedom in regard to finite realities in the world is actually freedom in relation to God. Freedom is ultimately «either self-realization in the direction of God or a radical refusal of self to God»[22]. Freedom is a fundamental option for or against God.

Freedom, as a fundamental option for God, is freedom to choose as the absolute either God or a finite reality. To regard and select a finite reality as the absolute would be a self-contradictory practice of freedom. For, insofar as God is the condition of possibility of freedom, freedom is always meant to be freedom for God. As the infinite horizon of freedom, God is the source and term of freedom. On the other hand, to opt for God would mean to acknowledge God as the absolute; it eventually indicates the love of God. We can choose and accept God, according to Rahner, precisely because God's self-communication is already given in the mode of an offer to everyone of us prior to our

---

[19] K. RAHNER, *Foundations of Christian Faith*, 94.
[20] Cf. K. RAHNER, *Foundations of Christian Faith*, 98.
[21] K. RAHNER, «Theology of Freedom», 182.
[22] G. A. MCCOOL, ed., *A Rahner Reader*, 255.

freedom, i.e., supernatural existential[23]. Therefore, to opt for God and to accept God's self-communication means to live according to God, who dwells in us by means of the divine self-offering (grace). God can be understood, in this sense, as an intrinsic, constitutive principle, which leads us toward God and at the same time, «retains in itself its own essence absolutely intact and in absolute freedom»[24]. In short, freedom in a genuine sense is freedom to choose to love God, to accept God's self-communicating love, and to live according to God indwelling in us.

1.2.2 The Love of God and the Love of Neighbor

One may ask how our fundamental option for God and love of God are realized in the act of our freedom with regard to concrete realities. Rahner holds that it is in the love of neighbor that the love of God is actualized, stressing a unity between these two loves. «The love of neighbor is not merely the preparation, effect, fruit and touchstone of the love of God but is itself an act of this love of God itself»[25]. Nor is the love of God only «an old-fashioned, mythological expression for love of neighbor», which can be dismissed if only the love of neighbor is practiced[26]. The love of God and the love of neighbor are intrinsically united with each other and condition one another: «There is no love for God that is not, in itself, already a love for neighbor; and love for God only comes to its own identity through its fulfillment in a love of neighbor»[27].

To comprehend properly the unity of these two loves, we must recall that the human being is at once a being in transcendence and a being in history in such a way that one's transcendentality is always historically mediated in one's knowledge and freedom[28]. Transcendentality is actualized in history and history is the event of transcendentality. Therefore, the transcendental experience of God is always given to us

---

23 Cf. K. RAHNER, *Foundations of Christian Faith*, 126-133. Supernatural existential can be construed as God's self-communication given to everyone as an offer. This is «the necessary condition which makes its acceptance possible» (at 128).

24 K. RAHNER, *Foundations of Christian Faith*, 121. See also J. O'DONNELL, «The Mystery», 307: «Rahner speaks of a quasi-formal causality to indicate that God becomes a co-constitutive element of man without ceasing to be God».

25 K. RAHNER, «Reflections», 236.

26 K. RAHNER, *The Love of Jesus*, 71

27 Cf. K. RAHNER, *The Love of Jesus*, 71.

28 Cf. K. RAHNER, *Foundations of Christian Faith*, 140.

in our categorical experience in the world, primarily in our encounter with other human beings. We always have a transcendental experience of God, implicit as it is, in the love of neighbor if it is genuine[29]. Hence, «we encounter him [God] unexpressed, unthematic, unobjected and unspoken in all of the things of the world, and therefore and especially in our neighbor»[30]. It can now be held that a fundamental option for God grounded in God's self-communication is realized in the love of neighbor in our daily life.

The love of neighbor, which is the actualization in the world of the love of God, has a social aspect as well as a personal one. In fact, we cannot completely divide these two aspects from each other insofar as the human being is at once social and personal. The love of neighbor is «an act which has to permeate all the social dimensions of human life, and which implies soberly and realistically giving others their due and respecting their freedom in the social sphere as well»[31]. Rahner was worried about the privatization of the love of neighbor and its deterioration into egoism.

> if man is essentially a 'political' being – this love of one's neighbor must not be the mere inclination of the affections or private intercommunication, which can be the most sublime form of egoism precisely because it can be so intimate and bring such happiness, but must become the sober service of 'political' love as well, whose concern is the whole of mankind, turning the most distant person into the nearest neighbor and having occasion to hold the nearest person sternly at a distance[32].

Political love holds that the love of neighbor must reach «the whole of mankind» beyond one's personal relationships. Political love rejects a naïve illusion of love which may turn into «the most sublime form of egoism», and it builds a sober viewpoint on love. The love of neighbor as political love does not always evoke or guarantee immediate satisfaction or happiness. It implies that we must not be satisfied with loving only those whom we know personally and are inclined to love. The political dimension of love demands that the priority of our commitment to neighbor be decided from a global perspective from which to take the whole humankind into account. Therefore, the love of neighbor must include as an essential element concern for social struc-

---

29 K. RAHNER, *The Love of Jesus*, 245-246.
30 K. RAHNER, *Foundations of Christian Faith*, 98-99.
31 K. RAHNER, «The Function», 240.
32 K. RAHNER, «Christian Humanism», 188.

tures in which our neighbors – the entire humankind – live. If our love of neighbor is to be genuine, we must be concerned about injustice in the world and make every effort to uproot it. In this regard, the love of God and the love of neighbor include our criticism of any unjust socio-economic structures and our protest against them[33].

Although Rahner developed the issue of social concern in the context of the function of the church as a critic of society, it is important to note that everyone is involved in the duty of social concern, insofar as it is a genuine expression of the love of neighbor and God. For the love of neighbor and God is grounded in the human freedom and God's self-communication given to every human being as an offer. Put otherwise, social concern belongs to an existential dimension of the human being. No one is exempted from the duty of social concern.

1.3 *The Inference of Ecological Concern from Social Concern*

The love of neighbor is actualized in diverse forms according to different historical situations such as «Christian nonviolence, environmental protection, responsible family planning, health care, political responsibility, and so forth»[34]. The love of neighbor for Rahner can be found particularly in his concern for the poor. He construes poverty primarily as a public issue throughout the world rather than a private issue among individuals[35]. He also understands poverty as a structural problem: «right from the outset they [the poor] have never been given the possibility of a start in human or economic terms [...]»; «the conditions and structures of wealth and power make some wretched and pitiful while according unjust privileges to others [...]»[36]. He makes a criticism, in regard to our attitude to poverty, that we are unwilling and reluctant to help the poor. For it demands that we share what we possess with the poor and that we ourselves become poor in that measure: «We say we cannot when what we really mean is we will not»[37]. There are many diverse factors that cause poverty in the world. Rahner points out straightforwardly, as one fundamental and plain fact, that we are rich precisely because many are poor: «still we, who cannot number

---

[33] Cf. K. RAHNER, «The Function», 241.

[34] K. RAHNER, *The Love of Jesus*, 74. It can be held that Rahner is at least aware of the environmental issue, in relation to the love of neighbor.

[35] Cf. K. RAHNER, «The Unreadiness».

[36] K. RAHNER, «The Unreadiness», 271. 272.

[37] K. RAHNER, «The Unreadiness», 276.

ourselves among these poor, are rich [...] moreover because [...] those poor people are poor»[38]. This observation demands from the rich a more just distribution of wealth and a more frugal way of living. It also implies that economic development alone cannot resolve the grave problem of poverty in the world. What is critical to cope with poverty consists, from this standpoint, not in how much we produce but in how justly we distribute what we produce. This remark leads us to realize soberly a fundamental limit of the earth. It reminds us that the natural resources of the world are limited, so that the only way of eliminating or alleviating poverty is to share them as fairly and modestly as possible, not to compete for them. It is morally wrong that only a few maintain a way of living which most people cannot afford. It is a grave sin in that this material extravagance virtually deprives the poor of basic needs for living.

A case was made that social concern as a concrete expression of the love of neighbor is grounded in the freedom of the human being as a fundamental option for God. Hence, social concern belongs to an existential dimension of the human being. Moreover, Rahner has explicitly expressed his concern for the poor in the world as a global and structural issue, which requires our specific effort such as solidarity with the poor through the just distribution of material wealth. At the same time, as he recognizes, the love of neighbor is actualized in diverse ways and forms according to different situations. For the transcendental experience of God such as a fundamental option for God is always given to us in our concrete experience in a specific condition of the world. We may further expect, grounded in these observations, that Rahner would have expressed explicitly his thought on ecology if the ecological deterioration had been as serious a historical situation in his day as the issue of poverty. We can then conjecture, on the basis of his perspective on the world, what his stance on ecological concern and its relationship with social concern would be.

Rahner's perspective on creation was characterized in chapter three by the dynamic unity of spirit and matter. All creatures in the world are grasped in a single process of self-transcendence in which matter develops into spirit in virtue of God's immanence in the whole creation[39]. There still exists an essential difference between humankind and nature. This dissimilarity does not override, however, a unity which

---

[38] K. RAHNER, «The Unreadiness», 271-272.
[39] Cf. K. RAHNER, «The Unity»; ID., «Christology».

precedes and underlies it. Human self-consciousness is regarded as what the cosmos has achieved in humanity, i.e., cosmic self-consciousness; human beings participate physically in the cosmos through their body and thus are seen to have cosmic bodily presence. The entire world is construed as one cosmic whole in its origin, history, and end[40].

It can then be asserted without violence, I hope, that Rahner would say that ecological concern must be practiced today together with concern for the poor. For humanity and nature are intrinsically and inevitably related to each other. Still, one may feel somewhat remote and awkward the claim that the love of neighbor must reach nature. In this regard, it must be recalled that the love of neighbor, which is far from one's emotional inclination, is that which turns even the most distant one into our nearest neighbor. Who becomes our nearest neighbor depends on historical situations[41]. Today, I believe, one of our nearest neighbors must be nature, together with the poor.

Finally, one may add that Rahner provides an important motive rooted in the gospels, which can encourage us to practice our concern for nature and the poor in the world where injustice seems to overshadow and overwhelm justice. He points out that «the gospel is always and essentially a gospel of the Cross as well, of the acceptance of failure and death within this world in a spirit of faith and hope». The gospel of the cross may indicate two things in this context. It confirms again the function of the Church and of every Christian as a critic of society. He remarks that although Jesus did not die as a social revolutionary, his death was not merely private. It was «a political event». He died in «a hostile confrontation with the social forces and institutions then prevailing»[42]. Therefore, the discipleship of Jesus the crucified one must not be restricted to a personal realm. It inevitably entails a political character, and in that measure, it is always accompanied by a certain amount of risk. The gospel of the cross in this sense helps us understand soberly what the discipleship of Jesus demands. It does not always assure those who follow him of success, security, or satisfaction. Insofar as the following of Jesus means the following of the crucified Christ in the assent of faith and hope, we must venture to commit ourselves to what is just but also arduous and even dangerous.

---

[40] Cf. K. RAHNER, «Christology».
[41] Cf. K. RAHNER, «Christian Humanism», 188.
[42] K. RAHNER, «The Function», 241.

2. The Compatibility of Ecological Concern and Social Concern from the Perspective of Jürgen Moltmann

2.1 *Introduction*

One can get a glimpse of the stance of Moltmann on the third proposition from his comment on liberation theology: «the perception [...] has begun to make its way in Latin American liberation theology that economy and ecology belong indivisibly together, and that it is suicidal to despoil and consume the foundations on which one's own life is based»[43]. This comment brings to light the inseparable link of destitution to ecological devastation and the significance of ecology as the foundation of humanity's existence. A great number of human beings and nature have been exploited in the current capitalist economic system; injustice and the breakdown of integrity have been inflicted on society and nature respectively. As far as the global capitalist market economy, which enforces the aggressive exploitation of the environment and the poor, prevails in the world, a gap and conflict between the rich and the poor will deepen and the situation of the environment will be aggravated. «Without social justice between the First and the Third Worlds, there will be no peace; and without peace in the world of human beings there will be no liberation of nature»[44]. This view of society and nature corresponds to the biblical perspective that humanity is so intimately related to nature that they influence each other (cf. Gen. 3:17; Hos. 4:1-3). In fact, the human world and the natural world form a dialectical relationship, so that demographic, economic, political, technological, and ideological changes in society affect the natural environment. The resultant change in nature causes further changes in society[45]. It can be said that our way of relating to other human beings influences and is reflected in the way we deal with nature, and *vice versa*. If we conceive other humans primarily as a means by which we may make a profit, this conception is projected on our attitude toward nature. Similarly, insofar as we do not regard and ensure the integrity of nature and continue to view the earth simply as a warehouse of raw

---

43 J. MOLTMANN, *God for a Secular Society*, 63.

44 J. MOLTMANN, *God for a Secular Society*, 95.

45 Cf. C. MERCHANT, *Death of Nature*, 43: «Theories about nature and theories about society have a history of interconnections. A view of nature can be seen as a projection of human perceptions of self and society onto the cosmos. Conversely, theories about nature have historically been interpreted as containing implications about the way individuals or social groups behave or ought to behave».

materials for our sake, we will inevitably be engaged in a struggle to conquer and dominate other humans in order to take «more». Violence in nature leads to violence in society. Justice in society and justice in nature are indispensable to each other. They are essential to peace in the whole world.

In the face of widespread poverty and the environmental degradation of the earth, we must acknowledge that we can resolve neither by means of the economic development that we pursue at present. It is a somber but undeniable fact that the way of living that some in rich countries maintain is not possible for all human beings simply because the earth cannot afford it. Nor is that way of living morally right in the situation that a great number of people are starving. The material affluence of a few in the present situation is only possible at the expense of many. It is but an exploitative affluence. We need an alternative way out of poverty and ecological disruption. «Only a universal 'equalization of burdens' can lead to a common standard of living and a sustainable development»[46]. The natural resources of the earth will soon be depleted if rich countries retain their current way of living and poor countries seek to catch up with them by economic development. In this situation, poverty prevalent in the world must be mitigated through a just distribution of wealth, not through a rapid growth of economy, if the sustainability of nature is to be guaranteed. The alleviation of poverty is also important with regard to the environmental issue. It is known that impoverishment generally leads to over-population because children are the only means of security for the poor[47]. Over-population will deplete available natural resources more rapidly and put more pressure on the global environment. As people are relieved from poverty, the depletion of natural resources is expected to slow down in the long run. We need an international effort and cooperation that will ensure «a universal equalization of burdens» in order to break the vicious cycle of poverty and ecological deterioration.

I will in this section reflect on the significance of the sabbath in Judaeo-Christian tradition, having in mind the ecological devastation of the earth as well as global poverty. I will first consider the sabbath as the anticipatory redemption of creation. On that basis, I will focus on the messianic sabbath, which indicates the redemption of creation. I will then seek to associate Jesus of Nazareth, especially the kingdom of

---

[46] J. MOLTMANN, *God for a Secular Society*, 93.
[47] J. MOLTMANN, *God for a Secular Society*, 94

God that he had in his mind and his ministry, with the messianic sabbath. The kingdom of God and his ministry will take on a cosmic
significance in the light of the messianic sabbath. I will conclude this
reflection with a remark on the discipleship of Jesus grounded in the
messianic sabbath, which will invite us to a commitment to both ecological justice and social justice.

2.2 Creation and the Sabbath

2.2.1 The Sabbath: The Anticipatory Redemption of All Creation

The sabbath, the weekly day of rest and abstinence from work, was a
cornerstone of Jewish religious tradition from earliest times, as shown
in the Pentateuch. In the Old Testament are found two major motives of
the practice of the sabbath: «a memorial of God's resting from the work
of creation» (cf. Gen. 2:1-3); «the need to give servants, strangers, and
work animals an opportunity to rest» (cf. Ex. 23:12; Deut. 5:14-15)[48].
In this regard, the personal, social, and ecological dimensions of the
sabbath can be found. As a personal dimension, the sabbath is «an
excellent therapy for our own restless souls and tense bodies»[49]. On the
sabbath day of every week can we get away from our work and competition with others so that we, as God's creatures, may rest and find
peace in God. It is only in the spirit of the sabbath that we can perceive
and appreciate what we could not do if we were engaged in the restless
pursuit of power and wealth, such as the goodness and beauty of nature
and our affinity with nature as the same creation of God. The sabbath
has a social and ecological dimension as well. The sabbath day, the
sabbath year, and the jubilee year protect the poor, animals, and land
and aim at the liberation of them from abusive exploitation (cf. Ex.
23:10-12; Lev. 25). The sabbath laws provide practical safeguards that
prevent the poor from being abused and periodically grant an opportunity for each one to regain freedom and equality. The sabbath ordinances also have a function to protect the life of land, its fertility,
through the wisdom of fallowing. The spirit of the sabbath aspires to
the liberation and well-being of all creatures.

In relation to creation, the sabbath may be understood as the completion, blessing, and sanctification of creation, and the feast of redemption[50]. In the first creation account of Genesis, although we have al-

---

48 D.A. GLATT-GILAD – J.H. TIGAY, «Sabbath», 954.
49 J. MOLTMANN, God for a Secular Society, 114.
50 Cf. J. MOLTMANN, God in Creation, 276-296.

ready heard that God made everything on the sixth day, we are told again that «on the seventh day God *finished* the work that he had done» (Gen. 1:31-2:2). Given this point, it can be held that the project of creation was not completed with the last creating act of God. Rather, it is in the sabbath rest that it came to completion: «and he rested on the seventh day from all the work that he had done» (Gen. 2:2). It is out of this rest that God blessed and hallowed the sabbath (cf. Gen. 2:3). Moltmann points out that the sabbath as the completion of creation has been overlooked in the Christian tradition of the West. He holds that without the sabbath rest, God is inevitably viewed only as creating God. The God who blesses, sanctifies, rejoices over, and rests in creation recedes in the background and is forgotten. As a result, it is in their work alone that those who regard themselves as the image of God find the ultimate meaning of life. The other important aspects of life that the sabbath indicates, such as rest, joy, and celebration in stillness, are suppressed as useless[51]. It is worth mentioning that God did not bless or hallow specific creatures but the seventh day, i.e., time[52]. Given that time is equally given for all, it implies further that God's blessing and sanctification of the sabbath are for all creatures, not only in the present but also in the future. The sabbath is for the whole creation. It is in the sabbath rest that we can perceive the world as the blessed and sanctified creation of God. Only then can we recognize that God loves and cherishes all creatures.

The sabbath is the feast of the redemption of creation as well that we anticipate at present and celebrate in advance: «creation is aligned towards its redemption from the very beginning; for the creation of the world points to the sabbath»[53]. Creation is destined to salvation because creation is intimately connected with the sabbath. The redemptive character of the sabbath is found in the sabbath ordinances, which seek to manifest and actualize in advance the future redemption to a certain extent. Hence, the sabbath celebrated in the present can be understood as a prefiguration of salvation in the future. It can be said that the feast of redemption is celebrated in anticipation as long as we remain faithful to the spirit of the sabbath. This redemptive aspect of the sabbath brings to light a dynamic perspective on creation. The sabbath as an anticipation of salvation implies that the completion of creation in the sabbath

---

[51] J. MOLTMANN, *God in Creation*, 277.
[52] J. MOLTMANN, *God in Creation*, 281-287.
[53] J. MOLTMANN, *God in Creation*, 5.

must not be understood as its perfection, which would imply a static
view of creation that the cosmos was created once and for all. Rather,
the standpoint of the sabbath as the anticipated future redemption
makes plain that creation is open to the future and in dynamic process
toward its final fulfillment.

The sabbath laws dictate how to maintain and restore the original
order implanted by God in society and nature. The sabbath day ensures
that slaves, aliens, and domestic animals are permitted rest: «you shall
rest, so that your ox and your donkey may have relief, and your home-
born slave and the resident alien may be refreshed» (Exod. 11:12; cf.
Exod. 20:8-11; Deut. 5:12-15). The sabbath year allows land to rest and
enables wild animals as well as the poor to survive: «the seventh year
you shall let it rest and lie fallow, so that the poor of your people may
eat; and what they leave the wild animals may eat». (Exod. 23:11; cf.
Lev. 25:1-7; Deut. 15:1-18). The year of jubilee is a period during
which a more profound restoration of the original order in society and
nature is achieved through rest and the release of debts (cf. Lev. 25:8-
35). Land lies fallow, slaves are released, and original right to one's
property is restored. Jubilee ordinances remind us that the entire creation belongs not to humankind but to God: «the land shall not be sold in
perpetuity, for the land is mine» (Lev. 25:23). The Psalmist sings the
same: «The earth is the Lord's and all this in it» (Ps. 24:1). The spirit of
the sabbath day, the sabbath year, and the jubilee year consists not
simply in rest but in the restoration through the life-giving liberation of
the original good order that God embedded in creation.

We are told that if it obeys the ordinances of God, Israel will be
blessed; otherwise, it will be punished (cf. Lev. 26:3-33). We continue
to hear that these blessings and punishments extend to nature. As long
as Israel holds fast to the divine ordinances, nature will thrive. Otherwise, nature will suffer. As a consequence of Israel's disobedience,
land became desolate and Israelites were scattered. However, this was
precisely for the rest of the land: «Then the land shall enjoy sabbath
years as long as it lies desolate, while you are in the land of your enemies; then the land shall rest» (Lev. 26:34). It is noted that the sabbath
laws share with the prophet Hosea the same intuition and stance on the
intimate connection of social corruption and ecological catastrophe. It
must be remembered, at the same time, that it is not nature but Israel
that suffers and perishes in the end if it is disobedient to God. It seems
to be a stern warning that nature can survive without humanity, but not
vice versa.

2.2.2 The Messianic Sabbath: The Redemption of All Creation

In the sabbath ordinances, a coherent movement toward the just order and liberation of creation is found[54]. The sabbath day points beyond itself to the sabbath year; the sabbath year to the jubilee year. The extent of liberation that one expects is intensified and broadened as one proceeds from the sabbath day to the sabbath year to the year of jubilee. At the same time, the sabbath norms, which are periodically applied in its own cycle of seven days, seven years, and fifty years, signify that neither the removal of exploitation nor the perfection of liberation in the world is achieved once and for all. The perfect liberation of creation, which the sabbath alone cannot bring forth, calls forth in us a craving for the messianic sabbath which will achieve the redemption of creation: «this sabbatical year, in its turn, points in history beyond itself to the future of the messianic era»[55].

The messianic era can be rendered as «new heavens and a new earth» where even the carnivorous and herbivorous animals live together in peace, as the prophet Isaiah proclaimed (Isa. 65:17; cf. Isa. 65:25; 11:6-9). The messianic vision calls for the messianic mission in order that this vision may come true. Hence, Isaiah also announced: «The spirit of the Lord God is upon me, [...] he has sent me to bring good news to the oppressed, to bind up the brokenhearted, to proclaim liberty to the captives, and release to the prisoners; to proclaim the year of the Lord's favor» (Isa. 61: 1-2a). This is what Isaiah envisaged to occur in the world as the messianic era comes. He proclaimed the liberation of all in affliction such as the oppressed, the brokenhearted, the captives, and the prisoners. What he envisioned is the fulfillment of what the jubilee laws dictate. It is the messianic sabbath and the redemption of all creation.

Given that the messianic sabbath indicates the redemption of creation, which began in Jesus of Nazareth, how can Jesus and the messianic sabbath be related to each other? It can be claimed first that Jesus is closely linked to the messianic sabbath and thus to all creation, not only to human beings. We are told that Jesus took up the passage of the prophet Isaiah above and read it (cf. Luke 4:16-19). This act of Jesus is

---

[54] It is in fact doubtful whether the laws of the sabbath year and jubilee have ever been put into practice. Nevertheless, the sabbath tradition is still of great significance in that it provides a model of ecological justice and social justice with a redemptive character. See R.R. RUETHER, *Gaia and God*, 213.

[55] J. MOLTMANN, *God in Creation*, 6.

of great significance in conceiving how Jesus is related to the messianic sabbath: «It was with the proclamation of the messianic sabbath that the public ministry of Jesus of Nazareth began»[56]. If we see this scene, which can be viewed as the inauguration of his public ministry, in the light of the messianic sabbath, the horizon and significance of his life is opened up to the entire creation. This suggests that we must consider his ministry from the standpoint of the messianic sabbath if it is to be properly understood. Meanwhile, it is also the case that we must place his ministry in the context of the kingdom of God if it is to be integrally grasped. For God's kingdom is the centerpiece of his whole life, at least according to the synoptic gospels[57]. The kingdom of God is the ultimate cause and goal which guided his ministerial activities and accorded them a coherent significance. It can be held, therefore, that there is an intimate association of the messianic sabbath on the one hand, and God's kingdom and Jesus on the other hand.

2.3 Creation and Jesus

2.3.1 The Kingdom of God:
The Fulfillment of the Messianic Sabbath for All Creation

Jesus proclaimed the good news of the kingdom of God: «The time is fulfilled, and the kingdom of God has come near; repent, and believe in the good news». (Mark 1:15). However, this passage alone does not deliver clearly to us what God's kingdom means. What is particularly ambiguous is the phrase of «has come near», because it is not clear whether this phrase indicates the present or near future[58]. To understand properly what the kingdom of God was to Jesus, how he understood it,

---

[56] J. MOLTMANN, *God in Creation*, 6; Cf. *Ibid.*, 290-292.

[57] Cf. J.P. MEIER, *A Marginal Jew*, II, 238. According to Meier, the significance of the kingdom of God in Jesus' life is demonstrated simply by «the number and spread of occurrence of the phrase in the sayings of Jesus». See also J. FUELLENBACH, *The Kingdom of God*, 4: «The kingdom is not only the central theme of Jesus' preaching, the reference point of most of his parables, and the subject of a large number of his sayings, it is also the content of his symbolic actions». The word «kingdom» is the traditional English translation of *basileia* in Greek. It may give a false impression or inaccurate idea of the kingdom as a territory or a space. However, another English translation «reign» indicates that the kingdom of God must be understood as a dynamic notion rather than as a static one, although it does not exclude the latter completely. Some avoid the expression of «kingdom» because it is a masculine and monarchical term.

[58] Cf. M.D. HOOKER, *The Gospel according to Saint Mark*, 55-58.

and why he dedicated himself to it, we must consider his teachings and remarks concerning it, which are scattered in the synoptic gospels[59]. This is also true of the ambivalent, temporal character of God's kingdom. The Lord's Prayer makes clear, for example, that Jesus understood God's kingdom as a reality in the future. He taught his disciples to pray that God's kingdom come to the earth (cf. Matt. 6:10). Jesus' saying at the Last Supper is another important evidence for the future kingdom: «I will never again drink of the fruit of the vine until that day when I drink it new in the kingdom of God» (Mark 14:25). Sensing his imminent doom, Jesus expressed his hope that he would drink wine in the kingdom to come in the future. We must not fail, however, to give heed to the fact that God's kingdom is a reality in the present as well. Jesus emphasized that the kingdom has already been mediated to this world and become tangible through him: «But if it is by the finger of God that I cast out the demons, then the kingdom of God has come to you» (Luke 11:20). The act that Jesus cast out demons by God's power signifies that God's kingdom has already begun to affect this world. In another occasion, Jesus answered: «in fact, the kingdom of God is among you» (Luke 17:21). God's kingdom is not like a kingdom in the world. It is not so much a static or spatial reality as a dynamic reality. It is the reign of God «among us» in this world. It can then be said that the kingdom of God is a reality which is already active in the present and will be fulfilled in the future. The kingdom of God «has come so close that the signs of the messianic era are already visible: the sick are healed, demons are driven out, the lame walk, the deaf hear, the poor

---

[59] Cf. J. FUELLENBACH, *Kingdom of God*, 25; J.P. MEIER, *A Marginal Jew*, II, 243-52. Given that Jesus too was a man of his age, it can be held that he must have shared what his contemporaries had in mind regarding the kingdom of God. Although the term «the kingdom of God» itself is rarely found in the Old Testament, the image is deeply rooted in it and Israel's history. See also D.J. HARRINGTON, «Kingdom of God», 509. Harrington suggests a perspective on the kingdom of God that a first-century Jew might have had: «a new heaven and a new earth where goodness and justice will prevail», «God's future display of power and judgment», and «the final establishment of God's rule over all creation». This notion of God's kingdom is predominantly future-oriented. Despite certain continuity with his contemporaries, we must not overlook the uniqueness which Jesus had about God's kingdom. Jesus was different in critical points from the Pharisees, the Zealots, the Essenes, and other apocalyptic movements of his day. For instance, Jesus affirmed the involvement of this world in God's kingdom, while the Essenes had a completely negative view of this world and insisted on withdrawal from it. See also J. FUELLENBACH, *Kingdom of God*, 67.

have the gospel preached to them»[60]. All these events are the signs of God's kingdom in this world, which is already active but not fulfilled yet.

It is well known that Jesus used parables to illustrate the kingdom of God. These kingdom parables give us important clues to understand God's kingdom properly. The parables of the mustard seed and yeast, for example, reveal both the present and future dimensions of God's kingdom: «It is like a mustard seed that someone took and sowed in the garden; it grew and became a tree, and the birds of the air made nests in its branches»; «It is like yeast that a woman took and mixed in with three measures of flour until all of it was leavened» (Luke 13: 19, 20). They imply that God's kingdom will end up in greatness (in the future), though it looks tiny now (in the present). Insofar as its completion is concerned, the kingdom is a reality in the future; insofar as it is «sown» and «mixed», it is a reality in the present. Both aspects of «already» and «not yet» must be retained in God's kingdom. God's kingdom is not an entire, otherworldly reality. Nor can it be identical with this world. Instead, we must perceive that God's kingdom is already present in this world and transforms it gradually. The kingdom, as a mustard seed, is sown in the field (this world) and grows out of it. The kingdom, as yeast, is mixed in with flour (this world) and leavens it. God's kingdom is the power of God that transforms creation and brings it to completion. It must be noted that these parables emphasize the significance of this world in relation to God's kingdom.

The parables which Jesus used in order to illustrate who God is are also important to understand the kingdom of God that he envisioned. For they help us conceive concretely how God reigns. They highlight God's forgiving love for all and special concern for the vulnerable. The parables of the lost sheep, lost coin, and lost son tell us that God is the God of the sinners and the least (cf. Luke 15). The episode of the owner and workers in the vineyard presents the God who provides everyone with what is necessary to live as the human being (cf. Matt. 20:1-16). The story of the Good Samaritan challenges us to practice love beyond all discrimination, racism, and prejudice (cf. Luke 10:25-37). The story of the last judgment even identifies God with the least one (cf. Matt. 25:31-46). The Old Testament as a whole is in fact a testimony to this God, who is love: God always forgives the Israelites who break the covenant and wants them to come back to the divine loving care; at the

---

[60] J. MOLTMANN, *The Way of Jesus*, 97.

same time, God cares in a special manner for the widow, the orphan, and the foreigner.

How can we conceive of God's kingdom where this God reigns? One thing that can be conjectured from the kingdom parables is that no one will be alienated in the kingdom of God. Every creature will become what it is meant to be and enjoy perfect communion with other creatures and God. The messianic sabbath renders this still vague and abstract picture of God's kingdom in concrete and vivid expressions: «the laws of the year of liberty contain a programme for a complete social reform, designed to do away with indebtedness and enslavement among the people, and to end the exploitation of the earth»[61]. With the prohibition of the excessive use of land, the social reform of jubilee turns into the ecological reform. The divine peace and joy will prevail in creation with the fulfillment of the messianic sabbath, as the prophet Isaiah envisioned (cf. Isa. 61:1-4; 65:17-25). At the same time, the kingdom of God discloses some hidden aspects of the messianic sabbath. The present and future dimensions of God's kingdom call to mind that the messianic sabbath is not what is achieved once and for all nor is it completely a future reality. These two temporal dimensions show that the messianic sabbath is already brought into effect due to the presence of God in this world through Jesus, although it will be fulfilled in the future. The complete actualization of the messianic sabbath and the perfect liberation of all creation will be achieved in the coming kingdom of God. The kingdom of God is the fulfillment of the messianic sabbath for all creation, while the ministry of Jesus is its mediation to all.

2.3.2 The Ministry of Jesus:
The Mediation of the Messianic Sabbath to All Creation

The ministry of Jesus as a whole can be grasped differently according to the two temporal dimensions of God's kingdom. As far as its future dimension is concerned, his ministry is a visible indication of the kingdom of God which is to come. It is «the fore-tokens of the all-comprehensive salvation, the unscathed world, and the glory of God»[62]. However, insofar as its present dimension is concerned, it is the mediation of the kingdom of God to this world. It makes God's kingdom present here and now, imperfect as it is. This aspect is

---

[61] J. MOLTMANN, *The Way of Jesus Christ*, 120.
[62] J. MOLTMANN, *The Way of Jesus Christ*, 107.

disclosed by what Jesus replied to the disciples of John the Baptist: «the blind receive their sight, the lame walk, the lepers are cleansed, the deaf hear, the dead are raised, the poor have good news brought to them» (cf. Luke 7:22). All these occurrences can be understood as the transformation of the present world in virtue of God's reign mediated to this world through Jesus. What must be noted is that the messianic vision was being realized through him. Hence, he was mediating the reign of God to this world to the extent that he brought the messianic vision into effect. We can understand in the same context Jesus' saying: «this scripture has been fulfilled in your hearing» (Luke 4:21). The messianic sabbath was already occurring in this world by virtue of him, although it was not perfect yet. In short, the present dimension of God's kingdom informs us that Jesus' ministry has a real significance and effect in this world. It is not only a sign that points to the coming kingdom of God. It influences the world; it transforms the world. One can assert, moreover, that in the light of the messianic sabbath, the influence and transformation of God's reign reach all creation, both human and nonhuman.

The ministry of Jesus, like the kingdom of God, reveals a cosmic significance when it is viewed in the light of the messianic sabbath. Put otherwise, his ministerial activities such as healing, exorcism, and the fellowship with the outcast, seen in the context of the messianic sabbath, take on a cosmic importance in relation to deteriorating nature. We must recall again the passage of the prophet Isaiah that Jesus read. It can be supposed that Jesus, as a Jew, was aware of what this passage means. What he proclaimed is «the year of the Lord's favor», which can be interpreted as the jubilee year, the supreme moment of the sabbath tradition[63]. The benefit of jubilee is meant for the whole creation as well as for humanity. Therefore, it can rightly be expected that Jesus' public ministry ultimately aims, at least implicitly, at the liberation of the whole creation as well. It includes both humankind and nature.

Those who were sick and possessed by evil spirits must be understood as part of the marginalized in society. We are told that the sick became healed and demons were cast out in the presence of Jesus. They went back to their community and found themselves accepted (cf. Mark 1:43-44). They became who they were meant to be as God's creatures.

---

[63] Cf. R.J. KARRIS, «The Gospel According to Luke», 690; L.T. JOHNSON, *The Gospel of Luke*, 79.

Alienation was ended, and their relationship with others was restored. It can be said, analogously, that today nature is sick due to humanity's violent exploitation. The healing act in the light of the messianic sabbath suggests that nature too needs healing so that it can recover its integrity. Jesus enjoyed abiding and eating with the outcast or the sinners (cf. Matt. 9:7-13; Luke 19:1-10). They were denied dignity as the human being. In this regard, his table fellowship with them can be regarded as a healing act. It tore down the alienation which had dehumanized them and gave them back a sense of the human being. They were healed in this process of reconciliation. Alienation was ended, and their human dignity was regained. It can be said, analogously, that today nature is denied its due regard and degenerated into a warehouse of material resources. The table fellowship in the perspective of the messianic sabbath indicates that nature too must be given due regard so that it can regain its value inherent in itself. The horizon of the messianic sabbath opens up the scope of Jesus' ministry to the entire creation: «When Jesus expels demons and heals the sick, he is driving out of creation the powers of destruction»[64]. In the same context, one can say that when he accepts the outcast and shares a meal with them, he infuses into creation the divine power of reconciliation. A case can now be made that the ministry of Jesus inspired with the vision of the messianic sabbath encompasses the whole creation, not only human beings.

The kingdom of God in the context of the messianic sabbath provides a sweeping perspective on the world from which we can grasp the intrinsic connection of humanity with nature and seek the integral liberation of all creation. The ministry of Jesus in the context of the messianic sabbath stimulates us to widen to all creation his option for the marginalized. The messianic sabbath, which Jesus sought to mediate through his ministerial activities to the world, is a breakthrough of a deep-rooted vicious circle of both the impoverishment of human beings and the exploitation of nature. Therefore, ecological justice and social justice will be fulfilled in the kingdom of God where the messianic sabbath is realized. What will finally sprout is God's peace among people and the earth[65]. The entire creation will be replete with the divine peace (cf. Isa. 2:4; 11:1-9; 65:17-24; Mi. 4:3-4). This is an eschatological picture of the world for which Jesus strove through his

---

[64] J. MOLTMANN, *The Way of Jesus Christ*, 98, 104.
[65] Cf. J. MOLTMANN, *The Way of Jesus Christ*, 121.

ministry, rooted in the power of God's kingdom and inspired by the vision of the messianic sabbath.

2.3.3 The Discipleship of Jesus: The Practice of the Messianic Sabbath to All Creation

Christians, as his disciples, are invited to follow the path that Jesus trod. Since he lived and acted in the spirit of the messianic sabbath, his discipleship too consists in the realization of the messianic sabbath in the world. The messianic discipleship is grounded in the presence of God's kingdom in this world as the transforming power of the world. Insofar as God's kingdom grows in this world, those who follow the way of Jesus are asked to contribute to the actualization of the messianic sabbath in this world. It is true that God initiates, manages, and will complete the kingdom of God. After all, it is the kingdom *of God*. As it is the earth that grows the seed, it is God who grows the kingdom (cf. Mark 4:26-29). It is God's enterprise and gift to us.

We must not forget, however, that we have our own task to accomplish. «It is God's work and gracious gift, but our actions on earth make a difference. [...] The content, the color, the design, will have our imprint since it will be made out of our history»[66]. Insofar as God's kingdom grows through the transformation of the world, our way of living and acting in this world make a difference. Our effort to change this world is of great significance to the kingdom of God. However, this task demands from us a radical change and firm resolution, here and now (cf. Matt. 13:44-45). We must renounce our old way of living, which may contribute to sustaining the current unjust socio-economic systems, which have enforced affliction on humans and nonhuman creation. We are challenged to choose a new way of living which can ensure justice and peace for the entire creation. For this, we need a radical change from the depth of our heart, because not a few of us are the very beneficiaries of the present unjust systems. Jesus demanded too that people repent first and then believe in the good news of God's kingdom (cf. Mark 1:15). Without a profound conversion to God, who wants the liberation of all creatures, we cannot relinquish our benefit which is attained at the cost of others. Nor can we select God's kingdom for the sake of all creation.

If we are to live and act in the spirit of the messianic sabbath that Jesus proclaimed, we must explore, opt for, and practice an alternative

---

66 J. FUELLENBACH, *The Kingdom of God*, 203.

to the present socio-economic system that does not ensure justice and sustainability to humans and nature respectively. Not a few recognize that the current global capitalist economy is sustained by the exploitation of a great number of people and at the expense of global ecology, only to satisfy the interests of a few. Nonetheless, only a few have the courage to denounce and reject it. Most of us accept this system simply as a given condition and adapt ourselves to it rather than confront and change it. But it is precisely an unyielding confrontation with unjust social forces and institutions that put Jesus to death on the cross. Jesus is an exemplar par excellence in holding fast to and practicing the spirit of the messianic sabbath and in mediating the kingdom of God to the world, in the midst of hostility. He recognized that his society was opposed to the spirit of the messianic sabbath, which stems from God's loving will for all creatures. He refused submitting himself to the unjust structure of the day. Instead, he opted for a radically different way of living which the messianic vision mandated and remained faithful to it to the end. He chose to stand on the side of the poor, the sick, the possessed, and the outcast.

If we are those who follow Jesus the crucified one, the way that led him to the cross must be our way as well. We must reveal by our radical rejection the unjust and violent character of the present socio-economic system to both humanity and nature. At the same time, we must explore and adopt an alternative way of living which presents and seeks alternative values and goal in accordance with the spirit of the messianic sabbath. We must live out this alternative so that it may spread over the world and transform it gradually. In this regard, the messianic discipleship must be practiced in two opposite directions. The first one is a radical distinction from this world[67]. The messianic discipleship must proclaim the kingdom of God and show a right direction to God's kingdom by distancing itself from this world and rendering itself a tangible reality of God's kingdom in the world. It is, in this sense, «the light of the world» (Matt. 5:14). The second one is an active insertion into the world to change it. The messianic discipleship must seek to embody the messianic sabbath and thereby contribute to the transformation of this world into God's kingdom. It must commit itself to the heart of this world in order to change it radically. It is, in

---

[67] Cf. J. MOLTMANN, *The Way of Jesus Christ*, 122: «It is a "contrast society," and through its existence it calls in question the systems of violence and injustice». For contrast (counter) society, see G. LOHFINK, *Jesus and Community*, 122-131.157-162.

this sense, «the salt of the earth» (Matt. 5:13). We Christians, who live in the spirit of the messianic discipleship, must be both the light and salt of the world until the messianic sabbath is fully actualized and thus God's kingdom is fulfilled.

3. The Compatibility of Ecological Concern and Social Concern from the Perspective of Leonardo Boff

3.1 *Introduction*

Liberation theology can find a strong motive to address the ecological crisis in the fact that the poor bear most of the burden of ecological disruption. «Eco-ethical concerns, because the fate of the poor and their land are interwoven, are, then, part of the fabric of liberation theology»[68]. In this sense, it can be said that the ecological concern of liberation theology always appears in the context of its concern for the poor: «enforced poverty and the subjugation of peoples are bound up with an assault on the natural environment»[69]. As Boff points out, liberation theology and ecological discourses begin with «the cry of the poor for life, freedom, and beauty (cf. Ex. 3:7), and the cry of the Earth groaning under oppression (cf. Rom 8:22-23)»[70]. Both the poor and the earth are under oppression, and to that measure, they are longing for liberation. Hence, liberation theology is particularly concerned about the common root of poverty and environmental degradation observed in the life of the poor: the oppression of the powerless by the powerful[71].

One may arrive at the same stance on the poor and nature from an integrated anthropological perspective that the human being is a being in nature as well as a personal and social being. It can be held from this standpoint that human liberation in a genuine sense must not consider only the personal and social dimensions of the human being. It must

---

[68] P. SMITH, *What are They*, 58.

[69] P. SMITH, *What are They*, 58.

[70] L. BOFF, *Cry*, 104.

[71] Deep ecology and ecofeminism, two influential environmental thoughts, have since long disputed concerning what is primarily responsible for the present ecological crisis: anthropocentrism and androcentrism, respectively (a more detailed account of the debate between deep ecology and ecofeminism will be given in the fourth section of this chapter). However, in a sense, liberation theology is in accord with both of them: liberation theologians «have in common with deep ecologists an attentiveness to the manner in which human hubris impacts nonhuman creation»; and with ecofeminist, «they share the recognition that systems of oppression wreak multivalent ill effects». See P. SMITH, *What Are They*, 57.

also take account of its cosmic dimension. Human liberation is not confined to the material, social, or purely spiritual realms[72]. Insofar as the integrity of nature is not ensured, a genuine liberation of the human being will not be attained. For the human being, as part of nature, is meant to live in constant interaction with it. Boff maintains that liberation theology has been aware of this point from the outset: «It has been the merit of liberation theology to have maintained its comprehensive scope since its origins; it did so because it was correctly interpreting what human liberation is about [...]»[73]. In this regard, «liberation theology and ecological discourse need each other and are mutually complementary»[74].

Given this intimate connection of poverty and ecological deterioration, I will in this section examine what perspective is attained if we view the present, global ecological disruption of the world from the vantage point of liberation theology. For this, we need first to look at a method and process of liberation theology, which is divided, according to Boff, into three stages of socio-analytical, hermeneutical, and practical mediations. I will take up the Amazon region, as he describes it, as a concrete social reality to which socio-analytical and hermeneutical mediations are applied. I will then hold that an emerging perspective on nature and the poor shows that one and the same logic is at work both in poverty and ecological disaster and that concern for nature and the poor are not conflicting but compatible. Finally, I will consider in the same context the notion of sustainable development. A conclusion will be drawn that sustainability and development are not compatible but conflicting insofar as the current, predominant conception of development is retained.

3.2 The Process of Liberation Theology: Socio-analytical, Hermeneutical, and Practical Mediations

In his methodological account of liberation theology, Boff stresses that what comes first is practice (experience) and then theological discourses (theory) follow it[75]. Liberation theology is rooted in and

---

[72] Cf. L. BOFF, *Cry*, 108.

[73] L. BOFF, *Cry*, 108.

[74] L. BOFF, *Cry*, 114.

[75] Cf. L. BOFF – C. BOFF, *Introducing Liberation Theology*, 22-23. It can be held that this remark applies not only to liberation theology in particular but to theology in general in the sense that theology seeks to express faith experience of believers in precise and theoretical terms.

starts with life in faith with the poor. Only then the concrete realities of the poor are brought into view and reflected upon in the light of faith. Liberation theology comes to a conclusion which provides a proper response to a given situation by means of observations and reflections illuminated by faith. The process of liberation theology can be divided into «three basic stages, which correspond to the three traditional stages involved in pastoral work: seeing, judging and acting»[76]. In sum, liberation theology starts with practice and leads again to practice.

Boff calls these three stages socio-analytical mediation, hermeneutical mediation, and practical mediation respectively.

Socio-analytical (or historico-analytical) mediation operates in the sphere of the world of the oppressed. It tries to find out why the oppressed are oppressed. Hermeneutical mediation operates in the sphere of God's world. It tries to discern what God's plan is for the poor. Practical mediation operates in the sphere of action. It tries to discover the courses of action that need to be followed so as to overcome oppression in accordance with God's plan[77].

First, socio-analytical mediation is the stage of reading, analyzing, and interpreting a social reality in which the poor live in order to know the cause of their poverty and suffering. It is also called historico-analytical mediation since «this approach focuses on the poor not only in their present situation, but as the end-product of a long process of plunder and social marginalization»[78]. A social reality at a given moment has its own history. Different kinds of method can be employed for the analysis of a concrete social reality[79]. Liberation theology seeks by means of social analysis to arrive at a deeper grasp of a social reality[80]. As a consequence, liberation theology understands poverty as an outcome of oppression, not of individual laziness or underdevelopment: «poverty as the product of the economic organization of society itself, which *exploits* some – the workers – and *excludes* others from the production process – the underemployed, unemployed, and all those marginalized»[81]. This understanding of poverty alludes to conflicts and struggles

---

76 L. BOFF – C. BOFF, *Introducing Liberation Theology*, 24. See also L. BOFF, Cry, 109-110, where Boff adds another element of celebrating as the last stage.

77 L. BOFF – C. BOFF, *Introducing Liberation Theology*, 24.

78 L. BOFF – C. BOFF, *Introducing Liberation Theology*, 27.

79 Cf. L. BOFF – C. BOFF, *Introducing Liberation Theology*, 25-27: Boff presents three types of analysis: empirical, functional, and dialectical explanations. See also L. BOFF, *Salvation and Liberation*, 6-7.

80 A.F. MCGOVERN, *Liberation Theology and Its Critics*, 121.

81 L. BOFF – C. BOFF, *Introducing Liberation Theology*, 26.

between those who possess capital and means of production, on the one hand, and those who provide labor, on the other hand. At the same time, liberation theology comprehends poverty as a structural problem that can be resolved only through the introduction of an alternative to the present socio-economic system[82]. The stage of social analysis provides material for hermeneutical mediation.

Second, hermeneutical mediation is the stage of reading in the light of faith the material that is provided by socio-analytical mediation. It is a theological interpretation of «a text – in this case, the socio-analytical "text" of reality»[83]. How can socio-economic material be interpreted theologically? This is what theology, as a reflection on faith experience, must carry out. It must be noted that faith does not add any theological material to a given socio-economic reality. Rather, faith enables us to see and grasp in a given social reality a hidden theological significance and implication[84]. «It is the task of Christian reflection to unveil and extract this hidden theological element, to bring it to the light of day in reflection, in liturgical celebration, in an expression of prayer»[85]. In this phase, a socio-economic reality is interpreted in the light of faith. This is a theologizing phase of an analyzed social reality. For example, a social structure which enables the excessive accumulation of wealth by a few and produces mass poverty may be regarded as a sinful situation through the eyes of faith in God, who loves all human beings[86]. Hermeneutics occurs in the reverse direction as well. In other words, the Christian tradition is read and interpreted in the context of a social reality from which the poor suffer, such as poverty and oppression. For instance, a reading of the Bible through the eyes of the oppressed may inspire a new insight or interpretation[87].

---

[82] Cf. L. BOFF – C. BOFF, *Introducing Liberation Theology*, 26-27. It is in socio-analytical mediation that liberation theology comes into contact with and employs various theories of social analysis such as Marxist analysis and dependency theory. It must be remembered, however, that liberation theology adopts social analysis theories purely as an instrument for social analysis: «liberation theology freely borrows from Marxism certain "methodological pointers" that have proved fruitful in understanding the world of the oppressed, [...] Liberation theology, therefore, maintains a decidedly critical stance in relation to Marxism» (*Ibid.*, 28).

[83] L. BOFF, *Salvation and Liberation*, 9.

[84] L. BOFF, *Salvation and Liberation*, 55.

[85] L. BOFF, *Salvation and Liberation*, 17.

[86] Cf. L. BOFF, *Salvation and Liberation*, 9.

[87] Cf. L. BOFF – C. BOFF, *Introducing Liberation Theology*, 32-33.

Third, practical mediation is the stage that leads back to a practice that is efficacious to a given situation[88]. There are many factors in this stage that must be considered in order that actions may be effective: «A decision as to what is *historically viable* [...]»; «Defining one's *strategy and tactics* [...]»; «Drawing up a *program* (blue print) for action», and so forth[89]. This stage is extremely complex because every element depends on a specific circumstance. It needs prudence and resolution based on experiences. This final stage of liberation theology goes beyond the scope of this study and will not be dealt with. This must be discussed and determined by those who are engaged in specific issues in their own concrete circumstances.

In a nutshell, liberation theology starts with practice and ends with practice. Practice in faith (praxis) leads one to do reflection in faith (theology), and the latter in turn stimulates one to commit oneself to the former. This does not mean, however, that faith can be reduced merely to practice by action or reflection by reason. There is in faith another element that comes from the depth of one's heart, which may be expressed as celebration, praise, petition, and worship. Faith touches the whole of one's being in front of the absolute Being. Faith includes as its most critical part the contemplation and celebration of the divine. Therefore, liberation theology must lead one «up to the Temple. And from the Temple it leads back once more to the practice of history, now equipped with all the divine and divinizing powers of the Mystery of the world»[90]. Action without heart would be but militant; reflection without heart would be but speculative. And faith would wither eventually. Practice and theology must be nourished by the celebration of faith.

3.3 *Liberation Theology and the Ecological Crisis*

3.3.1 Socio-analytical Mediation

What is the present world like in which we live? Socio-analytical mediation seeks an answer to this question. It can hardly be denied that poverty is pervasive today all over the world as well as in poor countries. Drawing on various socio-analytical methods, liberation theologians seek to arrive at the root of poverty. An oft-quoted social analysis theory is «dependency theory». Dependency theory was developed as a

---

[88] L. BOFF – C. BOFF, *Introducing Liberation Theology*, 39-41; L. BOFF, *Salvation and Liberation*, 11-12.
[89] L. BOFF – C. BOFF, *Introducing Liberation Theology*, 40.
[90] L. BOFF – C. BOFF, *Introducing Liberation Theology*, 39.

reaction to the so-called modernization model or developmentalism, which had been presented to overcome poverty in Latin America after World War II[91].

> If the developed nations of the center are to keep up their pace of development and their level of goods, they must keep the peripheral nations in a state of dependence in order to extract what they need for their own affluence. There are many reasons for our underdevelopment [...] But the decisive factor is the system of dependence, which comes down to oppression and domination. It is internalized in the various peripheral countries with the help of those who represent the imperial center[92].

Dependency theory comprehends the whole economic order of the world primarily in terms of domination, oppression, and exploitation, which center countries impose on periphery countries. «Through various mechanisms (unequal exchange, foreign debt, transnational corporate profit remittances and brain drain), the productive surplus from the

---

[91] Cf. A.F. MCGOVERN, *Liberation Theology and Its Critics*, 118. Dependency theory is known to have originated in United Nations Economic Commission on Latin America and its director Raul Prebisch after World War II. Diverse versions of dependency theory based on «center-periphery» conception developed, mainly according to the respective importance of external (center) and internal (periphery) factors. For instance, some may place the entire blame on the center countries, while some others may regard internal factors in periphery countries as significant as external ones. The relationship of liberation theology to dependency theory is different according to periods and individual theologians. Many liberation theologians, including Gustavo Gutiérrez, adopted dependency theory at the outset. However, for example, Gutiérrez mentioned clearly in 1988 that dependency theory is no longer an adequate tool, because «it does not take sufficient account of the internal dynamics of each country or of the vast dimensions of the world of the poor» (G. GUTIÉRREZ, *A Theology of Liberation*, xxiv). Boff also expressed his own reserved and nuanced attitude to dependency theory, although he agreed basically with what dependency theory points out in regard to massive poverty in Latin America: «It is only a theory, not an established truth. It is one stage in an ongoing investigation and has its own intrinsic limitations. It offers a good diagnosis of the structure of underdevelopment, but it does not do much to offer any viable way out» (L. BOFF, *Liberating Grace*, 66). Despite its limitations such as ideological factors that impede scientific understanding of social reality, excessively simplistic hypotheses of center-peripheries, and its lack of capability to present a solution, one can still hold that dependency theory made a contribution to disclose the structural dimension of poverty in the world. In this section, dependency theory will be regarded simply as one of social analysis theories adopted by liberation theologians, particularly by Boff. For an exposition of dependency theory (and also Marxist analysis) in the context of liberation theology, see A.F. MCGOVERN, *Liberation Theology and Its Critics*, 105-176.

[92] L. BOFF, *Jesus Christ Liberator*, 276.

periphery is systematically extracted by the core countries to further their development at the expense of development of the periphery»[93]. According to dependency theory, unlike the claim of developmentalism, poverty is not a state of underdevelopment. Nor can it be alleviated or eradicated by development. «Underdevelopment is the reverse side of [...] development and a consequence of it. It is the product of development as conceived in capitalistic terms»[94]. In this economic structure of the world, the underdevelopment of poor countries contributes to the development of affluent countries; the latter presupposes and demands the former. It is not true, from this standpoint, that poverty can be overcome by personal effort alone without a fundamental change of the socio-economic structure that produces both development (affluence) and underdevelopment (poverty). Dependency theory holds that poverty can be eradicated only through a substantial change in the exploitative economic structure of the world. It emphasizes the necessity of fundamental change in the socio-economic order of the world, which will be accompanied by conflict between the rich and the poor. Notwithstanding controversy surrounding validity in its details, dependency theory reveals that massive destitution has at the core an undeniable structural cause and that the present mode of development cannot liberate the poor from destitution.

Insofar as nature is concerned, the exploitative structure of the current world economy has contributed to the global ecological crisis and will continue to aggravate it. A structural assault, i.e., what Boff refers to as «a form of socio-economic and political violence», has been made on nature as well as on a great majority of people in the world[95]. Both capitalism and socialism are to blame for the deterioration of the environment due to the obsession of economic development: «All modernity, in both free-market-capitalist or Marxist-socialist variants, lives on this common assumption: it is imperative to grow, expand markets, and fill them with goods and services»[96]. «Both these models of society have broken with the Earth. They have reduced it to a supply of raw materials and natural resources»[97]. Capitalism now seems to dominate the entire economic order of the world, as socialism has virtually dis-

---

[93] This is quoted from www.uap.vt.edu/classes/uap4764/session5.htm, the website of Urban Affairs & Planning, Virginia Polytechnic Institute & State University.

[94] L. BOFF, *Jesus Christ Liberator*, 276.

[95] L. BOFF, *Ecology and Liberation*, 27.

[96] L. BOFF, *Cry*, 67.

[97] L. BOFF, *Cry*, 68.

appeared, at least as an institutional form of economy. The current version of capitalism can be regarded as a global capitalist economy characterized by the global market, which is dominated and manipulated by enormous multinational companies and transnational capital. The economic growth propelled by the current process of globalization will never provide a way out of poverty and environmental degradation, because it is predominantly biased to the pursuit of profits of those who possess capital at the expense of the poor and nature[98].

I will take up the Amazon region as a concrete locus to see what impact market capitalist economy brings about to the people and the natural habitat of this region and how it takes place[99]. Let us briefly follow Boff to get an idea of what the Amazon is. The Amazon is the largest nature reserve, or more specifically, the largest tropical rain forest on the planet: its total size is estimated as «2.5 million square miles»; «three-fifths of the area of Brazil» is covered by the Amazon; and «the Amazon River is the longest river in the world, 2,200 miles»[100]. What is the Amazon? Boff seeks first to strip the Amazon of two myths. The first myth is that the Amazon is «the *lungs of the world*». Instead, the oxygen produced in the plants of the Amazon by day is consumed by these plants and other living organisms because it is in a state of «dynamic equilibrium». It does function, however, as a «large carbon dioxide filter», absorbing in the process of photo-synthesis a great amount of carbon, which is regarded as the main cause of the greenhouse effect of the planet. Without the Amazon, therefore, «there would be mass death of live organisms»[101]. The second myth is that the Amazon is «the *storehouse of the world*», which is not true, either. «The forest remains lush because the chain of nutrients is closed». The Amazon region is based on complex and fragile balance. The topsoil is very shallow. «It is not the soil that nourishes the leaves, but rather the trees that nourish the soil». Without the forest, therefore, «the Amazon could become a huge grassland or even a desert». In short,

---

[98] It can be held that dependency theory is valid in the present situation, at least in a macroscopic sense, to the extent that wealth is accumulated in the hands of a few by means of globalized, exploitative market mechanisms.

[99] Cf. L. BOFF, *Cry*, 86-103.

[100] L. BOFF, *Cry*, 87.

[101] L. BOFF, *Cry*, 90.

the Amazon is not the storehouse of the world. Instead, it can and must remain as «the temple of the greatest biodiversity on the planet»[102].

Boff remarks that the greatest threat to the Amazon is deforestation by means of clear cutting and burning. It actually happened in the Brazilian Amazon, for example, to export trees in the form of charcoal, to grow foreign plants which bring short-term profit, to develop mines, and to construct dams for the production of hydroelectric power. At the heart of these projects are the Brazilian government, Brazilian and multinational companies, i.e., an oppressive political regime and exploitative economic powers. Deforestation in this region has made rapid progress. A large influx of foreign laborers into various projects resulted in ruining the life of indigenous peoples, causing vast poverty among new settlers, and devastating the natural environment[103].

Boff presents the Grande Carjas Project as a representative of many projects in the Amazon. This project is for mining, agro-industries, and tree farming. It was headed by a large state-owned company and multinational mining companies including the U.S.A., Japan, Canada, and so forth. The oil crisis in 1972 forced these countries to look for another place where basic metal such as aluminum could be produced at low cost. The Amazon was an excellent alternative location due to its abundant resources, cheap labor force, and geological advantage for transportation. There is also another advantageous side effect which rid these countries of harmful industry. The forest was cut down to set up and operate metal producing foundries. It was rapidly cleared for the agro-industrial and animal raising projects as well. Indigenous people were expelled. To speed up clear cutting, destructive chemical agents were sprayed from planes, polluting soils and rivers and killing many people. Agro-industries and cattle projects have caused permanent damage to the ecosystem of the Amazon such as «erosion, compacting, and leaching of the soil, silting of rivers and dams, air pollution produced by huge fires»[104].

---

[102] L. BOFF, *Cry*, 90-91. The significance of biodiversity in an ecosystem would be straightforward from the perspective of the first proposition that all things are interconnected. From this perspective, every one is in constant interactions with others through relationships. Therefore, the extinction of one species in an ecosystem would not mean merely the disappearance of that species from an ecosystem or the world. It would mean a further, wider influence upon others to which that species was related and an ecosystem as a whole.

[103] Cf. L. BOFF, *Cry*, 91-98.

[104] L. BOFF, *Cry*, 95-98.

Some comments can be made on what has occurred in the Amazon region. First, the structural aspect of poverty is observed in these development projects in the Amazon. It is plain that poverty is not a private issue in the case of the Amazon. The poor in this region are not responsible for the poverty from which they suffer. Rather, one must say that poverty is imposed and inflicted upon them. Poverty bears and reveals an oppressive and exploitative character. It is an inevitable consequence of violent exploitation, in the name of development, of ordinary people by a conjunction of political power (government) and economic power (multinational capital). Poverty can never be overcome through personal effort and diligence alone insofar as this exploitative system is sustained. For this system produces wealth on the one side and poverty on the other side. It can be surmounted only through a radical change of the unjust social, political, and economic structures which bring systematically extreme affluence to a few at the cost of many. Second, the harmful effects of exploitative development impact not only on people in the forms of poverty, expulsion from homeland, disease, and so forth. The natural environment also suffers from this development. Nature is devastated and degraded due in great part to the reckless extraction and consumption of natural resources and the pollution caused by industrial production. Moreover, it is generally the poor who bear the burden of degraded natural environment, while those who get most benefits from the exploitation of people and the environment maintain a pleasant life in environmentally safe and comfortable places. In sum, this type of development causes poverty and ecological disruption together, and the poor suffer from the consequent degradation of the environment.

Poverty and ecological deterioration are intrinsically related to each other. In other words, the same logic of domination and exploitation forces people into destitution and ravages the natural environment. What has occurred in the Amazon testifies that it is the endless pursuit of profit by market-oriented capitalist economy that has brought disastrous effects to people and nature. «The logic that exploits classes and subjects peoples to the interests of a few rich and powerful countries is the same as the logic that devastates the Earth and plunders its wealth [...]»[105]. Therefore, as we now see, we must consider and deal with massive poverty and the global ecological devastation together, which are caused by one and the same oppressive and exploitative system.

---

[105] L. BOFF, *Cry*, xi.

The Amazon case witnesses that the present type of development is unjust as well as wrong. It pronounces «how misguided it is to pursue development along the lines of modernity»[106]. The current model of development is not a way out of poverty and the ecological crisis. We must acknowledge an urgent need for an alternative model of development. This alternative must be «a kind of development for all of humankind, whose starting point is the centrality of ecology, which provides the basis for dealing with economic, political, cultural, and other aspects of a civilized society»[107]. A new model of development must be «for all of humankind», not for a few with power and wealth. It must profoundly acknowledge and appreciate «the centrality of ecology», without which even the survival of humankind is not possible. The Amazon case also awakens us to realize an extreme gap between the rich and the poor in the world: «too much consumption by the rich and too little consumption by the poor. It means the global crisis of the life-system, from the destruction of forests [...] to the contemporary indifference toward the drama of millions of starving people [...]»[108].

The damage that some have imposed and inflicted on a great number of people and nature in the pursuit of their profit, as shown in the Amazon case, illustrates vividly how distorted our way of seeing others is and how prevalent in us this distorted perspective is.

> Through the economics of growth, nature is degraded to the level of mere «natural resources», or «raw materials», at the disposal of humankind. Workers are seen as «human resources» and as a mere function of production. Everything is governed by an instrumental and mechanistic vision: persons, animals, plants, minerals. All creatures, in short, lose their relative autonomy and their intrinsic value[109].

The root cause of the current catastrophe must be found in this extreme, utilitarian attitude toward others, together with a sense of disconnectedness, as mentioned at the outset of this study. The ecological crisis in conjunction with massive poverty reveals «the crisis of profound meaning in our way and system of life, and in our model of society and development»[110]. Speaking in terms of liberation, «it is not only the poor and oppressed that must be liberated; today all humans must be

---

[106] L. BOFF, *Cry*, 101.
[107] L. BOFF, *Cry*, 86.
[108] L. BOFF, *Cry*, 73.
[109] L. BOFF, *Ecology and Liberation*, 24.
[110] L. BOFF, *Ecology and Liberation*, 37.

liberated. We are hostages to a paradigm that places us – against the thrust of the universe – *over* things instead of being *with* them in the great cosmic community»[111]. We need an alternative perspective from which to see others, both human and nonhuman. We see here again the utmost significance of the ecological perspective on the world that envisions all things as interconnected. This ecological worldview will curb the prevalent, reckless utilitarian standpoint on others. While the ecological viewpoint acknowledges in all beings an instrumental aspect due to the interconnectedness of all, it always recalls us to a more profound attitude to others, which must precede an instrumental attitude, i.e., gratitude and due regard.

3.3.2 Hermeneutical Mediation

What is the present world like in which we live, in the light of faith? Hermeneutical mediation seeks an answer to this question. What theological significance and implication can we find in the social reality that we observe and analyze, and how? For this, I will reflect in the light of the Christian tradition on what socio-analytical mediation presents in the case of the Amazon, which I believe somehow represents what occurs to the poor and to nature. It is important in hermeneutical mediation to recall and bear in mind that historical, i.e., socio-economic, liberation is intrinsically connected with salvation in Jesus Christ, although the two must be distinguished from each other. «Historical liberations are thus anticipations and concretizations, ever limited, but real, of the salvation that will be full and complete only in eternity»[112]. In other words, salvation is not identified *with* historical liberation, but the former is identified *in* the latter[113]. Liberation makes salvation in the future palpable and visible, though not perfect, here and now in history. This perspective on salvation and liberation is pivotal to liberation theology since it grants theological significance to human efforts in history for liberation and justice[114].

Calling to mind that the trinitarian perspective on creation provides a theological motif of the liberation of creation, let us look at the current situation of the world, demonstrated by the Amazon, through the mystery of the Trinity. For our concern the trinitarian relationship of

---

[111] L. BOFF, *Cry*, xii.
[112] L. BOFF, *Salvation and Liberation*, 18-19.
[113] L. BOFF, *Salvation and Liberation*, 32.
[114] L. BOFF, *Salvation and Liberation*, 19.

perichoresis is the core of the trinitarian doctrine. *Perichoresis* states that the three divine persons are in perfect mutual indwelling in virtue of perfect openness to each other. It must be recalled that *perichoresis* is the principle of life, love, inclusiveness, and equality (or due regard). In this trinitarian relationship, there is no room for negativities such as selfishness, domination, exclusion, marginalization, and death. The community of the triune God can be conceived as the perfect egalitarian communion full of life and love. As a reflection of the trinitarian community creation is meant to be a community where life, love, solidarity, and equality are respected, maintained, and promoted. The trinitarian vision of community provides us a prototype for a just society with harmonious relationship with nature.

In the face of massive, extreme poverty imposed upon human beings and global, severe deterioration inflicted upon nature, as observed in the Amazon, the message of the trinitarian doctrine is crystal clear. The trinitarian perspective on creation asserts definitely that what happened in the Amazon is against the nature of the triune God and thus against that of creation as well. What occurred in the Amazon is death, selfishness, alienation, and exploitative domination instead of life, love, inclusiveness, and due regard. What we find there is «little sharing, less communion, and a great weight of oppression placed on the poor»[115]. This is obviously an enormous scandal to the triune God of *perichoresis*. This is a grave sin. The whole creation needs and longs for liberation from this sinful situation. This is what we are told about our world by the trinitarian doctrine. The trinitarian doctrine operates also as inspiration and aspiration to the liberation of creation, not only as the condemnation of the oppression of creation. The trinitarian communion among the divine persons, i.e., «the union between them in love and vital interpenetration, can serve as a source of inspiration, as a utopian goal» for all those who aspire to liberation[116]. The trinitarian perspective on creation awakens us to the sinfulness of the present situation. At the same time, it encourages us to take up the cause of the poor and groaning nature and to follow in the midst of oppression and exploitation a path to which the triune God invites us.

The kingdom of God as well can be regarded as a model which creation is ultimately meant to be. God's kingdom is the leitmotif of Jesus, and he perceived it as the ultimate future of the world. Let us see

---

115 L. BOFF, *Trinity and Society*, 11.
116 L. BOFF, *Trinity and Society*, 6.

briefly how Boff understands the kingdom of God that Jesus had in mind[117]. The kingdom of God is not so much a spatial reality as a dynamic reality. «It does not mean a territory but the way in which God acts, the means by which God makes himself Lord of all creation»[118]. It is the reign of God over the whole creation. Jesus proclaimed that this kingdom of God had already begun in this world through him, though not yet fulfilled (cf. Luke 4:18-21; Matt. 11:2-5). This respect is well indicated in Jesus' kingdom parables such as the parable of a mustard seed and the yeast (cf. Matt. 13:31-33). As a mustard seed turns into a tree and the yeast swells the whole flour, God's kingdom will be brought to completion through the transformation of the world, not through its annihilation. The whole creation will completely be renewed and turn into God's kingdom with its fullness, the seed of which has already been sown and growing here.

> The kingdom of God is a total, global and structural transfiguration and revolution of the reality of human beings [...] The kingdom of God is not to be in another world but is the old world transformed into a new one. [...] The kingdom of God does not simply signify the annihilation of sin but the annihilation of all that sin means for human beings, society, and the cosmos[119].

It must be noted that what is to be transformed into the kingdom of God is not only human beings but the whole creation. An anthropocentric view of salvation is not allowed or justified from the perspective of God's kingdom. The kingdom of God is theocentric, i.e., the reign of God over the entire creation, which embraces not only humanity but the entire cosmos.

What is this kingdom of God like, as a transfigured world? It must be mentioned first that it is the reign over all creation of the God who is love and mercy (cf. Luke 15). The kingdom of God is a banquet which this loving and merciful God grants to all creatures (cf. Luke 14:15-24). Every creature enjoys the fullness of life in this banquet; everyone is loved as such; no one will be excluded from the invitation of this feast; no one is treated unjustly. Since the God who holds the banquet is the creator of heaven and earth, this feast is open to all creatures, not only to human beings. It is like a feast to which all creatures are called to

---

[117] For a detailed account of the kingdom of God, see the second section of this chapter.

[118] L. BOFF, *Trinity and Society*, 28.

[119] L. BOFF, *Jesus Christ Liberator*, 53.

come and in which they enjoy cosmic kinship under the parental love and care of God (cf. Isa. 11:6-9; 65:17, 25). This eschatological banquet will be «the feast at which all sit together to celebrate, the new city in which all are brothers and sisters, with God in the midst of these sons and daughters, serving them all. So images of communion and sharing describe the form God's rule will take»[120].

In confrontation with the disastrous situation in the world, as seen in the Amazon, the message of God's kingdom is obvious, too. The reign of God, who is love and mercy, asserts strongly that what occurred in the Amazon is against the kingdom of God, the ultimate future of creation, and thus against creation. What occurred in the Amazon is oppressive alienation and exclusive possession instead of communion and sharing. This situation is an astounding scandal to the God who serves all, instead of being served. This is a grave sin. The whole creation needs and aspires to liberation from this sinful situation. This is what we are told about our world by the kingdom of God, which is «the exercise of God's power to liberate from everything that denies or rebels against God and to bring God's final plan to fruition: a life of sharing, solidarity and justice»[121].

The kingdom of God, like the trinitarian doctrine, operates as inspiration and aspiration to the liberation of creation, not only as the condemnation of the oppression of creation. It is in the future that a total transformation of the world will happen. Therefore, the kingdom of God is continually the object of hope and supplication (cf. Matt. 6:10). At the same time, insofar as it grows here and now, it is also the case that the kingdom of God is present in this world (Luke 17:20-21). This suggests that there is our share and task in building God's kingdom to the extent that it is present in the world. Jesus himself dedicated his life to the actualization of the kingdom in this world through his public ministry, especially with the poor, the sick, and the marginalized. Jesus also called and invited people as his disciples so that they might commit themselves to the building of God's kingdom. Jesus continues to call us to the cause of God's kingdom. It demands a radical change, i.e., a conversion, from those who respond to his call. «Conversion means changing one's mode of thinking and acting to suit God, and therefore undergoing an interior revolution»[122]. It is only with our conversion that God's kingdom begins to germinate in us, as Jesus proclaimed it

---

[120] L. BOFF, *Trinity and Society*, 28.
[121] L. BOFF, *Trinity and Society*, 28.
[122] L. BOFF, *Jesus Christ Liberator*, 64.

with a demand of conversion (cf. Mark 1:14-15). Conversion to the kingdom of God bears not only a personal but a social and cosmic significance since the kingdom is a reality comprising all creatures. Conversion to God's kingdom requires that we attune completely to God our way of being in the world, i.e., thinking and acting, so that we may see the world with self-offering heart, instead of self-centered eyes. Only then can we perceive the kingdom of God in the world stained with sinfulness. Only then can we commit ourselves, with unyielding hope, to the building of God's kingdom in the world.

3.4 A Radical Change in a Perspective on Nature and the Poor

The socio-analytical mediation of the Amazon reveals that destitution and ecological deterioration have one and the same root cause: an oppressive political and exploitative economic structure. Poverty and the ecological degradation are primarily structural issues although personal aspects, such as individuals' way of living (this is still influenced to a great extent by a socio-economic structure), cannot be ignored. Without a radical change of the prevalent economic and political structure, these problems can hardly be settled. They are also political issues in the sense that they can be resolved only by our decision to opt for just distribution and proper ecological care, not by the current economic development that brings forth both poverty and affluence, as dependency theory claims.

The hermeneutical mediation of the Amazon region affirms that massive poverty and the ecological degradation of the earth are sinful situations, which are against God's will and plan for all creation. The trinitarian perspective on creation maintains that the current situation of the world has severely deviated from what creation as a reflection of the trinitarian community is meant to be. The kingdom of God holds that the present situation of the world is against what Jesus had in mind for the ultimate future of the world. In short, the present world is fundamentally wrong in the light of Christian faith. In this context, we Christians must reflect critically upon our basic assumption or perspective on the world that we have long since taken for granted: «profound worldwide changes are needed, embracing a new economic order, a new concept of ownership, and different social and ecological relationships – in short, a new humanity»[123]. A radical change is demanded today.

---

[123] L. BOFF, *Ecology and Liberation*, 103.

3.4.1 Ecological Concern and Social Concern: Not Conflicting but Compatible

Poverty and the ecological devastation have been disclosed to have one and the same root. A conclusion can now be drawn that ecological concern and social concern are intrinsically intertwined and must be practiced together. It is here that liberation theology meets ecological discourses and is allied with them. Liberation theology now raises a cause for groaning nature as well as for the poor; ecological discourses are now equipped with the systematic methodology of liberation theology. Liberation theology reveals, through socio-analytical mediation, that poverty and ecological degradation are systematically produced by the current, predominant socio-economic structure and that the poor are the first victims due to the ecological disruption. Liberation theology comes to recognize how nature is related to poverty: the more the natural environment of a region deteriorates, the more the poor who live in the region suffer. Material wealth is meant to benefit only the powerful and rich. Liberation theology, with an ecological perspective on the world, testifies to a silent but miserable reality of the world where a great number of human beings are crushed by dire poverty and nature is torn away by human violence with an obsession to possess.

Grounded in social analysis and out of an elevated ecological awareness, liberation theology asserts: «What should prevail instead is ecological justice – respect for the otherness of beings and things and their right to continue to exist – and constant social justice, respect and concern for people [...]»[124]. Ecological justice and social justice support and stimulate each other. Some may make the criticism that a claim for ecological concern obscures the urgent issue of poverty. However, ecological concern does not eclipse the desperate situation of the poor. Rather, concern for the environment highlights the poor, because they cannot leave their environmentally devastated region and must bear most of its burden. An escalated concern for nature does not mean a lowered concern for the poor. «Since the human race is part of the environment, social injustice goes hand-in-hand with ecological injustice. [...] without a minimum of social justice it is impossible to make ecological justice fully effective»[125]. Conversely, one may say the other way around that without a minimum of ecological justice it is

---

[124] L. BOFF, *Ecology and Liberation*, 77.
[125] L. BOFF, *Ecology and Liberation*, 88.

impossible to make social justice fully effective. Ecological justice and social justice are reciprocally related to each other.

Ecological concern makes us alert to the limited amount of the natural resources of the earth as well as to the rapid deterioration of the global environment such as air, water, and land. Ecological concern awakens us to heed how justly the scarce resources of the planet are distributed and who suffers the most from the environmental degradation. Ecological concern turns into social concern, which claims the just distribution of material wealth. Social concern sounds the alarm also to the degradation of the environment as well as to poverty. Social concern leads us to pay attention to the aggressive and exploitative use of nature, which benefits only the powerful and rich. Social concern turns into ecological concern, which claims the integrity of nature.

The world seen from the trinitarian perspective on creation, in which life, love, inclusiveness, and due regard are expected to be ensured, demands that society proceed in a direction that ecological justice as well social justice is built and promoted. The world seen from the perspective of the kingdom of God, in which God's ultimate plan for the future of all creation is expected to be finally achieved through its transformation, calls upon us to commit ourselves to the cause of ecological justice as well as social justice. In accord with socio-analytical mediation, these two Christian traditions in hermeneutical mediation help us keep ecological concern and social concern in balance.

3.4.2 Sustainability and Development: Not Compatible but Conflicting

The current, predominant socio-economic structure cannot ensure and actualize justice in society and nature. Moreover, the present type of economic development based on the extravagant consumption of material resources (especially, nonrenewable ones) cannot be sustained indefinitely because of the very limit of the natural resources of the earth. We need an alternative to the present developmental and societal model: «we have to move toward an economy of sufficiency, which focuses on the life of the human person and of nature, the participation of all in the production of the means of living, and solidarity with those persons and those creatures that have lived or suffered through pathological and harsh subsistence conditions»[126]. What we must seek is an

---

[126] L. BOFF, *Ecology and Liberation*, 28.

alternative economic order which can ensure one's basic needs to survive, a possibility of one's becoming a subject of one's life, concern for the vulnerable and marginalized, and sharing with them. In fact, one can say, this conception of economy is more faithful than the present one to the meaning of the word *oikonomia* in Greek, in which the world «economy» originates. *Oikonomia* can be interpreted as «the management of the household so as to increase its use value to all members of the household over the long run»[127]. The scope of the household must be expanded, in our context, to include nature. Hence, economy must be concerned not only for human beings but for nature. This conception of economy is in accordance with the community that the divine communion suggests in that it includes the entire creation. This is in harmony with the kingdom of God that Jesus had in mind as the ultimate future of the world in that it embraces the whole creation.

An urgent need for an alternative economic model brings to light the notion of sustainability. The term «sustainability» originates in biology. «The category of *sustainability* has been worked out in the realm of ecology and biology to define the trend of ecosystems toward dynamic equilibrium sustained in the web of interdependencies and complementarities flourishing in ecosystems»[128]. Sustainability is only possible under the condition of «the dynamic and self-regulating balance (*homeostasis*) that is inherent in nature as a result of the chain of interdependencies and complementarities among all beings, especially living things that depend on resources that are continually recycled and hence are sustainable without limit»[129]. The Amazon would be an example.

> Materials are decomposing on the soil [...] These things are enriched by the water dripping from the leaves and running off the trunks. These two kinds of water wash and carry off the excrement [...] There are also huge numbers of fungi and [...] microorganisms that [...] resupply the roots. It is through the roots that the food substance passes into the plants[130].

It must be noted that the sustainability of an ecosystem is critically dependent on the recycling of all that lives and exists in that ecosystem. Even a slight deviation of the recycling circle could inflict disastrous impact on the sustainability of an ecosystem. Sustainability is possible

---

127 H.E. DALY – J.B. COBB, JR., *For the Common Good*, 138.
128 L. BOFF, *Cry*, 66.
129 L. BOFF, *Cry*, 101.
130 L. BOFF, *Cry*, 90-91.

only with sophisticated and vulnerable balance among all beings in a region.

In the course of seeking an alternative to the present developmental model that turned out destructive to the sustainability of nature both locally and globally, sustainable development has come to the foreground. However, we must be careful to distinguish what sustainable development originally means and what it actually comes to mean. *Our Common Future*, the report issued by the WCED (the so-called Brundtland Commission), made the term «sustainable development» widespread. It describes sustainable development as «a process of change in which the exploitation of resources, the orientation of investments, the paths of technological development and institutional change are in accordance with current and future needs»[131]. One can hardly find in this understanding and rendering of sustainable development any serious concern for the integrity of nature itself[132]. What one may perceive is, instead, an implicit but deep-rooted anthropocentric assumption to which modern human beings have long been accustomed. The aim of change in the scope of resources, investments, technologies, and institutions that this report mentions is in great measure motivated by and geared at human need. It considers the future, but predominantly for the sake of the future generations of humanity. Its basic presumption seems to be that «development» must continue. The aggressive notion of development regarding nature seems to be not discarded but only mitigated. It can be held that this conception of sustainable development is not «deep» but «shallow». Above all, sustainable development in this sense will not be sustainable.

Boff himself is critical of the perception of sustainable development in this report. He raises a question whether the two terms «sustainable» and «development» can ever be put together: «Can the term *sustainability* be applied to the kind of modern development and growth whose logic is based on plundering Earth and exploiting the labor force?»[133] This suspicion stems from the basic viewpoint of the report on development, which he believes «still remains a captive of the

---

[131] WCED, *Our Common Future*, 46.

[132] Cf. WCED, *Our Common Future*, 43. As already mentioned at the outset of this chapter, one can find in this document another description of sustainable development, but only with the same connotation and orientation: «sustainable development is development that meets the needs of the present without compromising the ability of future generations to meet their own needs».

[133] L. BOFF, *Cry*, 66-67.

development-and-growth paradigm»[134]. According to him, the report assumes: «poverty and ecological deterioration mutually affect one another and occur in tandem. What pollutes [...] is extreme poverty. Therefore the more development advances, the less dire poverty there will be, and the less dire poverty there is the less pollution there will be, to the betterment of ecology»[135]. The report seems to claim that economic development based on the extravagant consumption of unrenewable, material resources must continue in order that both poverty and the ecological crisis may be alleviated and eradicated in the final analysis. This is not the case according to what we have observed in the socio-analytical mediation of the Amazon. For it discloses that poverty and environmental degradation are caused by development itself. One may say that the report still understands poverty and environmental disruption from the perspective of the so-called developmentalism that economic development can mitigate and eventually eliminate poverty. It is certain, then, that whenever they come into conflict with each other, «it is always development itself that counts, even at the cost of ecological disorder», insofar as the present notion of development is maintained[136]. Sustainable development is then but a contradiction. We may now tell what sustainable development originally means and what it actually comes to mean. If sustainability is to be seriously considered, sustainable development must mean a development which seeks and ensures the sustainability of nature. For this, we must radically change our perspective on development. But what sustainable development actually comes to mean is the sustainability of development, not that of nature. Then, we need not change our standpoint on development, but eventually at the cost of the sustainability of nature.

In short, insofar as we do not radically change the traditional paradigm of development, sustainable development is nothing but a contradictory and impossible term precisely because of what development indicates. Moreover, we will never get out of the impasse of massive poverty and ecological devastation in the midst of economic development. At the same time, it must be remembered too that it is formidable for us to change profoundly a developmental model. For it is formed by and deeply rooted in the kind of society that we adopt and develop. This is in turn sustained by our basic convictions and values whereby

---

[134] L. BOFF, Cry, 66.
[135] L. BOFF, Cry, 66.
[136] L. BOFF, Ecology and Liberation, 22.

we see all realities. We now find ourselves back in a place which has been claimed to be the point of departure to grasp and deal with the present global ecological crisis: our way of seeing the world. For at the root of social injustice and ecological injustice in our age is our deep-seated and excessive, dualistic and instrumental perspective on the world. Only with an ecological perspective on the world, which requires a profound change in us, we can dispel a deep-rooted myth that economic development alone can uproot poverty in the world some day. Only then can we begin to build an alternative society in which respect for other human beings and due regard for nature are sought and practiced instead of blind economic development at the cost of many human beings and nature. Only then can we tread a path to which the doctrine of the Trinity and the kingdom of God invite us.

4. The Compatibility of Ecological Concern and Social Concern from the Perspective of Sallie McFague

4.1 *Introduction*

This section corresponds to the final stage of metaphorical theology where one experiments on a proposed metaphor in a new context which demands a new metaphor. In other words, I will in this section examine what the metaphor of God's body shaped by the Christic vision may imply with regard to the third proposition. Given that the current, predominant economic system is deeply related to poverty and ecological disruption, I will consider what significance and implication this body metaphor brings to an economic model, with a view to affirming the compatibility of ecological concern and social concern. I will first review the present, prevalent economic model and the worldview which undergirds it. As a result of the review, an urgent need of an alternative economic model will come to the fore. It will then be held that the metaphor of God's body suggests an alternative economic model. The body metaphor will bring to light the intimate connection of ecological concern with social concern. I will then reflect on the discipleship of Jesus in the light of the metaphor of God's body shaped by the Christic vision, with an emphasis on distributive justice and sustainability. Frugality will be presented as a concrete way of implementing the consequent discipleship. However, first of all, it is worth reviewing briefly the debate between ecofeminism and deep ecology, two crucial schools of environmental philosophy, over the root cause of humanity's domination and exploitation of nature. For we can get a glimpse in this debate of the viewpoint of McFague as an ecofeminist on the third proposition.

4.2 Ecofeminism and Deep Ecology

Insofar as her perspective on nature is concerned, McFague can be regarded as an ecofeminist[137]. Simply speaking, ecofeminism is «the name of a variety of different feminist perspectives on the nature of the connections between the domination of women (and other oppressed humans) and the domination of nature»[138]. There exist several streams in ecofeminism, according to different feminist perspectives, diverse views of nature, and various solutions to the ecological problems[139]. Nonetheless, ecofeminists have in common the view that there are «important connections between the domination of women (and other human subordinates) and the domination of nature»[140]. Deep ecology, which is known to have originated with the Norwegian philosopher Arne Naess, refers to the environmental philosophy which champions a radical biocentric or ecocentric egalitarianism of all human and non-human life forms on the earth[141]. Ecofeminism and deep ecology agree with each other that human beings must renounce the destructive exploitation of nature. Both of them challenge dualistic attitudes, logic, and practices that seek to dominate nature violently and recklessly. Both demand that the current, predominant perspective on the world be changed in order to restore the integrity of nature. However, they are different from each other in identifying the prime cause of humanity's exploitation of nature, suggesting different ways to uproot the current aggressive and excessive use of nature[142].

According to deep ecologists, it is an excessive anthropocentrism or human-centeredness that is to blame for the current environmental degradation. In order to root out the immoderate and violent exploitation of nature by humanity, they emphasize the equality of all beings grounded in their argument for the same intrinsic value of all. Deep

---

[137] Cf. P. SMITH, What Are They, 21-24.

[138] K.J. WARREN, «Ecological Feminist Philosophies», x.

[139] Cf. C. MERCHANT, Radical Ecology, 183-210.

[140] K.J. WARREN, «Ecological Feminist Philosophies», x.

[141] For an introduction of deep ecology and the controversy about it, see P. SMITH, What Are They, 5-18; C. MERCHANT, Radical Ecology, 85-109.

[142] For an overview of their debate, see P. SMITH, What Are They, 29-33. For a more detailed account, see R. SESSIONS, «Deep Ecology versus Ecofeminism»; V. PLUMWOOD, «Androcentrism and Anthropocentrism».

ecologists insist that we must acknowledge the same intrinsic value of all species as that of humanity. On this basis we must grant them a right to live and flourish. They demand that the use of nature be strictly restricted to vital human needs. From the perspective of deep ecology, humanity is but another species along many on the earth. On the contrary, ecofeminists are more concerned about a historical connection between the male domination of women and that of nature. They hold that it is not anthropocentrism but androcentrism or male-centeredness in patriarchal societies that is fundamentally responsible for the exploitation of both women (and other oppressed human groups) and nature. They claim that insofar as patriarchal androcentrism is not eradicated, the deterioration of nature will continue.

Ecofeminists criticize deep ecologists for their unfeasible assumption that the abusive domination of humanity over nature will disappear if all nonhuman species are granted equal right. Ecofeminists also criticize them for their lack of historicity, holding that what is problematic in human history is male domination over women and nature, not simply the domination of humanity over nature. They stress that there is a close connection between male domination over females and human domination over nature. Since females and nature are the victims of male domination, we cannot settle either issue if we fail to address both of them.

> the social domination of women and the ecological domination of the earth are inextricably fused in theory and practice. Hence the common statement that at the root of our ecological crisis is an overly anthropocentric view of the world is not quite accurate. It would be more precise to say that the problem lies in an androcentric view. Historically, not the superior identity of humanity in general but of man, understood as ruling class males in a patriarchal system, mandates the domination of nature[143].

Deep ecologists assert, on the contrary, that the notion of anthropocentrism basically encompasses androcentrism. For every type of domination emerges out of the perception that «I» am more human than «you» and thus superior to «you». They hold that this «you» can be women, slaves, other races, nature, and so forth. Androcentrism, deep ecologists argue, is eventually an anthropocentric view that the male is more human than the female. Deep ecologists also insist that the eradication of androcentrism does not automatically guarantee the elimination of

---

[143] E.A. JOHNSON, *Women, Earth, and Creator Spirit*, 16.

anthropocentrism, on the ground that one can imagine a society which is non-androcentric but still anthropocentric.

Each perspective may hold a part of truth, and some attempt to mediate these two stances. In practice, this debate itself can be regarded as meaningful in that it has evoked in us concern for the root cause of the ecological crisis. It is sure that both anthropocentrism and androcentrism are detrimental to nature. The merit of ecofeminists may be that they seek to base their argument on concrete historical observations. They are concerned about what has actually happened in history with regard to the exploitation of women and nature, and how it has happened. Deep ecologists, on the contrary, tend to ground their claim primarily on abstract ideas, and it is ambiguous how to put into practice their egalitarian argument for all species. Besides, they are often charged with a tendency of misanthropy[144]. Above all, focusing primarily on an egalitarian view of all beings and accusing human beings in general of the devastation of nature, deep ecology is likely to neglect the cries of the poor and powerless in the world, who are in many cases also the immediate victims of the ecological degradation. To that measure, it runs the risk of missing an intimate link between suffering human beings and groaning nature.

Despite this drawback, we must not ignore a positive contribution which deep ecology makes. McFague herself comments that the value of deep ecology lies not «in its conceptual adequacy but in its poetic power to make us feel unity»[145] It provides for us a vision to see the world drastically different from the present predominant worldview: «it radicalizes us into a new way of looking at the earth in which we are decentered as masters, as crown, as goal, and begin to feel empathy in an internal way for the suffering of other species»[146]. In this regard, deep ecology can be regarded as a prophetic voice that demands a profound change in our excessive instrumental attitude toward nature.

Given its perspective manifested in the debate with deep ecology, ecofeminists would affirm that concern for the poor is compatible with concern for nature. Poverty can be regarded as a grave consequence of the oppressive male domination of other humans, and then the poor belong to other oppressed humans, together with women. Hence, from ecofeminists' perspective, male domination is to blame in great part for

---

[144] Cf. P. SMITH, *What Are They,* 5-9.
[145] S. MCFAGUE, *The Body of God,* 125.
[146] S. MCFAGUE, *The Body of God,* 126.

poverty and the degradation of nature. Poverty and ecological deterioration are now viewed to be intrinsically interrelated so that one cannot
be resolved without the other. It can be assumed that McFague too
holds this standpoint insofar as she is in line with ecofeminism. In her
case, the compatibility of concern for nature and concern for the poor
was already suggested in chapter four when the scope of the Christic
vision was widened to the entire creation by the metaphor of God's
body, and conversely, the metaphor of God's body shaped by the Christic vision demonstrated that all creatures are interconnected in virtue of
God's compassionate love for all creatures, especially for the vulnerable.

4.3 *The Body of God and an Alternative Economic Model*

4.3.1 The Neo-Classical Economic Model and Its Worldview

Economics is deeply engaged in the present deterioration of ecology
as well as in mass poverty. It is often claimed, as a simple example, that
the environment must be exploited and impaired inevitably to some
measure in order to attain natural resources for economic growth,
which will bring the poor material wealth and thus alleviate poverty.
Ecological destruction is justified as an unavoidable reality for the
cause of economic development. On the contrary, some others hold that
the present economic model is responsible in large measure for poverty
and the degradation of nature. In either case, economics is viewed as an
important element that relates humanity to nature. Given that «economics [...] is the science whose subject is the gathering, cultivating, and
distributing of the earth's material resources, with a view to the survival
and thriving of human communities»[147], it is clear that both the human
element («gathering, cultivating, and distributing») and the natural
element («the earth's material resources») are intimately related to and
deeply influenced by economics and economic policies. In this regard,
it can be said that economics connects humankind to nature at a profound level («survival and thriving»).

The rendering of economics in this way implies that economics is not
value-free. Rather, one must say, economics depends on some fundamental values on the basis of which we collect, grow, and allocate the
material resources of the earth, which are basically scarce. In this sense,
economics is «about decisions concerning scarcity from the perspective

---

[147] C.F. HINZE, «Catholic Social Teaching», 171.

of a number of values, *one* of which is money»[148]. The way we distribute scarce resources depends greatly on our anthropological view and worldview, i.e., how we understand the human being and the world. A worldview informs us «who we are and how we should act in the world»[149]. A specific economic model assumes a worldview which undergirds it, and its concrete economic policies reveal a worldview that it assumes. As a simple example, if we view the human being primarily as an individual externally related to other human beings and regard nature principally as material resources to be possessed and consumed, then a method of gathering, cultivation, and distribution may well be grounded in the aggressive accumulation of material wealth through free competition.

An economic model predominant in the world today is grounded in neo-classical economics. The neo-classical economic model is basically market capitalism. The neo-classical economic model was conceived by some economists, represented by Adam Smith, in the eighteenth century and has since been developed[150]. Market capitalism can be rendered as «a giant machine operated by numerous investors, whose motives are neither vicious nor benign, who merely seek to maximize their returns»[151]. Given this, we can identify the corresponding worldview which undergirds the neo-classical economic model. First, the anthropological viewpoint of the neo-classical economic model is individualistic[152]. The neo-classical model holds that the human being is fundamentally an individual who competes with other humans, and is motivated by self-interest in order to get more of scarce commodities. It understands the human being basically as an individual with an insatiable desire for material wealth. The accumulation of wealth through fierce competition and the extravagant consumption of goods would be one's primary goal. Therefore, market capitalism brings to light the human being as a consumer. A society to which the neo-classical economic model leads would be a consumeristic society where the acquisi-

---

[148] S. MCFAGUE, *Life Abundant*, 75.

[149] S. MCFAGUE, *Life Abundant*, 72.

[150] Cf. www.bized.ac.uk/virtual/economy/library/theory/classical.htm: «The term "Classical" refers to work done by a group of economists in the 18th and 19th centuries. Much of this work was developing theories about the way markets and market economies work. Much of this work has subsequently been updated by modern economists and they are generally termed neo-classical economists [...]».

[151] N. KEYFITZ, «Consumption and Population», 485, as quoted in S. MCFAGUE, *Life Abundant*, 76.

[152] Cf. S. MCFAGUE, *Life Abundant*, 76-78.

tion and consumption of goods are pursued with little regard for the poor and nature.

Second, the neo-classical economic model presumes the mechanistic viewpoint on the world. As already mentioned, the conception of the world as a machine began in the West in the seventeenth century and replaced the medieval view of the world as an organism. The world is no longer viewed as a living organism with interrelated and interdependent members. Instead, it is regarded as «an object (not a subject), dead (not alive), with all its parts connected only in external ways [...]»[153]. The world is an inert object composed of many separate parts. The restraint that the organic view of the world laid on the reckless use of nature is removed. The world can be manipulated and exploited freely for the sake of humankind. This mechanistic worldview has brought about the anthropocentric view of the world. Nature appears from this perspective primarily as a source of materials for humanity.

Third, the goal of the neo-classical economic model seems to lie in economic growth without end. It holds that as economy grows, all will benefit from it. It is assumed that economic development will bring more people (eventually, to all) more material wealth and consumption. Therefore, the present market capitalist economy views «the planet as a corporation or syndicate, as a collection of individual human beings drawn together to benefit its members by optimal use of natural resources»[154]. No concern for the poor and the earth in the form of distributive justice and sustainability is found in the market-oriented capitalist economy[155]. The current, prevalent economic model pays no attention to the fact that natural resources are limited in the planet. Nor does it take heed of the necessity of the just distribution of wealth in society. It simply takes for granted the unlimited supply of material resources required for economic development. This is evidently not the case. With no concern about how to distribute the outcome of economic growth, it argues that poverty will disappear as economy grows. This is not true, either. In sum, the neo-classical economic model cannot be sustained indefinitely. Nor can it eradicate poverty.

---

[153] S. MCFAGUE, *Life Abundant*, 78.

[154] S. MCFAGUE, *Life Abundant*, 72.

[155] Cf. S. MCFAGUE, *Life Abundant*, 106-109. Sustainability and distributive justice will be regarded here as the concrete expressions of concern for nature and concern for the poor respectively. It can be held that sustainability aims at the integrity of nature and distributive justice seeks a right of everyone for a decent level of living by means of one's proper access to the material resources of the earth.

The current situation and prospects of the world are not as promising as the neo-classical economic model anticipates. We are already witnessing a huge, ever-widening gap between the rich and the poor and unprecedented environment ravage. A stern fact that only twenty percent of the entire population of the world uses more than eighty percent of the world's energy depicts succinctly the extremely unbalanced distribution of material wealth throughout the world and alludes to the rapid depletion of the natural resources of the earth[156]. In other words, twenty percent of the world population lives in a socio-economic structure which is arranged to waste too much natural resources and deplete them rapidly, while the remaining eighty percent of the population lives in dire poverty[157]. The standard and way of living that the neo-classical economic model suggests are neither possible nor desirable for us. In the first place, it is plain that all of us cannot afford this standard and way of living[158]. This is but an impossible dream because the earth cannot supply the sufficient material resources for this dream to come true. Nor can this type of life secure the sustainability and integrity of nature. The natural resources of the earth will be depleted entirely, and in the long run, nature itself will be devastated. The consumer society that the contemporary economic model and its corresponding worldview have pursued is not sustainable. It must be admitted that this is a realistic evaluation based on the limited availability of the natural resources, without which the current notion of economic development is not possible. In fact, these problems of market capitalism are already anticipated in its individualistic understanding of the human being and its anthropocentric view of development which ignore the material capacity and well-being of the earth[159]. What is common here is a dualistic perspective on others, both human and nonhuman. The individualistic anthropology of market capitalism drives everybody to fierce and endless competition. Its anthropocentric cosmology sepa-

---

[156] S. MCFAGUE, *Life Abundant*, xii.

[157] Cf. S. MCFAGUE, *Life Abundant*, 88. The following remark would make this fact more vivid: «Currently, Americans spend $8 billion annually on cosmetics and Europeans $11 billion on ice cream, a total more than it would cost to provide basic education ($6 billion) or water and sanitation ($9 billion) to the more than two billion people worldwide who do not have schools or toilets».

[158] Cf. S. MCFAGUE, *Life Abundant*, 80. The following remarks would make this fact more vivid: «For all the earth's people to enjoy a Western middle-class lifestyle, four more planets the size of the earth would be necessary as the resource base».

[159] S. MCFAGUE, *Life Abundant*, 94.

rates humanity from nature and results in the excessive extraction and extravagant consumption of material resources.

4.3.2 God's Body shaped by the Christic Vision: A Ground for an Alternative Economic Model

In confrontation with the disastrous consequences which the mechanistic worldview and the neo-classical economic model brought to human beings and nature, we must seek an alternative economic model. Given that the current market capitalistic economy lacks concern for nature and the poor, an alternative model must be inclusive in the sense that the condition of nature (sustainability) and one's basic needs for living (distributive justice) are seriously considered[160]. Bearing this point in mind, I will examine the metaphor of God's body to see what implications it may bring with regard to an alternative economic model. A case will be made that an economic model which satisfies our need of sustainability and distributive justice is mandated if we envision the human being and the world from the perspective of God's body shaped by the Christic vision. This will in turn affirms that the proposed metaphor of God's body can properly and effectively work in our age. In fact, its appropriateness has already been demonstrated to some measure in chapter four when the body metaphor broadened the scope of the Christic vision from humankind to the whole creation in order to meet an urgent need which our age raises.

It needs to be recalled that the perception of the world as God's body renders the world as one cosmic organism in which an immense number of individuals form radical unity in diversity. All are viewed to be organically connected to one another. In this organic conception of the world, unlike the mechanistic worldview, the world does not appear as a machine composed of separate parts or a collection of inanimate objects. Rather, the world is seen as a web of relationships in which all individual beings, including human beings, exist and live together. Each human being is not simply an individual who competes with others to amass material wealth. Rather, each one is primarily as a member of the community called creation where one's personal well-being is inseparably connected with the well-being of society and nature. The metaphor of God's body always renders an individual person in a wider, cosmic context. Therefore, the human being is always an individual in community. The notion of self in the metaphor of

---

[160] S. MCFAGUE, *Life Abundant*, 88.

God's body is broadened to include the whole world due to the organic interconnectedness of all. In this extended view of self, the goal of one's life consists not only in one's own well-being but also in that of the whole community by sharing material goods with other humans and giving due regard to nature[161]. In this respect, the metaphor of God's body contrasts sharply with the neo-classical economic model. It presents the human being as an individual consumer with an insatiable desire for material wealth and goods. One can hardly find in this individualistic viewpoint a sense of community and solidarity with others. In this individualistic standpoint of self, unlike in the extended view of self, the goal of one's life consists in one's own well-being which is ensured through the accumulation and consumption of material resources, not through the sharing of them with others[162]. Given that the destabilizing, inclusive, and nonhierarchical Christic vision demands a particular concern for the marginalized, i.e., the poor and exploited nature, this contrast becomes more striking.

The metaphor of God's body shaped by the Christic vision brings to the center distributive justice and sustainability. It demands that all creatures, especially the vulnerable, be given due regard and proper care. Distributive justice and sustainability are meant to secure the well-being of every human being, even the least in society, and the integrity of nature respectively. We must pay attention to both sustainability and distributive justice. Without sustainability for nature, human beings, both individually and collectively, cannot live well. Nor can distributive justice be ensured. The very source of material distribution will be in peril. At the same time, without distributive justice for each individual human being, nature cannot remain well. Nor can sustainability be secured. Those who are threatened to starvation will be forced, for survival, to use the natural environment in an exhaustive manner, without mentioning those who maintain an immoderate, consumption-oriented way of living which plunders nature systematically and rapidly. Concern for the poor (distributive justice) and concern for nature (sustainability) are mutually dependent.

If we hold fast to what the metaphor of God's body and the Christic vision indicate, what kind of economic model will come into view? This means that we conceive an economic model from a worldview which the metaphor of God's body shaped by the Christic vision brings

---

[161] S. MCFAGUE, *Life Abundant*, 105-111.
[162] S. MCFAGUE, *Life Abundant*, 81-85.

forth. An economic model thus conceived must be inclusive of all and have a special concern for the vulnerable. This economic model may be named the ecological economic model in that it is grounded in an ecological perspective on the world. The ecological economic model is deeply concerned for the well-being of nature as well as that of every human being. The ecological model seeks prosperity by sharing and sustaining the natural resources of the earth, not by amassing and wasting them as in the neo-classical model. The alternative model emphasizes sustainability and distributive justice, both of which are ignored or denied by the neo-classical model. The design principle of the ecological model is circular in the sense that it is aware that we live in «a circle composed of networks of interrelationship and interdependence with all other beings»[163]. This is also the way the metaphor of God's body conceives the world. On the contrary, the design principle of the neo-classical model is linear in the sense that it aims primarily at progress without end, which is in fact impossible. In sum, the metaphor of God's body shaped by the Christic vision encompasses the whole world, and at the same time, it shows a preferential concern for the vulnerable, both human and nonhuman. An economic model grounded in this body metaphor concentrates on how economic wealth must be allocated in society in order that the minimum decent level of living may be guaranteed to every human being (distributive justice) and how the integrity of nature can be maintained (sustainability).

From the perspective of God's body shaped by the Christic vision, it is plain that ecological concern and social concern must be practiced together. For the world is seen as a cosmic whole in which humankind and nature are organically related to each other. «Before all else the community must be able to survive (sustainability), which it can do only if all members have the use of its resources (distributive justice)»[164]. While extravagant way of living plunders natural resources for excessive consumption, the poor in extreme poverty too are compelled to destroy nature for survival. Conversely, all members must have access to natural resources, which is only possible if the community as a whole survives. Insofar as nature is not assured of sustainability, there is no material ground for distributive justice. Distributive justice and sustainability condition each other. We must

---

[163] S. MCFAGUE, *Life Abundant*, 106.
[164] S. MCFAGUE, *Life Abundant*, 100.

pursue distributive justice with a view to ensuring a decent way of living, which may also assure nature of sustainability.

The neo-classical economic model has failed to show a concern for the poor and nature. It disregards by its nature sustainability for the nature and distributive justice for the poor. It pays heed predominantly to the accumulation and consumption of material goods. The consequence is massive poverty and the ecological degradation of nature in the midst of the astounding material affluence that only a few enjoy. On the contrary, God's body shaped by the Christic vision demands an alternative economic model, which is grounded in «radical individuality» and «uncompromising community»[165]. The consequent, ecological economic model pays attention by its nature to both sustainability and distributive justice. «This model is as concerned with individuals as is the neo-classical view; the main difference is that the ecological model claims that individuals cannot thrive apart from the well-being of the whole – and the whole will not thrive unless the individuals are provided for»[166]. The ecological economic model is concerned for nature and every human being. All are seen as organically interconnected and thus interdependent. At the same time, the metaphor of God's body shaped by the Christic vision awakens the ecological economic model to a particular concern for the vulnerable.

4.4 The Discipleship of Jesus in the Light of God's Body Shaped by the Christic Vision

4.4.1 The Scope, Shape, and Way of Jesus' Discipleship

Given that we Christians seek to follow the way of Jesus in the current situation that the neo-classical economic model has brought about, we need to consider the discipleship of Jesus in the light of God's body shaped by the Christic vision. For this body metaphor demands and presents an alternative economic model. Hence, we will here examine what the metaphor of God's body shaped by the Christic vision may imply to the discipleship of Jesus today in the context in which the neo-classical economic model prevails and causes mass poverty and environmental degradation. First, the scope of Jesus' discipleship is extended to nature when it is viewed in the light of the metaphor of God's body. Traditionally, his discipleship has been considered and practiced only among human beings, epitomized by the

---

[165] S. MCFAGUE, Life Abundant, 104.
[166] S. MCFAGUE, Life Abundant, 105.

love of neighbor (cf. Luke 10:25-37; John 13:34-35). Since the metaphor of God's body indicates that human beings are organically related to nature, we cannot love our neighbor without due regard for nature, once we accept this organic way of conceiving the world. Moreover, the body metaphor further renders nature as our neighbor which is in need today because of the aggressive exploitation that the neo-classical economy inflicts on it. In this regard, the metaphor of God's body calls upon us to widen the discipleship of Jesus to reach the whole world including nature.

Second, the metaphor of God's body does not merely broaden the scope of Jesus' discipleship to include nature. The body metaphor, characterized by the destabilizing, inclusive, and nonhierarchical Christic vision which denounces the hierarchies and dualistic structures that are exploitative and oppressive, requires that the discipleship must bear a special concern for the vulnerable, both human and nonhuman. Therefore, it grants a proper shape to the discipleship, which is expressed as a preferential option for the marginalized, which includes nature.

Third, the neo-classical economic model is in practice such a powerful system that it will not easily allow any alternative system which stands opposed to it. Many of us may be driven to despair in front of this overwhelming power. However, the Christic vision of the cross powerfully reminds us that the discipleship is actualized in our being with the victims of the world and sharing their suffering. The way of Jesus' discipleship is solidarity and compassion with the poor and nature.

The ecological economic model, demanded by the metaphor of God's body shaped by the Christic vision, provides specific contents to the discipleship of Jesus. The ecological economic model holds that our primary concern must not consist in the accumulation of material wealth through fierce competition with others and the violent domination of them. Rather, it must consist in distributive justice for the poor and sustainability for nature. The discipleship of Jesus in the light of the ecological economic model leads us to a commitment to the cause of distributive justice and sustainability in the midst of mass poverty and the ravage of nature. The practice of social justice and ecological justice must be the concrete expression of the scope and shape of Jesus' discipleship today in the light of the ecological economic model. More concrete details concerning how to practice it, i.e., the way of discipleship, must be determined according to one's own situation. Finally, in practice we will be forced to make a choice between the issue of poverty and that of the environment. However, we must all the more recall that these two are intrinsically related to each other and always influence one another. Therefore, Jesus' discipleship calls for wisdom as regards how to act effectively and prudently in a concrete situation in order that we may grapple with a more urgent issue, either poverty or ecological degradation, while still retaining a deep concern for the other.

4.4.2 Frugality:
A Way of Jesus' Discipleship in a Consumeristic Society

Frugality or moderation as a specific way of living can be understood as a voluntary form of poverty[167]. In this regard, frugality refers to self-restraint about material accumulation and consumption, of which the current market capitalist economy persuades us powerfully. One may find the ideal model of frugality in the life of believers in the early church (cf. Acts 2:44-47; 4:32-37). Goods were distributed according to one's need, not to one's desire to possess, so that no one is in need. To possess what is more than one's need was harshly criticized (cf. Acts 5:1-11)[168]. Frugality is concerned for and aims at a decent life of individuals. At the same time, it demands that no one seek more than what is necessary for a decent living so that others may live likewise. Therefore, it can be said, frugality seeks sufficiency for both an individual and the community as a whole by means of voluntary abstinence from the immoderate accumulation of wealth and the extravagant consumption of material goods. In this respect, frugality is «a "sense of enough" and the willingness to live within material limitations so that others may also have enough»[169]. This means that those who practice frugality stand in opposition to the present, consumeristic society impelled by the neo-classical economic model. The neo-classical economic structure would not recognize a sense of sufficiency. Nor would it acknowledge the material limitation of the earth, within which all must live together. What it seeks is an economic growth without end and the consequent material affluence, only for a few.

---

167 Cf. J.B. COBB, JR., *Sustainability*, 17.

168 This stance on material possession is strongly reflected in the thought of such Christian writers as St. Basil, St. Augustine, St. Gregory the Great, St. Bonaventure, and St. Thomas Aquinas. Cf. VATICAN COUNCIL II, *Gaudium et Spes*, nn. 69-70; D. CHRISTIANSEN, «Ecology and the Common Good», 187-189.

169 S. MCFAGUE, *Life Abundant*, 116

I hold that frugality can be a concrete and effective way of actualizing the discipleship of Jesus which the metaphor of God's body shaped by the Christic vision indicates in our age, if frugality itself is illuminated and complemented by this body metaphor. A frugal way of living is «a response to solidarity, an affirmation of the truth of the ecological model that our lives are interdependent»[170]. Frugality as a sense of sufficiency and the willingness to live within material limitations is a radical refusal of the neo-classical economic model and what it presumes such as egoistic individualism with an unquenchable desire for material affluence. Frugality, which originates from a motive that others may also live a decent life, is an expression of social concern for others, i.e., solidarity with other people, especially the marginalized who are denied even the basic needs for living as a human being. However, a frugal way of living must not remain merely as a personal virtue to help the poor. The practice of frugality must be transformed into and lead to the communal effort to promote distributive justice. This is precisely that to which the Christic vision awakens us.

One must remark that if it is to be an effective and proper way of actualizing Jesus' discipleship today in the world where the ecological degradation is a pressing issue, the idea of frugality needs to be supplemented by the metaphor of God's body so that it may take nature into account. Today frugality must be practiced with a deep concern for the entire earth and its integrity. Frugality then, which comes out of a concern for nature as well as for the poor, is regarded as a manifestation of solidarity with groaning nature. However, a frugal way of living must not remain only as a personal virtue to care for nature. The practice of frugality must be transformed into and lead to the communal effort to enhance sustainability for nature. This is precisely what God's body shaped by the Christic vision mandates.

To live out frugality on a daily basis in our consumeristic society is a formidable task. It will not bring any convenience, not to mention any benefits, to those who practice it. In the world where global market capitalism and consumerism prevail, a frugal way of living is not what we can practice without difficulty. In principle, it may be the case that we can live frugality with our personal resolution alone. In practice, however, our predominant circumstance makes its actualization an arduous task, though not impossible. For it means to run counter to the present mainstream of global market capitalism and consumerism, and

---

[170] S. MCFAGUE, *Life Abundant*, 116.

to renounce the immediate convenience and benefits that they may provide. Hence, frugality demands from us conviction, courage, and patience to resist almost irresistible temptations to material affluence and the consequent convenience. Despite these difficulties, the metaphor of God's body shaped by the Christic vision empowers and encourages us to live out frugality. In this regard, a case can now be made that the proposed metaphor has proved itself to be proper for our age, which needs urgently an attitude of concern and due regard for others, both human and nonhuman. The motive of frugality originates from our solidarity with the entire creation, especially with the vulnerable, which is expressed as our concern for sustainability and distributive justice. It would be a modest but efficacious practice of our solidarity with others to share the suffering of the poor and to relieve the burden of nature by means of frugal way of living. The practice of frugality is a moderate but practical manifestation, with a cosmic significance, of the compassionate love of Jesus for the vulnerable and marginalized.

PART III

AN ECOLOGICAL VISION OF THE WORLD

CHAPTER VI

The Emergence of an Ecological Vision of the World

The Main Proposition: A Christian perspective on the world provides an ecological vision of the world that awakens and cultivates ecological consciousness in human beings in the age of the global ecological crisis.

We have reflected up until now on the three propositions that can support the main proposition and thereby contribute to the formation of an ecological vision of the world. These three propositions suggest how we must perceive the world in the context of the global ecological crisis, and our reflection on them is a process in which each of them is theologically examined, explicated, and supported. We are now seeing a vision of the world come into sight as a consequence of this theologizing process. What is expected is an alternative vision to the present, predominant perspective on the world, which is believed to be responsible in great measure for the current ecological crisis. With a view to assimilating into an alternative vision of the world what was considered in the preceding three chapters, I will in this chapter present how our theological reflections have bolstered and enriched these propositions. I will then show that these propositions in turn reinforce with their respective theological significance the main proposition, which affirms an ecological vision of the world grounded in the Christian tradition.

1. An Alternative Vision of the World:
The Interconnectedness of All Creatures

It has been submitted as Proposition I that all the finite beings in the world are interrelated and interdependent. The world seen from the vantage point of the first proposition discloses a deep sense of disconnectedness in us, which characterizes the way we view other human beings and nature. The sense of disconnectedness can be regarded as a heritage of the mechanistic worldview that has become influential since around the seventeenth century in the West. This mechanistic perspective grasps the world, except the human being (or the human mind), who confronts it, as a machine composed of inert objects and moved by external forces. All the parts of a machine are externally related to one another and replaceable with other equivalents. The mechanistic worldview bears inevitably a dualistic tendency that separates humankind, as a subject who manages nature, from nature, as an object which is controlled by humanity. It confers on humanity a sanction to manipulate nature freely and to extract recklessly material resources from it. The damage that human beings inflict on nature could somehow be repaired with more advanced technologies in the future. The mechanistic worldview leads eventually to an anthropocentric attitude toward nature. Nature is seen to exist primarily for the sake of humankind.

The first proposition supposes that a sense of disconnectedness, motivated by a dualistic and anthropocentric perspective on the world, is responsible in great measure for the present ecological degradation throughout the earth. In confrontation with a deep sense of disconnectedness and its fatal impact on nature, the first proposition suggests that we need an alternative perspective on the world which conceives all things in the world as intrinsically connected with each other. In this conception of the world, all beings are considered always in relation to the whole, and interactions among them are regarded as important to the whole as well as to themselves. A sensibility for the interconnectedness of all creatures is presented as the first element of an alternative vision of the world in the age of the global ecological crisis. The following thoughts are what can contribute to the issue of relationality.

1.1 *The Dynamic Unity of Spirit and Matter*

It is in the human being that the unity of spirit and matter is revealed and experienced. We humans as spirit are present to and conscious of our body as matter. As we observe in ourselves, we cannot separate spirit from matter, distinct as they are. If nature is conceived as matter, which is inescapably given to us, we as spirit are indivisibly united with nature, too. This macroscopic perspective on the unity of spirit and matter discloses that the human being is united with nature intrinsically and inevitably, not externally or incidentally. The unity of the human being and nature reaches a more profound level when it is considered how spirit and life come into being. If God, who is at once transcendent and immanent in regard to creation, is conceived as the ultimate source of the essential active self-transcendence of all creatures, matter can be regarded to develop into life and spirit. In other words, life and spirit appear out of matter. The entire creation is now seen as one coherent process in which matter transcends itself and develops into life and spirit in virtue of God's immanence. The dynamic unity of spirit and matter, which originates in the divine immanence, reinforces and deepens our understanding of the relationship that human beings form with nature.

Human beings have emerged out of nature. In that measure, we are part of nature. As humanity is part of nature, human history is part of cosmic history. This intrinsic and indivisible unity of humankind and nature enables the expression of cosmic self-consciousness and cosmic bodily presence for the cosmos and humankind respectively. It can be said that the cosmos has reached the state of self-consciousness in humankind and every human being assumes part of the universe physically, infinitesimal as it is. This interpenetrating connection between humanity and nature can be regarded to endure even after death, if the human being is regarded as the substantial unity of soul and body. Given that it is by its nature that the soul forms and fosters a relationship with matter, the soul can be viewed to maintain its connection to matter after death by opening its bodily connection to the entire universe. The soul and its relationship become pan-cosmic. Likewise the body, which is dissolved into the earth after death, can be viewed to relate to the universe pan-cosmically. The soul is then seen to retain a connection with the body, even after death, but always by the medium of the cosmos. Hence, the human being as a whole is viewed to maintain a wider and deeper relationship with all creation. In short, the viewpoint of pan-cosmic relationship in death presents a perspective which confirms and strengthens the intrinsic relationship of humanity with nature grounded in the dynamic unity of spirit and matter.

1.2 *The Pneumatological Vision of Creation*

If we conceive God, according to the trinitarian tradition, as the Spirit who creates and sustains all creation in virtue of the divine power rather than as the absolute subject in the monotheistic comprehension,

God is viewed to be present in creation. The perception of God the Spirit in creation brings about a radical change in our way of perceiving God and the world. God is no longer absent in creation from this standpoint. Nor is creation separated from God. God instills without cease life-giving and life-sustaining breath into creation. All creatures exist in the power of the Spirit. All of them are connected with each other in the sense that the same power of the Spirit penetrates and permeates them. The interconnectedness of all creatures is an internal and intimate relationship due to the way the Spirit acts in creation: penetration and permeation. We humans are no exception to this relationship insofar as we too exist and live in the power of God. The connection of humanity with nature becomes more clear and profound when we consider that the Spirit sustains every creature by pouring out the divine power on the whole creation. The Spirit sustains and enlivens all creatures, but always through others, i.e., through the relationships which connect them. Relationships in creation are disclosed to be life-supporting ones. They are not given to creation from without. Rather, they are embedded in the entire creation from within owing to the permeation of the Spirit in creation. The interconnectedness of all creatures is not an incidental or external relationship but an inevitable and internal one. All creatures are dependent on others for existence insofar as they are dependent on the Spirit. Humanity is related to nonhuman creation at the level of existence.

As the one who renews all creatures, the Spirit is also the ground and source of their newness including a radical change in their own nature, while still preserving a profound unity among them. This perception of the Spirit renders humankind as the one with unparalleled newness such as self-consciousness and freedom, and thus drastically different from all nonhuman creatures, but still united with them in a more profound sense. The penetration and permeation of God the Spirit into creation from the beginning does not allow an absolute dichotomization of humanity from nature.

1.3 The Trinitarian Perspective on Creation

The triune God forms perfect unity among the three divine persons. This perfect unity is characterized by the trinitarian relationship of *perichoresis*. *Perichoresis* indicates the three divine persons penetrate and indwell in one another in perfect measure. *Perichoresis* presumes and suggests perfect openness among the divine persons. The communion of the triune God is revealed to be an open communion. The triune God embraces the whole creation, and creation participates in the divine communion owing to the divine openness. To the extent that it participates in the divine communion, creation can be regarded as a reflection of the Trinity. The trinitarian relationship characterized by *perichoresis* is implanted in creation as a trinitarian reflection. As such, creation reflects the divine communion. Creation as an implantation and reflection of *perichoresis* does not only imply that all creatures are deeply related to each other and form a profound unity. *Perichoresis* is the principle of life, love, inclusiveness, and equality, in virtue of the divine openness. These trinitarian values are inscribed also in creation when it was created in a trinitarian process. They flesh out the inter-connectedness of all creatures. Seen from the perspective of *perichoresis*, relationships in creation no longer indicate that creatures are related to each other in a disengaged manner. Rather, it is disclosed that inter-connectedness in creation is meant for life, love, inclusiveness, and equality, the principle of which is the relationship of the triune God. This sheds light especially on the relationship of humankind with nature. We are not only connected with nature intrinsically and inevitably. Nor are we merely dependent on it for our living. Insofar as we understand creation as a reflection of the Trinity, we are asked to promote the trinitarian values, which were embedded in creation, i.e., life, love, inclusiveness, and equality (or due regard), in our interaction with nature. The trinitarian perspective on creation asserts firmly that we are responsible for letting all these values, which are inscribed in creation by the triune God, be preserved and thrive.

1.4 *The World as the Body of God the Spirit*

In accordance with the pneumatological and thus trinitarian perspective on creation, creation may be conceived as a cosmic body, which is penetrated by and steeped in the spirit. In this perception of creation as the body of God and God as the spirit of this body, the whole creation is viewed as an organic body in which all creatures form a web of relationships in virtue of the spirit. At the same time, the spirit preserves this organic body by infusing it with life-sustaining breath. This body-spirit perception for the world and God works as an antidote against a strong dualistic and anthropocentric tendency toward nature, which is still predominant in us. The spirit is seen to knit all creatures together as one organic body. The organic body brings to the center the internal interrelatedness and interdependence of all parts. Any dualistic view-point that tends to separate humans from nature is denounced as that which does harm to the whole body. Any anthropocentric standpoint that is biased to view nonhuman creation only for the sake of humanity is rejected as that which does damage to the entire body.

Space comes to bear a special meaning and importance from the standpoint of the world as a cosmic and organic body. Space as a purely geometric notion recedes and space as a habitat comes to the fore, in the light of the world as body. Space becomes the environment which is absolutely necessary for all creatures to exist and for all life forms to get basics for living. At the same time, the world viewed as one body makes obvious that space available for all creatures is limited. It further implies that because of the organic interconnectedness of all, if some seek excessive space, others inevitably lose ground for their existence, suffer, and die. Denied one's space, no one can remain well. Deprived of one's space, no one can exist. In this regard, sin is no other than a refusal to stay one's space and thereby to ensure the well-being and life of others. Sin is a rejection of the ecological unity that we are related to nature in the one organic body of the world. We must stay in our space so that other creatures, to which we are inseparably related and on which we are fundamentally dependent, may get space for existence and life, and thus thrive. Only then can we too continue to exist, live, and flourish.

2. An Alternative Vision of the World: The Intrinsic Value of All Creatures

It has been suggested as Proposition II that all the finite beings in the world have their own intrinsic, though not absolute, value. The world seen from the perspective of the second proposition reveals an excessive, utilitarian tendency in us, which portrays the way we relate to nature. This instrumental attitude can be regarded as a consequence of the mechanistic worldview still prevalent in our mentality to see the world. Nature as a machine presupposes implicitly that we human beings must control, dominate, and subject nature to our needs. Nature must serve humankind. Knowledge is understood primarily as power and a tool to achieve this purpose. The perception of nature as a machine composed of inert and replaceable parts is an underlying sanction for our free experiment with and exploitation of it. Nature as a collection of inanimate objects finally turns into a warehouse of material resources for commodities, to which we have free access. Insofar as an excessive instrumental viewpoint on nature prevails, one can hardly have concern for the intrinsic value of nature. One's benefit such as monetary profit, material affluence, and convenience may be the most important factor to be considered in regard to nature.

The second proposition supposes that an extreme utilitarian attitude toward nature, stimulated by a dualistic and anthropocentric perspective on the world, is liable in great part for the current ecological deterioration. In confrontation with an excessive instrumental tendency and its devastating effects on nature, the second proposition suggests that we need an alternative perspective on the world from which we can acknowledge others primarily as they are, not as what they are for our sake. In this conception of the world, the intrinsic value of all beings emerges as that which we must properly recognize. The recognition of intrinsic value is presented as the second element of an alternative vision of the world in the age of the global ecological crisis. The following thoughts are what can contribute to this issue of intrinsic value.

2.1 *The Absolute Savior and the Incarnation*

From the perspective of salvation history, creation is the history of God's self-communication, which is the other aspect of creation's self-transcendence toward God. Given this viewpoint on creation, the event of the absolute savior as the irrevocable and irreversible event in the history of God's self-communication and human acceptance is conceivable. The event from which the absolute savior appears can be regarded as the incarnation. Put otherwise, the idea of the incarnation is transcendentally conceivable. Therefore, the idea of the absolute savior helps to accept the incarnation soberly. Since the absolute savior emerges out of creation and is part of it in that measure, creation is the material ground of the incarnation. Creation as the physical ground of the incarnation suggests strongly the goodness of creation. In virtue of the incarnation and owing to the dynamic unity of spirit and matter, not only that part of creation out of which the absolute savior appears but also the whole creation is united to the divine, divinized, and sanctified. The world seen from the perspective of the incarnation is already a transfigured world. This transfiguration of creation is a powerful confirmation of the intrinsic value of all creatures.

As regards the incarnation that occurred in history, the standpoint of salvation history leads one to view creation and the incarnation as two different stages of one single process toward the fulfillment of creation in the future: creation is a deficient mode of the incarnation; the incarnation is a perfect mode of creation and as such its final goal. This perception of creation and the incarnation brings to light the aspect that creation is in a process toward its fulfillment, as is shown in the incarnation, although it is uncompleted and imperfect. It discloses a hidden value of creation, which must be preserved. Without the present imperfection, there could be no future perfection, either. In this regard, the incarnation is the divine pledge to the perfection of the whole creation, which assures all creatures of intrinsic value. This relationship between creation and the incarnation also sheds light on the aspect of creation as the corporeal ground of the incarnation, without which the incarnation itself cannot occur. This aspect further confirms the goodness and value that the incarnation has pledged to creation. The goodness of creation is finally approved by the fact that an infinitesimal part of creation, as the ground of the incarnation, was actually assumed by God, who accepted it as God's own reality that it truly expresses God and lets God be present in the world. Again, in virtue of the dynamic unity of spirit and matter, the consequence of the incarnation, in which God took on a segment of creation, reaches the whole creation. Indeed, the world is a transfigured world.

If it is considered that the significance of Jesus' life to the entire creation, inaugurated by the incarnation, is finalized in his death, Jesus' death too must have brought a profound change in the world. In terms of the pan-cosmic relationship that the soul forms with the cosmos after death, Jesus was inserted, in his death, into the world and became the permanent destiny, intrinsic principle, heart, and center of the world. Jesus' death infused the effect of the incarnation to every single part of creation through his pan-cosmic relationship. In other words, his death deepens what the incarnation brings about to the world. It is then held that the entire creation shines forth with its ineffable dignity, which springs from its transfiguration that the incarnation has carried into effect and Jesus' death has intensified.

2.2 *The Christological Vision of Creation*

The christological vision of creation is to view creation in the light of Christ, through, in, and for whom all things have been created. Creation is understood, in this perspective, as a dynamic reality, which begins with initial creation and proceeds continuously toward the new creation.

Throughout this movement, Christ undergirds creation as the mediator, the upholder, and the lord of creation. As such, Christ is the ground of the original creation, the source of continuous creation, and the assurance of the new creation respectively. These profound relationships of Christ with the whole creation throughout its dynamic process awaken us to the inherent value and goodness of this world notwithstanding its present, obvious drawbacks. Creation seen from this dynamic standpoint appears as a promise for the final fulfillment in the future. Creation as a not-yet-fulfilled-promise also enables us not to lose sight of its goodness and value despite its defects in the present. In the future fulfillment, defects will disappear and goodness will be brought to perfection.

The christological vision of creation is inclusive in that all creatures are viewed to be under the affectionate concern and care of Christ. This Christ is viewed as the firstborn of creation, the reconciler of creation, and the firstborn from the dead. As the firstborn of creation, Christ is the eldest brother of all creatures. As such, he regards all creatures with affectionate concern and care. Christ cherishes all of them as they are because they are his brothers and sisters. As the reconciler of creation, Christ is the advocate of all creatures. As such, he offered his life for all creation and achieved peace and the reconciliation of all creatures with God. All are so precious to him that he surrendered even his life for them. This testifies persuasively that Jesus himself acknowledged and appreciated deeply the inherent goodness of creation. As the firstborn from the dead, Christ is the pioneer and assurance of the new creation. As such, he made the eschatological promise of the new creation present and palpable in this world. Christ has manifested in the present a radical transformation of creation in the future, promised the future fulfillment of creation, and confirmed its value as it is now. The cosmic concern of Christ for all creation is in accord with the love of the earthly Jesus. Therefore, the universal concern of Christ powerfully proves that even the vulnerable, i.e., nature and the poor, have been granted intrinsic goodness and value by God.

2.3 *The Panentheistic Perspective on Creation*

The trinitarian perspective on creation leads to the panentheistic perspective that God is in all and all is in God. The panentheistic conception of God and creation can be regarded as an outward manifestation to creation of the divine relationship of the triune God, i.e., *perichoresis*. The panentheistic perspective brings to the fore nature as a sacrament of God. As such, it provides a fundamental ground for the intrinsic value of nature, based on the intimate relationship of nature to God. It also provides a safeguard against an instrumental perspective on sacramentality to regard it only as a means to ascend to God. The panentheistic standpoint stresses that the divine presence in nature is as real and enduring as nature and therefore does not depend on our perception or imagination of it. This solidifies a ground for the intrinsic value of nature. As sacramentality is dependent not on humans but on God, the intrinsic value of nature is not at our disposal. It is God who inscribes intrinsic value in every creature, different as it is. Finally, from the panentheistic perspective, the disengaged presence of God in nature recedes, and instead the affective presence of God comes to the fore. It discloses more concretely what the divine presence in the world means. The presence of God in creation indicates, from the panentheistic viewpoint, that the trinitarian values which *perichoresis* effects are embedded and reflected in creation. What *perichoresis* brings forth is life, love, inclusiveness, and equality. These values embedded in creation in virtue of the divine, affective presence further support the intrinsic value of all creatures. The whole creation is suffused with the trinitarian values, although they may seem vague to us. For us to perceive nature as a sacrament of God would demand that we cherish and foster the intrinsic value of nature characterized by these values of the triune God, who is present in it.

2.4 *The Christic Vision and God's Body*

The Christic vision and the metaphor of God's body complement each other to bring into relief a concern for nature. The vision that Christ had at heart is a destabilizing, inclusive, and nonhierarchical vision for the poor and the marginalized, which is against and denounces oppressive and exploitative worldviews and structures. It must be noted, however, that the scope of the Christic vision, which perceives clearly the inherent and effaceable dignity of all human beings, particularly those who have no voice, is still restricted to the human world. The metaphor of God's body awakens a cosmic dimension in the Christic vision, broadens its horizon, and enables it to encompass nature within its scope. The Christic vision with an extended range of destabilization calls for the end of the oppressive and exploitative, anthropocentric view of nature and the socio-economic structures which infringe violently on nature. It demands that we replace them with a more harmonious and symbiotic view and an ecologically sensitive structure so that its own goodness may be regarded and preserved. It means a radical change in our perspective to see nature. The Christic vision with a broadened horizon of inclusiveness makes obvious that every creature has its own place to exist in the world. This aspect of inclusiveness reminds us that God loves all, particularly the marginalized, because they are in desperate situations. It leads us to reach out to them, one of which today is nature. This mandates that we let it live and thrive. The Christic vision with a widened scope of nonhierarchy implies that Jesus' solidarity and compassion, expressed in his death on the cross, include all creatures in the world. This encourages us to stand on the side of nature despite of disadvantages or risks that may accompany us.

The Christic vision reveals in the Christian context the significance of ecological unity, which is a basic perspective of the metaphor of God's body. In the conception of the world as God's body, the divine immanence is revealed as God's love for creation. God is present in the whole creation because God loves all creatures. In the light of the destabilizing, inclusive, and nonhierarchical Christic vision, ecological unity among all creatures does not only show that all creatures are interconnected. It also reveals that they are interconnected so that all of them, even the least, can exist in virtue of ecological unity. In this regard, ecological unity is an actualization of the Christic vision in the world. Ecological unity illuminated by the Christic vision does not simply hold that we are part of nature. It also requires us to give due regard to all creatures so that even the least can exist. The metaphor of God's body shaped by the Christic vision reinforces the goodness and intrinsic value of all creatures, especially those of the least in the world, both human and nonhuman.

3. An Alternative Vision of the World:
The Compatibility of Ecological Concern and Social Concern

It has been presented as Proposition III that concern for nature is compatible with concern for the poor. The world from the standpoint of the third proposition shows that a deep sense of disconnectedness and an excessive utilitarian attitude, underlaid by the mechanistic worldview, has brought calamities to both humanity and nature. The disaster inflicted on humanity and nature can be characterized by mass poverty and the ecological disruption of the earth in the midst of unprecedented material affluence. It is the case that there are two different voices: one voice for the priority of the poor; the other for that of nature. In confrontation with a deep sense of interconnectedness, an excessive utilitarian tendency, and their disastrous consequences on humanity and nature, on the one hand, and those two different voices, on the other hand, the third proposition holds that we must maintain and practice ecological concern and social concern together. This proposition convinces us that poverty and the ecological crisis must be grappled with and overcome together because both of them have occurred out of the same root. In this conception of the world, poverty and ecological degradation are regarded not as two separate realities competing for priority but as two different phenomena that originate from the same cause called a deep sense of disconnectedness and an excessive utilitarian attitude toward others. We are asked on this basis to pursue ecological justice and social justice together. The compatibility of ecological concern and social concern is presented as the third characteristic of an alternative vision of the world in the age of the global ecological crisis. The following thoughts are what can contribute to the issue of compatibility.

3.1 *Freedom as a Ground of Social Concern and Ecological Concern*

Given an integrated perspective on the world grounded in the dynamic unity of spirit (the human being) and matter (nature), a case can be made from the standpoint of freedom that ecological concern is mandated once social concern is demanded. Freedom in a profound sense means a fundamental option for God whereby one accepts God's self-communication and lives according to God' will. This act of freedom indicates one's love for God. Hence, freedom in an authentic sense leads eventually to the love of God. Meanwhile, it is in the love of neighbor that the love of God is actualized and manifested. For it is in our concrete experience in the world, primarily in our encounter with other human beings, that we have the transcendental experience of God. Furthermore, the love of neighbor bears inevitably a social and political character and extends to all human beings in the world, insofar as we are a socio-political being. In short, social concern, whose origin consists in the human freedom, belongs to an existential dimension of the human being. No one is exempt from the duty of social concern. If we view social concern from an integrated perspective on the world grounded in the dynamic unity of spirit and matter, the scope of social concern is widened to nature. For nature and humankind are distinct but more profoundly united with each other. The love of neighbor, as a concrete realization of the love of God, reaches nature and demands justice for its sake as well as for the sake of humanity. Eventually, our freedom is a freedom to dedicate ourselves to building a socially and ecologically just world.

3.2 *Jesus and the Messianic Sabbath*

Jesus and the kingdom of God must be understood in the light of the messianic sabbath, to the measure that he proclaimed in his life and ministry the inauguration of the messianic sabbath and dedicated himself to its actualization in the world. The messianic sabbath illustrates the kingdom of God in terms of the perfect liberation of humanity and nature. God's kingdom in turn implies that messianic sabbath is already brought into effect, incomplete as it is. The reign of God is the fulfillment of the messianic sabbath for both humankind and nature. The demand of the messianic sabbath reveals a hidden, cosmic dimension of Jesus' ministry. We can thereby understand more comprehensively what he ultimately sought. In the light of the messianic sabbath, his affectionate concern for human beings, particularly for the vulnerable, is revealed to embrace the whole creation. As the pioneer of the messianic sabbath, he is seen to strive for the liberation of all creation, encompassing nature as well as humanity. In this regard, the ministry that he carried out must be seen as a mediation of the messianic sabbath to all creation. The messianic sabbath demands a breakthrough of a deeprooted vicious circle of both the impoverishment of human beings and the exploitation of nature. One may say that Jesus in his life and ministry is steeped explicitly in social concern and implicitly in ecological concern, both of which the messianic sabbath mandates. Insofar as Jesus is viewed to live in the spirit of the messianic sabbath, our discipleship must consist in the realization in the world of the messianic sabbath for which he strove and struggled. If we are to live and act in the spirit of the messianic sabbath that Jesus proclaimed and lived, we must explore, opt for, and practice an alternative to the present, predominant socio-economic structure that ensures neither justice to humanity nor sustainability to nature.

3.3 *The Trinitarian Community and the Kingdom of God*

According to the trinitarian perspective, creation is modeled on the divine community of the triune God. Creation is a reflection of the trinitarian community. As such, creation is meant to be a community suffused with the trinitarian values that the trinitarian relationship of *perichoresis* brings forth, i.e., life, love, inclusiveness, and equality. All these values must be respected, maintained, and cultivated in the whole creation. If they are violated in either nature or society, the consequence is not restricted to either. It eventually affects both. For we are so inextricably related to nature that the way we deal with other human beings is reflected in nature and *vice versa*. As the ideal model of creation, the divine community of the triune God condemns injustice in society and nature as a grave sin which suffocates those trinitarian values. As the prototype of creation, at the same time, the trinitarian community gives us inspiration and aspiration to the liberation of all creation. It awakens us to the sinfulness of the present situation and encourages us to stand on the side of the poor and nature. It demands that we act in the world in a direction that ecological justice as well as social justice is built and promoted.

The kingdom of God is referred to as the ultimate future of creation. It can be compared to a feast to which all creatures are invited and in which they enjoy cosmic kinship under the parental love and care of God. The value of communion and sharing, two prominent kingdom values, are to be preserved, respected, and promoted in the world, which is transformed into the kingdom of God. As the ultimate future of the world, the kingdom ôf God condemns injustice such as oppressive domination and excessive possession as a grave sin which stifles communion and sharing in the world. At the same time, it infuses us with inspiration and aspiration to the liberation of all creation, whereby we can dedicate ourselves to the promotion of social justice and ecological justice.

3.4 *God's body and the Christic Vision*

The conception of the world as God's body renders the world as one cosmic organism in which an immense number of individuals form radical unity in diversity. All are viewed to be organically interconnected. In this organic perception of the world, the world does not appear as a collection of inanimate objects. Rather, it is seen as a web of relationships in which all individuals, including human beings, exist and live together. In this world, the human being is not primarily an individual who competes with others to amass material wealth. Rather, the human being is understood primarily as a member of the community called the world where personal well-being is inseparably connected with the well-being of other human beings and nature. The human being is always an individual in community. Moreover, humanity as a whole is inseparably related to nature and absolutely dependent on nature. In this perception of the world, human beings and nature must thrive together. Otherwise, neither can flourish. The destabilizing, inclusive, and nonhierarchical Christic vision, which denounces oppressive and exploitative worldviews and structures, further raises a particular concern for the vulnerable and marginalized. Today, one may say, they are the poor and exploited nature.

God's body shaped by Christic vision brings to light distributive justice and sustainability. Distributive justice and sustainability are meant to ensure the well-being of the individual human being, even the least in society, and the integrity of nature respectively. We must give attention to both. Without sustainability for nature, human beings cannot live well individually or collectively. Nor can distributive justice be ensured. The very source of material distribution will be in peril. At the same time, without the distributive justice for each individual human being, nature cannot remain well. Nor can sustainability be secured. Those who are threatened to starvation are forced to use the natural environment in an exhaustive manner for survival, without mentioning those who maintain an immoderate, consumption-oriented way of living which plunders nature systematically and rapidly. Concern for the poor (distributive justice) and concern for nature (sustainability) are mutually dependent.

4. The Emergence of an Ecological Vision of the World

At the outset of this study, a premise has been made that we need an alternative vision to the present, excessively dualistic and anthropocentric perspective on the world in order to overcome the ecological crisis of the earth. It has been submitted, then, as the main proposition that a Christian perspective on the world provides an ecological vision of the world that awakens and cultivates in us ecological consciousness in the age of the global ecological crisis. Subsequently, three propositions have been suggested to make a case for this main proposition. The first proposition regarding the interconnectedness of all creatures, the second one concerning the intrinsic value of all creatures, and the third one about the compatibility of ecological concern and social concern have been considered, explicated, and supported theologically, as seen previously.

What is attained as a consequence of this theological reflection is *a perspective on the world*. With regard to the premise, the attained perspective is definitely an *alternative* vision to the current, excessively dualistic and anthropocentric worldview, in that it is inclusive and cosmocentric. As an inclusive vision of the world grounded in the first proposition, it requires that we shift our focus from the distinctiveness of humanity from nature to their interconnectedness. As a cosmocentric vision based on the first and second propositions, it informs and reminds us that we are part, rather than the center, of the universe and dependent on it. It also demands that we give due regard to nature and all those in it. Insofar as the current, prevalent perspective on the world is responsible in great measure for the present environmental degradation of the earth, this inclusive and cosmocentric vision can help us overcome the ecological crisis at the root.

With regard to the main proposition, the alternative perspective thus attained is a *ecological* vision of the world in that it is relational and inclusive. First, the alternative perspective is an ecological vision in an epistemological sense. It recognizes that all creatures in the world are interrelated and interdependent in virtue of the divine immanence. God, the creator of all, is also the God who sustains, empowers, and renews all creatures. This perspective considers seriously relationality in the world. Relationship is viewed as real as being. Interconnectedness is what is embedded in creation by virtue of God's immanence, and in that measure, it is real. It is a life-giving, enduring, and renewing relationship. Moreover, this perspective is inclusive in that it regards every creature seriously, even the least. If all creatures are recognized to be intrinsically connected with each other, the aspect of inclusiveness is already suggested and expected. Since all creatures are interrelated and interdependent, the interactions to which each one contributes through this relationship in its own way are important to all of them and the whole creation. Conversely, all creatures are interconnected so that even the least creatures may not be alienated.

Second, the alternative perspective is an ecological vision in an ethical sense. It admits that all creatures in the world have intrinsic value in their own degree, grounded in their relationship with God. God the creator is the God who loves all creatures so deeply that God became a creature as well as God is immanent in creation. Every creature forms somehow profoundly a relationship with God in virtue of this love of God. In that measure, everyone has its own reason and importance to exist. Every creature is good for one's own sake. From this standpoint, all creatures must be regarded seriously no matter how little it may look. This perspective is inclusive of all. It demands that the intrinsic value of all creatures rooted in God be properly regarded and respected. Meanwhile, no one is self-sufficient, and to that extent, every creature needs others and is dependent on them, as already implied by interconnectedness in creation. Therefore, this perspective also admits one's instrumental value for others, but always insofar as one's intrinsic value is ensured.

Third, the alternative perspective is an ecological vision in the sense of praxis. It holds that concern for nature is compatible with concern for the poor. Humanity and nature are intrinsically related to each other in virtue of God' immanence in creation. Both of them have their intrinsic value in virtue of their relationship with God. This perspective also perceives that the poor and nature are the victims of the unjust socio-economic structures and power. The interconnectedness of all creatures and the consequent interactions among them suggest strongly that injustice on the one side will eventually impact on the other side. This vision mandates therefore that we seek justice both in society and nature. In this respect, relationality is an essential element to this vision. It is also inclusive of all, both humankind and nature. God has inscribed in the human being a dynamism toward God, which is actualized in one's concern for others, both human and nonhuman. Jesus Christ, the incarnate God, strove for the liberation of all creatures. The entire world, as a reflection of the trinitarian community and as a seed of the kingdom of God, is permeated with the trinitarian and kingdom values, which must be preserved and promoted. As such, the alternative vision understands that justice must be practiced and realized in both society and nature.

It can now be observed that these three propositions are reciprocally related to each other and form unity among themselves. The interconnectedness of all creatures grounds and supports the intrinsic value of all creatures, and it renders compatible ecological concern and social concern. The intrinsic value of all creatures stimulates and promotes justice in nature as well as in society. The motive of justice is strengthened by the interconnectedness of all. Ecological justice and social justice ensure the intrinsic value of all and maintain intact the interconnectedness of all. In sum, the three propositions do not speak of three different realities in creation. They express one and the same reality, the love of God for all creation, in three different ways.

What we have now obtained is an ecological vision of the world, which is expected to instill in us ecological consciousness. It must be noted that this ecological vision of the world is *Christian* in that all theological reflections up until now are explicitly or implicitly rooted in the trinitarian conception of God, which is properly Christian. The source of interconnectedness is found eventually in God's immanence in creation. It is in virtue of the triune God that all creatures are connected with one another. The ground of intrinsic value consists in one's relationship with God, who was incarnated and is immanent in creation. It is in virtue of the triune God that all creatures deserve their own intrinsic goodness and value. This integrated perspective, which is based on interconnectedness and intrinsic value and thereby comprehensive of humanity and nature, awakens us to cosmic justice, which embraces both social justice and ecological justice. This cosmic justice mandates our concern for nature as well as concern for the poor. In short, it can be held that at the root of this ecological vision of the world is the triune God.

It has been mentioned that an ecological vision of the world is a cosmocentric vision. As such, it contains an effective restraint to an excessive, anthropocentric and instrumental attitude toward nature. It can now be said that an ecological vision of the world grounded in the trinitarian conception of God is in a more profound sense a theocentric vision. For the source, ground, and motive of one's cosmic concern consist in God, who created, sustains, and leads to fulfillment the world. Therefore, as a theocentric vision, an ecological vision of the world also functions as a restraint to an immoderate, cosmocentric attitude toward nature, another extreme attitude in regard to nature.

In sum, an ecological vision of the world which has finally come into view is the trinitarian vision of the world. This vision can be referred to as the perspective of the triune God, who contemplates the world as a whole[1]. It is the vision of God, who created the world out of love. It is the vision of God, who became a creature out of love. It is the vision of God, who is present in creation out of love from beginning to end. We human beings, who are made in *imago Dei*, are invited to share in the trinitarian and ecological vision of the world.

---

[1] Cf. ST. IGNATIUS OF LOYOLA, *The Spiritual Exercises*, n.102.

CHAPTER VII

A Christian Spirituality and Life
Grounded in an Ecological Vision of the World

1. Christian Spirituality and Life

The term «spirituality» is such a vague and vexing word in its meaning and usage that it often evades an exact definition. Nonetheless, we need a description of it, at least in a broad sense, as we begin to explore a Christian spirituality and life grounded in and motivated by an ecological vision of the world. A simple and broad description of spirituality may be given as «the authentic human quest for ultimate value»[1]. This rendering of spirituality implies that spirituality belongs to a fundamental and existential realm of the human being. When we ponder on the ultimate meaning of life and seek to live in accordance with it, we are somehow engaged in what spirituality means. «On this existential level spirituality is constituted by the actual way any given person leads his or her life. [...] Spirituality is thus a general anthropological category»[2]. In this regard, spirituality refers to «the experience of consciously striving to integrate one's life in terms not of isolation and self-absorption but of self-transcendence toward the ultimate value one perceives»[3]. Spirituality is conceivable, in this sense, without any explicit recognition of God, although it is already implicitly associated with God in its reference to «the ultimate value». In sum, spirituality is primarily concerning one's way of living with regard to a profound meaning and purpose of life and one's experience from it.

---

[1] M. DOWNEY, *Understanding Christian Spirituality*, 14.
[2] R. HAIGHT, «Sin and Grace», 135.
[3] S.M. SCHNEIDER, «Theology and Spirituality», 266.

In addition to this experiential level of spirituality, there is an abstract and reflective dimension in spirituality, which refers to «the theory of how human life should be led»[4]. Therefore, spirituality comprises «both a lived experience and an academic discipline»[5]. This division of spirituality can be classified in more detail: first, «a fundamental dimension of human being»; second, «the full range of human experience as it is brought to bear on the quest for integration through self-transcendence»; third, «the expression of insights about this experience»; and fourth, «a disciplined study»[6]. This classification can be regarded as four different phases in one and the same process in which one recognizes, actualizes, expresses, and articulates what is called spirituality. It is in experience that spirituality is recognized and actualized; it is experience that is expressed and articulated by spirituality as an academic discipline. Therefore, experience emerges as a critical element in all these four phases of spirituality.

One can speak, to be sure, of Christian spirituality. For this, one may understand in the Christian context what has been remarked on spirituality in general. Christian spirituality may then refer to that which «has to do with *our way of being Christian*, in response to the call of God, issued through Jesus Christ in the power of the Holy Spirit»[7]. Simply speaking, Christian spirituality is «living according to the Holy Spirit»[8]. The ultimate value that one pursues is informed by the revelation of God manifested through the person of Jesus Christ and kept alive in the power of the Spirit. Christian spirituality too is inseparable from experience, which occurs in relation to God revealed through Jesus in the Spirit. If we Christians follow Jesus Christ in the Spirit, we are already living a Christian spirituality[9]. Therefore, Christian spirituality is not restricted to a so-called spiritual realm, which is contrasted with a realm where our ordinary life unfolds. If we recall what Rahner has mentioned, i.e., the transcendental experience of God is always given to us in our categorical experience in the world, we can and must live a

---

[4] R. HAIGHT, «Sin and Grace», 135.

[5] J.W. CONN, «Spirituality», 972.

[6] M. DOWNEY, *Understanding Christian Spirituality*, 43.

[7] R.P. MCBRIEN, *Catholicism*, 1020.

[8] J. SOBRINO, *Spirituality of Liberation*, 124.

[9] M. DOWNEY, *Understanding Christian Spirituality*, 31. Cf. *Ibid.*, 44: «Christian spirituality is not anything other than Christian life in the Spirit: being conformed to the person of Christ, and being united in communion with God and with others».

life of spirituality in every historical event and moment, no matter how minute it may be[10].

In regard to the reflective dimension of spirituality, it can be held that «human experience is the very *"stuff"* of spirituality»[11]. «At the root of all spirituality is a spiritual experience [...]»[12]. Spirituality, especially as an academic discipline, builds on living experience as theology does. In fact, the experience of Christians on the one hand, and theology and spirituality on the other, are mutually related to each other and bolster one another. The praxes of Christians provide concrete materials upon which theology and spirituality ponder and build themselves. Theology and spirituality in turn illuminate this experience in the light of the Christian theological and spiritual traditions and encourage Christians to live their faith more authentically. «Here the meaning of spirituality approaches the meaning of theology insofar as theology has bearing on Christian life»[13]. Besides, spirituality and theology support each other. Theology must be grounded in spirituality and nourished by it. Otherwise, it would become speculative and have little influence on Christian life. Spirituality must in turn be informed by theology and rooted in it. Otherwise, it would run the risk of losing its identity as specifically *Christian* spirituality. In sum, Christian theology, spirituality, and life are interwoven with each other and influence one another.

Given the intimate connection of Christian theology, spirituality, and life, I will in this chapter consider how an ecological vision of the world, which is a consequence of theological reflections on the three propositions of this study, brings forth and fosters a specific Christian spirituality and life[14]. What is intended here is not a study on Christian spirituality or life in general, which goes beyond the scope of this study. Rather, I will reflect on how the three propositions that constitute an ecological vision of the world may help us grapple with the grave reality which we face today. More specifically, I will examine how these three propositions can contribute to forming a spirituality of life and peace and to fostering a Christian life committed to justice in order to dispel the power of death, violence, and injustice, which shadow the whole world densely.

---

[10] Cf. K. RAHNER, *Foundations of Christian Faith*, 140. See also M. DOWNEY, *Understanding Christian Spirituality*, 33.

[11] M. DOWNEY, *Understanding Christian Spirituality*, 91.

[12] J. SOBRINO, *Spirituality of Liberation*, 56.

[13] R. HAIGHT, «Sin and Grace», 135.

[14] Spirituality here refers to a reflective level of spirituality.

2. A Fragmentary Thought on the World: Life, Peace, and Justice

It has been mentioned that a sense of disconnectedness and an excessive, instrumental attitude toward others prevail in us today. A widespread and deep-rooted phenomenon today that characterizes our world is an excessive, consumeristic tendency, which pursues immoderate material wealth and consumption[15]. Market capitalist economy is known to have contributed in great measure to this consumeristic tendency[16]. An economic model and a way of living that strive only for the exclusive accumulation of wealth and the extravagant consumption of goods are in line with and solidified by a sense of disconnectedness and an extreme utilitarianism. In this situation, all beings that exist, even human beings as well as nonhuman life forms and the natural environment, are eventually viewed as the means of producing wealth and commodities. One's value is dependent on one's utility and decided by market mechanism. Human rights and dignity in society, without mentioning due regard for nature, have dropped in the background. What is considered vital is material profit and interests. In this context, the sacrifice of many without power would be taken for granted for the benefit of a few with power. Justice has been lost in society; integrity is no longer found in nature. Justice, if any, means only the justice of those who have power. With the loss of justice, peace can hardly put down roots in the world. Peace for the sake of all, not peace only for the sake of a few with power, cannot germinate and thrive unless all are given due regard and respect. In the Christian context, it can be held that peace depends on the right order and harmony inscribed in creation by God the creator. Justice can be conceived in this sense as what maintains intact this God-given order and harmony, out of which peace emerges and in which it remains.

Our present world may be compared to a world where a few dominate and control many in order to possess material affluence exclusively. The world is stained with an extreme unbalance in the possession and distribution of wealth[17]. This is not possible except by the exploitation of others, both human and nonhuman. Many human beings

---

[15] Cf. JOHN PAUL II, *Centesimus Annus*, n. 37. Here consumerism is understood in a close connection with the ecological problem.

[16] Cf. C. MERCHANT, *Radical Ecology*, 44-45.

[17] Cf. S. MCFAGUE, *Live Abundant*, 80.88. More updated data in this respect can be obtained by access to websites such as those of the Worldwatch Institute and World Resources Institute.

are denied human rights and dignity that they deserve; nature is denied due regard that it deserves. This situation cannot be sustained except by violent oppression on those exploited. The world with this grim reality deviates greatly from the order of creation, according to which all creatures are meant to live in harmony. Justice receded from our world and injustice prevails in it. War and violence prevalent in the world today are in fact nothing but a pertinacious attempt to protect and increase the affluence that a few have exclusively accumulated at the expense of many human beings and nature. Their wealth is a face of their greediness. It is nourished by the abuse and exploitation of an immense number of the poor and nature. It is an exploitative affluence, which is not possible without the forced sacrifice of the poor and nature.

Insofar as one's right to exist and live is denied, peace will eventually be broken. Peace, if any, would be a disguised or coerced peace that is enforced by oppression and violence. Without peace, life cannot endure and flourish, either. The ecological crisis today too can be conceived as a consequence of the lack of peace and life. As Pope John Paul II points out in his message concerning ecology, «the lack of respect for life» underlies the present ecological problem[18]. One can hold in accordance with him that a sense of respect in us for life is disappearing. It has been noticed that life, which used to be conceived and respected as mystery, is no longer viewed and dealt with as such by many, for various reasons. Moreover, today, even life has come to be regarded as a means for economic wealth. It may be said that life turns into a commodity. In a word, a sense of awe for life has disappeared. Instead, a power of death seems to prevail in our world. The world where life and peace are trampled and suffocated testifies to the loss of justice. Violence and death are unjustly inflicted on the vulnerable, i.e., the poor and nature, for the sake of a few. The voices that claim concern for nature and the poor are overshadowed by the logic of efficiency and development. Many in the world are groaning under the violent power of death, aspiring to life, peace, and justice. Without justice, peace is not actualized; without peace, life is stifled. This is a reality, grim as it is, that comes into view when we ponder upon our world seriously and earnestly.

Paradoxically, the dismal situation that we have observed awakens us to an urgent need of spirituality. «It is our profound awareness of evil

---

[18] JOHN PAUL II, *Peace with God the Creator,* n. 7.

[...] that has the most profound implications for spirituality today»[19]. We need a spirituality which can encourage us to hold fast to an unyielding hope for life and peace so that we may not give way to the power of death and violence. We need a spirituality which can empower us to dedicate ourselves to the realization of justice so that violent, death-imposing power may finally be vanquished and life and peace may thrive. If we recall that Christian spirituality indicates «living according to the Spirit», we must ground a spirituality of life and peace in our faith in and experience of God, who created and sustains all creatures and will lead them to the final fulfillment. An authentic spirituality of life and peace, firmly rooted in the God of life and peace, leads to the praxis of justice, which will in turn bring forth life and peace in the world.

3. An Ecological Vision of the World and a Spirituality of Life and Peace

In his letter to Romans, St. Paul mentions two types of people, who live according to either the flesh or the Spirit (cf. Rom. 8:5). He continues: «To set the mind on the flesh is death, but to set the mind on the Spirit is life and peace» (Rom. 8:6). It is first noted that the consequence of being adherent to the Spirit is life and peace. Given that Christian spirituality is living according to the Spirit, any genuine Christian spirituality is expected to bring forth life and peace as its consequence. Spirituality as an option for a specific way of living is also noticed, as implied in living according to *either* flesh *or* the Spirit. We are asked to choose an actual way we lead our life, which belongs to spirituality at the existential level. The prototype of Christian spirituality in this sense is found in Jesus of Nazareth, a man who was born in the power of the Spirit and lived with the Spirit. Insofar as he lived in the Spirit, he can be understood to bring forth life and peace in the world. Christian spirituality, as a concrete way of living of those who follow Jesus, is inseparably related and unexceptionally invited to his discipleship. Now let us take a look at how the interconnectedness and intrinsic value of all creatures, which constitute the epistemological and ethical dimensions of an ecological vision of the world, inspire and contribute to a spirituality of life and peace respectively.

—

---

[19] M. DOWNEY, *Understanding Christian Spirituality*, 16.

3.1 *A Spirituality of Life: The Interconnectedness of All Creatures*

God, who creates, sustains, and renews all creation, is the God of life (cf. Gen. 1:1-2; Ps. 104:29-30). All that exists gets existence from God; all living creatures get life from God. This God of life is the God of love as well, and as such, God gives life to the world. «For God so loved the world that God gave his only Son, so that everyone who believes in him may not perish but may have eternal life» (John 3:16). Jesus, the only Son of God, declared himself life (cf. John 14:6). He gives «a spring of water gushing up to eternal life» (John 4:14). God is also the God of liberation. Jesus, whom the Spirit of the Lord anointed, proclaimed liberation from poverty, captivity, blindness, and oppression. This liberation is the liberation of all creation from all that oppresses, which is expected in the year of the Lord's favor (cf. Luke 4:18-19). This act of liberation is directed toward life. Various human situations, from which Jesus proclaimed liberation, such as poverty, captivity, blindness, and oppression, ultimately manifests death[20]. Oppression means death; liberation means life. The kingdom of God that Jesus proclaimed in his words and mediated in his acts is the kingdom of life and liberation as well. In the reign of God, everyone is liberated from all that is oppressive, and thereby everyone is given life to the full. God vindicated Jesus and confirmed his deeds by raising him from the dead. «The resurrection of Jesus is the sign to the world that God indeed does reign, does give life in death, and that the love of God is stronger even than death (Rom. 8:36-39)»[21]. Jesus is thus «the Author of life, whom God raised from the dead» (Acts 3:15), as St. Peter preached. The risen Jesus became «a life-giving spirit», as St. Paul claimed (1 Cor. 15:45).

The triune God, revealed through Jesus Christ in the Holy Spirit, is the God of life. The three divine persons penetrate thoroughly each other. Each divine person gives oneself to the others ceaselessly and completely, and thereby one lets the others dwell in the one perfectly. The divine life consists in the divine communion. Life is possible only in communion, as the divine life supremely manifests. Exclusion or alienation only brings about death. To live is meant to live *with* and *for* others, as is shown in the divine communion[22]. To live *over* others brings death to them. Life comes out of the relationship of communion.

---

[20] G. GUTIÉRREZ, *The God of Life*, 8.
[21] NCCB, *The Challenge of Peace*, n. 50.
[22] G. GUTIÉRREZ, *The God of Life*, 12.

In this regard, the first proposition of interconnectedness ultimately leads to life. Each one of us exists in virtue of others, i.e., through our relationships with others, whether we are aware of it or not. In this sense, all the reflections in regard to the first proposition contribute, in their own way, to respect for life. The dynamic unity of spirit and matter demonstrates the intrinsic and inevitable relationship of humanity and nature, at once spatially and temporally. The pneumatological vision of creation discloses relationships in the world as the source of existence, life, and evolution in virtue of the Spirit in creation. The trinitarian perspective on creation fleshes out relationships in creation with the trinitarian values of life, love, inclusiveness, and equality. The body of God the spirit pictures the world as one organic body and brings to the center the importance of space for existence and life.

For a specific example, let us think of the trinitarian perspective on creation in regard to the issue of life. From this standpoint, creation is viewed as a reflection of the trinitarian community. As such, the values that the trinitarian relationship brings forth, i.e., life, love, inclusiveness, and equality (or due regard), are regarded to be inscribed in the world. These trinitarian values reflected in creation are meant to be nourished by the relationships that all creatures have among them in the world. If we live according to what the interconnectedness of all creatures dictates, all these values are expected to thrive in the world. Otherwise, we would obstruct and even smother them.

In fact, all these values are intrinsically interwoven. Love always tends toward life, and life is the supreme actualization of love. To love others means, in a profound sense, to let them have life abundantly. Life and love will not allow anyone to be alienated. Alienation would be a gradual, but certain, process to death. Instead, life and love would embrace all that exists. This inclusiveness does not merely mean that we must be included in the world in a physical sense. Rather, it indicates that we must be given our due respect as the human being. Due regard for all creatures would ensure life to all. This would be possible only when domination and oppression, which will eventually bring about death, are vanquished. Equality means that we renounce living *over* others, choose to live *with* them, and let them have life abundantly as we have. In this understanding, life, love, inclusiveness, and equality, which are inscribed in creation, are in fact four different expressions of one and the same reality, the divine communion of the triune God. In this respect, our relationships with the world and our unique and prominent place in the world are never meant to satisfy our indulgent or extravagant desire at the expense of others. They are, in a profound sense, are intended to let life flourish abundantly, which originates in the divine communion. If we distort or deviate from this relationship only for our sake, we stifle life in the present and will eventually impede the appearance of life in the future. This is an indirect and gradual, but comprehensive and certain, act of killing others. Our plunder and waste of nature hinder other human beings and life forms from attaining the basics that they need for living. We suffocate life-sustaining relationships rooted in the divine communion by what we extract from nature and what we waste. We are now threatening nature itself to death, which is filled with life, vague and ambivalent as it is.

In confrontation with the present world where the power of death overshadows life, which flows from God the source of life, we are asked to select either life or death. We cannot serve «God and mammon» together (Matt. 6:24). We must choose whether we live according to either the flesh or the Spirit. The former brings forth death; the latter life. In terms of the first proposition, it is in our concrete relationships with other human beings and nature that we are asked to choose the Spirit or the flesh. To choose the Spirit and thereby life would mean to live in accordance with what the interconnectedness of all creatures indicates and dictates. We would then consider interconnectedness as a life-sustaining relationship, which is given to all as God's gift. We would cherish and nourish it as a continuing source of life for others as well as for ourselves. To choose the flesh and thereby death would mean to live with disregard to what interconnectedness indicates. Instead, it would mean to live according to one's own desire. We would then distort the genuine significance of interconnectedness in creation and regard it merely as a commodity-producing relationship. We would turn a life-sustaining relationship into a doomed channel to death for all. So we are told today again: «I call heaven and earth to witness against you today that I have set before you life and death, blessings and curses. Choose life so that you and your descendents may live» (Deut. 30:19).

3.2 *A Spirituality of Peace: The Intrinsic Value of All Creatures*

Although it can be understood in diverse ways, peace in a profound sense cannot simply refer to the absence of conflict, violence, or war. Peace must be construed primarily as the actualization of justice: «The effect of righteousness [justice] will be peace» (Isa. 32:17; cf. Ps. 85: 11; 72:1-7). Vatican Council II renders peace as follows:

Peace is not merely the absence of war. Nor can it be reduced solely to the maintenance of a balance of power between enemies. [...] Instead, it is rightly and appropriately called «an enterprise of justice» (Isa. 32:7). Peace results from that harmony built into human society by its divine Founder, and actualized by men as they thirst after ever greater justice[23].

It is evident, according to the understanding of peace as «an enterprise of justice», that justice is what brings forth peace. Peace, if it is to be genuine, must be rooted in justice. Justice seeks to actualize in the world the harmony that was built in creation by God, from which peace emerges. Peace cannot be sustained and will eventually disappear when the good order of creation is disrupted. The disruption of the good order means that the relationships in creation are distorted. According to the first proposition of interconnectedness, these relationships originate from the way God relates to creation, for example, God's penetration and permeation of all creatures. Given this, the tarnish of relationships among creatures ultimately indicates the impairment of the relationship of creation to God. Considered that peace is also an indication of the status of one's relationship to others, peace is ultimately connected with one's relationship with God. For Christians, therefore, «peace will imply a right relationship with God, which entails forgiveness, reconciliation, and union»[24]. A right relationship with God calls for and brings about a right relationship with others through «forgiveness, reconciliation, and union» (cf. Matt. 6:23-24). From here will peace sprout and thrive among us.

God grants creation good order and harmony, which undergird peace. But it is we humans who actualize this good order and harmony in our world and let peace germinate, grow, and flourish. Hence, peace is at once a divine and human enterprise. There is always a yearning in us for «ever greater justice». If peace is achieved by our longing for justice, the substance of peace must be justice. The peace that is enforced or coerced is not peace in a genuine sense. This also implies that peace is not achieved once and for all: «peace is something that is built up day after day, in the pursuit of an order [...] a more perfect form of justice among men»[25]. It is in salvation that peace will be brought to fulfillment. Peace in this sense is an eschatological reality, which points

---

[23] VATICAN COUNCIL II, *Gaudium et Spes*, n. 78.

[24] NCCB, *The Challenge of Peace*, n. 27.

[25] PAUL VI, *Populorum Progressio*, n. 76.

to «a final, full realization of God's salvation when all creation will be made whole»[26].

This comprehensive understanding of peace is in accord with what *shalom* in the Old Testament means. The Hebrew word *shalom* refers to «peace, wholeness, well-being. It describes the ideal human state, both individual and communal, the ultimate gift from God»[27]. It is used in the Old Testament to indicate «harmony with nature, self, others, and God; [...]; and life»[28]. In sum, *shalom* means «a state of wholeness and integrity, a condition of life that is in harmony with God, other people, and nature»[29]. Peace as *shalom*, which consists in the right relationship with God, other humans, and nature, is an indispensable condition that ensures life. For life emerges out of relationships in creation, i.e., the inter-connectedness of all creatures. Therefore, peace will be attained as we reject all that impairs and disrupts the relationships built in creation. It needs our rejection of all that disturbs the relationships which bring forth life in creation. Peace will grow as we support all that contributes to these relationships. It needs our affirmation of all that fosters them. This reminds us that peace is a human enterprise as well as a divine enterprise. It demands our dedication to the preservation and promotion of justice.

Jesus himself affirmed the aspect of peace as a human enterprise when he said, «Blessed are the peacemakers» (Matt. 5:9). Jesus invites us to this peacemaking: «We are called to be peacemaker [...] by our Lord Jesus»[30]. This is in fact an inherent part of our vocation as a Christian: «The Christians has no choice but to defend peace [...] This is an inalienable obligation»[31]. Jesus also mentioned the persecution that may accompany the peacemakers who work «for righteousness' sake» (Matt. 5:10). Our commitment to justice demands our rejection of all that threatens and damages the interconnectedness of all creatures, and our action may incur violent reactions from those who seek to distort and appropriate this relationship only for their sake. In fact, this is what Jesus did and what happened to him. What Jesus did is to proclaim and actualize the kingdom of God in the world; what happened to him is a violent persecution, i.e., his death on the cross.

---

[26] NCCB, *The Challenge of Peace*, n. 27. See also *Ibid.*, nn. 32-39
[27] J.M. EFIRD, «Shalom», 1003.
[28] M. MCMORROW, «Creating Conditions of Peace», 45.
[29] G. GUTIÉRREZ, *The God of Life*, 126.
[30] NCCB, *The Challenge of Peace*, n. 333.
[31] NCCB, *The Challenge of Peace*, n. 73.

It has been held that the kingdom of God is understood as the fulfill-ment of the messianic sabbath, the perfect liberation of all creation, since Jesus lived in the spirit of the messianic sabbath. Perfect libera-tion would mean that all distorted relationships are abolished in crea-tion. It would indicate the perfection of the relationships that have originally been built in creation. For example, the value of communion and sharing in the kingdom of God indicate that the interconnectedness of all creatures, which gives, empowers, and sustains life, will be brought to perfection. Therefore, the kingdom of God can be imagined as the fullness of peace and life (cf. Isa. 11:6-9).

The peace that Jesus sought to bring in the world is different from the peace that the world gives (cf. John 14:27). We are told that he came to the earth to bring not peace but division. Only after the peace of the world is burnt out by the fire he brought to the world, the peace of Jesus, *shalom*, will be realized (cf. Luke 12:49-51). Jesus dedicated himself to peacemaking and was persecuted to death. But even death cannot stifle life and peace, the source of which is the God of life and «Prince of Peace» (Isa. 9:6). Jesus Christ has become the reconciler of the entire creation to God by «making peace through the blood of his cross» (Col. 1:20; cf. 2 Cor. 5:18-20; Eph. 2:13-22). His resurrection shows what his peace is like, which was achieved by his death. The peace that he promised to us is a peace which even death cannot break. Jesus' gift of peace must be understood in the light of «the fullest demonstration of the power of God's reign over all kinds of violence, particularly the power of death, demonstrated in the resurrection of Jesus»[32]. Indeed, Christ is our peace (cf. Eph. 2:14)

It was mentioned that the task to build peace in the world by actualiz-ing the good order and harmony which God founded in creation has been entrusted to us human beings. To keep harmony in creation may begin with our effort and attitude to recognize others as they are and to give them their due regards. Our right relationships with others, both human and nonhuman, can be sustained by the recognition of their rights to exist and live, if we view all of them in the light of God's creation. In this regard, the second proposition of intrinsic value even-tually leads to peace. «A firm determination to respect other men and peoples and their dignity [...] are absolutely necessary for the estab-lishment of peace»[33]. Insofar as we disregard the right of others rooted

---

[32] NCCB, *The Challenge of Peace*, n. 51.
[33] VATICAN COUNCIL II, *Gaudium et Spes*, n. 78.

in their intrinsic value, we will inevitably disrupt the order and harmony of creation. Justice will eventually be tarnished and impaired. Instead, conflict and violence will germinate and prevail. Peace will disappear. Without peace, life cannot grow and thrive, either. Our due respect for the intrinsic value of all creatures is indispensable to peace.

In this sense, all the reflections in regard to the second proposition contribute, in their own way, to the promotion of peace. The transcendental idea of the absolute savior in regard to the incarnation brings to the fore the profound goodness and intrinsic value of creation by the sober affirmation of the incarnation and the relationship of creation with the incarnation. The christological vision of creation confirms the value of creation as a promise-laden reality which will be brought to fulfillment in the future and in which all creatures are under the loving concern and care of Christ in the present. The panentheistic perspective on creation deepens the meaning of God's presence in nature by the trinitarian values and thereby further strengthens the intrinsic value of creation. God's body shaped by the Christic vision solidifies the inherent goodness of all creatures by throwing light on God's love for all creatures, particularly for the vulnerable.

For a specific example, let us review the christological vision of creation with regard to the issue of peace. Jesus of Nazareth, who dedicated himself to peacemaking, was recognized in his resurrection as the cosmic Christ. This cosmic Christ is conceived to be profoundly engaged in the entire creation from beginning to end. The cosmic Christ is regarded as the firstborn of creation, the reconciler of creation, and the firstborn from the dead. All these three titles illustrate vividly the intimate relationship of Christ with creation and his affectionate concern for creation. Christ, the firstborn of creation and as such the eldest brother of all creatures, cares for each one of them with brotherly affection. No one evades the all-embracing, loving concern of Christ, no matter how little it may appear. Christ, the cosmic reconciler and as such the advocate of all, offered his life in order to reconcile them to God by making peace through his death. Christ is the one who dedicated to peacemaking, even up to his death, for the sake of all creation. This commitment powerfully approves how profoundly he has appreciated all creatures and their goodness. Christ, the firstborn from the dead and as such the pioneer and assurance of the new creation, has made palpable in this world what the new creation is and promised it to all creation. Christ is the pledge to the future fulfillment of all creation.

The conception of the world in the light of the cosmic Christ brings to light the intrinsic value of creation grounded in the relationship of Christ to creation. This relationship could be characterized by the loving care, sacrifice, and promise of Christ for all creation. All creatures are the beloved of Christ, reconciled to God, and filled with promise and hope for the future fulfillment. This view of creation gives us a strong motive to give due regard to nonhuman creation as well as to other human beings. This helps us regain and keep the integrity of nature that has been disturbed. This conception of creation urges us to respect the way Christ relates to all creatures, what he has achieved for them, and what he has promised to them. The first step we may take would be to make our own the eyes and heart through which Christ sees all creatures. We will then be able to appreciate the profound goodness of creation, to acknowledge its inherent value, and to relate to it accordingly. With this, we can put a robust ground upon which peace may thrive. Insofar as we are faithful to this vision of Christ, the present violent infringement on the right and value of nature and the poor will recede. Only then will peace grow from the good order and harmony of creation founded by God.

In confrontation with the world where power is justice and this power disrupts the good order and harmony of the world with violent means such as exploitation, abuse, and war, we are asked to choose peace rather than to give way to the violent power which will destroy peace and life and which will effect death. Again, we must decide whether we live according to either the flesh or the Spirit. The former brings forth death, the latter peace. In terms of the second proposition, we are asked to make a decision about our attitude towards others. We can grasp others primarily from an instrumental perspective to consider our own interests alone. The consequence will be the violent domination of other human beings and reckless exploitation of nature. On the contrary, we can see others as God's precious creatures with their own intrinsic goodness and value, vague as they are. We will then give due regard to them, reconcile ourselves to them, and foster peace together with them. We are invited to make «every effort to maintain the unity of the Spirit in the bond of peace» (Eph. 4:3). We Christians are called to follow the Christ who is himself the reconciler of the cosmos and has given us the ministry of reconciliation so that the peace of Jesus may flourish in the world (cf. Col. 1:20; 2 Cor. 5:18-20).

4. An Ecological Vision of the World and Cosmic Justice

The spirituality of life and peace invites us to a dedication to the praxis of justice. Justice provides a ground upon which peace and life grow. It has been mentioned that experience is an essential aspect of spirituality. To that measure, spirituality builds on our experience and leads to praxis in our life. Otherwise, our spirituality would become vain. At the same time, praxis must be nourished by spirituality. Otherwise, praxis becomes sterile or cannot endure. It is submitted here that a spirituality of life and peace be expressed and actualized as a commitment to ecological justice and social justice. Peace must be secured in order that life may sprout and thrive. Justice is what brings forth peace. Peace and life are guaranteed only when we pursue and practice justice. At the same time, an ecological vision of the world requires that the justice for which we strive be comprehensive of both humanity and nature. What is needed today is both social justice and ecological justice, i.e., cosmic justice, which embraces nature and humans. A spirituality of life and peace rooted in interconnectedness and intrinsic value invites us to dedicate ourselves to ecological concern as well as social concern. Now let us conceive how the third proposition of an ecological vision of the world, i.e., the compatibility of ecological concern and social concern, leads us to Christian life dedicated to cosmic justice.

God is revealed in the Scriptures as «a God of justice» (Isa. 30:18). God loves justice (cf. Isa. 61:8; Ps. 11:7; 33:5; 37:28; 99:4). God also demands justice from us (cf. Deut. 16:20). This indicates clearly that our relationship to neighbors is bound up with our relationship to God. Jesus made this point clear by saying that our love of God is manifested in our practice of love for others (cf. Mark 12:28-34; Luke 10:25-37). Particularly, God shows a deep concern for the vulnerable in society, who are typically designated as widows, orphans, and strangers (cf. Exod. 22:21-24). God «maintains the cause of the needy, and executes for the poor» (Ps. 140:13). God emerges as «the liberator of the oppressed and the defender of the poor»[34]. Jesus put into practice this concern of God by his ministries, especially his being and eating together with the marginalized. He even identified himself with the least (cf. Matt. 25:31-46).

---

[34] SYNOD OF BISHOPS, *Justice in the World*, n. 30.

Basically, justice suggests «a sense of what is right or of what should happen»[35]. Justice even in this basic sense does not simply mean legal justice whereby everybody is given one's due. Rather, in accordance with the previous reflections on life and peace, one must say that justice is always bound up with life and peace. What is right and what should happen for living creatures would be to sustain life, which is given by God as a gift (cf. Matt. 20:1-16). All creatures deserve to exist and live insofar as God creates them as such. To acknowledge this and to let them exist and live would be to practice justice in a profound sense. We will actualize by this justice the good order and harmony that God has founded in the cosmos. Here come out peace and life (cf. Isa 11:1-9). Justice in this sense is another expression of love, the love of God the creator. This love and justice instill life and peace into all creation. This justice is cosmic justice, which seeks life and peace both in the human world and the natural world. This cosmic justice will be manifested and actualized in our ecological concern and social concern.

In this regard, the third proposition of the compatibility of concern for nature and concern for the poor leads directly to cosmic justice. Hence, all the reflections in regard to the third proposition contribute, in their own way, to our dedication to a socially and ecologically just world. The human freedom provides a transcendental ground for social and ecological concern. Jesus lived in the spirit of the messianic sabbath, and as such he was filled with social and ecological concern. He strove for and aspired to the liberation of all creatures. The trinitarian community and the kingdom of God condemn as a grave sin what is inflicted on nature and the poor. At the same time, they inspire us to move forward in a direction that they indicate as the ideal model and ultimate future of creation. The body of God shaped by the Christic vision brings into relief distributive justice and sustainability for human beings and nature respectively.

First of all, in order to solidify our effort to build justice in society and nature, we need to recall that our dedication to cosmic justice was understood in this study to belong to an existential dimension of the human being. Freedom as a fundamental option for God discloses that social concern, which is an expression of our love of neighbors, is an essential aspect of every human being. An ecological vision of the world grounded in the dynamic unity of spirit and matter opens the

---

35 NCCB, *Economic Justice for All*, n. 39.

scope of this social concern into the whole creation, awakening us to its inseparable connection with ecological concern.

As a specific example, let us now see what the metaphor of God's body shaped by the Christic vision indicates with regard to justice. The conception of the world as God's body renders the world as one cosmic and organic body. Both human beings and nature appear as the members of one and the same body. As such, one cannot enjoy life while others are dying. As such, one cannot remain in peace while others suffer. The vision of God's body integrates the human world and the natural world into one organic world. It demands that justice be retained in both in order that this one body may sustain and enjoy life in peace. The destabilizing, inclusive, and nonhierarchical Christic vision holds, moreover, that justice must mean primarily justice for the least, i.e., for nature and the poor. Justice thus established must be concretized in our age as sustainability and distributive justice for nature and individual humans respectively. Without either, neither nature nor humans will remain well. The metaphor of God's body shaped by the Christic vision presents specific contents to the discipleship of Jesus with regard to the praxis of justice today. First, the metaphor of God's body tells us that the scope of the discipleship must be the whole world embracing nature and human beings. Second, the Christic vision demands that the discipleship be characterized by a special concern for the vulnerable, which include nature as well as the poor according to the metaphor of God's body. Third, the metaphor of God's body shaped by the Christic vision indicates that the discipleship is realized in our solidarity with and compassion for the poor and nature, which sometimes require our own risk to run.

Frugality can be proposed as a concrete practice of the discipleship that we may conceive in regard to distributive justice and sustainability. Frugality can be understood as a voluntary form of poverty with a sense of enough in attaining material wealth and consuming material goods. It comes from the willingness to live with a certain limit of material affluence for the sake of others. It is a radical refusal to immoderate consumerism, which pursues excessive material wealth and consumption in an exclusive manner. It is a definite resolution to let others have enough. It is stimulated and supported by the Christic vision, which emphasizes our solidarity with the poor. Frugality is, therefore, an expression of social concern for others, which must lead to distributive justice. At the same time, the metaphor of God's body supplements and widens this conception of frugality to embrace nature. Frugality today must be practiced with a deep concern for the earth as well as human beings, which must lead to sustainability. Frugality in this sense must be viewed to originate in one's acknowledgement of the right and value of others to have basic needs for living. It will then contribute to the promotion of peace and life. In this respect, frugality is not only a personal virtue. Rather, it is the praxis of justice, which begins both with a personal resolution and with a social and cosmic vision, i.e., distributive justice and sustainability for the poor and nature respectively.

In confrontation with the world where nature as well as the poor is denied their inherent value and right and thereby even their life is threatened, we are asked to take the cause of justice and dedicate ourselves to it. In terms of the third proposition, we must show and practice both ecological concern and social concern. If we are ever to follow Jesus, who lived in the spirit of the messianic sabbath and longed for the liberation of all creatures, the praxis of justice is not an option but a mandate to us: «Action on behalf of justice and participation in the transformation of the world fully appear to us as a constitutive dimension of the preaching of the Gospel [...]»[36]. Our faith must be always «the faith that does justice». We are told to «let justice roll down like waters, and righteousness like an ever-flowing stream» (Amos 5:24). It is by our active participation in the enterprise of justice that this ardent aspiration of the prophet Amos can be realized in the world. It is only then that peace and life too will flourish in the world.

---

36 SYNOD OF BISHOPS, *Justice in the World*, n. 6.

EPILOGUE

The whole process of this study, which is composed of three parts, may be compared to building a house. The first part corresponds to the stage of preparing construction. As the condition of the ground upon which a house is built and its surroundings are examined beforehand, the context in which this thesis would be developed was reviewed in the first part. The second part is equivalent of the phase of building a house. I was initially given the final shape of the house, i.e., what the house must be like, and the three pillars with which I began to build the house. I began this study with the main proposition which says what the final outcome of this study must be like and the three propositions with which I would build up the main one. Other diverse materials were needed, to be sure, in order to build a house. All the other theological materials needed to complete the thesis were attained from the four resource theologians. It was crucial to select proper materials for this study among all that these resource persons may provide. These theological thoughts thus chosen were, however, still raw materials. They needed to be processed through critical reflections on them in order that they can support those propositions theologically. The third part can be regarded as the occasion to examine and appreciate the house as a whole which is now completed and to ponder how the house may be used more effectively. First, it was affirmed that the final outcome, which was attained out of the preceding process of theological reflections, is an ecological vision of the world, as the main proposition requires. Second, I sought to show that this ecological vision of the world can contribute to forming and fostering a spirituality of life and peace and to our commitment to transform our broken world into a socially just and ecologically sustainable world.

We build a house, not merely to look at it but actually to live in it. What remains is to live in the house, once a house has been built. The main proposition too must be lived out, once it has been formed and affirmed. It is only when we live it in our life that an ecological vision of the world will begin to change our broken world. Hence, I have to say now, it is time for me to proceed from the theological reflections which I have done to the theological praxis which these reflections demand, together with those who are willing to live an ecological vision of the world.

ABBREVIATIONS

1. The Abbreviations of the Bible[1]

Acts	The Acts of the Apostles
Col.	The Letter of Paul to the Colossians
Deut.	Deuteronomy
Exod.	Exodus
Gen.	Genesis
Heb.	The Letter to the Hebrews
Hos.	Hosea
Isa.	Isaiah
Jer.	Jeremiah
John	The Gospel According to John
Lev.	Leviticus
Luke	The Gospel According to Luke
Mark	The Gospel According to Mark
Matt.	The Gospel According to Matthew
Mi.	Micha
Ps.	The Psalms
Rom.	The Letter of Paul to the Romans
1 Cor.	The First Letter of Paul to the Corinthians
2 Cor.	The Second Letter of Paul to the Corinthians
1 John	The First Letter of John

2. Other Abbreviations

cf.	confer
CH.	Chapter
COBE	Cosmic Background Explorer

---

[1] Scriptural citations are from the *New Revised Standard Version of the Bible*, New York 1994.

d.	decree
ed.	editor(s)
HCBD	*The HarperCollins Bible Dictionary*, ed. P.J. Achtemeier, New York 1996.
HeyJ	*Heythrop Journal*
Ibid.	*Ibidem* (that is, «at the same place»)
ID.	*Idem* (that is, «the same»)
i.e.	*id est* («that is»)
MA	Massachusetts
n. (nn.)	number(s)
NASA	National Aeronautics and Space Administration
NCCB	National Conference of Catholic Bishops
NDCST	*The New Dictionary of Catholic Social Thought*, ed. J.A. Dwyer, Collegeville 1994.
NDT	*The New Dictionary of Theology*, ed. J.A. Komonchak – M. Collins – D.A. Lane, Wilmington 1987.
NJBC	*The New Jerome Biblical Commentary*, ed. R.E. Brown – J.A. Fitzmyer – R.E. Murphy, Englewood Cliffs 1990.
SacMun	*Sacramentum Mundi*
sic	so, thus
TheoIn	*Theological Investigations*
UN	United Nations
U.S.A.	United States of America
USCC	United States Catholic Conference
WCC	World Council of Churches
WCED	World Commission on Environment and Development

BIBLIOGRAPHY

1. Works of Karl Rahner

1.1 *Books*

Foundations of Christian Faith. An Introduction to the Idea of Christianity, New York 1978.

Hominization. The Evolutionary Origin of Man as a Theological Problem, London 1965.

The Love of Jesus and the Love of Neighbour, New York 1983.

On the Theology of Death, New York 1961.

1.2 *Articles*

«Christian Humanism», in *TheoIn* 9, 187-204.

«Christology in the Setting of Modern Man's Understanding of Himself and of His World», in *TheoIn* 11, 225-229.

«Christology Today», in *TheoIn* 21, 220-227.

«Christology Today?», in *TheoIn* 17, 24-38.

«Christology within an Evolutionary View of the World», in *TheoIn* 5, 157-192.

«Current Problems in Christology», in *TheoIn* 1, 492-200.

«A Faith That Loves the Earth», in *Everyday Faith*, New York 1968, 76-83.

«The Function of the Church as a Critic of Society», in *TheoIn* 12, 229-249.

«Incarnation», in *SacMun* 3, 110-118.

«Natural Science and Reasonable Faith», in *TheoIn* 21, 16-55.

«On the Theology of the Incarnation», in *TheoIn* 4, 105-120.

«The Theology of Freedom», in *TheoIn* 11, 178-196.

«The Theology of Symbol», in *TheoIn* 4, 221-252.

«The Unity of Spirit and Matter in the Christian Understanding of Faith», in *TheoIn* 6, 153-177.

«The Unreadiness of the Church's Members to Accept Poverty», in *TheoIn* 14, 270-279.

«Reflections on the Unity of the Love of Neighbor and the Love of God», in *TheoIn* 6, 231-247.

2. Works of Jürgen Moltmann

The Coming of God. Christian Eschatology, Minneapolis 1996.

God for a Secular Society. The Public Relevance of Theology, London 1997.

God in Creation. A New Theology of Creation and the Spirit of God, Minneapolis 1993.

Jesus Christ for Today's World, London 1994.

The Spirit of Life. A Universal Affirmation, Minneapolis 1992.

Theology of Hope. On the Ground and the Implications of a Christian Eschatology, London 1967, Minneapolis 1993.

The Trinity and the Kingdom of God. The Doctrine of God, London 1981.

The Way of Jesus Christ. Christology in Messianic Dimensions, Minneapolis 1993.

3. Works of Leonardo Boff

Cry of the Earth, Cry of the Poor, New York 1997.

Ecology and Liberation. A New Paradigm, New York 1995.

Jesus Christ Liberator. A Critical Christology for Our Time, New York 1978.

Introducing Liberation Theology, Kent 1987.

Liberating Grace, New York 1979.

The Prayer of Saint Francis. A Message of Peace for the World Today, New York 2001.

Sacraments of Life Life of the Sacraments. Story Theology, Washington D.C. 1987.

Saint Francis. A Model for Human Liberation, London 1985.

Salvation and Liberation. In Search of a Balance between Faith and Politics, New York 1984.

Trinity and Society, Kent 1988.

«Social Ecology: Poverty and Misery», in D.G. HALLMAN, ed., *Ecotheology. Voices from South and North*, New York 1994, 235-247.

4. Works of Sallie McFague

The Body of God. An Ecological Theology, Minneapolis 1993.

Life Abundant. Rethinking Theology and Economy for a Planet in Peril, Minneapolis 2001.

Metaphorical Theology. Models of God in Religious Language, Philadelphia 1982.

Models of God. Theology for an Ecological, Nuclear Age, Philadelphia 1987.

Super, Natural Christians. How We Should Love Nature, Minneapolis 1997.

5. General Bibliography

BARBOUR, I.G., *Myths, Models and Paradigms. A Comparative Study in Science and Religion*, New York 1974.

————, *Religion and Science. Historical and Contemporary Issues*, New York 1997.

BOHM, D., *Wholeness and the Implicate Order*, London 1995.

BROWN, B., «Toward a Buddhist Ecological Cosmology», in M.E. TUCKER – J.A. GRIM, ed., *Worldviews and Ecology. Religion, Philosophy, and the Environment*, New York 1999, 124-137.

CHRISTIANSEN, D. – GRAZER, W., ed., *And God Saw That It Was Good. Catholic Theology and the Environment*, Washington D.C. 1996.

CLIFFORD, A.M., «Creation», in S. FIORENZA – J.P. GALVIN, ed., *Systematic Theology. Roman Catholic Perspectives*, I, Minneapolis 1991, 195-248.

————, «Foundations for a Catholic Ecological Theology of God», in D. CHRISTIANSEN – W. GRAZER, ed., *And God Saw That It Was Good. Catholic Theology and the Environment*, Washington D.C. 1996, 19-46.

CLIFFORD, R.J., *Creation Accounts in the Ancient Near East and in the Bible*, Washington D.C. 1994.

————, «The Bible and the Environment», in K.W. IRWIN – E.D. PELLEGRINO, ed., *Preserving the Creation. Environmental Theology and Ethics*, Washington, D.C. 1994, 1-26.

CLIFFORD, R.J. – MURPHY, R.E., «Genesis», *NJBC*, 8-43.

COBB, J.B., JR., *Sustainability. Economics, Ecology, and Justice*, New York 1992.

CONN, J.W., «Spirituality», *NDT*, 972-986.

DALY, H.E. – COBB, J.B., JR., *For the Common Good. Redirecting the Economy toward Community, the Environment, and a Sustainable Future*, Boston 1994.

DODD, C.H., *The Parables of the Kingdom*, New York 1961.

DOWNEY, M., *Understanding Christian Spirituality*, Mahwah 1997.

EDWARDS, D., *Jesus and the Cosmos*, Mahwah 1991.

———, *Jesus the Wisdom of God. An Ecological Theology*, New York 1995.

EFIRD, J.M., «Shalom», *HCBD*, 1003

FOX, M., *Original Blessing*, Santa Fe 1983.

———, *The Coming of the Cosmic Christ. The Healing of Mother Earth and the Birth of a Global Renaissance*, New York 1988.

FUELLENBACH, J., *The Kingdom of God. The Message of Jesus Today*, New York 1995.

GLATT-GILAD, D.A. – TIGAY, J.H., «Sabbath», *HCBD*, 954-955.

GRUEN, L., «Revaluing Nature», in K.J. WARREN, ed., *Ecofeminism. Women, Culture, Nature*, Indianapolis 1997, 356-374.

GULA, R.M., *Reason Informed by Faith. Foundations of Catholic Morality*, Mahwah 1989

GUNTON, C.E., *The Triune Creator. A Historical and Systematic Study*, Grand Rapids 1998.

GUSTAFSON, J.M., *A Sense of the Divine. The Natural Environment from a Theocentric Perspective*, Cleveland 1994.

GUTIÉRREZ, G., *A Theology of Liberation*, New York 1973, New York 1988.

———, *The God of Life*, New York 1991.

HAIGHT, R., *Dynamics of Theology*, Mahwah 1990.

———, «Sin and Grace», in S. FIORENZA – J.P. GALVIN, ed., *Systematic Theology. Roman Catholic Perspectives*, II, Minneapolis 1991, 77-141.

HALLMAN, D.G., «Beyond "North/South Dialogue"», in D.G. HALLMAN, ed., *Ecotheology. Voices from South and North*, New York 1994, 3-9.

HARRINGTON, D.J., «Kingdom of God», *NDCST*, 509.

HAUGHT, J.F., «Ecology and Eschatology», in D. CHRISTIANSEN – W. GRAZER, ed., *And God Saw That It Was Good. Catholic Theology and the Environment*, Washington D.C. 1996, 47-64.

———, *Science and Religion. From Conflict to Conversation*, Mahwah 1995.

HILL, B.R., *Christian Faith and the Environment. Making Vital Connections*, New York 1998.

HINZE, C.F., «Catholic Social Teaching and Ecological Ethics», in D. CHRISTIANSEN – W. GRAZER, ed., *And God Saw That It Was Good. Catholic Theology and the Environment*, Washington D.C. 1996, 165-182.

HOOKER, M.D., *The Gospel according to Saint Mark*, London 1991.

JOHN XXIII, Encyclical *Pacem in Terris* (1963), in D.J. O'BRIEN – T.A. SHANNON, ed., *Catholic Social Thought. The Documentary Heritage*, New York 1995, 131-162.

JOHN PAUL II, Encyclical *Centesimus Annus* (1991), in D.J. O'BRIEN – T.A. SHANNON, ed., *Catholic Social Thought. The Documentary Heritage*, New York 1995, 439-488.

———, Encyclical *Redemptor Hominis* (1979), Boston 1979.

———, Encyclical *Sollicitudo Rei Socialis* (1987), in D.J. O'BRIEN – T.A. SHANNON, ed., *Catholic Social Thought. The Documentary Heritage*, New York 1995, 395-436.

———, Message *Peace with God the Creator, Peace with All of Creation* (1990), in D. CHRISTIANSEN – W. GRAZER, ed., *And God Saw That It Was Good. Catholic Theology and the Environment*, Washington D.C. 1996, 213-222.

JOHNSON, E.A., *Women, Earth, and Creator Spirit*, Mahwah 1993.

JOHNSON, L.T., *The Gospel of Luke*, Collegeville 1991.

LOHFINK, G., *Jesus and Community. The Social Dimension of Christian Faith*, Philadelphia 1984.

KARRIS, R.J., «The Gospel According to Luke», *NJBC*, 675-721.

KATZ, E., «Judaism and the Ecological Crisis», in M.E. TUCKER – J.A. GRIM, ed., *Worldviews and Ecology. Religion, Philosophy, and the Environment*, New York 1999, 55-70.

KEENAN, M., *From Stockholm to Johannesburg. An Historical Overview of the Concern of the Holy See for the Environment*, Vatican City 2002.

KEYFITZ, N., «Consumption and Population», in D.A. CROCKER – T. LINDEN, ed., *Ethics of Consumption. The Good Life, Justice and Global Stewardship*, Lanham 1997, 476-500.

KUHN, T., *The Structure of Scientific Revolutions*, Chicago 1970.

LANCASTER, L., «Buddhism and Ecology: Collective Cultural Perceptions», in M.E. TUCKER – D.R. WILLIAMS, ed., *Buddhism and Ecology. The Interconnection of Dharma and Deeds*, Cambridge, MA 1997, 3-18.

MCBRIEN, R.P., *Catholicism*, New York 1994.

MCCOOL, G.A., ed., *A Rahner Reader*, New York 1989.

MCDONAGH, S., *Passion for the Earth*, New York 1994.

——, *The Greening of the Church*, New York 1990.

MCGOVERN, A.F., *Liberation Theology and Its Critics. Toward an Assessment*, New York 1989.

MCMORROW, M., «Creating Conditions of Peace», in G.F. POWERS – D. CHRISTIANSEN – R.T. HENNEMEYER, ed., *Peacemaking. Moral and Policy Challenge for a New World*, Washington D.C. 1994, 41-56.

MEIER, J.P., *A Marginal Jew. Rethinking the Historical Jesus*, II, New York 1991.

MERCHANT, C., *Earthcare. Women and the Environment*, New York 1995.

——, *Radical Ecology. The Search for a Livable World*, New York 1992.

——, *The Death of Nature. Women, Ecology and the Scientific Revolution*, New York 1980.

MURPHY, R.E., *The Tree of Life. An Exploration of Biblical Wisdom Literature*, Grand Rapids 1996.

MÜLLER-FAHRENHOLZ, G., *The Kingdom and the Power. The Theology of Jürgen Moltmann*, London 2000.

NASH, R., *The Rights of Nature. A History of Environmental Ethics*, Leichhardt 1990.

NCCB, Pastoral Letter *Economic Justice for All* (1986), in D.J. O'BRIEN – T.A. SHANNON, ed., *Catholic Social Thought. The Documentary Heritage*, New York 1995, 572-680.

——, Pastoral Letter *The Challenge of Peace. God's Promise and Our Response* (1983), in D.J. O'BRIEN – T.A. SHANNON, ed., *Catholic Social Thought. The Documentary Heritage*, New York 1995, 492-571.

NORTHCOTT, M.S., *The Environment and Christian Ethics*, Cambridge 1996.

O'DONNELL, J., «The Mystery of Faith in the Theology of Karl Rahner», *HeyJ* 25 (1984) 301-318.

——, *The Mystery of the Triune God*. London 1988.

PAUL VI, Encyclical *Populorum Progressio* (1967), in D.J. O'BRIEN – T.A. SHANNON, ed., *Catholic Social Thought. The Documentary Heritage*, New York 1995, 240-262.

PIUS XI, Encyclical *Quadragesimo Anno* (1931), in D.J. O'BRIEN – T.A. SHANNON, ed., *Catholic Social Thought. The Documentary Heritage*, New York 1995, 42-79.

PLUMWOOD, V., «Androcentrism and Anthropocentrism: Parallels and Politics», in K.J. WARREN, ed., *Ecofeminism. Women, Culture, Nature*, Indianapolis 1997, 327-355.

RUETHER, R.R., *Gaia and God. An Ecofeminist Theology of Earth Healing*, New York 1992.

SANTMIRE, P., *The Travail of Nature. The Ambiguous Ecological Promise of Christian Theology*, Minneapolis 1985.

SCHNEIDER, S.M., «Theology and Spirituality: Strangers, Rivals, or Partners?», *Horizons* 13/2 (1986) 253-274.

SESSIONS, R., «Deep Ecology versus Ecofeminism: Healthy Differences or Incompatible Philosophies?», in K.J. WARREN, ed., *Ecological Feminist Philosophies*, Bloomington 1996, 137-154.

SMITH, P., *What Are They Saying About Environmental Ethics?*, Mahwah 1997.

SOBRINO, J., *Spirituality of Liberation. Toward Political Holiness*, New York 1988.

SOCIETY OF JESUS, *Documents of the Thirty-Fourth General Congregation of the Society of Jesus*, St. Louis 1995.

SWIMME, B. – BERRY, T., *The Universe Story. From the Primordial Flaring Forth to the Ecozoic Era – A Celebration of the Unfolding of the Cosmos*, New York 1992.

SYNOD OF BISHOPS, Statement *Justice in the World* (1971), in D.J. O'BRIEN – T.A. SHANNON, ed., *Catholic Social Thought. The Documentary Heritage*, New York 1995, 288-300.

TIMM, R.E., «The Ecological Fallout of Islamic Creation Theology», in M.E. TUCKER – J.A. GRIM, ed., *Worldviews and Ecology. Religion, Philosophy, and the Environment*, New York 1999, 83-95.

TRACY, D., «Theological Method», in P.C. HODGSON – R.H. KING, ed., *Christian Theology. An Introduction to Its Tasks and Traditions*, Philadelphia 1985, 52-59.

TUCKER, M.E. – BERTHRONG, J., ed., *Confucianism and Ecology. The Interrelation of Heaven, Earth, and Humans*, Cambridge, MA 1998.

USCC, Pastoral Statement *Renewing the Earth* (1991), in D. CHRISTIANSEN – W. GRAZER, ed., *And God Saw That It Was Good. Catholic Theology and the Environment*, Washington D.C. 1996, 223-243.

VATICAN COUNCIL II, Pastoral Constitution *Gaudium et Spes* (1965), in D.J. O'BRIEN – T.A. SHANNON, ed., *Catholic Social Thought. The Documentary Heritage*, New York 1995, 166-237.

VORGRIMLER, H., *Dimensioni Politiche del Cristianesimo*, Roma 1992.

WALLACE, M.I., «The Wounded Spirit as the Basis for Hope», in D.T. HESSEL – R.R. RUETHER, ed., *Christianity and Ecology. Seeking the Well-Being of Earth and Humans*, Cambridge, MA 2000, 51-72.

WARREN, K.J., «Ecological Feminist Philosophies: An Overview of the Issues», in K.J. WARREN, ed., *Ecological Feminist Philosophies*, Bloomington 1996, ix-xxvi.

WCED, *Our Common Future*, Oxford 1987.

WHITE, L., JR., «The Historical Roots of Our Ecological Crisis», *Science* 155 (1967) 1203-1207.

INDEX OF NAMES

TABLE OF CONTENTS

PART II: IN SEARCH OF AN ALTERNATIVE VISION OF THE WORLD

PART III: AN ECOLOGICAL VISION OF THE WORLD

CHAPTER VI: *The Emergence of an Ecological Vision of the World*.......... 255

CHAPTER VII: *A Christian Spirituality and Life*
              Grounded in an Ecological Vision of the World.............. 273

TESI GREGORIANA

Since 1995, the series «Tesi Gregoriana» has made available to the general public some of the best doctoral theses done at the Pontifical Gregorian University. The typesetting is done by the authors themselves following norms established and controlled by the University.

Published Volumes [Series: Theology]

1. NELLO FIGA, Antonio, *Teorema de la opción fundamental. Bases para su adecuada utilización en teología moral*, 1995, pp. 380.

2. BENTOGLIO, Gabriele, *Apertura e disponibilità. L'accoglienza nell'epistolario paolino*, 1995, pp. 376.

3. PISO, Alfeu, *Igreja e sacramentos. Renovação da Teologia Sacramentária na América Latina*, 1995, pp. 260.

4. PALAKEEL, Joseph, *The Use of Analogy in Theological Discourse. An Investigation in Ecumenical Perspective*, 1995, pp. 392.

5. KIZHAKKEPARAMPIL, Isaac, *The Invocation of the Holy Spirit as Constitutive of the Sacraments according to Cardinal Yves Congar*, 1995, pp. 200.

6. MROSO, Agapit J., *The Church in Africa and the New Evangelisation. A Theologico-Pastoral Study of the Orientations of John Paul II*, 1995, pp. 456.

7. NANGELIMALIL, Jacob, *The Relationship between the Eucharistic Liturgy, the Interior Life and the Social Witness of the Church according to Joseph Cardinal Parecattil*, 1996, pp. 224.

8. GIBBS, Philip, *The Word in the Third World. Divine Revelation in the Theology of Jen-Marc Éla, Aloysius Pieris and Gustavo Gutiérrez*, 1996, pp. 448.

9. DELL'ORO, Roberto, *Esperienza morale e persona. Per una reinterpretazione dell'etica fenomenologica di Dietrich von Hildebrand*, 1996, pp. 240.

10. BELLANDI, Andrea, *Fede cristiana come «stare e comprendere». La giustificazione dei fondamenti della fede in Joseph Ratzinger*, 1996, pp. 416.

11. BEDRIÑAN, Claudio, *La dimensión socio-política del mensaje teológico del Apocalipsis*, 1996, pp. 364.

12. GWYNNE, Paul, *Special Divine Action. Key Issues in the Contemporary Debate (1965-1995)*, 1996, pp. 376.

13. NIÑO, Francisco, *La Iglesia en la ciudad. El fenómeno de las grandes ciudades en América Latina, como problema teológico y como desafío pastoral*, 1996, pp. 492.

14. BRODEUR, Scott, *The Holy Spirit's Agency in the Resurrection of the Dead. An Exegetico-Theological Study of 1 Corinthians 15,44b-49 and Romans 8,9-13*, 1996, pp. 300.

15. ZAMBON, Gaudenzio, *Laicato e tipologie ecclesiali. Ricerca storica sulla «Teologia del laicato» in Italia alla luce del Concilio Vaticano II (1950-1980)*, 1996, pp. 548.

16. ALVES DE MELO, Antonio, *A Evangelização no Brasil. Dimensões teológicas e desafios pastorais. O debate teológico e eclesial (1952-1995)*, 1996, pp. 428.

17. APARICIO VALLS, María del Carmen, *La plenitud del ser humano en Cristo. La Revelación en la «Gaudium et Spes»*, 1997, pp. 308.

18. MARTIN, Seán Charles, *«Pauli Testamentum». 2 Timothy and the Last Words of Moses*, 1997, pp. 312.

19. RUSH, Ormond, *The Reception of Doctrine. An Appropriation of Hans Robert Jauss' Reception Aesthetics and Literary Hermeneutics*, 1997, pp. 424.

20. MIMEAULT, Jules, *La sotériologie de François-Xavier Durrwell. Exposé et réflexions critiques*, 1997, pp. 476.

21. CAPIZZI, Nunzio, *L'uso di Fil 2,6-11 nella cristologia contemporanea (1965-1993)*, 1997, pp. 528.

22. NANDKISORE, Robert, *Hoffnung auf Erlösung. Die Eschatologie im Werk Hans Urs von Balthasars*, 1997, pp. 304.

23. PERKOVIĆ, Marinko, *«Il cammino a Dio» e «La direzione alla vita»: L'ordine morale nelle opere di Jordan Kuni i , O.P. (1908-1974)*, 1997, pp. 336.

24. DOMERGUE, Benoît, *La réincarnation et la divinisation de l'homme dans les religions. Approche phénoménologique et théologique*, 1997, pp. 300.

25. FARKAŠ, Pavol, *La «donna» di Apocalisse 12. Storia, bilancio, nuove prospettive*, 1997, pp. 276.

26. OLIVER, Robert W., *The Vocation of the Laity to Evangelization. An Ecclesiological Inquiry into the Synod on the Laity (1987), Christifideles laici (1989) and Documents of the NCCB (1987-1996)*, 1997, pp. 364.

27. SPATAFORA, Andrea, *From the «Temple of God» to God as the Temple. A Biblical Theological Study of the Temple in the Book of Revelation*, 1997, pp. 340.

28. IACOBONE, Pasquale, *Mysterium Trinitatis. Dogma e Iconografia nell'Italia medievale*, 1997, pp. 512.

29. CASTAÑO FONSECA, Adolfo M., *Δικαιοσύνη en Mateo. Una interpretación teológica a partir de 3,15 y 21,32*, 1997, pp. 344.

30. CABRIA ORTEGA, José Luis, *Relación teología-filosofía en el pensamiento de Xavier Zubiri*, 1997, pp. 580.

31. SCHERRER, Thierry, *La gloire de Dieu dans l'oeuvre de saint Irénée*, 1997, pp. 328.

32. PASCUZZI, Maria, *Ethics, Ecclesiology and Church Discipline. A Rhetorical Analysis of 1Cor 5,1-13*, 1997, pp. 240.

33. LOPES GONÇALVES, Paulo Sérgio, *Liberationis mysterium. O projeto sistemático da teologia da libertação. Um estudo teológico na perspectiva da regula fidei*, 1997, pp. 464.

34. KOLACINSKI, Mariusz, *Dio fonte del diritto naturale*, 1997, pp. 296.

35. LIMA CORRÊA, Maria de Lourdes, *Salvação entre juizo, conversao e graça. A perspectiva escatológica de Os 14,2-9*, 1998, pp. 360.

36. MEIATTINI, Giulio, *«Sentire cum Christo». La teologia dell'esperienza cristiana nell'opera di H.U. von Balthasar*, 1998, pp. 432.

37. KESSLER, Thomas W., *Peter as the First Witness of the Risen Lord. An Historical and Theological Investigation*, 1998, pp. 240.

38. BIORD CASTILLO Raúl, *La Resurrección de Cristo como Revelación. Análisis del tema en la teología fundamental a partir de la Dei Verbum*, 1998, pp. 308.

39. LÓPEZ, Javier, *La figura de la bestia entre historia y profecía. Investigación teológico-bíblica de Apocalipsis 13,1-8*, 1998, pp. 308.

40. SCARAFONI, Paolo, *Amore salvifico. Una lettura del mistero della salvezza. Uno studio comparativo di alcune soteriologie cattoliche postconciliari*, 1998, pp. 240.

41. BARRIOS PRIETO, Manuel Enrique, *Antropologia teologica. Temi principali di antropologia teologica usando un metodo di «correlazione» a partire dalle opere di John Macquarrie*, 1998, pp. 416.

42. LEWIS, Scott M., *«So That God May Be All in All». The Apocalyptic Message of 1 Corinthians 15,12-34*, 1998, pp. 252.

43. ROSSETTI, Carlo Lorenzo, *«Sei diventato Tempio di Dio». Il mistero del Tempio e dell'abitazione divina negli scritti di Origene*, 1998, pp. 232.

44. CERVERA BARRANCO, Pablo, *La incorporación en la Iglesia mediante el bautismo y la profesión de la fe según el Concilio Vaticano II*, 1998, pp. 372.

45. NETO, Laudelino, *Fé cristã e cultura latino-americana. Uma análise a partir das Conferências de Puebla e Santo Domingo*, 1998, pp. 340.

46. BRITO GUIMARÃES, Pedro, *Os sacramentos como atos eclesiais e proféticos. Um contributo ao conceito dogmático de sacramento à luz da exegese contemporânea*, 1998, pp. 448.

47. CALABRETTA, Rose B., *Baptism and Confirmation. The Vocation and Mission of the Laity in the Writings of Virgil Michel, O.S.B.*, 1998, pp. 320.

48. OTERO LÁZARO, Tomás, *Col 1,15-20 en el contexto de la carta*, 1999, pp.312.

49. KOWALCZYK, Dariusz, *La personalità in Dio. Dal metodo trascendentale di Karl Rahner verso un orientamento dialogico in Heinrich Ott*, 1999, pp. 484.

50. PRIOR, Joseph G., *The Historical-Critical Method in Catholic Exegesis*, 1999, pp. 352.

51. CAHILL, Brendan J, *The Renewal of Revelation Theology (1960-1962). The Development and Responses to the Fourth Chapter of the Preparatory Schema De deposito Fidei*, 1999, pp. 348.

52. TIEZZI, Ida, *Il rapporto tra la pneumatologia e l'ecclesiologia nella teologia italiana post-conciliare*, 1999, pp. 364.

53. HOLC, Paweł, *Un ampio consenso sulla dottrina della giustificazione. Studio sul dialogo teologico cattolico luterano*, 1999, pp. 452.

54. GAINO, Andrea, *Esistenza cristiana. Il pensiero teologico di J. Alfaro e la sua rilevanza morale*, 1999, pp. 344.

55. NERI, Francesco, *«Cur Verbum capax hominis». Le ragioni dell'incarnazione della seconda Persona della Trinità fra teologia scolastica e teologia contemporanea*, 1999, pp. 404.

56. MUÑOZ CÁRDABA, Luis-Miguel, *Principios eclesiológicos de la «Pastor Bonus»*, 1999, pp. 344.

57. IWE, John Chijioke, *Jesus in the Synagogue of Capernaum: the Pericope and Its Programmatic Character for the Gospel of Mark. An Exegetico-Theological Study of Mk 1:21-28*, 1999, pp. 364.

58. BARRIOCANAL GÓMEZ, José Luis, *La relectura de la tradición del éxodo en el libro de Amós*, 2000, pp. 332.

59. DE LOS SANTOS GARCÍA, Edmundo, *La novedad de la metáfora κεφαλή – σῶμα en la carta a los Efesios*, 2000, pp. 432.

60. RESTREPO SIERRA, Argiro, *La revelación según R. Latourelle*, 2000, pp. 442.

61. DI GIOVAMBATTISTA, Fulvio, *Il giorno dell'espiazione nella Lettera agli Ebrei*, 2000, pp. 232.

62. GIUSTOZZO, Massimo, *Il nesso tra il culto e la grazia eucaristica nella recente lettura teologica del pensiero agostiniano*, 2000, pp. 456.

63. PESARCHICK, Robert A., *The Trinitarian Foundation of Human Sexuality as Revealed by Christ according to Hans Urs von Balthasar. The Revelatory Significance of the Male Christ and the Male Ministerial Priesthood*, 2000, pp. 328.

64. SIMON, László T., *Identity and Identification. An Exegetical Study of 2Sam 21–24*, 2000. pp. 386.

65. TAKAYAMA, Sadami, *Shinran's Conversion in the Light of Paul's Conversion*, 2000, pp. 256.

66. JUAN MORADO, Guillermo, *«También nosotros creemos porque amamos». Tres concepciones del acto de fe: Newman, Blondel, Garrigou-Lagrange. Estudio comparativo desde la perspectiva teológico-fundamental*, 2000, pp. 444.

67. MAREČEK, Petr, *La preghiera di Gesù nel vangelo di Matteo. Uno studio esegetico-teologico*, 2000, pp. 246.

68. WODKA, Andrzej, *Una teologia biblica del dare nel contesto della colletta paolina (2Cor 8–9)*, 2000, pp. 356.

69. LANGELLA, Maria Rigel, *Salvezza come illuminazione. Uno studio comparato di S. Bulgakov, V. Lossky, P. Evdokimov*, 2000, pp. 292.

70. RUDELLI, Paolo, *Matrimonio come scelta di vita: opzione – vocazione – sacramento*, 2000, pp. 424.

71. GAŠPAR, Veronika, *Cristologia pneumatologica in alcuni autori cattolici postconciliari. Status quaestionis e prospettive*, 2000, pp. 440.

72. GJORGJEVSKI, Gjoko, *Enigma degli enigmi. Un contributo allo studio della composizione della raccolta salomonica (Pr 10,1–22,16)*, 2001, pp. 304.

73. LINGAD, Celestino G., Jr., *The Problems of Jewish Christians in the Johannine Community*, 2001, pp. 492.

74. MASALLES, Victor, *La profecía en la asamblea cristiana. Análisis retórico-literario de 1Cor 14,1-25*, 2001, pp. 416.

75. FIGUEIREDO, Anthony J., *The Magisterium-Theology Relationship. Contemporary Theological Conceptions in the Light of Universal Church Teaching since 1835 and the Pronouncements of the Bishops of the United States*, 2001, pp. 536.

76. PARDO IZAL, José Javier, *Pasión por un futuro imposible. Estudio literario-teológico de Jeremías 32*, 2001, pp. 412.

77. HANNA, Kamal Fahim Awad, *La passione di Cristo nell'Apocalisse*, 2001, pp. 480.

78. ALBANESI, Nicola, *«Cur Deus Homo»: la logica della redenzione. Studio sulla teoria della soddisfazione di S. Anselmo arcivescovo di Canterbury*, 2001, pp. 244.

79. ADE, Edouard, *Le temps de l'Eglise. Esquisse d'une théologie de l'histoire selon Hans Urs von Balthasar*, 2002, pp. 368.

80. MENÉNDEZ MARTÍNEZ, Valentín, *La misión de la Iglesia. Un estudio sobre el debate teológico y eclesial en América Latina (1955-1992), con atención al aporte de algunos teólogos de la Compañía de Jesús*, 2002, pp. 346.

81. COSTA, Paulo Cezar, *«Salvatoris Disciplina». Dionísio de Roma e a* Regula fidei *no debate teológico do terceiro século*, 2002, pp. 272.

82. PUTHUSSERY, Johnson, *Days of Man and God's Day. An Exegetico-Theological Study of ἡμέρα in the Book of Revelation*, 2002, pp. 302.

83. BARROS, Paulo César, *«Commendatur vobis in isto pane quomodo unitatem amare debeatis». A eclesiologia eucarística nos* Sermones ad populum *de Agostinho de Hipona e o movimento ecumênico*, 2002, pp. 344.

84. PALACHUVATTIL, Joy, *«He Saw». The Significance of Jesus' Seeing Denoted by the Verb εἶδεν in the Gospel of Mark*, 2002, pp. 312.

85. PISANO, Ombretta, *La radice e la stirpe di David. Salmi davidici nel libro dell'Apocalisse*, 2002, pp. 496.

86. KARIUKI, Njiru Paul, *Charisms and the Holy Spirit's Activity in the Body of Christ. An Exegetical-Theological Study of 1Cor 12,4-11 and Rom 12,6-8*, 2002, pp. 372.

87. CORRY, Donal, *«Ministerium Rationis Reddendae». An Approximation to Hilary of Poitiers' Understanding of Theology*, 2002, pp. 328.

88. PIKOR, Wojciech, *La comunicazione profetica alla luce di Ez 2–3*, 2002, pp. 322.

89. NWACHUKWU, Mary Sylvia Chinyere, *Creation–Covenant Scheme and Justification by Faith. A Canonical Study of the God-Human Drama in the Pentateuch and the Letter to the Romans*, 2002, 378 pp.

90. GAGLIARDI, Mauro, *La cristologia adamitica. Tentativo di recupero del suo significato originario*, 2002, pp. 624.

91. CHARAMSA, Krzysztof Olaf, *L'immutabilità di Dio. L'insegnamento di San Tommaso d'Aquino nei suoi sviluppi presso i commentatori scolastici*, 2002, pp. 520.

92. GLOBOKAR, Roman, *Verantwortung für alles, was lebt. Von Albert Schweitzer und Hans Jonas zu einer theologischen Ethik des Lebens*, 2002, pp. 608.

93. AJAYI, James Olaitan, *The HIV/AIDS Epidemic in Nigeria. Some Ethical Considerations*, 2003, pp. 212.

94. PARAMBI, Baby, *The Discipleship of the Women in the Gospel according to Matthew. An Exegetical Theological Study of Matt 27:51b-56, 57-61 and 28:1-10*, 2003, pp. 276.

95. NIEMIRA, Artur, *Religiosità e moralità. Vita morale come realizzazione della fondazione cristica dell'uomo secondo B. Häring e D. Capone*, 2003, pp. 308.

96. PIZZUTO, Pietro, *La teologia della rivelazione di Jean Daniélou. Influsso su Dei Verbum e valore attuale*, 2003, pp. 630.

97. PAGLIARA, Cosimo, *La figura di Elia nel vangelo di Marco. Aspetti semantici e funzionali*, 2003, pp. 400.

98. O'BOYLE, Aidan, *Towards a Contemporary Wisdom Christology. Some Catholic Christologies in German, English and French 1965-1995*, 2003, pp. 448.

99. BYRNES, Michael J., *Conformation to the Death of Christ and the Hope of Resurrection: An Exegetico-Theological Study of 2 Corinthians 4,7-15 and Philippians 3,7-11*, 2003, p. 328.

100. RIGATO, Maria-Luisa, *Il Titolo della Croce di Gesù. Confronto tra i Vangeli e la Tavoletta-reliquia della Basilica Eleniana a Roma*, 2003, pp. 392.

101. LA GIOIA, Fabio, *La glorificazione di Gesù Cristo ad opera dei discepoli. Analisi biblico-teologica di Gv 17,10b nell'insieme dei capp. 13–17*, 2003, pp. 346.

102. LÓPEZ-TELLO GARCÍA, Eduardo, *Simbología y Lógica de la Redención: Ireneo de Lyón, Hans Küng y Hans Urs von Balthasar leídos con la ayuda de Paul Ricœur*, 2003, pp. 396.

103. MAZUR, Aleksander, *L'insegnamento di Giovanni Paolo II sulle altre religioni*, 2003, pp. 354.

104. SANECKI, Artur, *Approccio canonico: tra storia e teologia, alla ricerca di un nuovo paradigma post-critico. L'analisi della metodologia canonica di B.S. Childs dal punto di vista cattolico*, 2004, pp. 480.

105. STRZELCZYK, Grzegorz, *«Communicatio idiomatum», lo scambio delle proprietà. Storia, «status quaestionis» e prospettive*, 2004, pp. 324.

106. CHO Hyun-Chul, *An Ecological Vision of the World: Toward a Christian Ecological Theology of Our Age*, 2004, pp. 318.

Finito di stampare
nel mese di Maggio 2004

presso la tipografia
"Giovanni Olivieri" di E. Montefoschi
00187 Roma • Via dell'Archetto, 10, 11, 12
Tel. 06 6792327 • E-mail: tip.olivieri@libero.it